Published by Flatiron Publishing, Inc.

Published in the United States by Flatiron Publishing, Inc., New York.

ISBN 0-936648-55-4

Manufactured in the United States of America

First Edition, July 1994
Cover Designed by Saul Roldan
Printed at BookCrafters, Chelsea, MI.

Acknowledgments:

Client Server Computer Telephony was conceived as a straight-forward publication about "making your database talk." Although the talking database theme still has a chapter dedicated to it, the project grew far beyond its original scope. It became a showcase for the top experts in computation, telecommunications, and computer telephony. Some of my closest friends and long-time colleagues had a hand in producing this book. In lieu of acknowledging them all here, a short biography and other relevant information is listed at the end of each chapter. I am grateful for their help, because the end result is perhaps the most comprehensive collection of insights on the subject matter ever published in one manuscript.

This *industry sounding board* would not have been possible, however, if it were not for the encouragement and insights of Harry Newton. He is publisher of TELECONNECT, CALL CENTER, COMPUTER TELEPHONY and IMAGING Magazines. He is the author of several books, including the best-selling 1,120-page dictionary called "Newton's TELECOM Dictionary." He is also president and founder of Telecom Library Inc. Without a doubt, Harry's constant evangelizing, cajoling, deal-making and energy has had more to do with the overall spirit of this once-fledgling industry than any other person. He has been banging the open architecture drum for over a decade, and it was this happy noise that eventually compelled me to write this book. One has only to look at Mr. Newton's long list of telecom industry associations to understand why he is our most popular speaker. He has spoken before, and continues to speak before virtually every telecommunications trade show and convention.

They include ADAPSO, Information Industry Association, American Bankers Association, Communications Networks, the SL-1 Users Association, NATA, NEHOSTA, Tele-Communications Association, Association of College and University Telecommunications Administrators (ACUTA), International Organization of Women in Telecommunications, Society of Telecommunications Consultants, United States Telephone Association, Midwest Telecommunications Association, Communications Managers Association of New York, New England Telecommunications Association, Armed Forces Communications and Electronics Association and South-Eastern Telecommunications Association.

Newton has been in the telecommunications industry since 1969, when the FCC handed down the MCI Decision and Bill McGowan, MCI's founder, convinced him to come into the industry. Newton holds a bachelor of economics degree from the University of Sydney and an MBA from the Harvard Business School. His research findings have been quoted in the *Wall Street Journal, Business Week, Fortune, Forbes, Newsweek, Inc, The New York Times*, and most communications trade publications. He appears regularly on NBC network news and feature shows as an expert on the industry. In May 1983, the Mayor of Indianapolis presented Newton with the key to the city.

I found one of my favorite quotes on Harry in a five-page cover story about him in Computerland's *On Communications.* They said: "With Harry, telecommunications is a metaphor for life... Every occupational group should have a Harry Newton. Harry is the patron saint of telecommunications, the exemplar of what can be. He addresses his audience members as if they were a family, chiding them and urging them to realize their potential. He really cares for them." My friend Harry has been a mentor to hundreds of entrepreneurs and fellow telecom enthusiasts like me.

Thanks, Harry. - Edwin "Magoo" Margulies

Table of Contents

FOREWORD

Our New Industry Erector Set Computer Telephony

by Harry Newton

Welcome to a new industry. Erector Set Computer Telephony. Our new industry will shortly become one of the world's largest. There are two parts.

First, "Computer Telephony" means the computer adds intelligence to your telephone call.

Second, "Erector Set" means you build this new computer intelligence as you build an Erector Set — with bits and pieces of commonly available parts. (In England, we call it Mechano Set Computer Telephony. In Japan, we call it Leggo Set Computer Telephony. In North America, Erector Set.)

This "Erector Set" analogy is not 100% accurate. There's only one maker of Erector Set toys. In contrast, there are many makers of Erector Set computer telephony building blocks (hardware and software). More are emerging daily. The good news is that all the building blocks are pretty well identified. Someone is working on them. They should be all available to buy by the time you read this.

Why add intelligence to the phone? Phones are stupid, though useful. Their "user interface" is friendly and irritating. Misdial a number. Hang up. Redial it. Even my two dollar calculator can do better. It lets me backspace, fix the offending digit, and go on. Not so with telephones. Voice mail is the "BIG" telephone innovation of the past 20 years. It can be a disaster. People hide behind it. They don't return messages. Their voice mail boxes fill up. Worse, voice mail is stupid. Big customer, little customer. All are treated the same. Everyone gets the same general message. Everyone gets dumped into the same box. Voice mail, promoted as an aid, has become an irritant.

There was a time years ago when everyone had a secretary. The boss had a button on the side of his phone. He pushed it. A bell rung outside his office. His secretary came running. "Get Joe, Harry and Saul on a conference call at 3:00 PM and make sure each of them have an agenda, have read it and have intelligent comments," he would say. Telephony's salad days!

No more. No one can afford secretaries. And even if they could, you can't find secretaries. At least literate ones. So we made machines to ape old-style intelligent secretaries. Touchtone dialers on phones. Auto dialers. Voice mail. Things without the intelligence of secretaries.

Erector Set Computer Telephony will get us the intelligence of secretaries, with some pluses and some minuses. Secretaries may be easier to train, but are more expensive. Computers never forget, can do things very fast, rarely get sick, never take a vacation, and, once taught, don't make mistakes.

I spend my life on the phone. I personally crave Erector Set Computer Telephony. I want to know who is calling. I want my calls to go to the right person, not always me. I want my computer to dial my phone calls. I want to call the right person at XYZ Company — the person our company has a great relationship with. I'd like my darling wife to call my office and get a different voice mail message from everyone else. I'd like my biggest customer to reach me at three in the morning, wherever I am.

As I write my computer telephony wish list, I realize how trivial my wishes sound. But then if somebody had said that I'd buy a $5,000 "typewriter" once a year to write articles and books, people would say I was crazy. Heck, I can do that with a yellow pad and a pencil.

There's a point. The computer is the first gadget that is not single purpose. A stove cooks. A vacuum cleaner cleans. A car goes places. But a computer can, from moment to moment, type my articles, check my stock prices (miserable), check the photos for our magazines, run a spreadsheet, dial my calls, set up my conference calls, tell me who's calling, etc.

Erector set computer telephony will let me add "intelligence" to my phone calls. What that intelligence will be will take me time to discover, as it did with my computer.

Today, in the summer of 1994, there are two ways of adding intelligence to my phone calls. I can put a telephone card into our PC and load some software to drive that card. Or I can put a card in the file server on my local area network, get my PC to talk to my file server, which in turn would speak to my telephone switch, which in turn would speak to and command the phone on my desk sitting next to my PC. This book is about the second setup — the Client Server telephony solution. My PC — the one on my desk — is the client. The one joined to my telephone switch is the Server.

The benefits of client server computer telephony fall into six broad categories. There may be 30 categories by the time you read this. For now, six is the conventional wisdom:

1. Synchronized data screen and phone call pop. My phone rings. The screen on my PC pops up with the name of the person calling, his photo, and all the notes about what we and everyone else in our company talked about. What his joys were. What his pleasures were. What his preferences were. What he last bought. What he's waiting on us for. My caller will think I have a superhuman memory. He'll be impressed with my service. He'll want to deal with my company. Moreover, if I'm taking orders over the phone, having his address, phone number, credit card, buying preferences, etc. will save me at least 30 seconds a call. Which will allow me to get off faster — or sell a little harder. People hate answering, "Where do you live? What's your great grandmother's maiden name?" They'd much prefer to buy my "special of the day."

2. Integrated messaging (voice, fax, e-mail, image, video). Also called unified messaging. I arrive in the morning. I turn on my PC. It logs onto my LAN and its various servers. In seconds, it gives me a screen listing all my messages — voice mail, electronic mail, fax mail, reports, compound documents. Anything and everything that came in for me. Each is one line. Each line tells me whom it's from. What it is. How big it is. How urgent. Cursor down. Click. Click. My PC loads up the application. My LAN hunts down the message. Bingo, it's on screen. If it contains voice — maybe it's a voice mail or compound document with voice in it — it rings my phone and plays the voice to me. Or, if I have a sound card, it plays the voice through my PC's speakers.

Messages are deluging us. To stop them is to stop progress, to lose sales, to annoy my boss. But run my eye down the list. Pick the key ones (like the one from my boss.) Junk the junk ones. Postpone the others. It gets better. I'm out. I dial in with my laptop. Skim my messages. Click on the ones I want. Listen to those on voice mail. Have my faxed messages sent to my laptop. If I'm not on a laptop, I can dial in, have my desktop PC play my voice mail messages, read my electronic mail and faxed messages. It has built-in OCR (Optical Character Recognition).

A LAN server is a perfect repository for messages. It can search for them, assemble them, process them, store them, convert them, compress them, shape them, shuffle them, interpret them. It can store them once, but let many people get to them (my choice). Marshall R. Goldberg, Developer Relations Group at Microsoft, says "Voice mail systems that could benefit through integration with the personal computer largely remain isolated, difficult to use, and inflexible. Browsing, storing messages in hierarchical folders, and integration of address books — functions just about everyone could use — are either unavailable or unusable." No more.

3. Database transactions. Customer lookups. My friends at Expert Systems in Atlanta call it "Giving Data A Voice." Catchy. There are bank balances, ticket buys, airline reservations, catalog requests, store locations, movie times, shipping information, inventory status, etc. All sorts of information that people want. My thesis: no one buys the product any longer. They buy the information that surrounds the product. I call it "The Surround Stuff." There are many overnight delivery organizations. But, for those of us who want information on where our package is at this very moment, there's no better company than Fedex. We care that our package wasn't delivered. We care much more that no one knows where it is.

Doing business over the phone is convenient. The caller touchtones in his request or responds with recognized speech. The system responds with speech and/or fax. Today, callers to TV stations don't speak to people to buy advertised baubles. They "speak" to machines and prefer them. They're faster. Repairmen don't carry heavy manuals. They carry portable fax machines. When they need info on how to fix something, they dial from the handset of their fax machine, punch in some touchtones, and hit "Start." Bingo the machine disgorges the best tips on how to fix the broken cash register.

4. Telephony work groups. We work in groups. Telephony today is BIG. One giant phone system for the building. Everyone shares the same automated attendant, the same voice mail, the same ubiquitous, universal, generic telephone features. They shouldn't. Salespeople need phones that grab the caller's phone number, do a look-up on what the customer last bought and quickly route the call to the appropriate (or available) salesperson. The one who sold the customer last time.

The company's bill collectors need phones that dial the debtors quickly. They need phones that pick answering machines from real people. pick busies from noise. The company's help desk needs a front-end voice response system that asks for the customer's serial number, some indication of the problem and tries to solve the problem by instantly sending a fax or encouraging the caller to punch his way to one of many canned solutions. "The 10 biggest problems our customers have." When all else fails, the caller can be shunted to a live human, expert at diagnosing and solving his pressing problem. A development group might need e-mails and faxes of meeting agendas sent, meeting reminder notices phoned and scheduled video conferences set up. All automatically.

When the history books are written, I suspect we'll see more telephony groupware applications than computer groupware applications. As I write this in the summer of 1994, Lotus Notes and desktop conferencing whiteboarding software were the rage. In two years, telephony workgroups will be the rage.

5. **Desktop telephony.** A group rolodex. A company Rolodex. A personal Rolodex. There are enormous personal productivity gains to running my phone from my PC. I can dial by name. I can have it automatically reply to faxes. I can even backspace erase. I can go on endlessly. You get the message. My favorite (yours may be different) is that I can run my messages like a tape recorder. I can rewind, slow down, speed up, etc. All with the on-screen interface of a super intelligent tape recorder. How would you like at the end of a conversation a message on your screen, "I've recorded this conversation. Would you like it saved? Would you liked it transcribed in Word 6.0 or WordPerfect 8.0?"

6. **The compound document.** The media we work in daily — voice, fax, video, paper, spreadsheets, etc. — are today all separate. How about combining them? The power of persuasion (why else do we write this stuff?) is magnified exponentially. Here's a spreadsheet. Click on the lousy fourth quarter numbers and hear my voice with a feeble explanation of why the results are so awful. Join fax to voice mail. Throw in a video clip of a tour around our new plant. Or a trip around our new house. Or a demo of our new product.

It's all here. And it's all happening.

This book is a beginning journey into client server computer telephony. The authors of each of the chapters read like a Who's Who of computing, telecommunications, voice processing and networking — all the pieces of computer telephony. I hope you enjoy our efforts. If you have questions, comments, suggestions, improvements, please contact me or Ed. There'll be many updates, many editions. This is one fantastic journey we're all embarking on.

Harry Newton
New York City
Summer, 1994
My Internet address:
HarryNewton@MCIMail.com

1

The Client-Server Revolution

Client-Server Computer Telephony is a phrase describing an approach to modern solutions for superior customer service. The phrase itself combines a variety of complex technical and business issues which are being attacked by hundreds of experts in the fields of telephony, computation, and networking. Some of the best talent in the communications industry helped explore, define, and demystify the concepts outlined here.

Whether you are a vice president of customer service, the customer service systems analyst, or a product manager, there is something for everyone who wishes to gain a competitive edge for their products and services. But first, let's take a look at the reasons why these concepts are important to understand and master. By taking advantage of new offerings in the disciplines of client-server and *computer telephony*, you can:

- Radically upgrade customer service for your company
- Save thousands of dollars in business process re-engineering
- Achieve optimal "rightsizing" of people and computers
- Master the confluence of computing and communications

In this chapter, a discussion of the prevailing drivers for the modern enterprise is explored. This sets the tone for the remainder of the book, which gets into the specifics of how you can take advantage of client-server technology itself. You will also see how client-server technology is becoming rapidly absorbed by the communications network and *computer telephony* marketplace.

Focus on Customer Service

Every business serves a master, and that master is the customer. It doesn't matter if the goods being delivered are hard products or services, because in order for a business to survive, the cash has to continue to roll in, and in virtually every case, it's customers who stoke the flames of profitability. In most businesses, the function of customer service is manifest in a variety of duties that are carried-out by every department. These functions revolve around the goal of customer satisfaction, which is essential to retaining existing customers and attracting new ones.

Figure 1.1 Customer Service Model

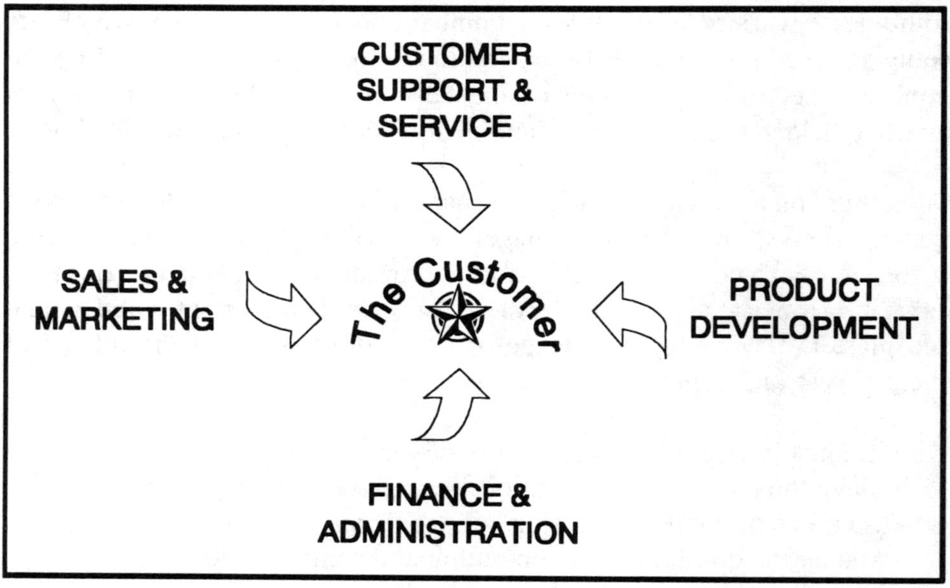

The customer's view is framed by the overall experience in dealing with the enterprise, not by an intimate knowledge of who reports to whom within the enterprise. The customer service function attracts the most attention for symptoms of disorganization, lost profits, and competitive pressure. These problems are not typically the fault of the *customer service department*, but rather a failure of the entire enterprise to be customer-oriented from the inside-out.

It is a good idea to take a look at some of the general issues in customer service at this point in order to focus on the relationship between customer expectations and the design of business process. Client-Server Computer Telephony also comes into play as an enabler of superior customer service. But more on that later.

Customer service is usually provided by some intermediary who is an employee of the business enterprise in question. This employee could be a sales person, agent, clerk, manager, or anyone who comes in contact with customers in some way. It is this "agent" who must utilize all of the appropriate information stores of the business in order to provide information or services to the customer.

Over the past decade, however, there has been a move toward automating some of these services, so that the customer can gain access to needed information on their own. The call processing industry has done much to aid in this automation, such that customers can 'self-navigate" through the same information that typically requires the intervention of an agent.

Regardless as to the mode of providing the information, the customer expects to be able to:

- Obtain product and service information
- Get specific order or account status information
- Order, cancel, or change requests for products
- Complain, remark, or give advice about service
- Change or update their customer profile

These generic categories apply to virtually any enterprise. Typical examples include customers who call airlines to inquire about flight status, or utility workers who call a centralized service center to ask about where hidden cables may be buried before starting construction. The overall premise is that a customer needs access to information that may be distributed across the entire enterprise itself, or scattered across a number of enterprises.

This cross-enterprise information gathering is certainly true of order entry applications, for example. If a prospect calls a phone-in catalog store, their credit card number may be checked, product inventory will be checked, and shipping will be scheduled. The card approval will most likely be authorized as a result of several queries to both a local database, and an off-site service bureau. The availability of product will sometimes include queries to outside vendors, and lastly, the shipping may be scheduled with a distributor or fulfillment house. A happy customer, of course, will want to be shielded from the details of how the order is fulfilled and orchestrated between all of these processes. The more seamlessly these processes interact, the more seamless the transaction will be for the customer.

In some cases, the customer actually has to initiate multiple transactions just to get the desired result. This is often the case in ordering services from a bank. For example, if a bank client wishes to transfer funds from his or her line of credit to a checking account, and also get payment information on a credit card, it often takes several phone calls to complete the transaction. This problem is being addressed by some “bank-by-phone” services.

With each subsequent phone call or visit to the bank, the ugly specter of dissatisfaction looms. This is true because of the law of averages - the more times a customer has to repeat information such as name, account number, and social security number in a short period of time, the more annoyed that customer becomes.

It is clearly important, then, to discover *what* the customer wants as soon as possible during the initial stages of a transaction, but it is also equally important to find out *who* they are. Although this sounds fundamental, it is at the very core of superior customer service. Account profile information can be retrieved in a more timely fashion by using a variety of technologies, such as ANI (Automatic Number Identification), DNIS (Dialed Number Identification Service), CTI (Computer-Telephone Integration), and IVR (Interactive Voice Response).

Perhaps one of the most popular, if not controversial, means for doing this is ANI. This is a means to capture information about what a customer's telephone number is when they call for help over the phone. This information is sent over the telephone network, and can be passed from the telephone lines over to the enterprise computer system.

The idea is to match the number with the customer's record, so that that record can be transferred automatically to the appropriate agent as the call rings-through.

The notion of ANI conjures-up issues of privacy and ethics in some circles, but it is nonetheless a staple technology used by hundreds of companies. Much valuable time can be saved both for the caller and for the company in question if the technology is used in an ethical way. DNIS works in the same fashion as ANI, however, the information being gathered is the telephone number that was dialed by the caller.

Figure 1.2 Who and What

This data can be used to share telephone lines that service calls for many types of products. By using ANI and DNIS together, long distance carriers, enhanced service providers, and companies with "800" numbers able to automatically determine the "who" and "what" of the transaction in order to provide speedy and efficient customer service.

That is to say, that once the *who* question is answered, it's sometimes easier to know exactly *what* the customer wants. This is certainly true if a customer profile has been established. Many times, a customer record or profile will contain information regarding customer preferences, buying behaviors, and historical ordering information.

Customer service systems can be built to capture this type of information, so that on each contact with the customer, the "database" on that customer can be updated and made more accurate.

This is important if the enterprise seeks to build a profile of the customer which closer approximates the customer's expectations for new services, satisfaction, future orders, and overall impression of the business relationship. Obviously, these items go far beyond the pressing needs of the immediate contact, but can also be used to improve customer relationships, which, in reality, is the key element that keeps the customer calling back time after time.

At this point, you may be wondering why these "little conveniences" are so important. The answer is that superior customer service may be the only thing that distinguishes your company from your competitor in the eyes of the customer. A number of studies have been conducted over the past forty years which profile the "stages of competency" of growing and successful organizations. In the beginning, companies establish themselves as a result of offering some attractive or competent service or product.

Figure 1.3 Stages of Competency

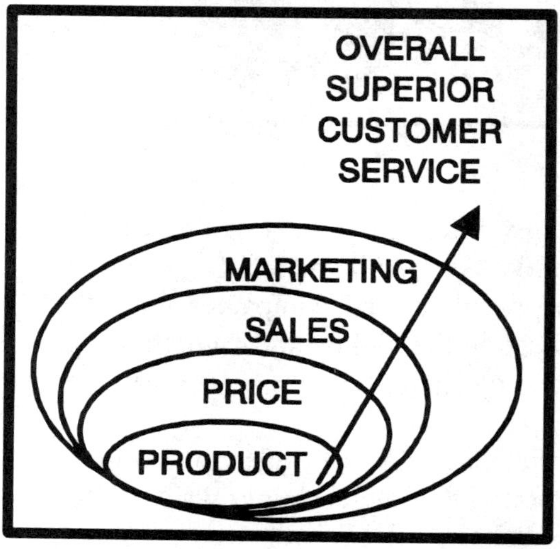

Sooner or later, a competitor comes around and does the same thing. The competitor may have come out with the exact same offering. The original company, having gotten a jump on the market, will sometimes change the pricing to more closely reflect their costs of manufacture, which by this time are lower due to volume. So, the second stage of competency is a *competitively priced* offering.

Most items don't sell themselves, so it is usual that after the offering itself is established and priced competitively, it is no long intuitively obvious why the customer should buy from company A versus company B. *Sales competency* is defined as the third stage. All of us have felt the sense of wanting to buy from one store, because the sales person seemed more knowledgeable about a product than the sales staff at another store. But alas, the most competitive companies usually "catch-up" after a while and establish a strong and competent sales force.

Once a good product, fair pricing, and competent sales staff is in place, the *marketing* of the product is what's most important. This is where many companies *"fall on their sword."* Many times, it is the way a product or service is promoted that is the singular distinguishing factor between competitors. Take, for example, the way we make decisions on where to buy clothing, and what to buy. Designer labels sometimes have nothing to do with the quality of the goods, yet we are sometimes compelled to drive from store to store looking for an article of clothing that has the right label on it regardless of cost or quality.

What is predictable in our shopping behavior is that we all like to get superior customer service. Sometimes, the designer labels are associated more with quality department stores, and so we equate good customer service closely with fine fashion. This is why you don't find as many designer labels in cut-rate or bargain department stores.

This is because the most fashion-conscious manufacturers of clothing only want to be associated with stores that offer superior customer service. For example, many manufacturers will not allow off-price or bargain retailers to mention the names of certain products in advertising. They regard this as degrading to their image. Thus, the marketing of a product appeals to our visceral and emotional response mechanisms, and actually sell us on how, fun, sexy, modern, or "cool" we are if we purchase a certain product.

It is for this reason that *customer service* is the ultimate expression of competitive competence. This is the holy grail for companies aspiring to greatness, because customer service is the one distinguishing characteristic of successful companies. A hallmark of competent customer service is the timeliness and accuracy with which information is gathered and utilized to fulfill an order.

An enterprise that touts excellent customer service has probably eliminated unnecessary (multiple) transactions or phone calls, and has the ability to complete transactions and get follow-up information during the same phone call. In short, customer service is a chief driver for the enterprise of the nineties and will likely remain that way well into the turn of the century.

A Prelude to Business Process Re-Engineering

In most customer service scenarios, there is some intermediary who navigates customers through a given *enterprise systems environment* in order to complete transactions. These intermediaries are commonly referred to as service agents, agents, or customer service agents.

From a systems perspective, service agents use synchronous or asynchronous character-based terminals, or some form of (gateway or emulation) terminal access to host computers. It is typical to find both 3270s (IBM mainframe terminals) and VT100s (asynchronous terminals for asynch hosts) on an agent's desk. In fact, there are some customer service centers where one can find several 3270 terminals and an additional one or two asynch terminals at one person's desk.

This proliferation of access devices is especially true of telephone companies, where a process-oriented view of information management has created one of the largest systems problems in modern history. In typical call center environments, the service agent must log on and off separate computer hosts in order to complete the most rudimentary transaction. An example of this is pictured in figure 1.4. For example, you may call for a hotel reservation and provide your name, the number of people in your party, and the length of your stay. Once the information is added to the database, the service agent may have to access another computer host to check for availability. The service agent must traverse several screens or log-off of one host session and re-establish the original one to discuss the alternatives. This is why so many agents actually have more than one terminal on the desk (in order to bounce back and forth between terminals to maintain simultaneous sessions with two separate host programs).

Figure 1.4 Typical Host/Slave Environment

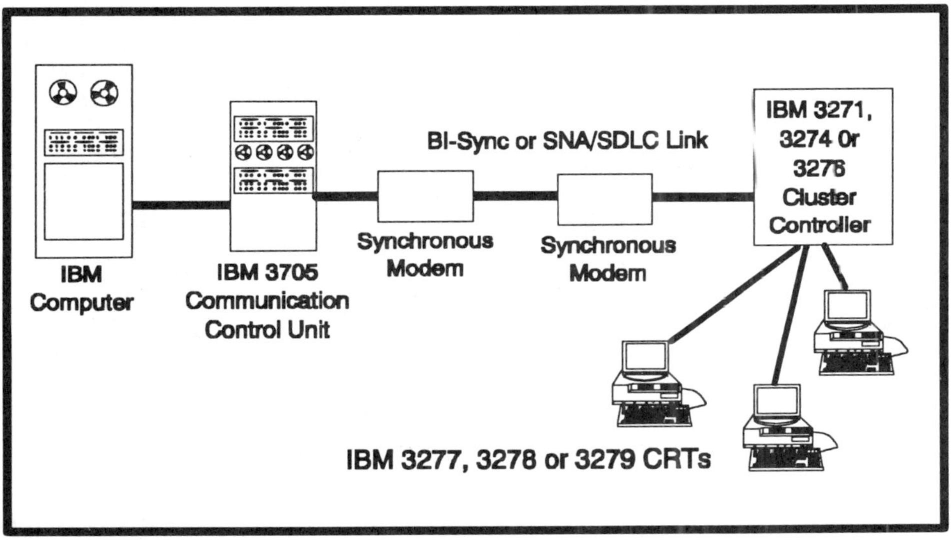

A more sophisticated approach is to maintain a current session with the (first) computer host while a second session is connected to the agent terminal. The service agent can then "ping-pong" between host computers all the time maintaining two or more on-line sessions. Figure 1.5 details the way in which some companies achieve this.

This is really a Band-Aid® to a pretty big problem, especially when you consider the on-line charges and performance issues of having all of your agents hooked-up to two or more host sessions simultaneously. The more the terminals, the more memory, disk, CPU power, and data communications facilities are required. It's no wonder that systems integration initiatives are so popular.

Figure 1.5 Typical Host/Slave Emulation

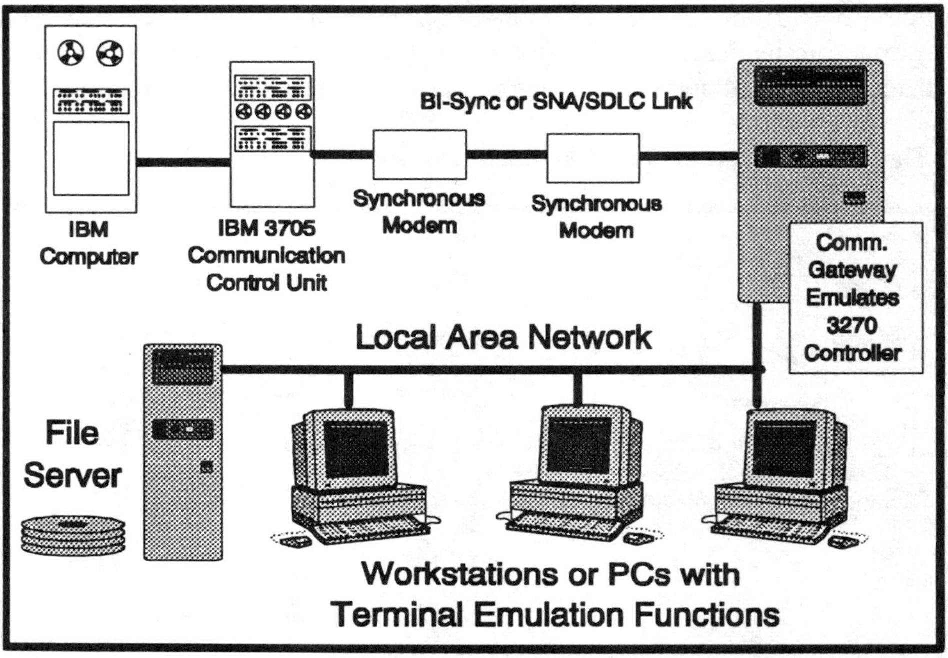

What's especially difficult for the agent in both of these cases is the inability to transfer or "cut and paste" data back and forth between sessions. In fact, many agents simply scribe information from one screen on a scratch pad - only to re-enter it on a subsequent session with a different host. Is it any wonder why there are so many misspellings, incorrect orders, and general dissatisfaction with how long it takes to complete a simple transaction?

This scenario exemplifies how human factors design (for the service agent and the customer) is woefully absent from most customer services environments. Service agents must be well-trained, experienced in more than one system, accurate, and quick. When customers have to be tolerant of mistakes with orders and patient when simple requests seem to take forever, they are generally dissatisfied with the results.

Telephone companies, for example, are largely dependent on disparate mainframe and minicomputer database access and programs. There are applications for service provisioning, engineering central office connections, assigning pairs of wires in the field, and dispatching personnel to name a few. In fact, there are no less than 80 major programs for each telephone company that are required to keep it running, yet virtually each and every program requires a separate terminal or some special gateway to gain access to the needed information. What's especially ironic is that much of the information that's stored in databases for these programs is redundant information that is simply replicated dozens of times throughout the enterprise. The problem here is that each program was invented to attack a specific set of tasks.

Once that program is installed, no one wants to deal with the inherent complexity of removing it. And since these process-oriented programs are installed in different departments, the management staff of that department views the software solution therein as his or her personal fiefdom.

In a way, what you end up with is dozens of small "countries" or "processing islands" that act as their own monolithic kingdoms. This situation typifies a process-driven view to computing and communications. *Process-driven* approaches to computing and communications are not inherently evil in their own right, but the thinking that goes behind this model is often flawed and short-sighted.

There is a trend toward binding separate processes through large-scale systems integration initiatives and newer technology. For example, the use of routers and mainframe gateways is more popular every day. In such a system, PCs are used to access "cluster controllers" on a local area network. These PCs often have displays that are able to maintain several "windows" which represent more than one concurrent session with the gateway.

This is also true of UNIX workstations, X-Windows terminals, and proprietary approaches. Unfortunately, these approaches rarely seek to unify or transfer data from one program to another, but are merely electronic versions of the paper pad mentioned earlier. These anomalies continue to exist because "legacy" systems are holding most companies and MIS directors hostage. Imagine the millions of dollars required to maintain these mainframes and minicomputers. The programs themselves represent millions of lines of code, and were often written 20-30 years ago by gurus who are either retired or in other lines of work. The fact that mainframes are still in use is a testimony to the overall reliability and basic utility of these offerings.

On the flip side, the fact that these systems were so expensive to establish and maintain often scares away endeavors to re-write the programs. This is one of the reasons why most service agents in call center environments are made to suffer with bouncing back and forth between these disparate systems in order to complete transactions on behalf of their customers. The prevailing attitude is that it's "tough luck" that agents have to do this: "Just think of all the money we're saving by having them continue this way." Ironically, this mentality has a negative impact on the image of customer service.

Some companies are beginning to realize the importance of at least streamlining these processes. This is especially true of operator service centers, for example. At one major telephone company, it was calculated that for every second that was shaved-off of each operator's typical directory assistance call, one million dollars of operational expense would be saved each year. Now that's the kind of money that sends managers scrambling for the drawing table!

Unfortunately, not every company stops long enough to take a look at other reasons there may be a benefit to re-engineering the storage and delivery of their customer service data. Namely, customer service can be used as a competitive weapon that helps to distinguish one enterprise from another. In fact, great customer service can turn former cost centers into profit centers by diversifying the function of service agents to include sales pitches, surveys, and customer profiling.

There are some critical questions that must be asked of an enterprise before employees are committed to "patching" a big process-driven model with systems integration.

Customer Service Pitfalls to Avoid

Avoid "throwing bodies" at the problem

Often times, customer service agents and sales staffing levels are artificially high because, in effect, employees are used to overcome the inadequacies of a poorly coupled information infrastructure. Customer contact personnel are used to act not only as intermediaries, but "protocol converters" between disparate data stores and internal processes.

By simply adding more bodies to the equation as a company grows, a false sense of efficiency is quickly realized. Staffing levels, then, are often a mask to the real problem of a basic undercurrent of systems inadequacy.

Decentralize operations, not intelligence

Many companies are restructuring their management and operational units such that localized autonomy can be achieved. This is a decent trend, however, too often the economy of scale afforded by cooperative computing is overlooked. For example, a customer records information retrieval system should not be replicated over diverse geographically separate systems.

Information such as employee data, inventory, and credit are often peculiar to a location, rather than shared by the entire enterprise. Most of the time, this can be overcome through the use of simple dial-up or dedicated access with data communications. As few as two or three locations can quickly recoup the cost of capital equipment and telecommunications costs with some planning.

Don't lose an opportunity to learn

Every customer contact is an opportunity to learn more about the patron's needs, buying habits, and other profile information. This data is essential for long-term growth of an enterprise. This is true even if each transaction is considered a "one-shot" sale, because the data can be used to ascertain demographic and market trend intelligence that is useful for product marketing and life-cycle planning.

Many times, a new systems integration effort overlooks the capture of critical information. Most systems integration efforts are put into place to force poorly designed systems to work together rather than rethinking the way an enterprise should be doing business with it's customers. This will be discussed in further detail later under the topic of resystemization.

Customer Service Planning Considerations

Now that we've discussed what to avoid, let's take a look at some of the critical success factors in upgrading or creating a modern customer service capability. This is where we begin to lead into the premise for client-server computer telephony, and how it is an integral part of your success in these ventures.

Systems Integration vs. Resystemization

There is a difference between systems integration and resystemization. Systems integration initiatives are primarily vehicles with which disparate systems are hobbled together. A systems integration initiative will often mask the totally separate nature of a telephone switch, mainframe, terminals, LANs, and voice response units.

A good systems integration job will mask the intricacies of the underlying computing and communications structure from both the customer and the service agent. To the customer's view, a seamless transaction may occur when calling for status of frequent flyer credits and subsequently ordering tickets with same.

This transaction may have been partially automated by collecting a frequent flyer number, providing account balance and award information through voice response, and then ultimately transferring the call to an agent for the actual ticketing.

In this scenario, most customers will have no idea that as many as three or four computers, multiple transmission lines, and complex switching went into this seemingly simple transaction.

The point here is for the systems planner to make a cognizant decision about the "phasing" of such an initiative. For example, the initial systems integration of an existing system may only fix the "front-end" of a customer service center and mask the inadequacies of an underlying "process driven" structure.

Figure 1.6 Phases Towards Resystemization

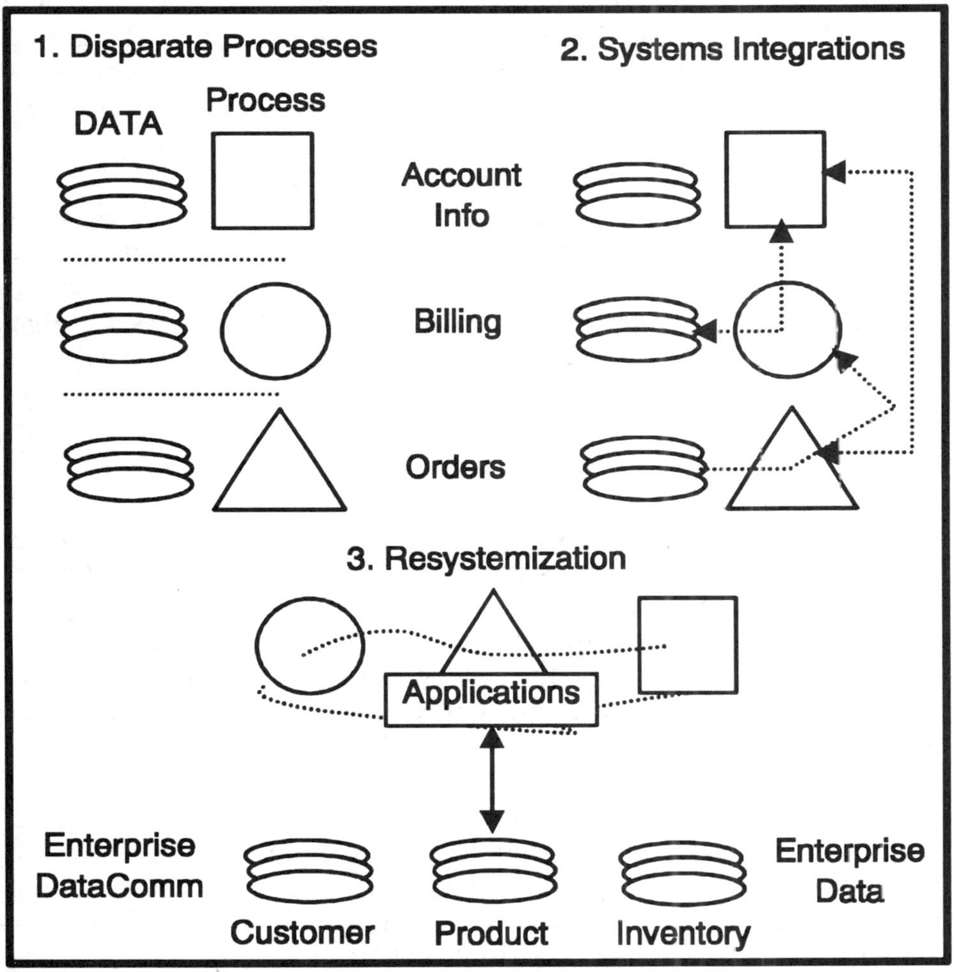

This is O.K. as a fist step, but the systems planner's job is certainly not done at this point. In reality, the "front-end" must be designed to adapt to an ever-changing computing and communication infrastructure, with flexibility and extensibility built in.

If the first phase of resystemization (which is almost always systems integration) is based on proprietary or custom solutions, critical opportunities for flexibility may be lost.

Reduce job stress

Any customer service planning initiative should be designed to reduce the overall level of stress that each customer contact employee faces each day. Ill-conceived initiatives will often simply eliminate positions and force more work on the remaining employees under the guise of improvements in efficiency. This is typified by rampant "downsizing" initiatives.

This is unfortunate, because it does not really serve the customer, which is the whole point of customer service in the first place. In other words, it is not a good idea to masquerade staffing reduction and efficiency initiatives under the guise of "improved customer service." Employees see right through this and loose confidence in the system planners and management when this occurs. This frustration always manifests itself in customer complaints.

The expectation of increased efficiencies needs to be separated from the overall human factors issue. Systems need to be specifically designed to accommodate human beings, as opposed to forcing people to adapt to the idiosyncrasies of machines. Too often the whim of a systems analyst or programmer results in years of frustration and stress for users of the system. This kind of thinking must be flushed-out from the very start. Chapter 12 discusses "evaluating potential solutions" and we'll revisit this issue in more detail there.

It is important to reduce job stress in order to maintain an image of consistency and maturity with your customer base. Employee turnover is very expensive, because of the general disruption, training, and spin-up time in bringing new employees on board. In addition, by reducing job stress, you will maintain better employee relations than your competitors. The issue of maintaining a competitive edge extends also to attracting and keeping good employees. It is an undeniable truth that some employees will quit to join a competitor who has a less stressful working environment, all other things being equal.

This concept of stress reduction can also be directed at the customer. Just take a look at what's happened to bank teller lines over the past fifteen years. ATM machines have provided the catalyst for a fundamental shift in the way people bank. Balances, deposits, transfers, and other simple transactions can be "self-navigated," so lines are shorter and only more complex transactions are carried-out inside the bank. Much is the same of bank-by-phone usage, although many people still prefer face-to-face transactions. The overwhelming fact is that the stresses associated with a long wait in line to merely get cash or check on balances have been reduced.

Involve multiple technologies

It is critical to embrace all that technology has to offer, assuming that the technology in question is reliable and economically feasible. Don't be afraid. The computer telephony industry is approaching $4 billion this year alone, and over $80 million worth of commercial grade fax and image servers were sold last year alone. Surely, there must be a substantive value in this technology for so much product to be shipping. No "hoax" or "fad" technology takes hold of the marketplace like this.

The use of these multiple technologies will help your customers to "self-navigate" through the appropriate information stores that you have. For example, customers can call into your fax-on-demand number and have bulletins and data sheets automatically faxed to them. They can check on order status, confirm balances, leave messages, and a host of other functions that just ten years ago were unheard of without live intervention.

To put it more simply, what are you waiting for? Don't let your competitors drag you kicking and screaming into the 21st century! Take an inventory of your corporate thinking and clean house by kicking out old ideas such as "nobody wants to talk to a machine..." Most people don't want to talk to a machine when it's *appropriate* to speak with a human being.

This argument does not support the relentless use of technology for technology's sake; we all have encountered poorly designed voice response systems that leave you in endless (useless) loops and don't allow human interaction when it's needed. The fallacy is to blame this problem on the technology itself. The same thinking that went into putting the weight of bad systems design on the customer service agent is simply being shifted directly to the customer in this case. Good planning, attention to customer needs, and involvement of your customer contact personnel will overcome these pitfalls.

The key is to clearly articulate your enterprise's view of customer service and then carefully select the technology to enable that vision. The bottom line is not to let ignorance of the technology get the best of you.

Think "Information Asset"

Consider all of the information that is currently patched together from disparate machines and processes. Just how circuitous is the path between these information stores and the ultimate consumer of the data? Will you have to invest more money and corporate resources in integrating these systems than just starting from scratch? Is your current system serving departmental fiefdoms or the customer?

These are some pretty tough questions that become more complex and controversial as companies grow. The same considerations required for good customer service design is what's fighting you - namely human nature.

It is human nature to view *information as power*. We have a tendency to hoard it or claim the information as our own. This mentality extends to the department level and therefore spawns petty behavior which cascades into disparate processes and duplication of data stores.

This is not to say that distributed, cooperative computing is bad because it helps each working group to add value to common data. It suggests rather that your biggest enemy is human nature itself. It is not often that a rock-solid customer service system is facilitated without the cooperation of upper management (and the help of mostly every department in an enterprise, for that matter).

The best companies with the highest grade of service also have a tendency to fight monolithic thinking, if not only monolithic processes. Besides, machines only do what we tell them to do, right? The point here is to work together and rethink the way in which information is stored, managed, used, and delivered. No amount of technology will slay the beast of selfish, petty, and politically-based thinking.

Process Driven View of Computing and Communications

Process-Driven vs. Information Asset View

Perhaps one of the most important concepts in the approach to client-server computer telephony is the philosophical approach to the way we view our computing and communications infrastructure. We've only scratched the surface of the distinction between a process-driven view versus an information asset view, so now its time to take a closer look in order to build a premise for what is covered in the next chapter on the client-server acid test.

In most businesses, we look at the way we do our jobs (departmentally) as linked processes. This can be viewed in a variety of ways, including how we function as an internal client or as an internal vendor to other departments. This is often true of TQM (total quality management) initiatives.

We are forced to look at those we interact with in a company as customers or vendors of the processes we manage. Of course, this conjures-up the image of so-called cross-functional teams and the "empowerment" model of
modern business management. The irony in these systems is that the actual processes inside each department usually stay the same, and it's just the human interaction between departments that improves.

The process-driven view of computing and communications seeks to define and manage information that is critical to running a certain function, or department in a business. The number of processes that are the responsibility of a certain group of people roughly define the departmental fiefdoms that make-up the overall enterprise. In effect, there are a variety of "businesses" inside of each enterprise.

Each department tends to build internal systems for itself that are proprietary either by design or usage, thus limiting the sharing of that information in a cooperative manner. We have a tendency to automate these processes so that we can be more "efficient." The resulting efficiency gains produced by departmental initiatives are more likely to generate improvements in the process, but not in the delivery of important and timely information across the enterprise.

The net result of this thinking is the creation, care, and feeding of dozens and dozens of internal "businesses." These isolated businesses have their own information stores, access methods, human interfaces, and uses with wide-ranging quality and overall utility. Each application owns its own data and usage rules which typically disregard the overall utility of that knowledge for other departments. This is a reality that paints a highly parochial picture in which most of us are the typical subjects in today's enterprise.

Not surprising is the way in which the disciplines of science and academia tend to replicate this same process-driven mindset. Take, for example the cornucopia of information stores accessible through the Internet. Hundreds of scientific societies, agencies, universities, and individuals are established as entities on this free-for-all information highway, yet the processes which give birth to the information stores are entirely separate. No wonder it takes years to master simple navigation on the Internet so that a user is considered a savvy Internet "traveler."

Table of process driven characteristics

- Data and applications are process-specific and tailored by organization
- Pockets of processes have a tendency to become monolithic systems
- Data is optimized for the process that "owns" it
- Data is "passed" between processes
- Intense human interactions drive the creation of discrete process mechanization
- Data integrity and consistency rules are restated inside of each application
- Data synchronization is maintained without a master source
- Requirements for data communications are application-specific
- No overall architecture drives system development
- Presentation management tends to be cryptic and host-based

Despite the fact that the information sharing on the "net' is considered critical and forward-thinking, it nonetheless has no standardized format for sharing the data as a homogenous asset. This utopia, alas, may never be realized in science and academia - but it's realistic to strive for such a model within an individual enterprise. Perhaps the lack of an overall cohesive architecture is in itself the most daunting problem of the process driven view of computing and communications.

Figure 1.7 Process-Driven Silos

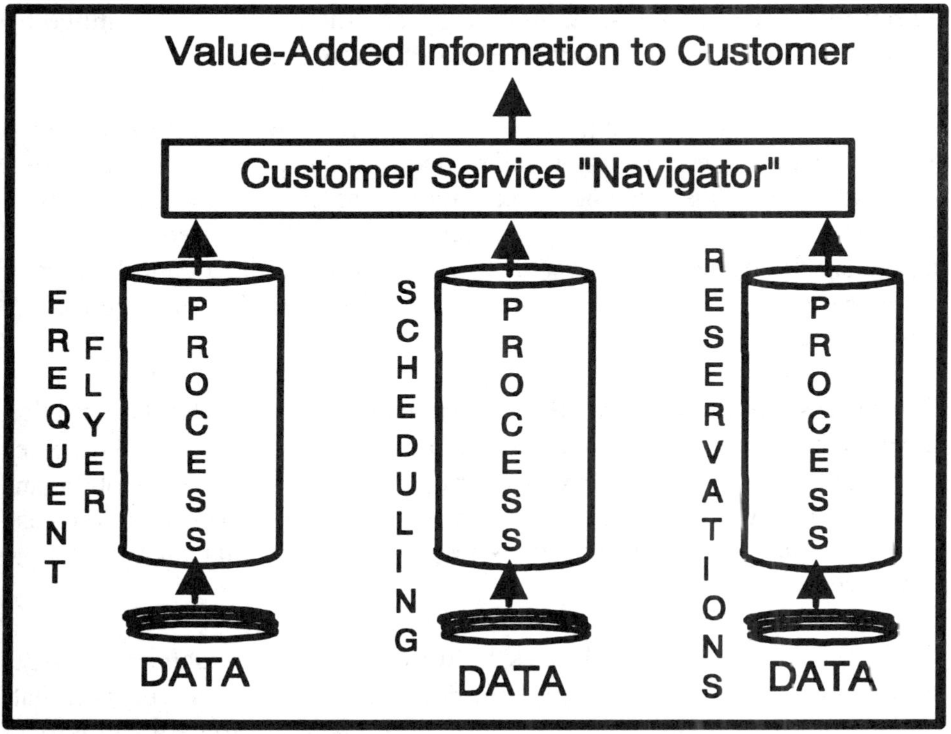

It would be a challenge for anyone to draw a flow diagram of such a view that represents a cohesive architecture within this mindset. The only one that comes to mind is represented in figure 1.7 as a collection of loosely-coupled "information silos." Unfortunately, the more silos there are in an enterprise, the more compounded the complexity of serving customers who have a thirst for information and service.

At best, this network of disparate processes and data stores is confounding, and at worst it is downright damning, especially in a highly competitive marketplace. One ever-present danger is corporate *downsizing*, because most of these initiatives are hell-bent on patching processes and automating ones that are inherently bad in the first place. In short, as the inimitable Mr. Banks would say: "We have a ghastly mess."

To further complicate the issue, the modular design of information asset re-use is animatedly limited by the hardware and systems that are currently in use or planned. This is because the hardware that was put into place from the get-go was not necessarily meant to be interoperable or cooperative with other platforms. In fact, even if interoperable and modular elements are put into place by well-meaning designers, their use may be limited by the process-driven view of how they should be used.

What's needed is for the data stores inherent in these systems to be looked at as an overall enterprise asset, rather than just a support mechanism for a set of processes. This concept is linked more to scientific thinking, inasmuch as the *data itself* in most scientific endeavors is the desired result. The trappings of support structure with which to derive the data are thought of as secondary or tertiary to the argument. This is certainly not the case in most businesses.

The process-driven view can be associated more with a cultural orientation rather than a technologically driven mindset. This is why we sometimes have a tendency to be wooed by faster, bigger, and better hardware platforms that may or may not have the right software to get the job done. In the case of the computer industry, one does not have to look that far to see how pervasive this thinking is.

How many computer companies hold onto proprietary schema that get faster and "better" in their own world, but offer no real (economical) interoperability outside of that model? Sure, there are some great vertical applications for order entry, general ledger, and so on that run on monolithic platforms, but separate maintenance, upgrades, and systems integration initiatives are required for an enterprise to adapt to the changing needs of their customers.

In the final analysis, the big question is whether or not incremental gains within a fundamentally flawed paradigm are a moot point. Perhaps this is what fueled open architecture initiatives such as OSCA (Open Systems Computing Architecture) at Bell Communications Research, and SCSA (Signal Computing System Architecture) within the computer telephony industry. Users of hardware and software are fed up with being held hostage by systems that don't allow them to be fickle.

As buyers, we want interchangeability, interoperability, modularity, scalability, portability - and all those other "bilities" the virtues of which have been touted by various international standards organizations over the years. One way of looking at the process-driven view is that we are held captive by our own cultural thinking, and that these problems become manifest in the systems that we buy, maintain, and adapt to. Computer manufacturers know this fact all too well, and we're mostly "cash cows" because of it.

Information Asset View

O.K. - let's climb down the soap box for a little while and present another approach to computing and communications. These models, by the way, are not being presented here for the first time. Modern thinkers have been espousing the virtues of the information asset view for some time now. In fact, many modern enterprises are beginning to embrace these views and have begun the slow process of resystemization. Examples of this can be seen at Dow Jones, GE Credit, and US West, all of whom have invested great talent and vision in some of these initiatives.

The idea behind the information asset view is to eliminate the inherent problems with individual fiefdoms of the enterprise. In this view, we seek to share information between internal "businesses" as a general asset, rather than something that is peculiar to one department. Some vendors don't like this idea, because requirements for more hardware platforms begins to go away as you realize the sanity of this approach...

Of course, some of you have the issue of security on the tip of your tongues and may want to rationalize the status quo because of this. In reality, security has more to do with the rules by which we create, access, and deliver information, so it's really not a paradigm argument. It's sufficient here to agree that security is extremely important, and obviously must be a critical capability of any model of computing and communications.

The driving force behind the sharing of this data is to help the enterprise to achieve competitive competence and to increase the overall success of the enterprise. To that end, you may not have to do this if have achieved same by some daily, timeless, miracle.

These characteristics are fundamentally different from the process driven view. Take a look at the way you manage your information systems. How do these models apply to the way in which you supply competitive customer service? Here is a snapshot of the characteristics that typify an information asset model:

Table of Information Asset View Characteristics

- Data is stored in subject-oriented databases
- Applications provide information via standard APIs
- Applications are packaged for extensibility and modularity
- Single-function applications that interoperate a development thrust
- Data fits the needs of the entire enterprise by design
- Control of data via *enterprise logical data model*
- Business rules either front-end data or are encapsulated in the data
- Data is converted into information by applications as required
- A clearly defined architecture drives systems development

At its very core, the information asset view demands the efficiency of modularity and rapid information delivery. In order to achieve this, the systems, databases, applications, and presentations used must be at least interoperable if not fully open-architected. This is why systems integration is required in the case of a heterogeneous environment where proprietary systems still exist.

Remember that systems integration is a stop-gap measure to overall resystemization, and in no way can be considered a panacea for a process-driven way of thinking. It is useful to compare and contrast the process driven view versus the information asset view of computing and communications. The table below provides a look at how you can logically separate the approaches to these paradigms from a systems perspective.

Note the differences between the two models in figure 1.8. The area of applications, presentation, communication, and data are stressed as differentiators. What comes to the surface almost immediately is the issue of modularity, re-use, and shared data. These elements are the basis with which client-server computing is based. Of course, these dame concepts are key for integrated computer telephony.

Figure 1.8 Process Driven vs. Information Asset Views

Process Driven View		Information Asset View
Applications and data are tailored to process flows within individual organizations such as marketing, sales, accounting, and manufacturing.	APPLICATIONS	Applications are designed to provide information through standard APIs. Only application specific data is "hidden" within (e.g. programming constants and data structures).
Every new application requires a restatement and reprogramming of "business rules" for maintaining data integrity, consistency , etc.	PRESENTATION	Interfaces to data are controlled via front-end systems that have access to the "business rules" in a self-standing rule base, semantic rule model, or through stored procedures or triggers.
Presentation management is generally host application driven with terminalsand/or PCs operating as terminals		Presentation management is done on end-user workstations. High-powered tools are used by end-user to create and customize the information views they desire.
Data is not sourced; it is difficult to determine where the master copy for data is in order to update, synchronize, or reference.	DATA	Data is sourced with a master copy and subordinate copies, all of which are synchronized and referential integrity is thus maintained.
Data is application specific and is embedded within the application or front-ended by it. Data is optimized for the processes involved.		Data is regarded as an asset and architected to fit the entire enterprise's needs.
Discrete processes are mechanized, usually wherever human interaction is most intense and potential cost savings are substantial. Collections of processes become monolithic systems.	COMMUNICATIONS	Applications are modularized and packaged in such a way as to become assets themselves. There is no need to reinvent the wheel every time a variation on a theme is needed.
Data communications requirements are application specific, thus proliferating many specialized networks. Data is passed from one application to the next.		Inter-system communication is accomplished via APIs and open architected protocol suites. Applications are abstracted from intricacies of underlying networks.

If enterprise data can be well structured, easy to access, and reasonably stable, then the applications which use this data can be more easily planned for and adapted. In fact, the applications themselves do not have to be born out of the peculiarities of a departmentally-owned database. Rather, the applications, presentation, business rules, and data can be completely separated - so each element can be re-used or replicated easily across the enterprise.

This is not to say that common enterprise data necessarily has to drive functions "back into the data center." Surely, some centralized processes make sense, but the point is that business-specific applications will be more cooperative and extensible with the information asset view.

The theme of modularizing all of the aspects of the environment is the ultimate death knell for proprietary systems. For example, the computing systems of yester-year stacked the data, applications, hardware, presentation, altogether inside of the same monolithic system. From a computer platform view, it may be easier to look at it as a value-added continuum, as pictured in figure 1.9. On the extreme left, we have the so-called monoliths - all the way over to a more modular open-systems view of things on the right.

This "breaking down" or modularizing of elements is inevitable in all marketplaces. It happened in word processing, computer-aided design, and general computing. It happened over the past 12 years in the computer telephony industry as well. It still has not altogether occurred in the telephone switch industry, which is about 10-15 years behind the computer industry in this respect.

The modularization possible within the constructs of the information asset paradigm help to foster greater flexibility, scalability, and overall enterprise utility. This lends itself to the idea of *rightsizing*, first coined by Sun Microsystems to describe an overall strategy for dealing with the proliferation of disparate platforms and computing models.

According to Sun, rightsizing is the process of re-evaluating information systems resources to see how they meet current business requirements and then evolving those resources to maximize cost-effectiveness and maintain the business's competitive advantage.

Figure 1.9 Modularity & Value-Added Continuum

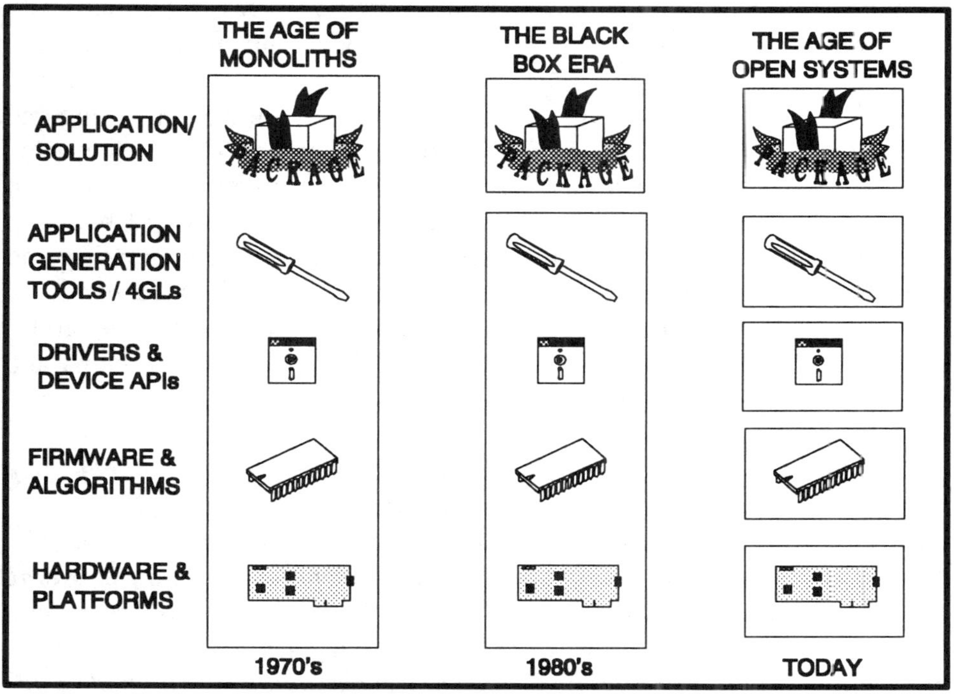

In particular, the rightsizing phenomenon describes the movement towards network-enabled client-server environments. Because the discipline of client-server computing is independent of hardware, rightsizing initiatives can span platforms of all kind.

By using the client-server model, original investments in existing equipment and software (whether they be proprietary or open architected), can be made more durable. As discussed earlier, business applications are either process driven or information asset driven. The information asset model stresses the importance of separating application, database, and user interfaces so these elements may interoperate and run on different platforms, if necessary.

With client-server forms of computing, the information asset view is much easier to implement, because applications are separated into components that interoperate regardless as to their physical location. For example, the database for a certain application or group of applications can reside on a mainframe, the application can be on a multi-user server, and the user interface can be accessed on desktop workstations. This approach has many advantages, none the least of which is improved processing efficiencies, conservation of time, and more modularity in development and growth.

So far, we've discussed some of the driving factors in the computing and communications infrastructure of the modern enterprise. These issues were primarily focused on customer service, however, virtually all aspects of business are impacted by business process re-engineering and planning considerations. Before we can master the confluence of computing and communications, however, it is important to explore the true nature of client-server. The next chapter provides a discussion of client-server architectures and a methodology for "testing" both your current systems and your thinking compared to this computing model.

Special thanks to both Gary Bradley and Carol McIntosh for their help with this chapter. They are both consummate experts in the field of resystemization and systems integration, having been involved in dozens of special projects with major computer companies and telephone companies. Along with their partner Rex Stringham, Gary and Carol founded the Enterprise Integration Group, a consulting firm that specializes in customer and communications management. The customer service initiatives outlined in this chapter and portions of chapter two are straight out of their open architecture doctrine.

Gary Bradley has over 25 years experience in the telecommunications and computer industries. In his first 10 years in telecommunications, Gary was responsible for both the day-to-day management and the staff support of a wide variety of residential and commercial customer service centers. He subsequently moved into the computer environment as a Director of Implementation for numerous customer service support systems.

These systems were provided by AT&T or developed within his operating company over a 5 year period. Gary rounded out his 21 years in telecommunications as a Director of Strategic Systems Planning and a Technical Director of Systems Engineering. In the latter role, he was responsible for the team which developed the distributed processing architecture currently being deployed across a 14 state region.

After exercising an early retirement option, Gary spent over 2 years as a Marketing Manager in the telecommunications division of a major computer OEM. In this role, he developed a solutions-oriented UNIX sales strategy and a platform-oriented approach to the deployment of distributed, customer service support systems. Over the last 2 years, Gary has been an independent consultant. A notable achievement during this period was his project management and creative contribution to a very comprehensive, cross-industry sales and marketing program for a major open systems OEM. This program is designed to go beyond common customer service requirements by providing a solutions-oriented approach to enterprise-wide customer management.

Carol McIntosh has over 25 years combined experience managing a variety of customer service, data, and billing centers, as well as developing systems to support customer service centers, and developing strategies for the re-systemization of legacy systems. Ms. McIntosh's career includes key positions at a Regional Bell Operating Company, as well as strategic consulting roles with major computer OEMs. Her expertise includes prototyping and rapid application development, including the design of state-of-the-art end user interfaces. As an open systems marketing consultant, she has conducted extensive primary and secondary research in the customer service market. She has also conducted numerous customer management and telecommunications seminars around the world.

2

The Client-Server Acid Test

There's much confusion afoot regarding the meaning of client-server. In fact, if you stop people on the street and ask them what they think it means, you're likely to get a hundred differing opinions on the subject. Actually, you're likely to get just as many opinions from self-appointed computer industry experts. Since this book goes into such detail on how client-server computer telephony can help you and your business, a straight-forward "acid test" has been devised in order to debunk, demystify, and otherwise establish some definitions on this sometimes controversial subject.

Distributed, cooperative processing

Client-server architectures help to facilitate the information asset view of computing and communications as discussed in the first chapter. The basic premise behind the information asset view is that data is shared by applications, data communications are shared by applications, and processes are modularized and re-used. In addition, business rules, synchronization, and transport protocols are abstracted from applications.

According to International Data Corporation, client-server computing is a "method for designing and implementing applications that are functionally separated into distinct processes. These functions can be placed on the same processor or (increasingly) distributed on multiple processors within a network. The location of function is transparent to the user."

In essence, distinguishing processes are distributed - but everything else is shared. It is to this end that client-server architectures are implemented. Remember, all of the trappings of a client-server paradigm can be purchased and installed, however, it is the intent and use of the gear and requisite software that makes a certain system conform to the client-server model.

Some people describe a client as a requesting process or application. The strict definition of a client describes it as a communications component which requests data on behalf of a process. In effect, a client "front-ends" a request for data submitted to it by a requesting (user) process for a certain job. In other words, conventional wisdom states that a client is the whole PC, Workstation, or whatever platform that needs shared resources. In effect, most of us personify the simple client function as an entire group of functions that are coupled. This is false, inasmuch as we use the word "client" not in the classic sense, but rather as a term of convenience.

So far, we could be talking about a dumb character-based terminal in a host/slave environment, but here is where the similarity ends: In a true client-server implementation, a requesting process (user) has the ability to massage data that is invoked from the client function and to further provide value-added capabilities. The phrase "value-added" suggests that some intelligence is required on the client side in order to massage the data. The client element itself is not the item that is doing the value-added, however.

Much like the client, a server is also a *communications component* that front-ends a foreign process or application. The process or application provides data to the server, which subsequently hands-off the data to the client. One of the subtleties of a true server function is that you cannot attribute a physical database as necessarily having inherent server characteristics.

In other words, the simple physical location of files on a so-called file server does not make the file server machine *itself* a true server. Some serving application or process needs to be in-between the physical database and the requesting (user) process such that business rules, consistency, security allow for *cooperative access* to the data.

For example, a PC connected to a LAN may locate some of its data files on a network drive, however, this alone does not constitute a true client-server relationship. Another way of drawing the distinction would be to consider how you might run a local copy of an RDBMS (Relational Database Management System) program on your LAN-connected PC. Let's say you use Telemagic, a popular sales contact management application. Telemagic allows you to change, store, and retrieve information on customer sales contacts. The application itself runs on a local PC as does the underlying Clipper-based database engine, and associated database files and index files.

Figure 2.1 Paradigm Shift in Networked Computing

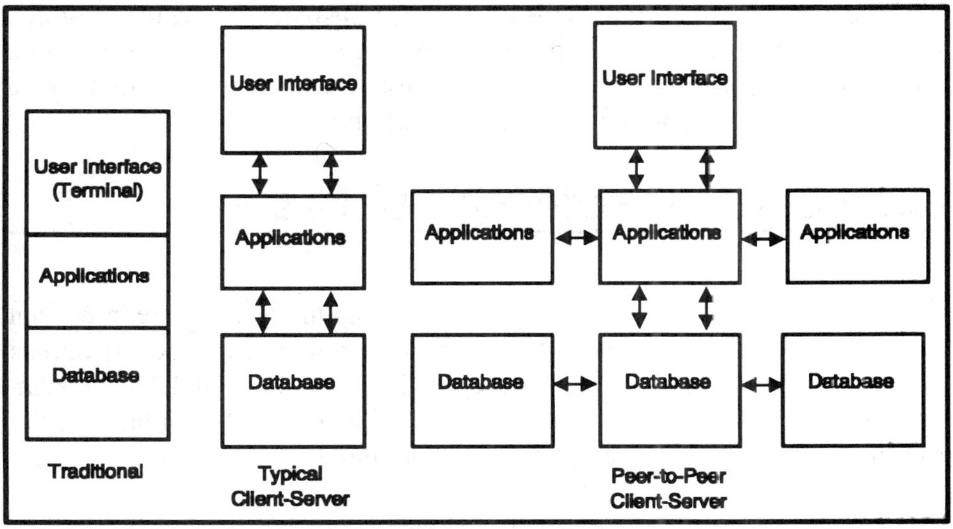

If you located just the files on a file server, then you still would not be operating in a true client-server model. This is because the required processing power and application for database search activities is still bound to the application inside the local PC. This is not the case with network versions of such products, where the database engine activity and processes reside on a foreign processing node (on the network). Thus off-loading local CPU cycles required for database engine activity to the foreign processing node allows for shared access to same by other users.

It's important at this point to say that you do not have to have a network, (local area or otherwise), to conform to a client-server model. For example, it is indeed possible to locate both client and server processes inside of the same host platform or PC.

In fact, it's the ability to separate these client and server processes between platforms *or* to combine them on one platform which is the very basis for the client-server acid test! Figure 2.1 shows the relationship between more traditional (host/slave) and client-server forms of networked computing. The paradigm shift in the way computers are networked is broken down in greater detail in this chapter.

In practice, pure client-server computing on an enterprise basis is not so easy. The reality of embedded minicomputers, mainframes, individual PCs, workgroups, and terminals dictates that client-server computing will grow in pockets and eventually provide a "web of transparency" inside of which new and existing computers and people can communicate. A truly effective client-server implementation can make access to data totally transparent, so the intricacies of a complex infrastructure are hidden.

Client-Server Relationship Definitions

There are several types of networked computing models that are important to understand before you can fully grasp the nature of client-server impact on computer telephony. Each of these relationships, or models, has instantiations in the marketplace from a variety of vendors. Individual vendor offerings can be roughly categorized in this manner:

- Level One - Traditional, or encapsulated
- Level Two - Basic Workgroup
- Level Three - Multi-Tiered / Departmental
- Level Four - Peer-To-Peer / Extended Enterprise

Level One - Traditional, or encapsulated

The encapsulated model typifies the environment which many stand-alone PCs, workstations, and other computer platforms use. In this case, the application, presentation, APIs, access to data, and rules governing the operation of the system are bound together in one monolithic process. The traditional model provides basic interconnection between devices, primarily in a host/slave relationship between ASCII terminals and asynchronous hosts or 3270-like terminals and mainframes.

This level also includes X terminal interconnection to asynch hosts. The common thread at this level of networking, is that the services provided to the so-called clients are completely host-based. A simplified representation of the traditional model is pictured in figure 2.2.

Figure 2.2 Traditional, or Encapsulated Model

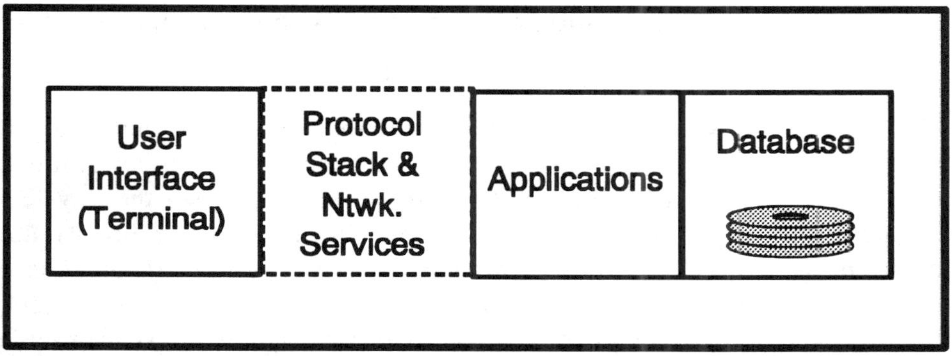

All application level intelligence and database services reside in a centralized computer, and the terminals are peripheral I/O devices. The key benefits to this type of networking is centralized maintenance and control, so applications must be designed for high "uptime." The criticality of applications in this type of environment is very high, since the entire computing infrastructure sometimes rests on a single platform. This is networked computing, however, it can be strongly argued that this does not represent a true client-server architecture, as the rest of this chapter will prove.

An enhancement of the traditional model is the use of "intelligent front-ends" which functionally replace and enhance the capabilities of dumb terminals. Environments using this level of networked computing are typified by the use of PCs as front-ends to CICS environments as discussed in chapter one (i.e., PCs as GUI replacements for character-based terminals, with "screen-scraping" capabilities).

The management of such an arrangement is still centrally administered, with the addition of a PC-based LAN, for example, with a mainframe gateway capability.

Depending on the functions implemented, it is possible to have limited client-server functions at this level, however, the "intelligent front-ends" are usually designed to mask the rough edges of a pre-eminent host/slave environment.

One way of looking at this is to consider the OSI application layer structure (reference model of computing and communications established by ISO 7498) and "collapse" it into virtually one layer. Of course, this may not apply if the system in question communicates with other processes over dedicated data links.

In the end analysis, one way of determining whether or not a given architecture can be called client-server is to consider this seven-layer model. If you can only identify three or less broad layers between the physical elements and the application, then the item in question is probably *not* conforming to a true client-server model. The seven-layer model is a universal way of distinguishing vendor and service offerings for equipment, software, and network services. It is rare to find one vendor who can provide hardware and software for all seven layers, so today's buyers must be expert at matching offerings that make-up a specific system design.

Basic client-server model

From a technical view, client-server refers both to processing and communications mechanisms to achieve interoperability between disparate components or platforms. At its very root, a local processing component (also termed "user" as identified in ISO 10031-1) submits a request for service. The local processing component invokes the services of its local "client," which is actually a communications component. This client then sets-up a peer-to-peer transaction with the server element, which is also a communications component. This server side of the transaction then establishes or invokes services from processing components on the foreign end of the link.

It is important to note that master/subordinate relationships are not the intent of client-server relationships. This is especially true of systems that establish one-to-many and many-to-one relationships concurrently. To treat either side of the equation as subordinate or superior actually limits the intended openness of distributed, cooperative computing.

Especially intriguing to buyers of computer telephony systems is this notion of distributed, cooperative computing. The implication is that computers, telephone switching functions, and networks can be widely distributed, yet interoperable. It is this premise that validates the use and reference to the OSI application layer model. Virtually any relationship between computers, databases, transport methods, and protocols can be explained in terms of this 7-layer model.

Traditional networked computing models can be articulated in terms of the 7-layer model as well as true client-server architectures. Perhaps the distinguishing factor between the two is the ability to abstract the users of the technology away from the lowest levels of the model.

For example, a service agent who accesses various hosts with two or three terminals and their associated (and keystroke intensive) log on sequences is not abstracted from these layers. On the other hand, the user of a workstation equipped with auto-logon software and multi-host server gateways probably has no idea where each host is and what the manual logon sequence is. That's the very point of implementing client-server technology... The OSI application layer structure is described in figure 2.3 below.

Although simplified in fewer than seven layers, figure 2.4 pictures a classic client-server logical model. This example is pictured as separate client and server machines (not to be confused with the actual elements). The "boxes" that provide the distinguishing characteristics of client-server elements are the ones labeled as "Client Management" and "Application Agent or Server Management." Note how these elements are separate from the APIs, Applications, and other processes. This is a key differentiator when you are reviewing a variety of vendor solutions and want a true client-server product.

If a vendor cannot articulate his or her product in these terms, then one of two things is apparent: 1) the product does not possess the requisite characteristics of client-server; or 2) the information you are reviewing may be high-level marketing collateral. If you suspect the later is the case, you need to speak with a technically astute person who works for the company in question and ask for a deeper explanation.

Figure 2.3 OSI Application Layer Structure

OSI layer	Examples	Functions
7 Application	APIs; Application process (AP); entities (AE), service elements (ASEs)	"Programming interfaces" invoked by applications in order to establish communication services
6 Presentation	X11; GUIs, etc.	"Language and dialect" elements including code conversion, encryption, and device emulation
5 Session	ASP (SS7)	"Logical sessions" to establish connections; synchronize transmissions from transport layer
4 Transport	TCP; UDP; SSCP (SS7)	"Packet assembly," set-up and tear-down of messages, segmentation of data stream, and error recovery
3 Network	CCITT Q.931, Q.932; ANSI T-1.607, 610; IP	"Packet routing," routing of data link-to-link; congestion control, node-to-node functions; call control in ISDN
2 Data Link	ANSI T-1.602; LAPB; SDLC; CCITT Q.921; 802.2 LLC ; 802.3-5 MAC, etc.	"Message packaging" and link management, flow control, framing, addressing, error checking, transfer between nodes
1 Physical	DS-0; V.35; 10BT; 802.x PHY ; RS-232, etc.	"Activate connection" at the mechanical/electronic level, send & receive bits; multiplex & allocate channel resources

Figure 2.4 Basic Client-Server Model

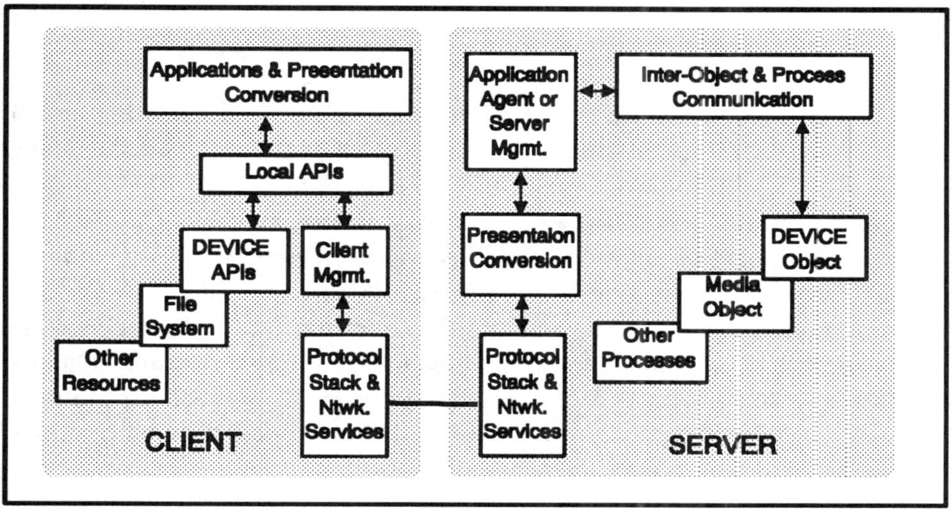

Level Two - Basic Workgroup

This level of networked computing operates at the workgroup level, or sub-department level. As such the domain is small and limited to specific, rather than enterprise-wide functions. Architecturally, a single tier of interconnection is typical.

The types of services provided as shared resources in this environment include simple print, file, and e-mail capabilities. The approach to managing such a system is fairly straight forward, since it is just for a small group of computers, however the management becomes more complex when these systems are interconnected with "out of group" networks and computers. The criticality of such a system is low, since the impact of down-time and other failures is limited to one workgroup.

Although tedious, a system using this model can be configured to avoid a single point of failure. This is the case since each node on the network has both client functions, server functions, and access to its own data stores in addition to others. In a way, this is a method for achieving "poor man's" fault tolerance. In other words, you can replicate numerous nodes and update them either manually or periodically to synchronize data in case one of the nodes crashes.

End-to-end response time between clients is minimized with this model because many of the functions required by each user are local, so the horsepower required to do a majority of the work is kept off the network. Of course, this is optimal only when casual use of another user's data is required. There are disadvantages of this approach, however. For example, system administration is made very difficult. A case in point would include software release control, and replication/synchronization of data. Since the data is entirely distributed, central maintenance is rarely an option. There's also the issue of high cost. With models of this kind, the need for multiple copies of (localized) application software, dedicated communication links, and per-node database management is a reality.

Figure 2.5 Basic Workgroup Model

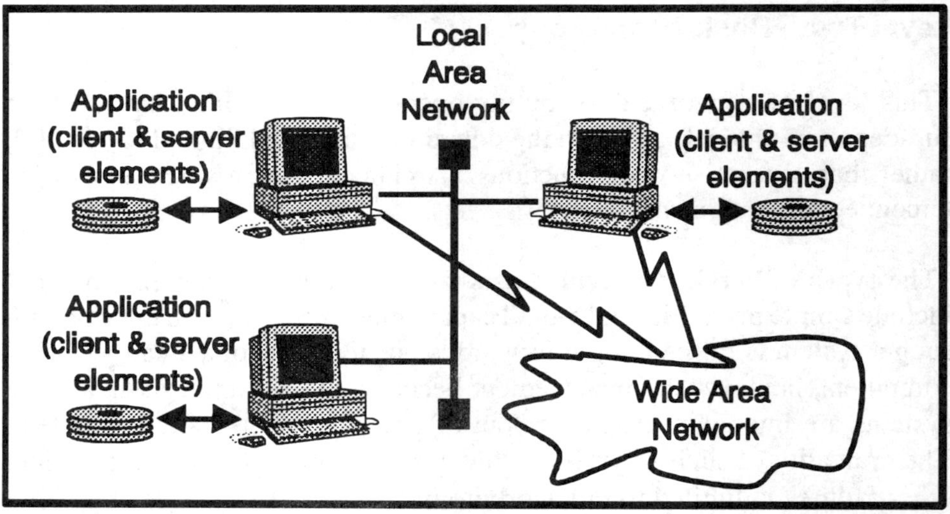

In many cases, this single-tier method of implementing client-server is just fine for locations where only several users are accessing the system. Take, for example, a small law office or auto parts store. If there's only two or three PCs, then a purchase of a file server, print server, or communication gateway may not be necessary.

Level Three - Multi-Tiered / Departmental Model

Management of a medium-sized domain at the departmental level can be fairly complex, and it is common to find nested networks and sub-networks which derive services from several servers. Applications are fairly sophisticated in such a domain, and the criticality of use is much more acute. For example, customer service, sales, and fulfillment services could all be in the same departmental domain at this level.

With a multi-tiered model, some of the meatier advantages of client-server computing become evident. For example, site licenses for network versions of software cost considerably less for system with as few as five nodes. In addition, system resiliency is much more robust, since redundant disk drives, CPUs, and power supplies can be shared across the network, thus limiting the instance of a single point of failure.

Multi-tiered models are also typified by a proliferation of "serving" nodes. For example, file servers, database servers, communication server, and fax servers to name a few. The driving force behind this proliferation of nodes on a network is the economy of scale inherent in shared resources. For example, a fax server may have four ports of computerized fax capability that can be shared across many client elements.

Likewise, it is a distinguishing characteristic of multi-tiered systems to isolate all RDBMS and communication server functions from the applications and presentation servers themselves. "Modem pooling" is a tried and true concept from the past generation that is replicated easily in today's communications server, who's serving communication element establishes logical connections to each client that needs datacom capability.

This "sharedness" can be taken a step further outside of the enterprise by establishing virtual connections with foreign servers via packet switched and frame relay networks as discussed in the next chapter.

The ratio between workstation and file servers in a multi-tiered system can range widely, depending on the memory and disk requirements of each requesting process. For example, the "paging" memory required for X terminals and graphics workstations can be a large drain on the servers in such a system. This has fueled the popularity of symmetrical multi-processors and memory-intense servers which are optimized to deal with much traffic on the LAN. Of course, regular Windows-based workstations have different constraints, but the balance of intelligence across the nodes on the system is different as well. One case for diskless workstations, however, is that they do not require the same administrative overhead as full-blown workstations.

Alas, there are disadvantages in a multi-tier scenario, none the least of which is long boot times and an average cost per seat that still does not approach the economies of peer-to-peer systems. The number of servers required, and the amount of memory on those servers is also a consideration, especially if system resiliency is an issue. In order to approach the same level of system redundancy and reliability associated with mainframe systems, duplicate hardware is required. For example, RAID arrays (redundant array of inexpensive disks), hot-swappable power supplies, and dual networks are not uncommon in order to achieve system resiliency.

Figure 2.6 Multi-Tiered / Departmental Model

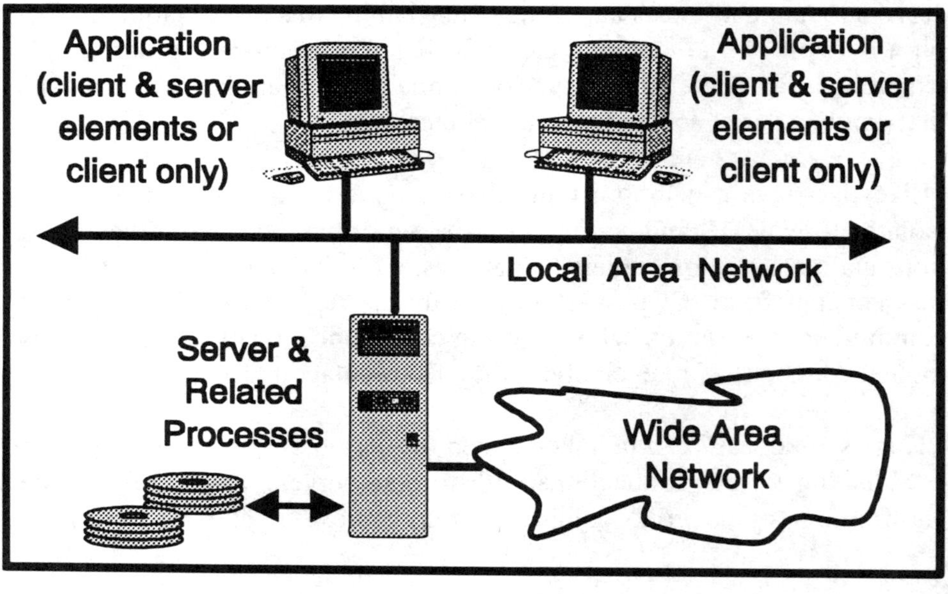

Some would argue that with all of this redundancy, that you'd do just as well to stay with a basic workgroup system and beef-up on hardware and memory at each seat. Perhaps the best way to determine which way to go is to consider the number of applications that each client needs to access and the actual size and CPU consumption of each program. Figure 2.6 shows how a typical multi-tiered architecture is put together.

Level Four - Peer-To-Peer / Extended Enterprise Model

A more sophisticated yet complicated approach to client-server computing is the *peer-to-peer* model. This level of networked computing is enterprise-wide and typified by use of complex topologies and advanced connectivity options for a variety of services. As with traditional models, the criticality of such a network is very high, since the entire business is dependent on its reliability.

Most medium to large sized companies have the challenge of interconnecting a variety of computers (including mainframes, minis, and PCs), so handling huge domains of this nature is a worldwide reality. The "extended" enterprise is a model for heterogeneous interoperability between vendors and suppliers.

A cluster of forth-level domains are interconnected so users of the system have a view of multiple enterprises and their associated processes. Hospitals, medical centers, insurance companies and testing laboratories, for example can participate in such a level of computing. Of course, all of these enterprises cannot be co-located, so telecommunications comes heavily into play.

Chapter three deals with telecommunications management and technology, so a discussion of the methods for interconnecting peer-to-peer domains is handled there. The management of these extended enterprises is very complex, since both local and global models of use and business rules need to be applied. Systems integration enthusiasts are especially fond of this model because "legacy" (traditional) systems, whether they be minicomputers or mainframes can be taken advantage of into the future.

Figure 2.7 Peer-To-Peer Client-Server Model

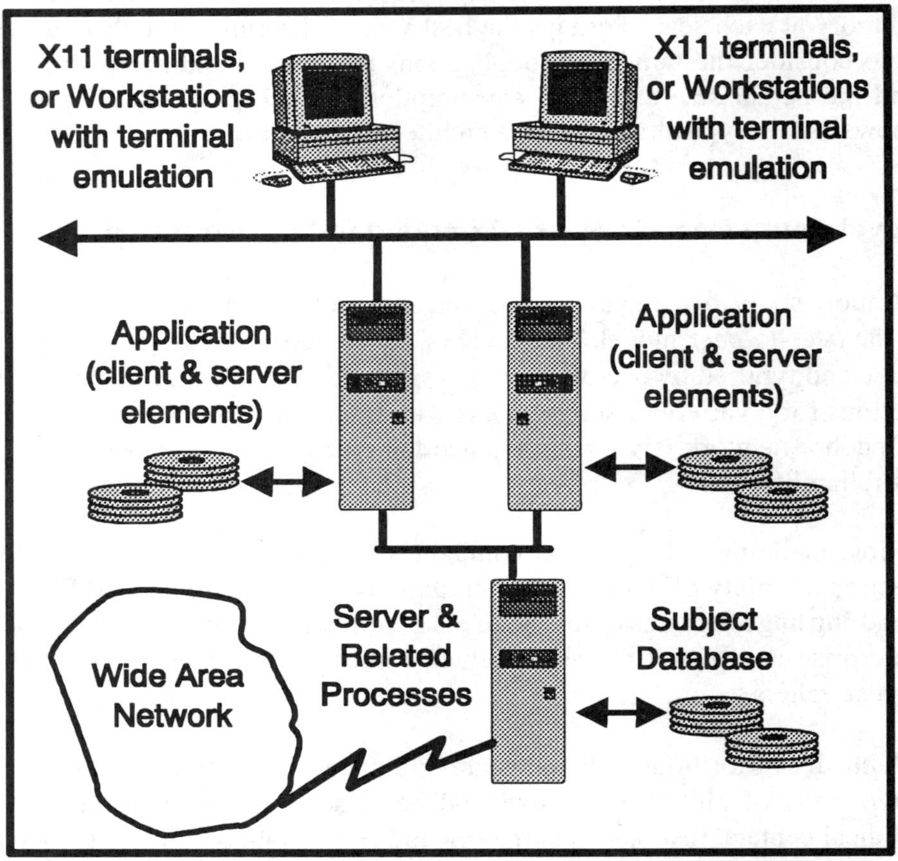

The peer-to-peer model exploits these systems as depositories for database rather than the drivers for applications. In this case, a transaction server is used to set-up OLTP (On-line Transaction Processing) sessions with host computers as an intermediary for the enterprise.

Multiple application processors and associated servers work in consort with lower tiers in order to deliver the required information to the workstation or terminal. In the case of an X-windows implementation, the cooperative computing is happening at the second and third tier and the terminals are used primarily for presentation and delivery of pre-massaged information. In effect, X-terminals act as if they were dumb character-based terminals, as described in the traditional model.

The similarity with older character-based terminals fades, however, when you consider the ability to traverse multiple screens, establish simultaneous sessions, and "scrape" data from one window in order to add it to another.

On To The Test

In reality, our industry would come to a screeching halt if every vendor had to conform to this crucible. Although client-server computing is elegant and modern, the author in no way is suggesting that everything should be scrapped in order to move ahead. To suggest this would certainly have a negative impact on customer service, which is the driving force behind considering client-server computer telephony in the first place.

Later in this book, you will be introduced to many vendors who have viable solutions for call centers, service bureaus, and stand-alone applications. Many of these offerings use client-server attributes, and some at least come close. You'll see a number of offerings that are in essence, host/slave (traditional) offerings, however they are listed because they provide migration paths to resystemization through system integration initiatives.

Take this simple test (figure 2.8) to see how close an offering (or your system) fits into the client-server paradigm. Each question scores points on a scale of one to five; five being true to client-server conventions, and one being not so true. Add the scores form each question to yield the final result. A total score between 28 and 35 is excellent. Scores between 21 and 27 suggest that the system in question is "trying hard." Any total yielding less than 17 is cause for a total rethink of your computing and communications infrastructure..

Figure 2.8 Client-Server Acid Test

"Acid Test" Question	**Circle Appropriate Score** *less true* *more true*
1. You can *describe* the system in terms of the OSI model	1 -- 2 -- 3 -- 4 -- 5
2. Client communication components can be distributed across *more* than one platform and call upon distributed server communication components	1 -- 2 -- 3 -- 4 -- 5
3. Server communication components can be distributed across more than one platform and called upon by one *or* more distributed client components	1 -- 2 -- 3 -- 4 -- 5
4. Both client communication components *and* server communication components can reside inside the same platform or can be wholly distributed across a network with no substantial degradation of service	1 -- 2 -- 3 -- 4 -- 5
5. Access to data communications, subject databases, computer fax resources, and computer telephony devices, are *not* dedicated by design	1 -- 2 -- 3 -- 4 -- 5
6. User processes *are* abstracted from protocol stack specifics by the client element	1 -- 2 -- 3 -- 4 -- 5
7. Master/subordinate relationships are *not* forced by design	1 -- 2 -- 3 -- 4 -- 5
TOTALS	

The author would like to thank Fabian Lubais and David Herington of SunSoft for their input on the Client-Server Acid Test. Much of the client-server modeling and examples were based on various white papers and other Sun Microsystems documents dealing with rightsizing and distributed cooperative computing. Thanks also to Carol McIntosh and Gary Bradley of the Enterprise Integration Group for their insights on resystemization and client-server paradigms.

3

Telecommunications Management ... for the 90's

This past century has been incredibly rich regarding the advances in telecommunications. Yet, despite our advances, there are many services available to businesses that are simply under-utilized or misunderstood. Fiber optics and advanced networks provide literally millions of times more throughput than the simple telegraph did one hundred years ago, yet many businesses operate as if nothing has happened. This chapter will help to clarify what is possible with modern communications networks and how they relate to computer telephony. Before you jump into the management of telecommunications, it's important to review some definitions.

Telecommunications

Telecommunications, or telecom for short, is the transmission or reception of signals, images, sounds, or intelligence of any nature by wire, radio, light pulse, or electromagnetic system. That just about covers virtually any means of transmission, regardless of source, channel, or media type. Telephony and *data communications* are subsets of telecommunications that are specific to computer-type transmissions and telephone-type transmissions, respectively.

Telephony

Taken from Greek root words meaning "far sound," telephony is the discipline of converting or transmitting voice or other signals over a distance, and then re-converting them to an audible sound at the far end.

Data Communications

This is a form of telecommunications that concentrates on the movement of encoded information from one point to another. This information is readable by machines, such as modems, computers, and fax machines as opposed to telephony, which is "readable" by the human ear.

Computer Telephony

Computer telephony represents the cooperative merger between telephony and data communications. It is a form of telecommunication that concentrates on the movement of both encoded and voice-related information from one point to another for the purpose of automating transactions between machines and humans, or between machines.

Interactive voice response, voice mail, and every type of host computer-to-switch integration scheme are examples of computer telephony. Because computer telephony requires both computers and telephones to work cooperatively, data processing is employed.

In general, data processing refers to the electronically automated processing of information wherein; 1) The information content or meaning of the data is in any way transformed and/or 2) The output information constitutes a programmed response to input information.

Figure 3.1 shows the relationships between data communications, telephony, and computer telephony. Note how these elements are all subsets of telecommunications. Although many people use these terms interchangeably, they represent distinct concepts.

Figure 3.1 Telecommunications Types

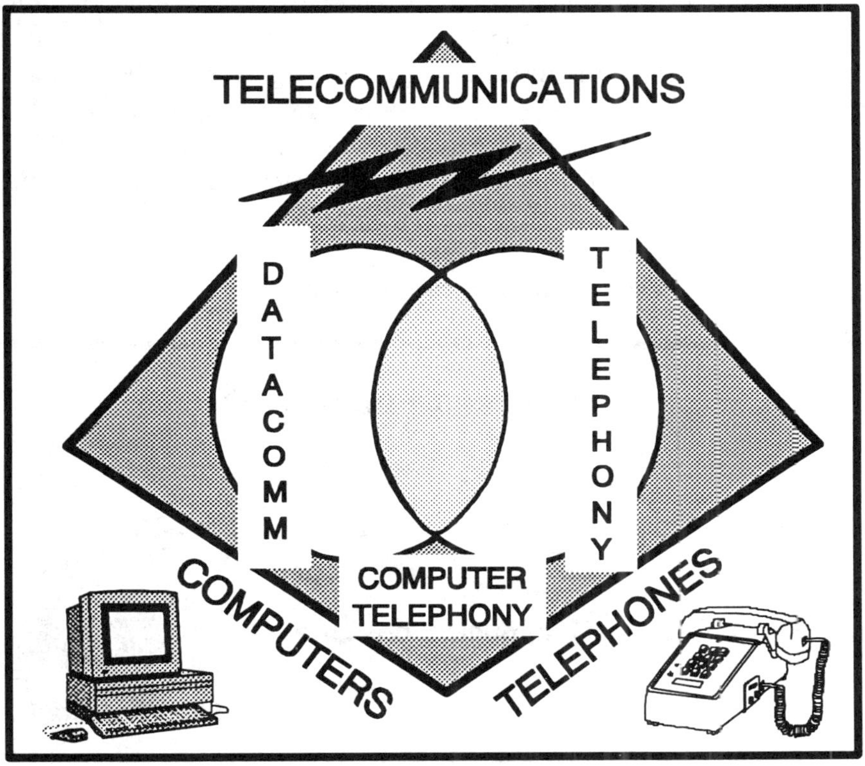

Figure 3.2 Elements of a Telecommunications System

Source: The transmitter of the information
Channel: The component that carries the information
Sink: The component that receives the information

As pictured in figure 3.2, any telecommunications system requires three basic elements: 1) the source, or transmitter of the information, 2) the telecommunications *channel*, and 3) the sink, or receiver of the information. In the case of a data communications system (figure 3.3), the source is a host computer, the channel could be copper pairs supporting an RS-232 data link, and the sink is a terminal. Likewise, the same relationship can be expressed in terms of a telephony-based system, as pictured in figure 3.4.

Figure 3.3 Basic Data Communications System

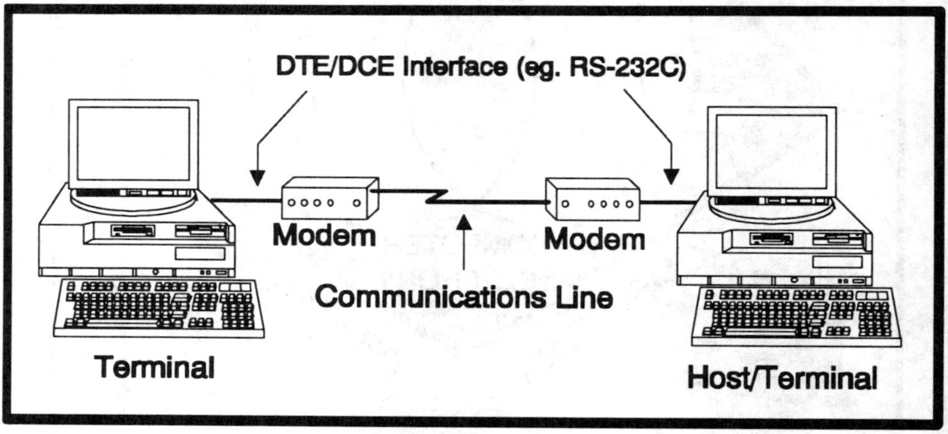

Figure 3.4 Basic Telephony System

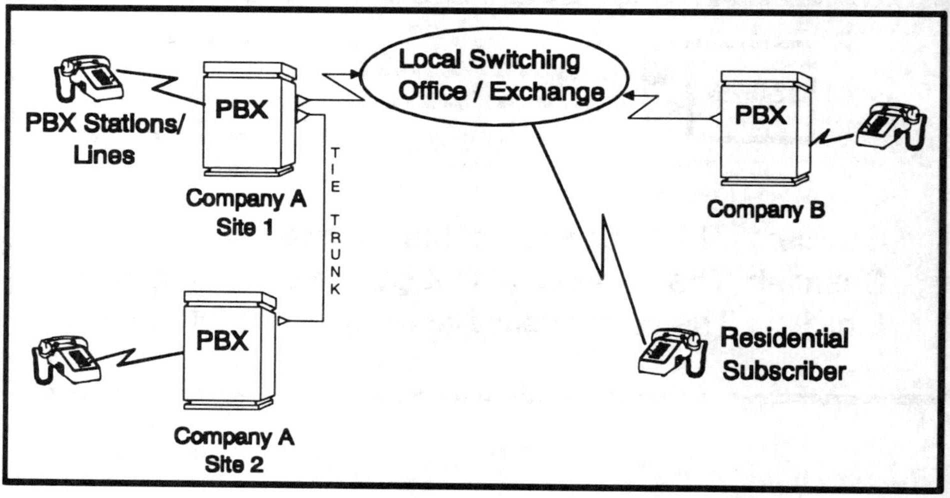

In this case, the telephone instrument is the sink, and copper pairs are often the channel. The switch behaves as the source, which provides "data" in the form of a voice communication transmitted from another telephone. It's easy to see how terminals can act in the role of source and sink simultaneously. Such is the case with a peer-to-peer client-server implementation, for example.

Telecommunications Channels

All telecommunications capabilities are dependent on channels to carry the payload, or information being transmitted. Even though pairs of copper wires seem primitive compared to fiber optic cables, they are nonetheless ubiquitous and the most common means for interconnecting station gear.

Much research and development has gone into the re-use of existing wire pairs. Considering the work that went into installing over 150,000,000 cables over the past 100 years, this is a worthy initiative.

In fact, both Basic Rate ISDN (BRI), twisted pair Ethernet (10BaseT), and T-1 circuits can utilize copper pairs. In some cases, these technologies can use the same copper pairs that were originally installed for voice-grade telephone circuits. This is largely due to innovations in station and switching gear now capable of correcting and enhancing transmissions in a fashion much superior to their predecessors.

The most popular types of telecommunications channels are detailed in figure 3.5. These channels have little to do with the actual protocol or routing capabilities of a specific network, and are associated with the low-level (physical layer) of the OSI application model. Therefore, it is possible for a single network to use most or even all of the types listed.

Figure 3.5 Telecommunications Channels

Channel Type	Description
WIRE PAIRS	Existing wire pair. Imbedded facilities cover the globe such that it is often more economical to re-use these facilities than to rebuild on the basis of new technology. Used for analog transmission and T-1 circuits.
COAXIAL CABLE	A single wire conductor. This is surrounded by an outer (cylindrical) conductor providing greater immunity to electrical and magnetic interference than common twisted pairs. A coaxial cable can typically carry information faster than wire pairs. Used for LANs, CCTV, and 327x systems.
MICROWAVE & CELLULAR RADIO SYSTEMS	High frequency radio waves. Point to point carriage of information travel in straight lines, therefore, relay stations must be arrange every 20 miles or so to compensate for the curvature of the earth. Cellular radio uses omnidirectional transmission towers linked with terrestrial circuits.
SATELLITE	Satellite communications are basically the same as microwave systems (the satellite acts as if it were a very tall microwave tower). Three satellites in geo-stationary orbits are able to cover the globe, which effectively eliminates the need for terrestrial relay stations. Satellite systems are nonetheless dependent on conventional circuits to carry data to the terminals and transmission stations, much like cellular telephone systems are dependent on terrestrial links.
LASER:	Lasers produce concentrated beams of light with bandwidth capabilities that outstrip over 100,000 microwave links, for example. Requiring point-of-sight alignment, the communication channel is susceptible to the vagaries of environmental conditions. Used in private networks and campus environments.
FIBER OPTICS:	Strands of glass that conduct light generated by lasers or light emitting diodes (L.E.D.s) at each end. Used in FDDI, MANs, Bypass, and SONET.

The Fit Between Telecommunications & Client-Server

The New York City police wear patches on their uniforms that read: "To Serve and Protect." It is as good a slogan as there could be for client-server computer telephony. It begins with the notion of *service*. Imagine the telephone network as the ultimate platform, not just for completing a call in response to dialed digits, but for providing a wide range of services. These include messaging, information retrieval, transactional services, entertainment, and assistance. Any telephone or terminal (and ultimately its user) is a potential client to wide world of services. It is the goal of this chapter to provide a snapshot of the array of new and existing networks services that are available such that you can match these outside services to your particular needs.

Protection, the other pillar upon which client-server computer telephony is built, refers to the use of a user interface to mask (thus protect) users from the complexities of network administration, database management, and transaction processing. For example, GUIs (graphical user interfaces) are integrated into PCs to provide "point-and-click" simplicity to their users while initiating all kinds of requests from network and computer resources. The mission of these enhancements is to *protect* [users from complexity] and *serve* [software, services, devices, processes, and other 'clients'].

Although not in keeping with the classic definition of the server as discussed in the last chapter, switching elements, voice response units (VRUs), telephone switches, and mainframes attached to the "public network cloud" are acting in the role of *servers*. Along the same line of thinking, people and telephones attached to the network are like *clients*.

In a way, if those people and telephones are "live" operators or telemarketing service representatives (TSR), then they, too are *servers*, since they are ultimately there to serve callers.

Figure 3.6 illustrates another view of this phenomenon as the evolution of the public telephone network through five Telecommunications Phases. This was first articulated by Dan Miller as three wider “epochs” in a 1992 report by New Science Associates, a division of Gartner Group. In the beginning, the public network was configured from three basic components:

- Terminals ("station gear")
- Network switching and control systems
- Transmission facilities and methods

Stations were predominately telegraph terminals until the telephone became prolific in the early half of this century. Telephone switching was the responsibility of switchboard operators, because there was no automated way of completing connections through the network until the electromechanical crossbar and step-by-step switches were invented during the second phase.

Phase two electro-mechanical devices were used to take the place of the switchboard operator. Later, so-called "adjunct" devices were appended to these devices to provide new features and functions, such as multi-carrier routing, call detail recording (CDR), Audiotex, messaging, or data communications services.

Gradually, the switches themselves slowly evolved into computers called electronic switching systems. Operators continued to play directory assistance roles and assisted in call completion, with help from more powerful technologies.

Today, the fifth phase of telecommunications is upon us. It brings an era in which the elements of the telephone network are defined by software that often runs on general purpose computers. The three-way division between station, switching, and transmission remains. However, new “switch-computer interfaces” have evolved to assist heretofore fragmented systems to interoperate more efficiently. Thus, the network and its elements have been deconstructed only to be recombined by new application software and interfaces.

Figure 3.6 Telecommunications Phases - 100 Years

Station Gear	Compute, Network & Switch Power	Transmission Methods	
1  Telegraph	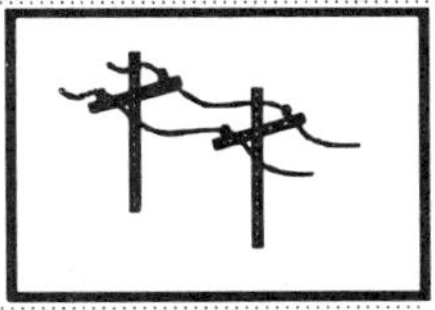 Manual connect	• Open Loop circuits	• Copper pairs
2  Telephones; TTY terminals	 Cordboards; crossbar switch	• Copper pairs • FDM	• Carrier Systems • Early data sets
3  327x terminals; feature phones; digital announce	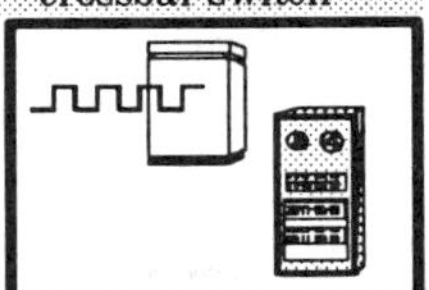 Digital switch; Stored program control; muxes; mainframes; Z80	• Low-Medium Datacom • Micro-wave • DDS • Coax	• TDM carrier • Sattelite • T-1; E-1 • SDLC
4  IVDTs; PCs; mobile phones; video conference terminals	 Mini/micros; x86, monolithic voice response; voice mail; SMP	• Switched 56K • BRI ISDN • Fiber Optics • Cellular	• LANs • PRI ISDN • Laser • VANs
5 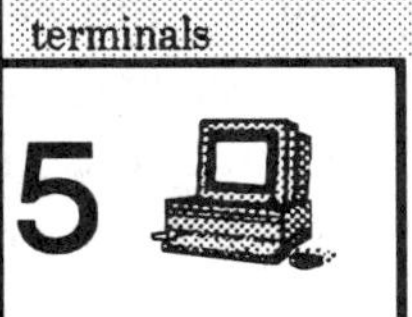 Multi-purpose workstations; PDA; mobile PC	 STPs & SCPs; LAN/WAN gateways; CTI	• SMDS • Frame Relay • SONET • FDDI	• SS7 • Fast Packet • AIN • ATM

Four major factors have driven us to this point. First, there is an irreversible movement toward end-to-end digital connectivity on the public network. Secondly, a shift away from closed, proprietary switching systems into "open" systems is apparent, owing to the lead taken by the computer industry. Third, telephone users (to wit virtually everybody) have become more comfortable with (or, at least, tolerant of) new telephone-based applications. For example, we retrieve bank balance information or leave messages over the phone without flinching.

Finally, the underlying voice processing, call processing, and signal processing technologies (computer telephony elements) are more affordable than ever before. Technological evolution has converted the ubiquitous telephone into a robust terminal. While it appears to be just above a pager in the telephony food chain, it is not as functionally-challenged as it first appears. Most lack full keyboards and displays. Yet, advances in digital signal processing (DSP) subsystems have accelerated the use of voice prompts and voice commands to accomplish everything from placing a collect call to providing checking account authorization.

Communications Service Types

To put this information into perspective, its relevance to communication service types is an important concept. The rest of this chapter provides a snapshot of transmission methods, speeds, and "feeds" that will help you to identify what services might be best for you.

Dedicated (Leased) Service

These circuits are permanently connected, so that no switching is required. They are leased for a monthly fee from the local or long distance carrier. For example, a group of terminals for an order entry application could be located at several geographically dispersed sites, yet "connected" to a centralized host via leased circuits.

Modems and multiplexors are used to combine the individual circuits onto one 56K data link or T-1 span. A mix of voice and data traffic can be achieved by using channel banks equipped with line cards that combine the separate voice and data traffic on twenty four (64K or DS-0) channels into a single T-1 span as pictured in figure 3.7.

Dataphone Digital Service (DDS), is available in one form or another under many service names from local telephone companies and common carriers. T-1 and T-2 services are provided via terrestrial links, while higher rates are provided via microwave. DDS uses standard PCM (Pulse Code Modulation) to convert analog data into digital form for transmission.

Figure 3.7 Dedicated Circuit Example

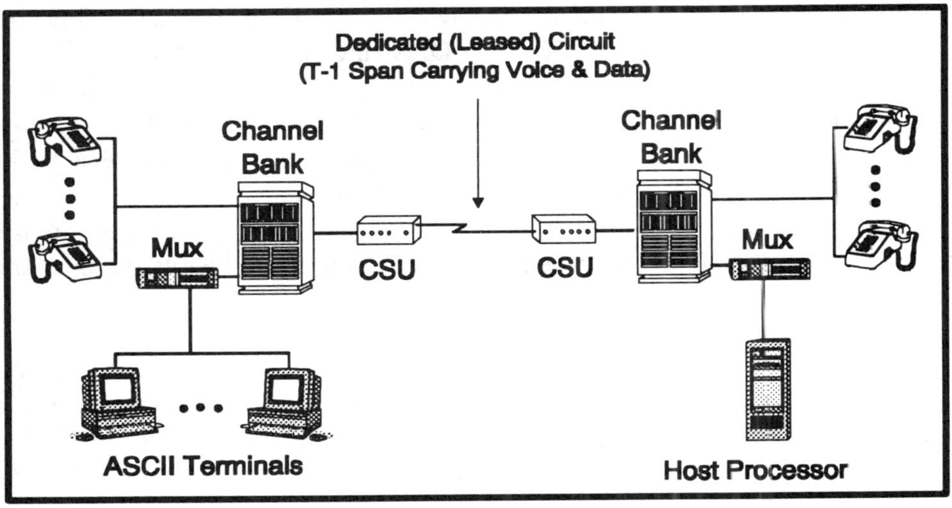

Although leased voice or data circuits provide predictable bandwidth, speed, and transmission economies - no alternate routing, redundancies, or other modern network benefits are available. The ability to dynamically allocate channels and bandwidth "on the fly" is not a capability of "nailed-up," dedicated circuits.

This "dedicated" bandwidth for transmission of voice and data can actually be emulated by "virtual" circuits in a *value-added* or *virtual* network. Virtual networks will be discussed in more detail under the section on switched services.

Figure 3.8 Leased Transmission Service Types

Carrier Speeds	Types of leased circuits
Low Speed	SERIES 1000; OPX lines
Medium Speed	SERIES 2000 & 3000; TTY; asynch terminals
Wideband	SERIES 5000 & 8000; point-to-point 9.6, 56K, dedicated T-1 multiplexor lines; DDS (Dataphone Digital Services

One of the most common uses of leased circuits is the OPX line, or off-premises extension for PBXs. An OPX line is a circuit that allows for the off-site extension of a regular telephone on your PBX or Key System. These circuits are often "loaded," or especially attenuated to deal with the resistance factor of metallic loops beyond the typical lengths of a PBX station line. Special cards are required to treat this type of circuit in the PBX, and the telephone company also treats the line for dedicated use by that PBX. Higher speed circuits required for data transmission are likewise engineered.

Switched Services

Switched services use the switching centers of common carriers to direct transmissions between originating and terminating points. Typified by services such as DDD (direct distance dialing), or dial-up service, switched services use no dedicated facilities except at the local loop. All other circuits are set-up and torn-down via the shared switching resources of common carriers.

Switched services fall into two broad categories: Circuit Switched and Packet Switched. Figure 3.9 is a diagram showing a variety of switched services, and the categories that will be explained in further detail here.

Figure 3.9 Switched Network Service Types

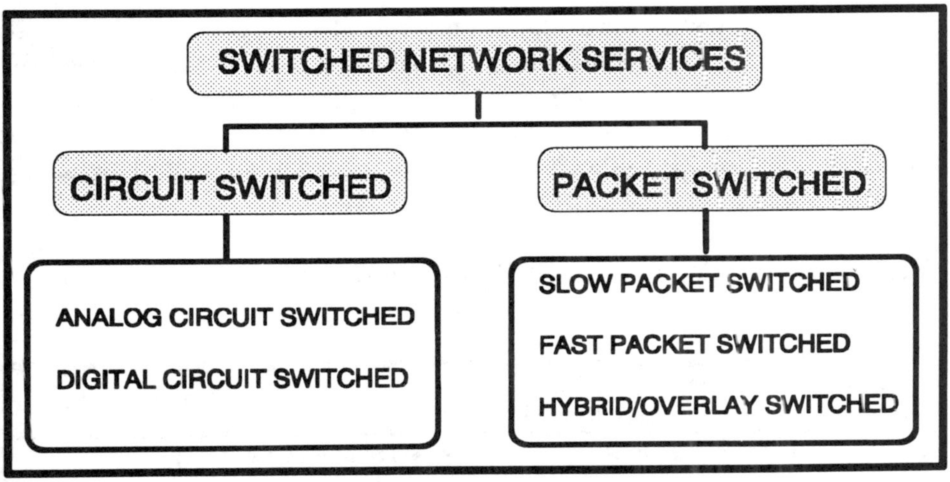

Analog Circuit Switched Network Services

The most common of all switched services is the circuit switched variety, especially the analog type. Analog switched services are sometimes called "POTS," or Plain Old Telephone Service. POTS services are regular dial-up telephone and data lines over the public switched network. The best example is DDD - what we all do when we pick up our home telephone to call our florist, dentist, or family. Regular telephones that are connected to analog circuits on PBXs are using POTS services when calling from extension to extension. Sometimes the switching system in the telephone network or PBX is using digital technology to multiplex and transmit the calls, but these are nonetheless baseline services.

Switched services offer a variety of benefits, none the least of which is low cost. POTS telephone service is between $9.00 and $18.00 for a single line at most homes, and they double as modem or fax lines, too. Literally thousands of computer telephony systems are hooked-up to regular POTS lines providing answering service, automated attendant, and other functions. Unless you have a high amount of data, voice, and imaging traffic that needs to be transported across wide areas, POTS service may be for you. Client-server enterprise computing can be "front-ended" by computer telephony gear that utilizes these common facilities and still help your company to provide a high grade of customer service.

Figure 3.10 shows the most common types of analog switched network service available. Depending on the local telephone company tariffed offerings, service types may come under the name of B-1, or 1FB business lines for regular POTS phone lines, or under the name of "Centrex" for analog versions of PBX-like features provided from the central switching office.

Figure 3.10 Analog Circuit Switched Service Types

Carrier Speeds	Analog Circuit Switched Services	Comments
2400; 9600; 14.4	Direct Distance Dialing (DDD)	POTS; analog Centrex; low- speed modems; fax
Voice grade	Operator assisted calls	411, L.D., TDD

Features like call forwarding, conferencing, speed dialing, and supervised transfers are all available on Centrex-equipped analog switched circuits, so don't be too quick to sign-up to sophisticated digital services unless the benefits are scrutinized thoroughly.

Digital Circuit Switched Network Services

Digital switched circuits combine the high-speed capabilities of leased data links with the convenience of dial-up capability. For example, DSDS (Dataphone Switched Digital Service) allows for 56kbps data links to be used for variable access to multiple hosts for transaction processing and bulk data uploads. This capability provides a significant advantage over paying for leased services, especially if the actual bandwidth being utilized is limited to several hours a day.

Whether the circuits are being used for circuit switched or packet switched services, there are some standard circuit and speeds that are used to carry the traffic. Figure 3.11 provides a snapshot of the bit rates and their associated circuits or voice channels. For simplicity, the number of circuits displayed assumes a 64kbps increment. Although submultiplexing of voice and data channels can be achieved below 64kbps, the table should give you an idea about the relative speeds of T-carrier E-1, and optical (SONET and SDH) circuits. These types of carrier circuits are the backbone for virtually every type of advanced network service. For example, Primary Rate ISDN, SS7, frame relay, and SMDS services use these common circuit conventions for the carriage of their respective payloads.

Perhaps the most popular of the digital switched services available is the T-carrier network. T-carrier networks use DS-0, DS-1, and DS-3 speeds, as outlined on the chart in figure 3.11. Basic T-1 circuits are the backbone for a variety of services, and are the basis for both private network and local carrier offerings.

Although the entry of new services such as SMDS and ISDN will create heavy competition for these stand-by services in the future, T-carrier will likely remain the "POTS" (Plain Old Telephone Service) of the digital switched service offerings.

The cost justification for installing T-1 circuits to handle voice and data traffic has steadily decreased with the entry of new service offerings. For example, over the past ten years, prices on local T-carrier have decreased enough to justify installation for carrying an equivalent 10 or fewer voice circuits. In other words, some local telephone companies actually charge more for 10 individual circuits to carry ten voice conversations than for an entire T-span, which will carry twenty-four.

If you have as many as ten voice lines, and a handful of data and fax lines, it is not too early to investigate these services. Give your local telephone company a call and make arrangements to speak with a Communications Consultant or Business Office Supervisor.

It may take a few calls to find the right person, but it's worth the trouble, because you can save as much as 30% or more on the flat rate portion of your phone bill and increase bandwidth simultaneously. The cost for T-1 circuits will decrease over time relative to newer service offerings, but it is still a good idea to look into it right away.

Figure 3.11 Digital Circuit Bandwidth

(N.A.) Signal Level / Carrier Type	BIT RATE	Circuits or Voice Channels
DS-0 / --	64kbps	1
DS-1 / T1	1.544mbps	24
DS-1C / T1C	3.152 mbps	48
DS-2 / T2	6.312 mbps	96
DS-3 / T3	44.736 mbps	672
DS-3A / T3A	89.472 mbps	1,344
DS-4 / T4	274.176 mbps	4,032
(CCITT) Signal Level / Carrier Type	**BIT RATE**	**Circuits or Voice Channels**
0 / --	64kbps	1
1 / E-1	2.048 mbps	30
2 / E-2	8.448 mbps	120
3 / E-3	34.368 mbps	480
4 / E-4	139.264 mbps	1,920
5 / E-5	565.148 mbps	7,680
SONET Signal Level / Carrier Type	**BIT RATE**	**Circuits or Voice Channels**
1 / OC-1	51.84 mbps	810
2 / OC-2	155.52 mbps	2,430
3 / OC-3	466.56 mbps	7,290
4 / OC-4	622.08 mbps	9,720
N / OC-*N*	*n* x 51.84	*N* x 810
(CCITT) SDH Signal Level / Carrier Type	**BIT RATE**	**Circuits or Voice Channels**
1 / SDH-1	155.52 mbps	2,430
4 / SDH-4	622.08 mbps	9,720
N / SDH-*N*	*N* x 622.08	*N* x 9,720

Figure 3.12 Digital Circuit and Packet Service Types

Speeds	Circuit Switched Services	Comments
DS-0	Dataphone Switched Digital Service (DSDS); Switched 56K	Polled SNA networks; alternate routing
DS-0 - DS-1	BRI/ISDN - PRI/ISDN	Voice & data grade; clear channel 64K w/D channel signaling
DS-1	SWIFT-DS-1	Voice & data grade; switched fractional T-1
DS-1, 3	T-carrier networks; TDM multiplexed data networks	Virtual/private networks
Speeds	**Slow Packet Switched**	**Comments**
4.8, 9.6, 56K	X.25-based networks	not suitable for bursty data or voice
56K	SNA (SDLC)	Polled terminal / 327x; typical CICS network
Speeds	**Fast Packet Switched**	**Comments**
56/64K; DS-1	Frame Relay CCITT I.122	"Connection Oriented" - low speed uses HDLC; high speed uses Q.921 ISDN data link. LAN/WAN bridges.
56/64K; DS-1, 3	SMDS (Switched Multimegabit Digital Service) "Cell Relay" MAN	"Connectionless Isosynchronous" uses 802.6-like data link
SONET; local connect	FDDI I, FDDI II	10 Mbps LAN; multi-LAN backbone
Speeds	**Hybrid / Overlay Switched**	**Comments**
DS-0; DS-1,3	SS7 - Signaling System # 7	Uses slow-packet 64K channels for out-of-band signaling and DS-0 - DS-*N* for voice and data carriage.

Packet Switched Services

Packet switching had its roots in the seventies, as corporate data communications users began to seek for a more economical means to share communications channels and optimize bandwidth for multiple terminals. The idea behind packet switching is to bundle small payloads of information and then transmit them across a network that supports variable routing for the data. X.25 streams of data are multiplexed ant the user site with software that segments data streams into packets.

These packets of information are typically multiplexed and then transmitted over data modems to a PAD (Packet assembler/dissembler). These PADS are connected to packet switches in the network that are responsible for delivering the packets to other network nodes. As packets travel throughout the network, the switches provide error correction, addressing, and re-transmission of data with the help of internal memory buffers. These packet buffers act as a holding tank for packets that need to be re-transmitted due to equipment failure, bandwidth blockage, and errors.

One disadvantage of this method is that the transmission is not "real-time," so it is not adequate for voice communication or multimedia transmissions. The wideband requirements of such media are served better by fast packet switching networks as discussed later in this chapter. Both SDLC and X.25 networks are the very basis for all subsequent packet switched network technologies. What's really changed is the efficiency and bandwidth of the newer services, however, the concepts have remained constant for about thirty years.

One way to drive your decision about which method to use is to gauge bandwidth requirements for your enterprise. For example, let's say you had a group of PCs each needing to transmit as many as 100 screens of data each hour (about 180,000 characters assuming 1,800 characters per screen). If such a terminal had it's own dedicated link, you would probably use a 4,800bps dedicated line. A 4.8K line carries 480 characters per second, taking into account start bits, stop bits, and an eight-bit word. This equates to 1,728,000 characters per hour (480 characters times 60 seconds times 60 minutes).

In this example, the effective utilization ratio of that data link would be 180,000 divided by 1,728,000, or just less than ten percent.

Figure 3.13 Sample Line Utilization Ratio Calculation

Data Link Bandwidth Calculation

4,800 bps line / 10 bits/char. = 480 char./sec.

480 char./sec. x 60 sec. = 288,000 char./min.

288,000 char./min. x 60 min. = 1,728,000 char./hr.

Terminal Needs Calculation

1,800 charaacters x 100 screens = 180,000 char./hr.

Line Utilization Ratio

1,728,000 char./hr. (line capacity) / 180,000 char./hr. (terminal needs) = 9.6% line utilization

Theoretically, as many as 10 terminals' worth of activity each hour would be required to fully utilize the bandwidth. Of course, this assumes that the bandwidth would not be required simultaneously, but rather spread more or less evenly over the specified time period. At any rate, it is easy to see how much waste would occur by providing each PC with its own dedicated data line, whether it was a dial-up line (which still, nonetheless requires it's own subscriber telephone line to the central office), or a dedicated leased line.

Unless a terminal needs to transmit full time, there is little need for a dedicated circuit, therefore, a dial-up (DDD) line may be worthwhile in this case. What with today's high-speed error-correcting modems, there's little worry in using dial-up lines to achieve this. If the number of terminals in the work group is more than a handful, you can easily justify the sharing of data communication line bandwidth by using slow packet switching.

Of course, the number of terminals attached at each site and the amount of traffic anticipated has an effect on the overall utility of one method versus another.

Figure 3.14 displays the relative cost savings of packet switching versus DDD and dedicated circuits. This assumes that the connections required do not demand full-time use of the circuit in question.

Figure 3.14 Relative savings of packet switching

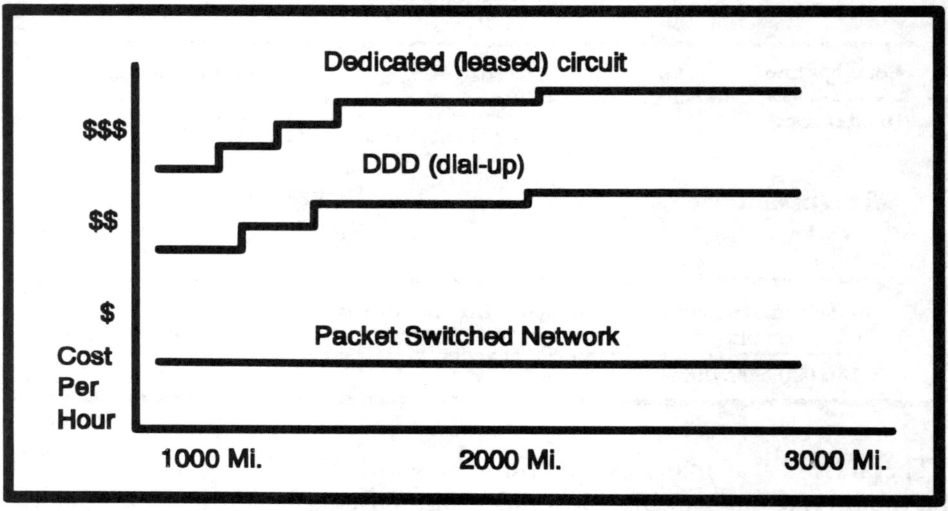

Slow Packet Switched Services

X.25-based and SNA (SDLC) networks are both categorized as slow packet switched services. Although their relatively slow speeds (4.8, 9.6, 56K) are not suitable for bursty data or voice, they are nonetheless popular in thousands of businesses. Many carriers provide these services under a variety of service names. For example, AT&T provides X.25 network service under their Accunet Packet Service. In addition, regional phone companies and other common carriers offer the same capabilities.

Remote time sharing of computers and shared transmission of common facilities drive the use of these services. There are a variety of additional value-added services that can be provided. For example: store and forward services, protocol conversion, and processing of data.

This is often the reason why the term value added network (VAN) is applied to the use of X.25. That is to say that the term VAN applies if the technology is used not only for simple data carriage, but other services as well.

Some additional (value-added) capabilities of these networks include alternate routing and error correction. Figure 3.15 shows how VANs provide this capability. When data is transmitted into a packet switched network, the packets are routed to their destination through a series of switches, called packet switches. The switches read the origination and destination address from each packet and then pass the packet along to the next switch according to predetermined routing rules.

An error correction scheme is used by buffering each packet after transmitting it in order to make sure it was received properly. An acknowledgment of the packet's receipt is sent back to each switch to let it know that it is all right to "dump" that particular packet by clearing the buffer. Of course, if the acknowledgment takes too long to come back, the switch may have already cleared the information due to buffer overflow or network failure.

Figure 3.15 Error Checking and Alternate Routing

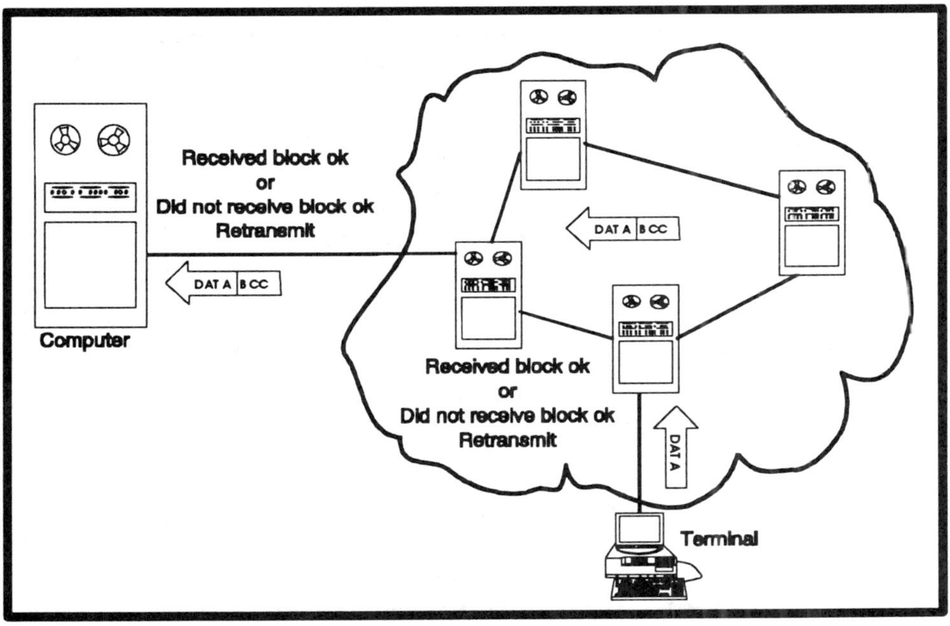

If a failure occurs on one transmission line, the sending switch can re-transmit the packet to another switch before its buffer overflows, so that the information can be routed along another path to its destination. This is called alternate routing. Alternate routing is used as a means to overcome heavy network traffic as well as error correction. Of course, the number and placement of packet switches in a network determines just how resilient the network is. If just two packet switches were used to act as the channel for a given network you would in effect have a point-to-point dedicated virtual circuit rather than an optimized packet switched network.

The same technology used for error correction and switching on packet switched networks can be applied to create multiple "virtual connections" to a variety of host computers. For example, a terminal can send and receive data through the same VAN for use with computers in New York, Los Angeles, and Dallas. The ability to display sessions from these separate hosts is limited to the capabilities of the terminal and its associated controller. Figure 3.16 shows how virtual connections are established with various hosts using packet switching. Some of the benefits of virtual connections include the ability to share common facilities, quicker log-on sequences, and alternate access to databases in the case of host down-time or traffic overload.

Figure 3.16 Virtual Switching

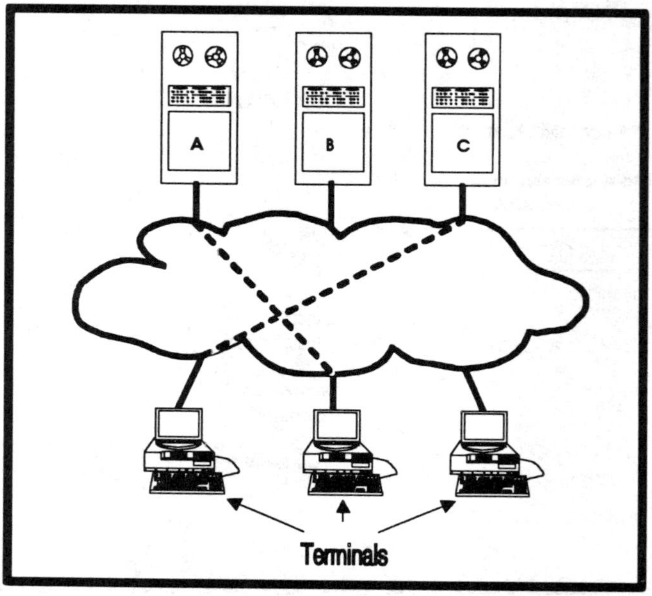

Virtual Networks

This technology can be explained in terms of a call center, or customer service perspective. A typical call center has both data communications and telephony requirements. Until the advent of fast packet switched networks, an enterprise treated the facilities for data communications and telephony as separate entities.

Over the past ten years, however, companies such as AT&T, Sprint, and MCI have offered hybrid network capabilities that allow for the mix or the transport channels over "virtually dedicated" circuits. The carriers use a variety of transport technologies to achieve this, including SS7 (Signaling System 7) and standard DS-1 and DS-3 T-carrier networking.

Virtual networks are software-driven, inasmuch as the routing, bandwidth allocation, and control of data communications and telephony channels is managed by computers and switches in the network dedicated to these functions. For example, AT&T's Software Defined Network (SDN) services are managed by Action Control Points and Network Control Points. These elements are equivalent to the STP (Signal Transfer Point and SCP (Service Control Point) as defined by SS7 conventions, respectively. Sprint provides similar services with its VPN (Virtual Private Network) offering, as does MCI with VNET (Virtual Network).

In general, virtual networks allow you and your company to customize a voice and data network to fit your needs. The carriers have plenty of network bandwidth that can be separated for use by your company on a nationwide basis. For example, you may require four T-Spans for voice during the business day, and just as much bandwidth for data file transfer and batch processing data transfer at night.

Carriers can allocate bandwidth in their networks dynamically, thus using the same basic access trunks and circuits to your facility for mixed voice and data traffic. In fact, you can siphon bandwidth from your virtual circuits and set it aside for video teleconferencing, bulk faxing, or other traffic-intense initiatives that cause traffic spikes.

This is preferable to running dedicated circuits to your facility that go unused most of the time. In addition to dynamic allocation of bandwidth, virtual networks also provide for on-net and off-net dialing. On-net dialing automatically forwards origination and destination addresses for inter-company calls.

Figure 3.17 Virtual Network Topology

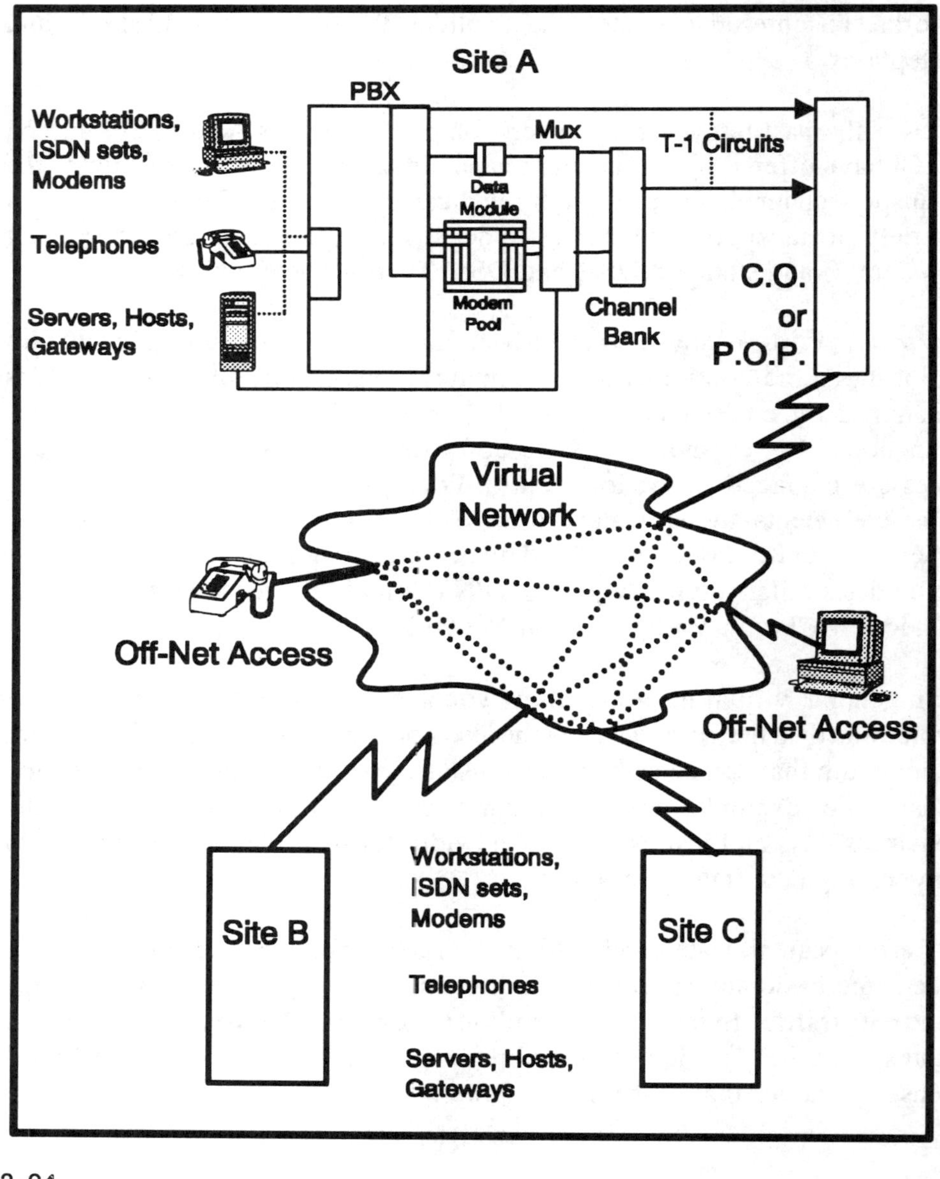

This on-net routing capability speeds the set-up and tear-down of calls as compared to DDD. Off-net dialing allows virtual network users to access network services from payphones or at home. Of course, this requires the input of codes, much like you would be required to do for third-party billed calls or operator assistance.

Figure 3.17 shows how a typical virtual network is put together. This diagram shows the user CPE (Customer Premise Equipment) perspective, depicting telephone, data modem, host, and peripheral accesses to the same network. There are a variety of devices that allow you to mix voice and data onto the same T-carrier or ISDN facilities. The most common devices used for doing this are channel banks, multiplexors, and special PBX data modules.

SS7 - Signaling System # 7

Signaling System #7 (SS7) is the basis for modern methods to route traffic with out-of-band signaling. Its forerunner, CCIS (Common Channel Interoffice Signaling), used 4,800bps data links to transmit call set-up and tear-down messages to switching office adjunct computers and packet switches. SS7 in itself is not a network service offering, but rather the underlying infrastructure with which many existing and proposed offerings are based. For example, local Basic Rate ISDN (BRI) services can tap into SS7, so 64kbps packetized data can be routed with the help of the networks out-of-band signaling capability. In addition, nationwide Primary Rate ISDN (PRI) services can use the same backbone.

At this time, regional telephone companies and long distance carriers have yet to ratify nationwide interconnection of all SS7 elements, so a "patchwork" of CCIS, SS7, and in-band techniques for signaling is the "rule." AT&T, Sprint, and MCI use SS7 technology in their own networks, and have provided its capabilities to large accounts. For example, operator services companies who use the large carriers for the routing of their operator-assisted calls use SS7 links to connect their switches to carrier Signal Transfer Points (STPs). In addition, there are direct links to Signal Control Points (SCPs) in order to speed billing and identification for these calls. STPs transmit packet data between SPs (Signaling Points) in order to "send ahead" messages for the purpose of setting-up and tearing down calls.

It's the SP's job to extract signaling data from the central office or tandem switch. Adjunct processors are sometimes used in older networks to transform in-band data into packets that are sent by the SP to the STP. Packet data on these systems operate at either 4,800bps, or in the case of SS7, at 56,000bps.

SCPs are used to access remote databases. In the case of virtual network use, the remote database will hold an enterprises' nationwide inter-office dialing plan, time-of-day routing information, and directory information. The SCP supplies all of the routing and translation data required to deliver advanced network services.

Figure 3.18 Signaling System #7 Topology

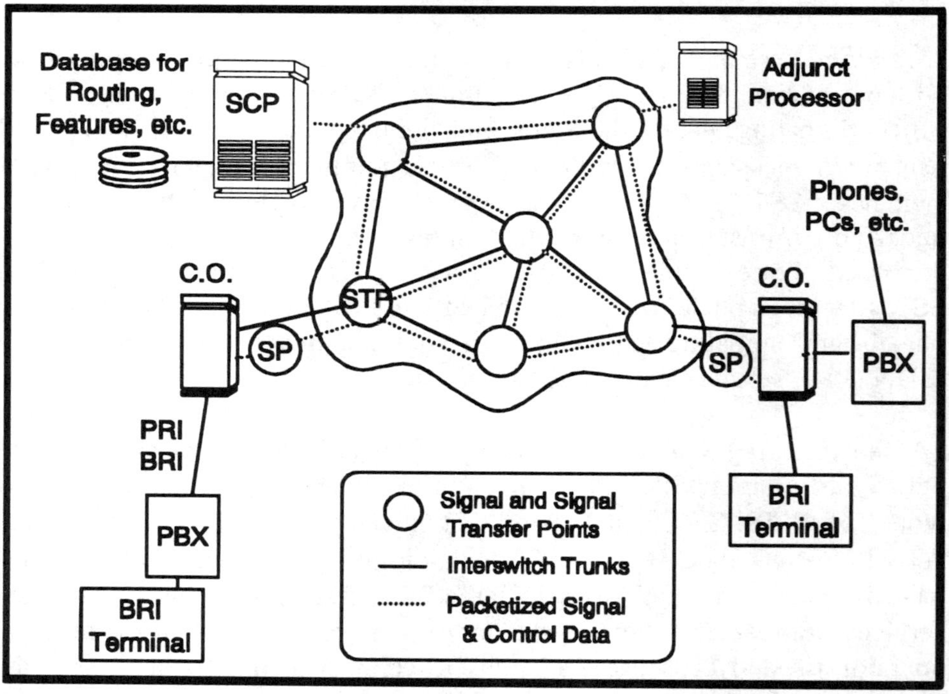

SCP implementations are the basis for 800 portability, in which translations of 800-type numbers can be cooperatively shared between carriers. For example, SCPs translate incoming 800 and 900 numbers into the required virtual routing number. The key concept here is that the SCP is wholly separate from the switching fabric itself, so customized services and call treatment can be put on-line for customers on a specialized basis. Figure 3.18 shows the relationship between the elements of a SS7-based network.

Fast Packet Switched Services

As discussed earlier in this chapter, the basic concepts of packet switching used in X.25 and SDLC-based networks are the basis for new packet switched services such as frame relay and SMDS. Some of these newer offerings provide the bandwidth and routing capabilities necessary to truly mix voice and data traffic in real-time. This capability makes fast packet switching suitable for video teleconferencing, remote sharing of desktop graphics applications, and real-time access to image databases. For example, fast packet switching can be used to interconnect geographically separate LANs such that remote and foreign virtual connections behave in every fashion as if they were locally connected. You can read, write, and append to files on remote servers as quickly and efficiently as if they were two feet away.

Although optimized primarily for data traffic, frame relay can handle bandwidth up to T-2 (4.5mbps). Based on CCITT I.122 standards, Frame Relay uses HDLC (High Level Data Link) control for lower speed implementations below the DS-1 level. Higher-speed frame relay networks employ Q.921 (ISDN) data link technology. This makes frame relay a viable technology for LAN/WAN bridges, so companies who wish to connect the LANs in separate cities can take advantage of each other's data in close to real time (or at least what *appears* to be real time to the network users).

Because frame relay is based on international standards that are commonly implemented, virtually all major carriers and local telephone companies are deploying some level of service with this technology.

For example, RBOCs (Regional Bell Operating Companies) have been busy interconnecting their local fast packet switches into long distance carrier networks over the past three years. British Telecom America, WilTel, and Sprint were the first carriers to introduce fast packet services at speeds up to T-1. In fact, you can now connect facilities between major continents, so global enterprises can even take advantage of the technology.

Unlike slow packet switched services like X.25 and SDLC, frame relay acts as a transparent pipeline for data, and therefore does not offer the error correction and protocol handling services of the older packet switched networks. In effect, frame relay is comparable to statistical multiplexing, inasmuch as the technology utilizes the full bandwidth of circuits and minimizes the delays associated with virtual connections.

Figure 3.19 Use of Frame Relay FAD

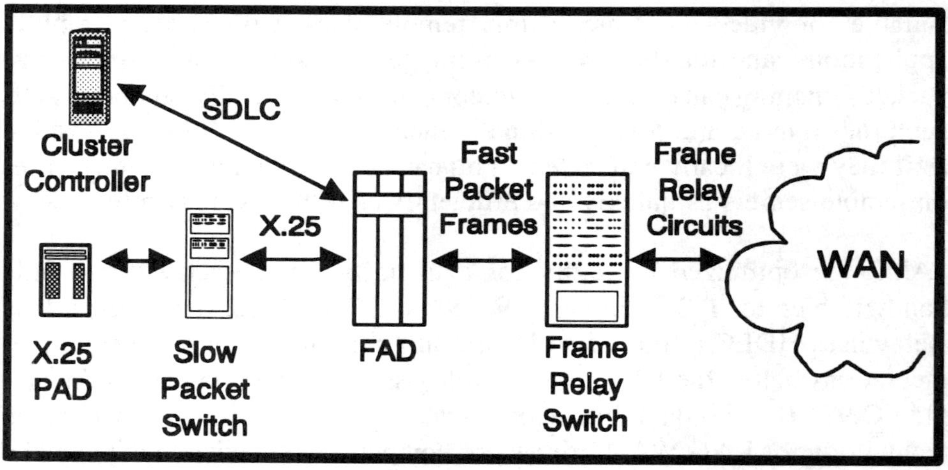

You can actually link facilities that are using slower packet switched technologies with frame relay, so the services are not incompatible with one another. For example, a service center with 3270-based terminals or ASCII terminals can link with FADs (Frame Assembler/Disassemblers) in order to achieve an efficient means for LAN/WAN bridging.

In practice, this is the way in which most companies take advantage of frame relay today, because retrofitting existing terminals with native fast packet elements is not yet viable on a wide basis. Figure 3.19 shows how localized slow packet technology is interconnected to a fast packet network with a FAD.

SMDS (Switched Multimegabit Digital Service)

Unlike frame relay and slow packet switching, SMDS uses a fixed packet length in order to utilize bandwidth as high as 45mbps. It is often referred to as a "connectionless" service, because the requisite overhead for set-up and tear-down of transactions typical in other networks is not used. In fact, cells are transmitted only with addressing information, so CPE equipment plays a large role in handling errors and requests for retransmission. Cell-oriented technology encapsulates groups of voice, data, and image packets of all types.

In practice, SMDS nodes scan every packet that is transmitted through the network and then filters only those with the correct address information for its associated site. Since cell-oriented technologies such as SMDS and ATM (Asynchronous Transfer Mode) are defined by higher-level protocols, cells can be passed through the same switches.

A cell is really a type of frame, with the one difference that its length is not variable, but rather of a short and constant rate. Because the cell size is constant, and handles speeds in the Multi-gigabit range, it is reasonable to predict the kind of bandwidth required to transmit voice as well as data. For example, if you know how much voice traffic is required on your network and can calculate the peak hour traffic, you can anticipate the requirements for the bandwidth on your SMDS network.

This capability allows for deterministic response times and transmission, so voice communications will not be interrupted in real-time. This predictability is not available on slower frame relay services, since variable length frames do not allow for deterministic bandwidth allocation. Of course, this is not as critical when you are transporting data, but then, computers are more suited to delays in transmission than we humans are in the middle of a conversation.

It is likely that SMDS will provide very compelling arguments for either delaying SONET and FDDI-II implementations, or perhaps displacing newly planned services, such as B-ISDN (Broadband ISDN). Carriers such as MCI and AT&T have already begun to offer SMDS, and the RBOCs have been trialing the technology with customers for several years. If your enterprise moves hundreds of circuits across town and requires the mix of real-time voice and data, SMDS services are a viable alternative to private networks.

Prelude to Implementation

Chapter four discusses how telephony-enabled personal computer and server applications move the PC-client into center stage. Microcomputers now have the ability to provide instructions to the switch and other network elements. In effect, computer telephony adjuncts, switch servers, and other CTI communications elements "serve" the handset as a ubiquitous client.

As witnessed by attendees of recent industry trade shows, the nineties are shaping up as the decade for this ultimate merger of technology. But the question remains: "What is it?" How about LAN-based call centers, visual voice mail on personal computers, and text-to-speech conversion of e-mail over the telephone? How about PC-based SS7 engines running on the desktop? It's easy to predict what could be a collision course between telecom management and LAN administrators.

In other words, these are very interesting times for telephony practitioners. To quote Harry Newton: "this is an industry exploding." Despite all of the excitement, one of our biggest challenges is to maintain some semblance of linguistic integrity.

Long-time telecommunications managers will find it difficult to believe that vendors no longer quote "price-per-port" for their systems. With the advent of client-server forms of computer telephony, the vocabulary used to discuss voice technology is now passé. The notions of *lines, ports, and telephone sets* has been replaced with the concept of *seats.*

More and more, systems are priced "per seat." This emphasizes the importance of knowing LAN jargon at this important point of transition to modern telecommunications. Once you become accustomed to referring to a telephone set as a "telephony client," you are well on your way.

It also helps to understand when to say "API" (for application programming interface) and when to say "driver." APIs are computer programs that are often ingrained or organized into a software developers' toolkit. They allow an application developer to write a program once and then have it interface to disparate types of equipment and applications in a repeatable fashion.

This does require cooperation between vendors, as there are many types of computer telephony APIs (to wit: chapters seven through ten of this book). Drivers, on the other hand, are used by vendors who want an application or device to interface a specific piece of equipment without the benefit of an API. Low-level drivers are almost always present below the API layer, but there use as a development vehicle is quickly fading.

When you go to buy client-server computer telephony products, you are definitely going to be confronted with two branches of the evolutionary tree. On one side of the trunk is "desktop telephony." "LAN-based telephony" is on the other. Think of desktop telephony as the single-user, grassroots approach, opening up a PBX to computer control by plugging individual PCs into phone jacks.

In contrast, LAN-based telephony is more of a departmental solution. It allows everybody on a LAN to use a personal computer to tell the PBX how to place and accept calls. The desktop direction is being driven by Microsoft with its Windows Telephony API (TAPI).

The LAN revolution is typified by market leader Novell. For example, Novell corroborated with AT&T, to release a set of "NetWare Loadable Modules" (NLMs) to its NetWare LAN software under the name "Telephony Services API" (TSAPI). The specific software engine is a Telephony Services function running as an NLM on a LAN-connected PC. The function is enabled by a set of PBX drivers inside the server, mirrored by software in the PBX.

The PBX drivers talk to the server using the European Computer-Supported Telecommunications Application (CSTA) API. On the other side, the all important TSAPI allows any client (e.g. workstations, facsimile machines, or telephones) to place and accept calls through the PBX by point-and- click (if it's Windows) or keyboard/mouse commands. In this architecture, no computer is directly connected to the PBX, but commands it through the LAN.

LAN-based telephony can emerge as an infrastructure for monitoring and managing the operations of a growing population of "informal call centers." This term refers to any business currently operating a LAN and performing unstructured albeit routine call handling. LAN-based telephony will provide a mechanism for automating and tuning the performance of such informal call centers without requiring the purchase of an ACD or predictive dialer.

Several PBX makers are already hopping on the TSAPI bandwagon. These include GPT, Alcatel, Mitel, Fujitsu Business Communications, and Comdial. The lure is the base of 30 million desks worldwide connected to Novell networks.

Microsoft's counter offer is that there's no need to wait for the office's LAN administrator to wire the office in order to embark on computer-aided telephony. TAPI-enabled PCs allow Window's users to place and take calls using a telephone connected to the PC through a serial port, for example. TAPI SDKs (Software Developers' Kits) have been shipping since late 1993 and "telephone enabled" Windows versions of Microsoft Office (a suite of software that includes word processing, spreadsheet, presentation graphics, database management and electronic mail) poised to begin shipping this year.

The number of Windows-based computer screens sporting buttons for dialing, bridging, screening, and otherwise manipulating telephone calls is growing steadily. Both desktop- and LAN-based visual telephony look the same on the screen. Both represent a powerful turbocharger for messaging, since they generate a visual "inbox" that can list voice mail, faxes, and e-mail messages on a single screen. This "visual voice mail" client will most likely be the one readily understandable application of screen-based telephony (no more listening to the header of calls in the order they are received).

Both of the flavors of client-server computer telephony suggest unavoidable performance and resource allocation questions. Digitized and recorded voice, even when compressed, has been known to take up significant disk space and transmission capacity (i.e. bandwidth). What's more, users must also ask themselves whether they will tolerate "LAN-like reliability" for their telephones.

As client-server telephony takes hold in the office, there is yet another universe that is being revolutionized by the new architecture. Local exchange and long-distance carriers have been in a race to upgrade the public telephone network to support so-called "Advanced Intelligent Network" (AIN) services. Although not intuitively obvious, the telcos want to turn the public telephone network into the ultimate backbone for a variety of servers. The underlying idea of AIN is to provide a way for public network providers to give third parties the opportunity to sit down at a workstation called a "Service Creation Terminal" (SCE) and use a mouse and icons to build new applications. MCI, Bell Atlantic, NYNEX, and BellSouth all demonstrated their respective SCEs at the Computer Telephony '94 Exposition.

AT&T is also busy adding intelligence into its network. The company recently cemented deals with General Magic for its Telescript (communications scripting language) and Lotus Development Corp. for *Notes*, its server-based software for administering and routing "intelligent messages." As such, AT&T wants to regard its long distance network as a wide area network (WAN). Here again, the mission of these enhancements is "to *protect* [users from complexity] and *serve* [software, services, devices, processes, and other 'clients']."

Whether you are considering dedicated, circuit switched, or packet switched services, it is necessary to spend some time carefully planning your telecommunications needs. Based on some of the technologies and services that are available, you can either continue to do business the way you are, or immediately embrace some of the newer technologies and services. Take a look at your needs for station gear and terminals, network switching and control systems, and your transmission facilities and methods. Try to keep the processing power, speed, and bandwidth capabilities of these telecom elements in line with one another. In most cases, some simple adjustments and upgrades can bring your overall customer service capabilities up to a whole new level of excellence.

Dan Miller, President of Opus Research, Inc., was instrumental in the completion of this chapter. As the Editor for the Kelsey Report, Dan's insights and observations are always astute when it comes to telecommunications. Dan has been researcher, analyst, and strategist for telephone companies, computer-makers, and interactive service providers since 1980, when he helped start the New Electronic Media Program at LINK Resources. Since then he has held positions in marketing, business development, and corporate strategy at Atari, Warner Communications, Pacific Telesis Group, and ARIX Corporation. He also oversees the publication of Telemedia News and Views, a newsletter covering events and trends that shape telephone-initiated entertainment, information retrieval, and transactions. Dan received his B.A. from Hampshire College and holds an M.B.A. from Columbia University.

The author would also like to thank Robert Lewis, Senior New Media Consultant for the Star Tribune Company, Minneapolis, Minnesota. Bob provided key editorial input and coaching on his lessons learned from client-server computing. Bob brings both a user perspective and a good deal of wit into every discussion on the paradigm shift from legacy systems to distributed, cooperative processing.

4

CTI and Client-Server Computing

Computer-telephone integration (CTI) is a subset of computer telephony. CTI has been with us since the first *computer-to-switch link* products were introduced in the late 1980's. Until recently, a CTI link usually connected a telephone system to a single computer system and served a single application running on that computer. Recent popularity of client-server computing has brought new application architectures with it, based on the interaction of many computers instead of the previous one-computer (encapsulated) model.

Designing a computer-telephone application in this new environment is a whole new ball game, requiring a new strategy for managing telephone events and using them to trigger application actions. This chapter explores these consequences of the client-server revolution, and suggests some ways of designing CTI applications in a client-server world.

The Growing Role of CTI with Client-Server Computing

In concept, client-server computing is straightforward: A *client-server* application is one in which a number of independent sub-systems interact to accomplish the desired task. This style of computing stands in stark contrast to the older, traditional *monolithic* method of application design, in which a single computer running one large software package was used to implement an application. The client-server design is so named because the interaction between the systems consists of queries from one subsystem or process, via a client, which are answered with replies from another subsystem or process, via the *server*. These need not be fixed designations; a single subsystem can house both client (initiating requests) and as server (responding to requests) capabilities.

Business applications tend to have a common set of functions, and these often form the basis of a division into client-server sub-systems. For example, a typical application might include the following major functions as pictured in figure 4.1:

Figure 4.1 Major Functions Relating to Client-Server CTI

Function	Examples
Data Storage	"Here is some data; please file it!" "Please fetch the record for customer X."
Application Logic	"Should we authorize another purchase for customer Y?" "Is there sufficient funds in this account to cover this check?"
Data Presentation	"Here is a list of part numbers; please display them in two columns." "Please draw a pie chart with the following segments..."

In a traditional monolithic application, all these functions would be performed inside one large software package, running on a single computer. As discussed in chapter two, a client-server application is more probably implemented with distributed software modules running on a combination of machines. In fact, one might have multiple database servers for different kinds of data, or multiple application logic subsystems for different kinds of processing.

Recall the discussion in chapter two regarding the *communication element* role of clients and servers. This speaks to the issue of how the client-server model applies primarily to *software* structure. In other words, a system is a client-server system if its software is divided into relatively independent modules which operate in parallel. Such a system is still a client-server system even if all of these modules are operating on a common machine. This is in essence, one of the key points in the so-called *client-server acid test*. The architecture in question is undoubtedly client-server if such a system could *also* be divided across multiple machines.

Arguably the single most important factor driving the popularity of client-server computing is the personal computer, and its suitability as a powerful data presentation processor. Data presentation is a very computation-intensive process, particularly when the presentation mode is high-quality graphics. Effective data presentation also requires substantial communication bandwidth between the software which is generating the presentation formats and the physical display or printing device. The personal computer answers both of these requirements admirably, suggesting an application design which splits processing tasks into at least two portions: a central database server, and a desktop presentation client. Application logic can be divided between these two systems -- forming a *multi-tier* client-server environment -- or on a third intermediate system layer, typical of a *peer-to-peer* environment. We will see examples of both organizations later.

One of the principal advantages of client-server design is its ability to adapt to change. A monolithic application is hard to change, because it consists of a single large software program. The structure of the program is usually complex, and changes to any one portion often have unanticipated side-effects in other portions. This occurs because the monolithic nature of the application does not force a careful modularization of functions in the initial design.

A client-server application, by contrast, is divided into segments in the initial design and the interactions between segments are carefully specified. This makes each subsystem a self-contained "black box" with defined inputs and outputs, and changes can be more successfully isolated to a specific module. Client-server applications are also more easily extended, because the extensions can often be implemented by adding additional modules rather than reworking existing ones.

All of these characteristics of client-server computing are useful in CTI applications. Call centers are the single focal point of customer communication, and agents handling these calls must tap into a wide range of existing company data systems.

CTI applications must change frequently to match new developments in customer support policies, product offerings or marketing programs. And these changes must be accomplished quickly, to maintain market competitiveness, and must be managed with minimal risk because system faults will result in revenue loss.

Client-Server Design and Legacy Systems

Most existing (or *legacy*) applications are of traditional monolithic design. But this does not mean that these applications must be discarded in order to adopt client-server principles. Instead, the legacy systems can be treated as database server subsystems, and additional client-server subsystems can be added around them.

For example, a bank's demand deposit accounting system (the system which tracks customers' checking account balances) would likely be programmed as a huge monolithic COBOL program, running on a large mainframe under the IBM CICS operating environment and driving 3270-type display terminals.

To convert this application to a client-server model, the bank might replace the 3270-type displays with personal computers. These PCs could then use 3270 communication protocols to retrieve database information from the mainframe, but instead of displaying the original screens an application running on the PC could analyze, edit and reformat the information.

Indeed, the PC application could retrieve data from several legacy applications running on multiple computer systems, and combine the data to make a single more useful display for the user. Furthermore, the data analysis and display methods can be changed as the user's requirements change, without requiring programming modifications on the original legacy application systems.

Introducing Computer-Telephone Integration

Computer-telephone integration is simply *the coordination of telephone and computing systems* so that their actions are synchronized. It's one of those ideas that seems perfectly obvious once you've thought of it.

For example, when a telephone call is presented to a certain telephone set, you might want a data screen displayed at the personal computer sitting beside it. Or when a call is transferred from one telephone to another, you might want the data displayed at the first agent's terminal to be moved to the second agent's terminal. The fact is, however, that the technology to accomplish computer-telephone integration (CTI) is just now becoming generally available in the marketplace.

The usual way to implement CTI uses third-party call control techniques, as shown in figure 4.2. This means connecting the telephone switch to a computing system with a point-to-point data link called a *CTI link*. This link carries call events and feature requests between the switch and the computer system, providing the basic capability through which the actions of the two systems can be coordinated.

Installing a CTI link requires the installation of a link option on the switch, as well as the installation of appropriate link protocol software on the computer. Several switch and computer vendors have offered CTI links since the late 1980s, but except for high-volume call center operators using standalone ACDs few customers have used them. This is now changing, with prices falling for the link options and several mainstream PBX vendors actively promoting the capability.

Some examples of currently available products are:

- AT&T's Passageway (formerly CallVisor)
- Northern Telecom's Meridian Link
- ROLM's CallBridge
- ASPECT's Application Link
- IBM's CallPath
- Digital Equipment's Computer Integrated Telephony
- Hewlett-Packard's Applied Computer Telephony

Figure 4.2 Third-Party Call Control

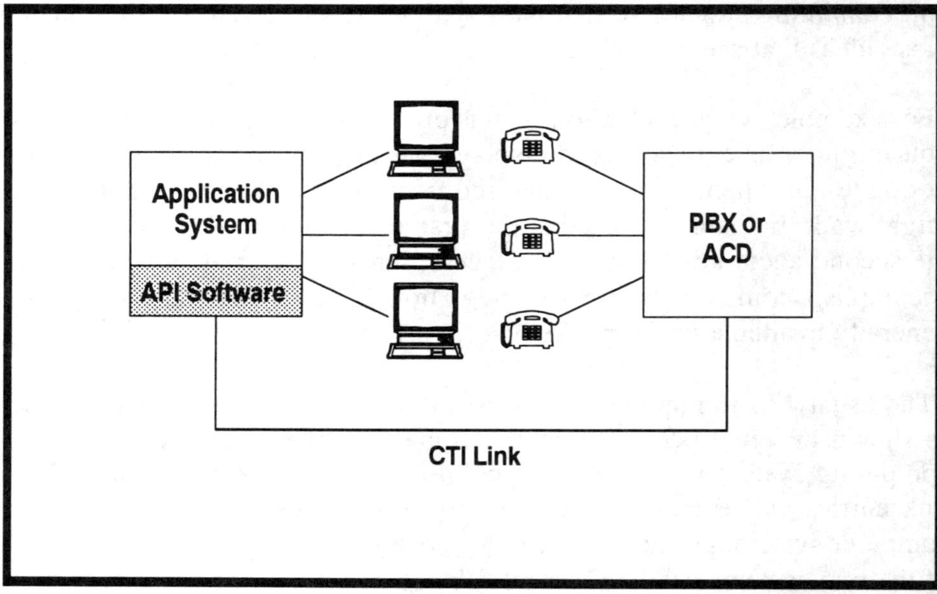

Meanwhile, a second method for CTI implementation is steadily gaining publicity: so-called first-party call control, which is usually accomplished by inserting an interface card into a personal computer so the computer can monitor the user's telephone line.

Whereas the third-party method allows the control of all telephones though a single CTI link (hence the name), the first-party method allows *only* the control of the user's individual telephone line. The first-party method is attractive to users who want to build a small application with only a few users, because there is no need to undertake a potentially expensive CTI link installation.

The disadvantage to the method is that fewer functions are available, and the scope of call control is limited to a single telephone line. This arrangement is shown in figure 4.3.

Figure 4.3 First-Party Call Control

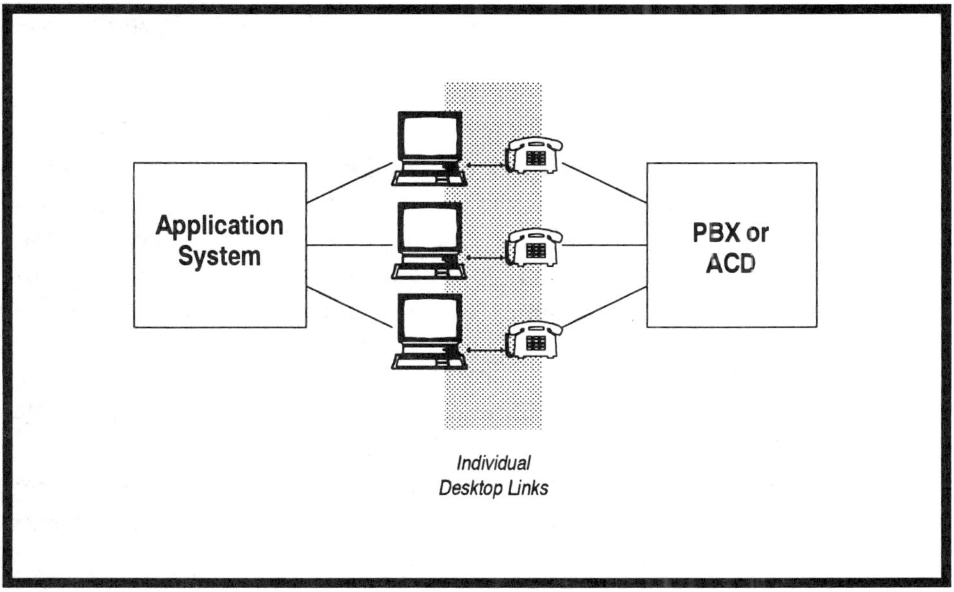

Most of the material in this chapter is devoted to third-party call control techniques, as these are better suited to high-volume applications and the client-server model.

CTI Standards

CTI standards are possible at two levels:

1. The physical connection between switch and computer, and
2. The *application programming interface* (API) used by the programmer.

Unfortunately, neither of these interfaces is standardized to any practical extent today, although work is proceeding in both areas. The interface between telephone and computer equipment is an issue of electrical standards and message protocols. Nearly every switch vendor has its own favorite, proprietary CTI link protocol, and even for different switches offered by the same vendor sometimes have vastly different arrangements. The digital telephony interfaces between switches and agent sets, used in first-party connections, is similarly proprietary. This means that you must be sure the computer system vendor you work with has an interface (either third-party CTI link or first-party set emulation) that matches the specific switch model you intend to use.

There is one published standard for third-party CTI links, called *Computer-Supported Telecommunication Applications*, or CSTA. This standard has been developed by the European Computer Manufacturers' Association (ECMA), and has been available for several years. A few switch manufacturers, including Ericsson and ROLM, have adopted it, and Digital Equipment Corporation offers computer software which implements the protocol.

The Telephony Services API recently announced by Novell and AT&T is also based on CSTA principles, although an implementation of the CSTA link protocol is not yet available. Another standard is under development by the American National Standards Institute (ANSI). This standard, called *Switch-Computer Applications Interface* (SCAI), has been under discussion for several years but has not yet been completed.

At the API level, standards discussions are only just beginning. Most of the major computer manufacturers have introduced APIs specific to their own product lines. And two software manufacturers in the personal computer and LAN marketplace have published proprietary APIs: Microsoft, working with Intel, developed their *Telephony Application Programming Interface* (TAPI); and Novell, working with AT&T, developed their *Telephony Services Application Programming Interface* (TSAPI).

All of these are tailored to suit each company's own product environment, so none is really an all-purpose API at this time. However, the ECMA CSTA study group is about to take up the question of a vendor-neutral API, so this situation could change soon. In addition to Microsoft and Novell, both Sun Microsystems and Dialogic Corporation have published specifications for APIs with CTI elements. All four of these emerging API standards are covered in detail later in this book.

Variations on CTI Link Implementation

In figure 4.2, we saw a single telephone switch, a single computer, and a single link connecting them. This is the simplest and most obvious possible configuration, but by no means the only one possible.

On the switch side, because most sites have a single telephone switch, not much variation is possible. Some switches permit multiple links, with the multiple paths used variously for traffic sharing, redundancy, or to connect multiple computer systems. In this latter case, however, most switches require the application designer to assign the individual links to non-overlapping groups of telephone lines.

On the computer side, however, more variations are possible. Whereas a typical installation has only one telephone switch, most installations have multiple computers. If more than one computer needs to receive telephone event information or make telephone feature requests, some arrangement must be found to distribute the CTI link messages among the appropriate application systems. The client-server model offers a ready solution, with a CTI server physically connected to the CTI link and client API modules installed on each application computer. This configuration is shown in figure 4.4. Using this approach, any number of applications on any number of computers can share the information supplied by a single switch CTI link.

Figure 4.4 CTI Link Server

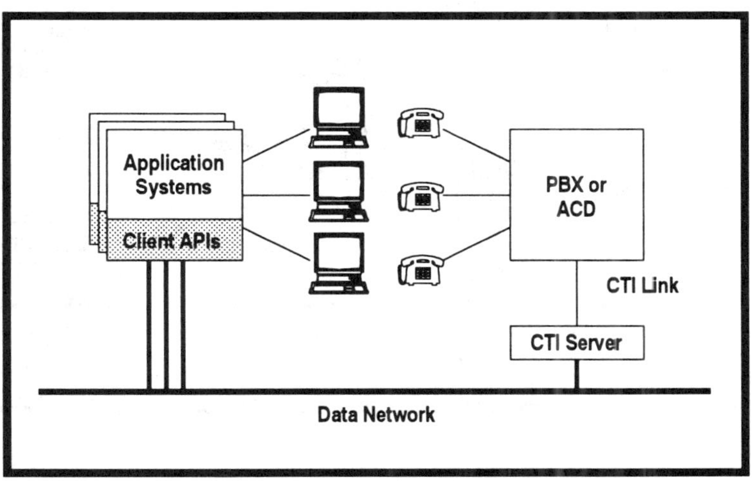

Avoiding Application Modification

While the client-server CTI design can distribute telephone information across the entire computer network, it still requires that the application software be changed to respond appropriately to these messages. This can be a significant issue when working with applications where changes are difficult or impossible due to the age of the application, the lack of a useful data network connection, or where the user organization has no access to application source code (for example, where the application is licensed from another party or where it is used remotely in a service bureau mode).

This difficulty can often be overcome by inserting a new application between the users and the original application as shown in figure 4.5. This new application, which could be termed a data distributor to emphasize its relationship to a call distributor, is the application which responds to telephone events and distributes the correct data to the proper desktop.

Figure 4.5 Data Distributor Application

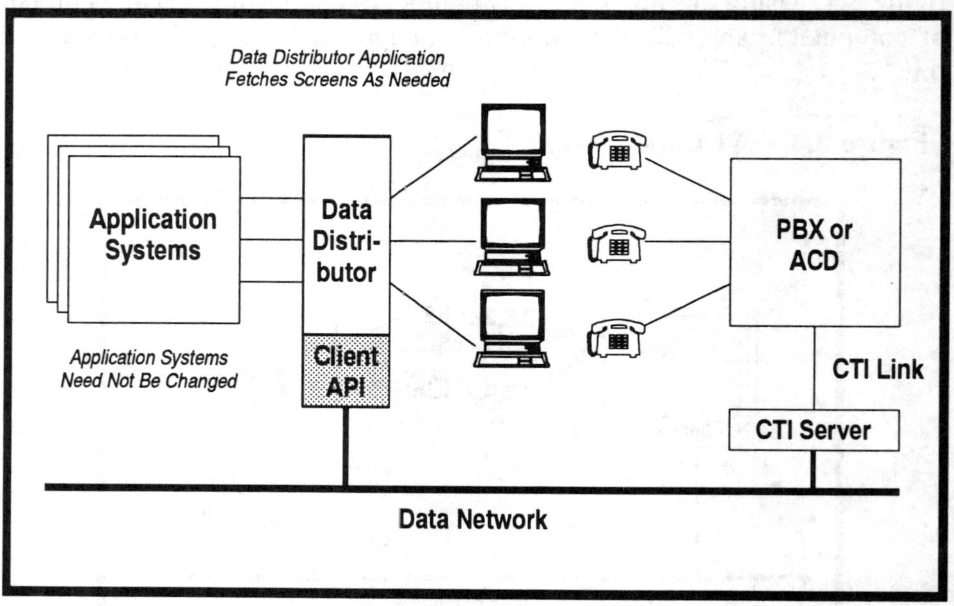

When a telephone call arrives, for example, a message from the CTI server is directed to the data distributor application, which in turn fetches information from one or more legacy applications and displays it on the user's terminal. Using this method, one can implement screen-pop and call-data transfer applications without modifying the legacy systems.

All the telephone-related logic appears instead in the data distributor application, which uses any available network connection (including terminal emulation connections) to retrieve information from the legacy systems.

Of course, with personal computers, the processing required by the data distributor application can take place on the desktop and a physically separate data distributor application machine is not required. The data distributor application, resident in the personal computer, operates exactly the same: Telephone events are forwarded to it by the CTI server, and the application uses network connections to the legacy applications to retrieve information and display it.

Using a personal computer for this task beings an added advantage, because of the large amount of commercial software available. Tasks which would have required significant custom programming on a minicomputer can often be done by combining several off-the-shelf PC software products.

One additional change must be made when substituting PCs for a central data distributor application: A repository must be provided where the data distributor applications running on all the PCs can share information about callers and call status. For example, when a call is transferred from one extension to another, the sending PC must write some information about the caller into this repository so that the second PC can retrieve it and display the caller information for the person answering the transferred call.

The most convenient method of doing this is to provide a *call status database* on a file server; the records in this database describe all of the calls being handled by the data distributor applications. This database can also be used as a historical log of all calls handled. This configuration, with the data distributor applications running in PCs and with a shared call status database, is shown in figure 4.6.

Figure 4.6 Desktop Data Distributor Application

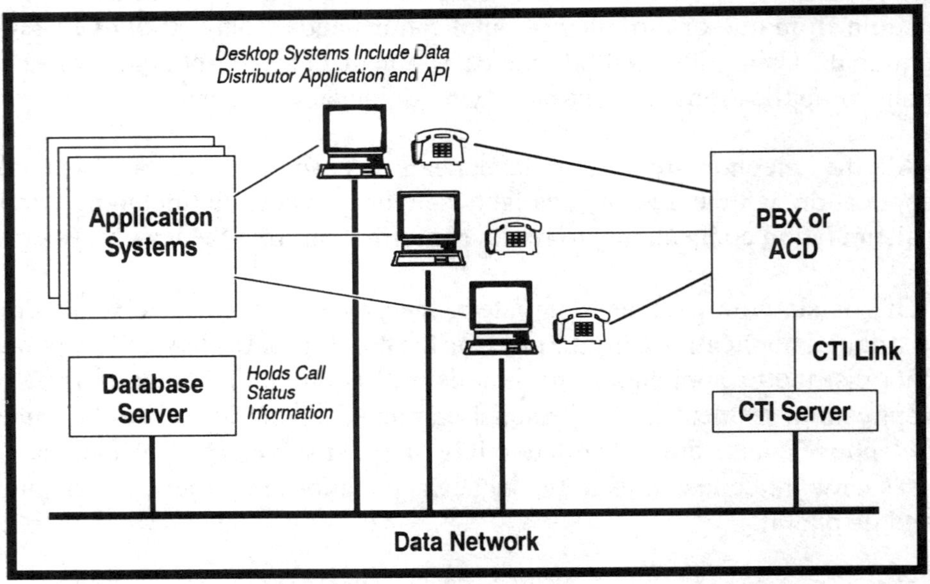

This configuration can easily be extended to support true file servers in addition to the terminal-emulation connections to legacy systems. This extension requires only that the file servers be connected to the same data network as the PCs, and that appropriate database access software be provided on the PCs. The data distributor applications on the PCs can then retrieve information from the legacy systems (via the terminal emulation connections) and from the true file servers (via the LAN connection), whichever is appropriate. This dual capability makes the migration from legacy systems to database-server applications much more manageable.

Adding Voice Response To A Client-Server CTI Configuration

So far, we have discussed only the handling of calls by human agents. Many applications also require calls to be handled by voice response units (VRUs) or by other signal-processing equipment such as facsimile servers. Increasingly, such calls must be transferred back and forth from human agents to signal processing equipment and back again without losing the context information which lets us know who the caller is, what he wants, and where he is in the call flow. CTI techniques are essential for maintaining this context.

In the client-server CTI model, signal processing equipment can be substituted for one or more agent positions very easily as shown in figure 4.7. The VRU system requires a total of three connections:

1. It must have a voice-path connection to the telephone switch, through which it receives calls.

2. It must have a data terminal connection through which it retrieves the legacy system information used during the call.

3. It must have a connection to the data network, through which it gains access to the call status database (to share information about the caller with other applications) and the CTI server (to get information about the status of telephone calls).

Figure 4.7 Adding Voice Response

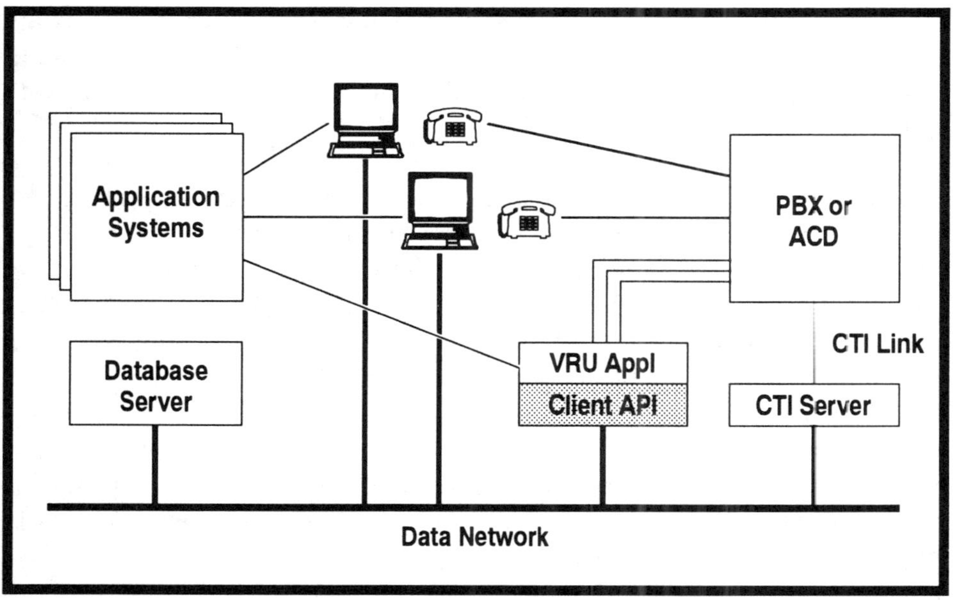

Most VRU systems on the market today provide the first two types of connection, but many do *not* provide the third type. This connection capability to the call status database is *absolutely essential* to the maintenance of the caller context as calls are transferred. This connection capability is more likely to be provided by an open VRU product built on a general computing platform, since it is easier to add physical LAN connections and networking software to such platforms. Shop carefully if you are buying a new VRU and wish to adopt a client-server application design! Make sure your new VRU comes client-server ready.

Differences Between Monolithic and Client-Server Designs

A comparison between typical mainframe legacy applications and client-server designs shows a subtle but extremely important difference:

In typical monolithic systems, information is pushed *out to a simple display device from a single source. But in client-server systems, information is* pulled *from many sources by an intelligent display device.*

In other words, in a client-server system, the client is in charge. It is the client that takes the initiative, and the servers respond. It is absolutely essential to keep this principle in mind when designing client-server CTI applications.

Designing a monolithic CTI application is relatively straightforward. A physical CTI link must be installed between the telephone switch and the application computer, and appropriate protocol software and application programming interfaces (APIs) installed. Then the real work begins: The application must be created or modified to react to the telephone events which the CTI software presents at the API interface.

In a typical screen-pop application, for example, the arriving call event must trigger much the same processing as if the user had manually entered an account number and hit the ENTER key. The data for that customer is retrieved and pushed out to the correct display terminal.

In a client-server application environment, the arriving call event is handled very differently. With this approach, the event which triggers the data retrieval is not sent to the database machine, since a server can take no action on its own; it must wait for a client to request an action. So in this model, it is necessary to send the arriving call event to the client -- in other words, the intelligent desktop. The client system receives the arriving call event, decides what data must be retrieved, and issues appropriate requests to the server machines. When the requests are fulfilled, the data which arrives back at the client is analyzed, edited and displayed.

The flow of events for a typical CTI screen-pop capability in both a monolithic application and a client-server application are shown in figure 4.8. Notice that in the monolithic example, the central application is in the center of the application flow; in the client-server example, the desktop system is in the center. These two diagrams illustrate the essential difference between the two approaches: a central application *pushing* information to the desktop, versus an intelligent desktop *pulling* the information it needs.

Figure 4.8 Monolithic vs. Client-Server Models

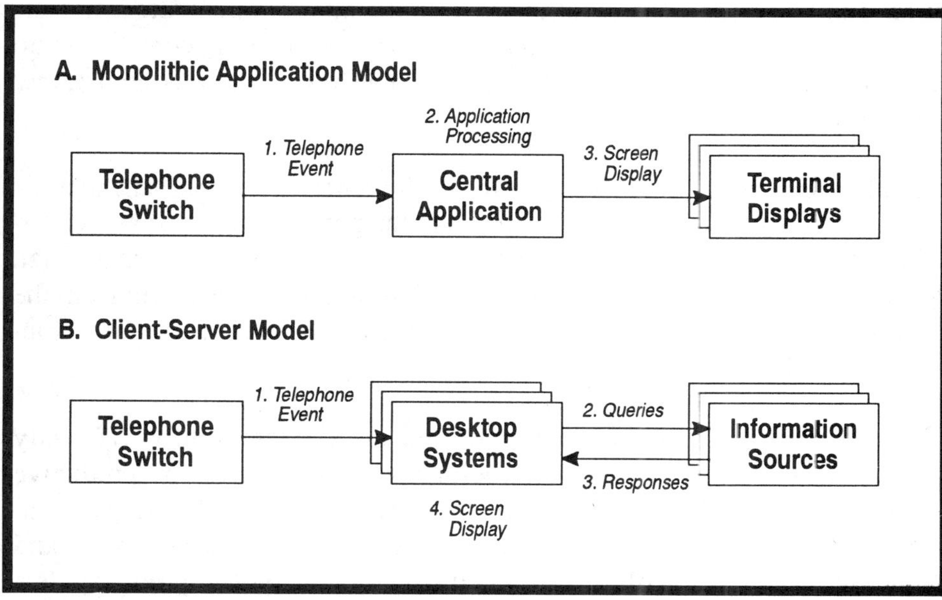

Outbound Calling In Client-Server Environments

Of course, all CTI applications are not inbound only. In many cases, the application must launch calls. Depending on the nature of the agent work-flow, these applications can use preview dialing or more sophisticated predictive dialing.

Preview dialing works just as its name indicates. A prospective called party is selected from a list, and the party's information is shown to the agent. When the agent is ready, the system dials the party. The call may be successful or not; if not, the agent goes on to the next name.

Predictive dialing can dramatically improve agent efficiency and aggregate talk time if the application's workflow permits its use. In predictive dialing, the agents do not see called party information before a call is placed. Instead, a background dialing algorithm continually launches calls to parties in a list. When a call connects successfully, an agent is selected and included into the call.

The agent sees the party's information at the same moment that the call is connected. Predictive dialing, if properly used, can improve efficiencies by several hundreds of percent because the computer application, not the agent, is launching and monitoring all calls. Agents are only connected into the call when the computer system is reasonably sure there is a customer to talk to.

Simple preview dialing is easy with the client-server model: The agent's PC selects a candidate from a list, displays the party's name and associated information for the agent to review, and waits for authorization to dial. When the agent gives the authorization, a dialing command is sent from the PC client to the CTI link server, and the call is automatically dialed from the agent's phone.

Predictive dialing is a bit more complicated, and is done slightly differently under the client-server model than with traditional standalone predictive dialers. Traditional predictive dialers are essentially monolithic applications. They handle dialing, call progress detection, agent selection, and agent data display all within one system. They also typically display data exactly as it would have appeared on a legacy system's display terminal, without any analysis or processing. The agent using the dialer sits 'behind' the dialer, rather than using a telephone set connected to an ACD. In fact, the agent usually cannot take inbound calls at all, but only those calls generated by the dialer and passed through to the agent.

Client-server application design offers a new way to handle predictive calling. This approach is strikingly similar to inbound call handling methods, making it easier to blend inbound and outbound call flows. This approach makes use of automatic call distributors (ACDs) to help handle the call routing after the calls have been dialed. Agents sit at normal ACD positions, and take the automatically-generated calls as they flow through normal ACD splits or gates. In fact, from the agents' point of view, they actually *are* taking inbound calls.

In the client-server model, outbound calls are generated by a *predictive dialing server*, which launches the outbound calls and then transfers successful calls into the appropriate ACD gate. (Gates used for outbound calling, of course, are configured for negligible wait times so they immediately flow through to a waiting agent.) The predictive dialing server paces the outbound calls to maintain this level of performance. The predictive dialing pacing algorithms are very similar to those used in standalone dialers; the only difference is the disposition of successfully connected calls. The standalone dialer connects the call to a captive agent; the predictive dialing server transfers the call into an appropriate ACD gate.

Figure 4.9 Predictive Dialing Server

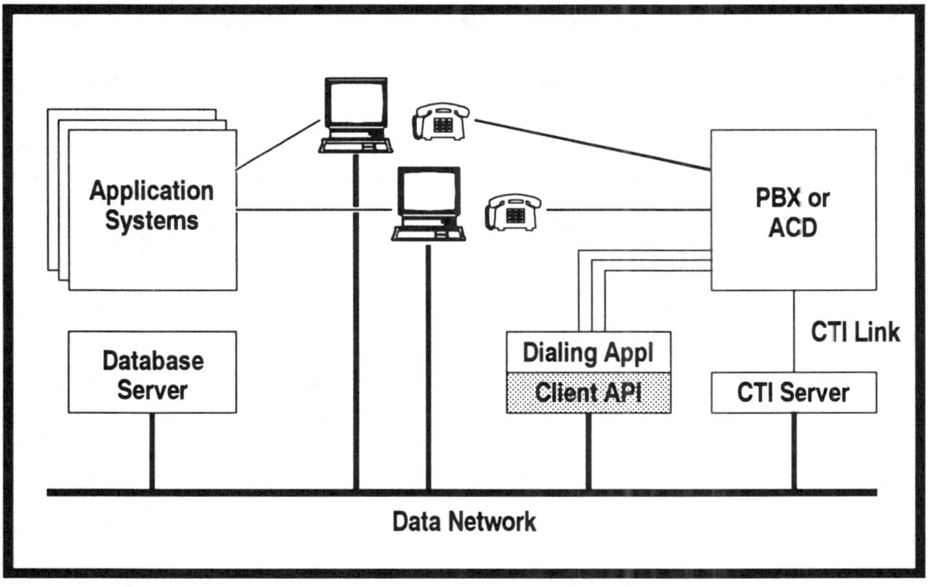

As with any transferred call, a CTI link capability is essential to maintain the context of the transferred call so that the receiving agent can be informed about the called party's identity. This means that the predictive dialing server, like the VRU, needs a data network connection to function in a client-server environment. Through this connection, the predictive dialing server exchanges call status information with the CTI server and uses a common repository database to store specific called party information for later use by desktop agent applications. This configuration is shown in figure 4.9.

The difference between standalone predictive dialing systems and predictive dialing servers is highlighted in figure 4.10. This diagram shows clearly how much easier it is to mix inbound and outbound agents using the client-server approach, and also demonstrates that a predictive dialing server arrangement generally requires fewer total ports than a standalone dialer and ACD used separately. This is because the server transfers the call into an ACD queue when a connection is sensed, so the dialer need not set aside ports to maintain calls while agents are talking. By comparison, with a standalone dialer the port is held for the duration of the call because the agent sits behind the dialer. Additional trunks are saved because both inbound and traffic can be blended across a common pool of trunks between the ACD and the public carrier.

Figure 4.10 Comparison of Predictive Dialing Methods

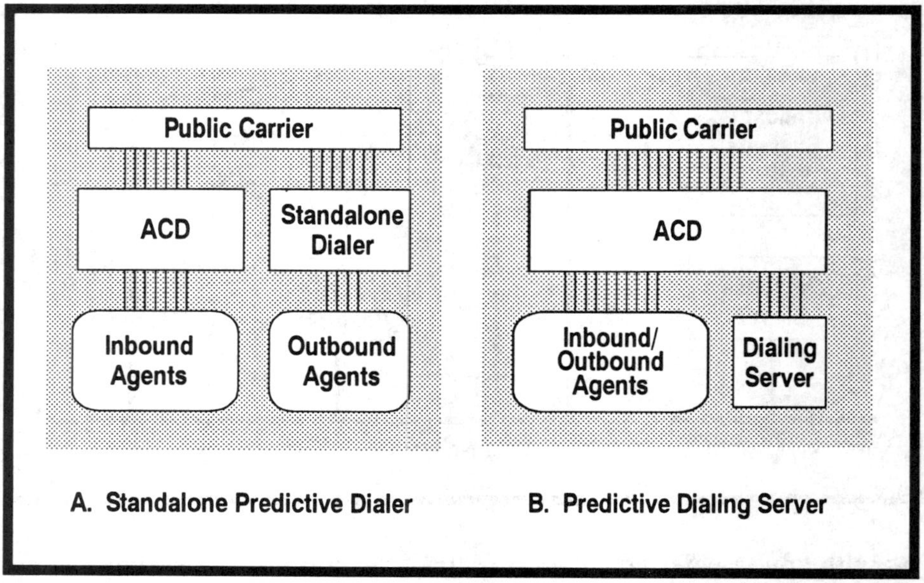

Rapid Application Development

One of the hidden advantages of client-server CTI applications is in the methodology of how they are created. The actual construction of large monolithic applications is generally preceded by an enormous amount of paperwork. Systems of this size are expensive, and are very difficult to change once built. Consequently, most development efforts spend a long time writing down every aspect of the proposed system in an attempt to ensure that everyone understands what will be built and agrees that it is the best design.

Unfortunately, this extended documentation process has two major disadvantages. First, it takes time. By the time a specification is agreed and construction is able to start, the underlying business situation has changed. An organization then has two equally distasteful alternatives: Build the obsolete system anyway, or set the completed design aside and start all over again. Clearly, this cycle could repeat over and over again and the system might *never* be completed.

Second, a system specification on paper does not accurately convey how it will operate in real life. Human factors issues are especially hard to judge from a functional specification document; system features that sound useful on paper often turn out to be less so, and potential efficiency aids are hard to identify during chalkboard walk-throughs. The only real way to find out if a system is helpful is to use it.

Client-server computing offers the potential of circumventing these difficulties. Because it relies strongly on desktop computing, a client-server CTI application can be tried at one desktop without disrupting others. Once the application is worked out at that single desk, it can be replicated at others. And the personal computer, together with the myriad of powerful application development tools now available, makes an excellent platform for translating automation ideas quickly into a working model.

The combination of these capabilities makes rapid application development a very powerful tool for building CTI applications. Let's look at an example of how this approach might be used. Take, for example, an insurance company wants to add some CTI automation to its customer service call center. They already have a voice response system, and they would like to have customer screens pop up when the VRU calls are transferred to live agents. This company could install a CTI link on its switch, and add a CTI server to its computing environment. Then it could set up a few test positions with personal computers.

Each personal computer would need a connection through a gateway to the legacy applications (probably on mainframes); and a small file server would have to be added to the LAN if not already available. If the existing VRU was not capable of client-server network connections as described earlier, a suitable small PC-based VRU system would be needed as well.

Once this set of base technology was assembled, the company would assign a small team of business and technical experts to build a sample automation application. This application would run on the PCs, using commercial application development tools. It would receive telephone events from the CTI server, caller information from the VRU via the call status database, and data records from the legacy systems via the gateways. It would present the proper information to the agent when each call arrives, and offer the agent some new capabilities beyond those of the legacy systems. Such an application could be completed in no more time than would be required to write a function specification document.

The advantage, of course, is that it is a working model. Customer service agents can sit at this position and take calls, providing excellent feedback to the designers on which features are valuable and which are lacking. Time-and-motion studies can be done to calculate the benefits of investing in a full-scale implementation. And potential difficulties, such as poor legacy system response times, can be identified and corrected. The whole process has a much greater "hands-on" feeling, and is much more likely to result in a system that successfully addresses the business situation.

In fact, the proof-of-concept system is likely to be so successful that users will want to begin with *it* instead of waiting for a full-scale implementation. This is not necessarily bad, assuming that there is some control over quality and the revision process. Companies who adopt these methods will likely find the line between demo systems and production systems will increasingly blur, and the systems development process will become much more closely inter-linked with the business operation. And *that*, of course, is a good recipe for competitive success!

Legacy Session Pooling

One improvement many companies will want to make as they move from proof-of-concept systems to full production is to better conserve legacy system resources. The terminal emulation techniques described earlier are easy to set up, and they are often the only path into an older system. But for many mainframe system environments, maintaining lots of terminal sessions is a very expensive proposition.

For example, a call center with 250 agents may need access to three different mainframe applications. Using terminal emulators, the call center would need the same number of sessions as with traditional 3270-type terminals: 250 sessions on each of three applications, for a total of 750 sessions. These are expensive resources, and they are probably only lightly used; the number of actual transactions entered by an agent in the course of a call is small.

This situation can be improved greatly through a technique called session pooling, shown in figure 4.11. With this technique, an additional server is placed between the agent applications and the gateway to the mainframe (In practice, the session pooling server and the communication gateway server can be the same physical equipment, running two different applications).

The session pooling server maintains a certain number of sessions to the legacy applications, and the agent applications send messages to the server requesting specific screens of information. When the server receives such a message, it grabs one of the available sessions, sends the query to the mainframe, collects the response, and immediately releases the session for use by someone else. The query results are then sent back to the requesting agent application.

This approach can reduce the number of sessions required by an astonishing degree -- frequently by a factor of ten or more. In our example, a session pooling server is likely to require only 20 or so sessions to each mainframe application, for a total of 60 sessions. This is a savings of 690 sessions, or more than 90 per cent! Such a savings is well worth the additional cost and complexity of a session pooling server for production systems. The same approach can also be used to handle the legacy system queries from VRU systems, with a similar magnitude of savings.

Figure 4.11 Session Pooling Server

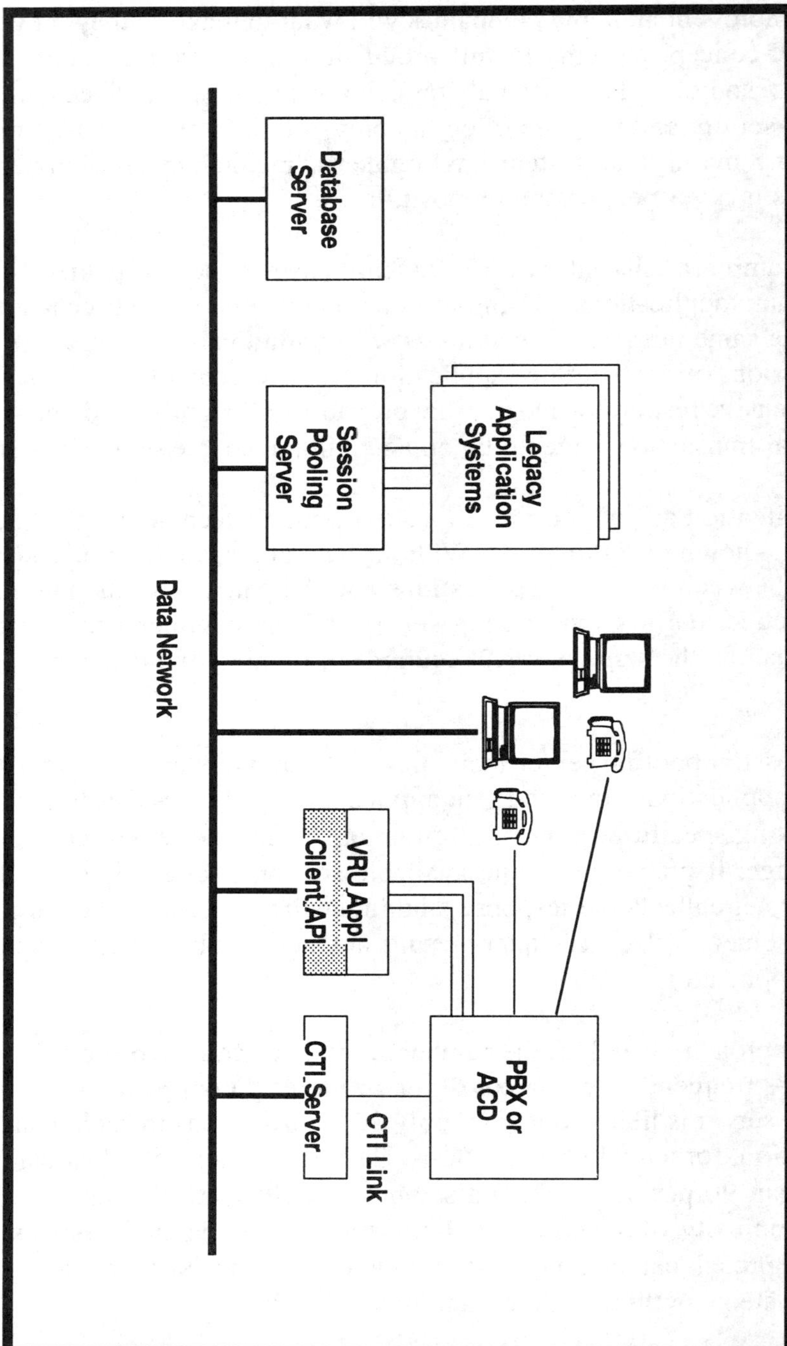

Putting It All Together

All of the configurations we have discussed can be combined into a single client-server call center environment. The result is shown in figure 4.12. This diagram combines:

- A telephone switch with a CTI link option
- A data network
- A CTI server
- Intelligent desktop systems
- Legacy systems
- A database server
- A voice response system
- A predictive dialing server
- A session pooling server

Other servers could be added as well -- for example, a facsimile server would fit into the configuration much like the VRU and dialing servers. Overall, the client-server computing model has a lot to contribute in typical CTI applications. The advantages of client-server computing help to meet the challenges of the fast-paced business environment usually found in marketing and customer service functions, and its ability to draw information from many sources -- including older legacy systems -- is very important.

CTI applications, however, must be completely rethought for a client-server environment. CTI links must be connected through servers rather than individual host computers, and the flow of information and event messages must be centered around the desktop or the special-function server rather than around a central application machine.

By adjusting your methods and procedures to fit this new model, however, you stand to gain considerable advantages in terms of rapid application development and adaptability to changing business situations. If your business depends on telephone contact with your customers, suppliers, or partners these advantages can translate directly to competitive advantage.

Figure 4.12 Complete Client-Server Call Center

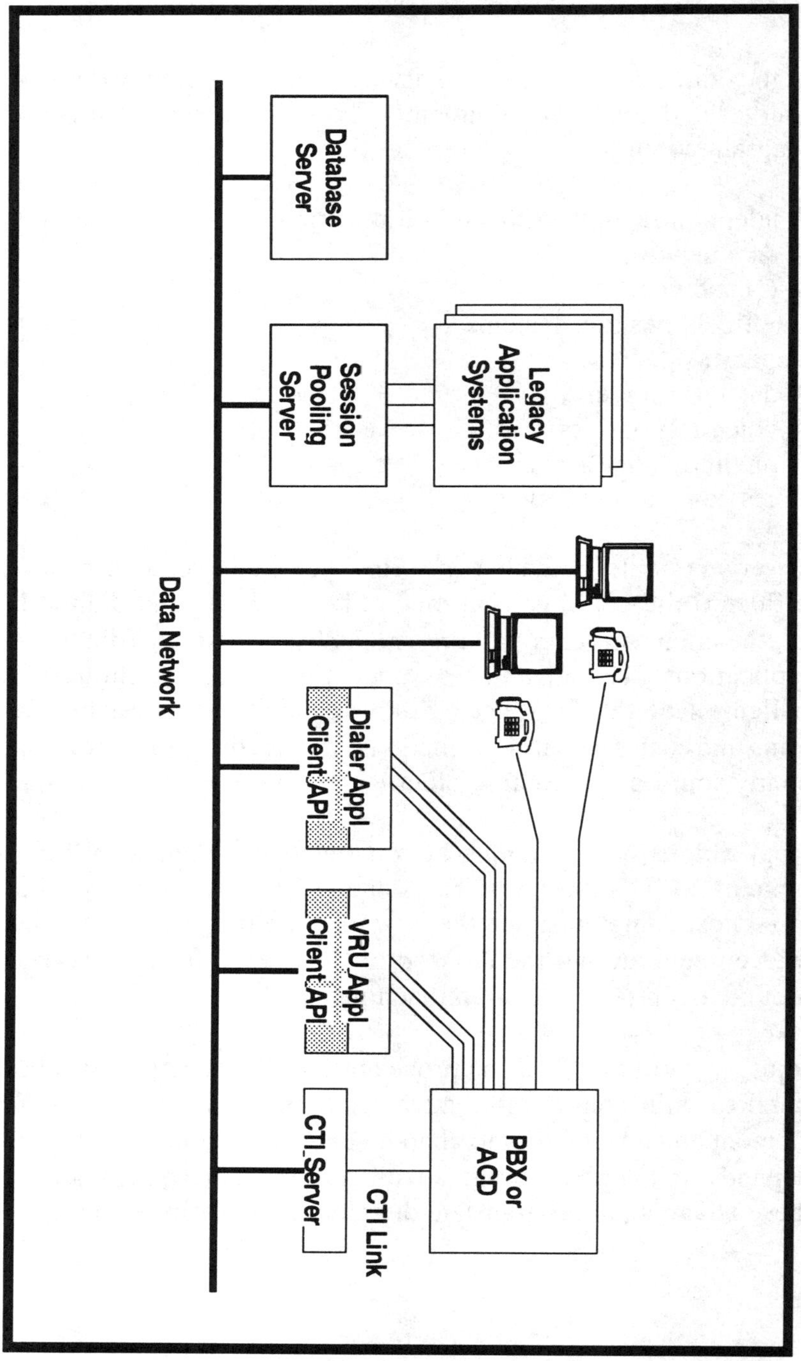

This chapter was made possible due to editorial contributions by Carl R. Strathmeyer. Mr. Strathmeyer is the Director of Marketing for Digital Equipment Corporation's CallCenterPLUS. In this position, he is responsible for determining and executing Digital's marketing strategy for integrated voice-data technologies and applications.

In his sixteen years with Digital, Mr. Strathmeyer has held a variety of management and technical positions in telecommunications applications marketing, computer network engineering, corporate telecommunications, and business systems design. Before joining Digital, Mr. Strathmeyer was a business systems consultant with Index Systems, Inc. (Cambridge, MA) and Casher Associates, Inc. (Brookline, MA). He holds a Bachelor of Arts degree from Dartmouth College (Hanover, NH) in mathematics and computer science, and is a member of the board of directors of the Alliance of Computer-based Telephony Application Suppliers (ACTAS).

Mr. Strathmeyer has written numerous papers and articles on message systems and voice-related computing which have appeared in publications of the International Federation for Information Processing (IFIP), the IEEE, and the trade press.

5

Making Your Database Talk

One of the most fundamental yet exciting prospects of *client-server computer telephony* is the ability to make your database talk. This is enabled by the use of client-based communications elements that make requests of server capabilities. In the case of a "talking database," these server capabilities are specific to xBASE, SQL, or other relational databases. The information gathered as a result of these requests is subsequently linked into the logic flow of a voice response application.

The traditional means for achieving this capability is to emulate a 3270 terminal in a traditional host/slave environment. In a traditional scenario, the mainframe computer houses both the application and the database in one monolithic system as described in chapter two. The terminals are really no more than peripheral I/O (input/output) devices that view and make changes to data as a result of keyed sequences that are recognized by the mainframe's application. An interactive voice response unit can behave as if it were a terminal and emulate all of the actions that a service agent would execute. The main difference is that the peripheral I/O is simply extended to the telephone keypad via the telephone network. Although not a true client-server implementation, this method has nonetheless been effective in automating voice response or adding automation into call centers with ACD adjuncts and CTI links as discussed in chapter four.

A client-server view of the same capabilities differs greatly because the voice response unit itself has intelligence. In fact, the basic transaction logic flow is usually in the VRU rather than the mainframe in this case. The physical database can reside in a number of places, for example:

- In the same platform as the VRU
- On a LAN-connected file server
- In a foreign database or mainframe computer

In most cases, the application and run-time engine for the voice response unit are on the client side of the client-server model. An example would be a Client *AP* (Application Processor) *System* developed by Telephone Response Technologies (TRT).

The company's Client AP System is an independent PC linked to at least one Resource Server System via a NetBIOS or SPX-compatible network. This client system is really a "super client," because many telephony clients can access the system and use its communication pipeline to the server as a shared resource.

The Resource Server System is another independent PC linked to at least one *Client AP System.* Its job is to accept and multiplex many simultaneous database requests from one or more *Client AP Systems.* The respective functions of these systems can be put into the same platform, if desired, and then later distributed for network-wide use. This will be discussed in greater detail later in this chapter.

Integrating voice applications and database access management permits a wide array of powerful solutions. For example, order entry, inventory access, and call center applications to name a few (see figure 5.1). This chapter will provide an overview of what elements and methodologies are required to link a database with computer telephony. Here's an overview of what is discussed:

- Database Design Elements
- Schema for Data Relationships
- Methodology for designing a database
- Overview of Pro/Found database access module
- Example of Call Center use of client-server database

Figure 5.1 Client-Server Database Application Examples

Application	Description
Order Entry	Systems that allow callers to place automated product and service orders.
Inventory Access	Allows callers to request structured information about products, prices and inventory.
Call Center	Coordinates telephone calls coming into a service center with matching records in a customer database. The critical information required to serve the customer is presented on-screen to a service agent. (Caller data can be taken from Automatic Number Identification [ANI] or from caller-entered DTMF digits.)

Database Design

The design of a database is frequently the single greatest factor in determining the performance, and therefore success, of a database. Just as it is important to plan an application before you delve into the writing of it, it is important to design your database before you begin implementing it.

This chapter contains theories and practical methods that will be useful to any developer of database-using applications. This is especially important for computer telephony applications that address CTI (Computer-Telephone Integration) functions. Careful database coordination is a necessary component for the routing of phone calls and screen-based transactions. In effect, this is where the "screen pop" lives. Poor choices in database design can seriously impede a system's performance or make application development far more difficult than need be.

The Basics of Data Relationships

Fields, records, and tables are the fundamental elements of any database. *Fields* are items of information (e.g., first name, last name, phone). *Records* are collections of fields (a *person* has a first name, a last name, and a phone). *Tables* are collections of records. A database design is generally represented in terms of the data involved and their relationships to each other. The conventional way to represent data relationships is with a simple diagram (or schema). The three basic types of data relationship are one-to-many, many-to-many, and *one-to-one*.

One-To-Many Relationships

In a one-to-many data relationship, one data element is related in some fashion to many other elements. A simple example of this relationship might be that of the student/teacher relationship as it exists in most United States elementary schools: One teacher to many students. This is graphically represented as a diagram in figure 5.2.

Figure 5.2 Schema for Data Relationships

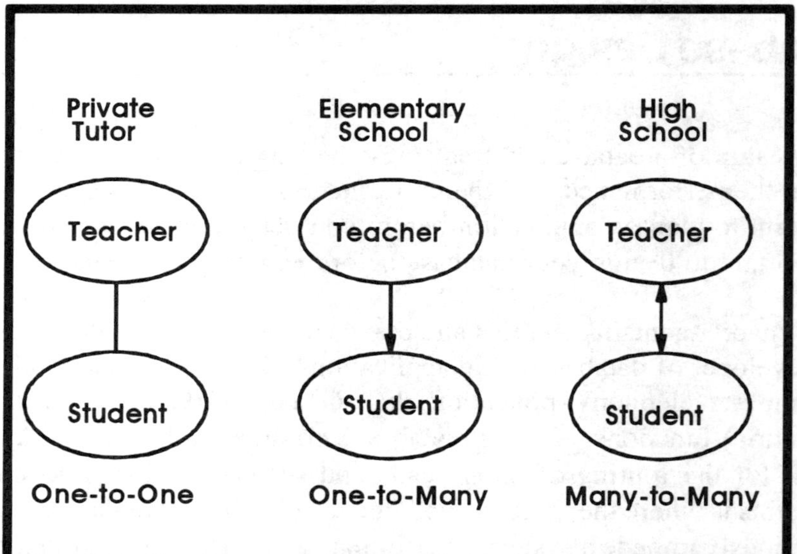

This schema indicates two record types, *Student* and *Teacher*. The relationship between these record types is indicated by the line connecting them: the end of the line with the arrowhead indicates multiplicity. Thus, there is a *one-to-many* relationship between *Teacher* and *Student*. In a database representing this relationship, each occurrence of a *Teacher* record may be accompanied by multiple *Student* records.

Many-To-Many Relationships

Although *one-to-many* relationships are the norm for most database applications, the real world is not often as simple. The world abounds with many-to-many relationships. For example, the same relationship between Student and Teacher becomes *many-to-many* when moved to the college or university environment. The only change between these two schemes is that the line representing the relationship now has an arrowhead at both ends. This notation is used to indicate *many-to-many* relationships.

One-To-One Relationships

Generally, one-to-one relationships are managed in a database by putting all of the related fields into the same record. For some applications, however, *one-to-one* relationships are represented using two separate records. Many times this occurs for historical reasons, such as when a new feature is needed after a database system is installed. Sometimes it is easier or better to add the new feature by adding a new table or record type which has a *one-to-one* relationship with an existing table rather than modify the structure of an existing table.

Steps to An Efficient Design

Because the design of a database plays such an important part in the success of the application of which it is a part, it is important to follow a structured plan to help design any nontrivial database. A simple plan is outlined below which will help in designing databases with minimal data redundancy and efficient access paths. For this tutorial, the given goal is to design a database structure (sometimes called a *schema*) for a database of *EMPLOYEEs*, *PROJECTs*, and *DEPARTMENTs*. We work under the following guidelines:

- Each employee is a member of one department
- More than one employee can work on the same project
- Employees can work on more than one project

Step 1: Define High-Level Relationships

Start by drawing the high-level relationships which will define the schema for the database. In this case, the schema can be represented as detailed in figure 5.3 below.

Figure 5.3 High-Level Relationships Defined

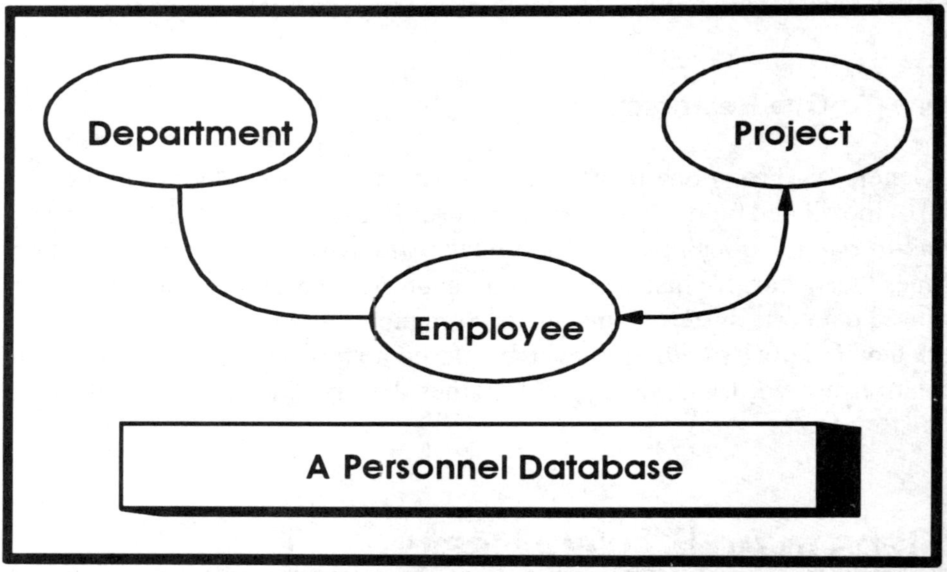

Step 2: List the Data Items

You should begin by creating a list of all of the data items to be included in the database. At this stage it is not necessary to group them into records. For this example, we simply define all of the fields that we want to track:

- Dept_Name
- EMPLOYEE_Name
- Date_Hired
- Salary
- Proj_Name
- Start_Date
- Due_Date

Step 3: Form Records

Using the list of data items created in Step 1, form separate lists of *one-to-one* relationships between items. Data items involved in *one-to-one* relationships should be grouped to form record types.

- DEPARTMENT = Dept_Name
- EMPLOYEE = EMPLOYEE_Name
- Date_Hired
- Salary
- PROJECT = Proj_Name
- Start_Date
- Due_Date

Step 4: Form More Records

Any data items not assigned to records in Step 2 are now made into record types of their own. At this point, each data item in the original list is assigned to one and only one record.

Step 5: Model the One-To-Many Relationships

Next, identify any *one-to-many* relationships between records. For each *one-to-many* relationship, establish the relationship between the two records by adding a field to the member (or "many") record that is a duplicate of a unique field in the owner (or "one") record. The field selected to establish the relationship should be one that uniquely identifies the owner record. For example, if the *department* record needs to be related to multiple occurrences of *employee* records, the field selected should be an *employee number* rather than the *employee's last name*, which might have duplicates among the other *employee* records.

In almost all cases, you should create an index for the member record based on the contents of the field which was used to create the relationship. This allows quick access to the secondary data once the owner record has been found. Figure 5.5 represents sample data for the *employee* and *department* tables.

Figure 5.4 Department and Employee: One-to-Many Relationship

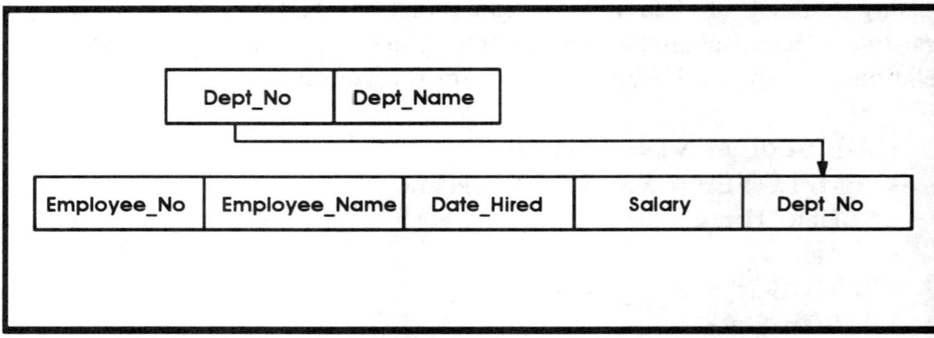

Figure 5.5 Sample Data for Employee and Department Tables

EMPLOYEE

Employee No	Employee Name	Date Hired	Salary	Dept No
00001	Smith	05/08/84	98000	00030
00002	Jones	02/04/93	13000	00010
00003	Rukeyser	06/12/91	97000	00030
00004	Kernighan	05/18/92	11000	00020
00005	Ritchie	11/11/85	14000	00020

DEPARTMENT

Dept No	Dept Name
00010	Support
00020	Programming
00030	Sales

Step 6: Create Many-To-Many Relationships

If at this point you have uncaptured relationships between record types, you can look for *many-to-many* relationships between records. Relational databases in general do not directly support many-to-many relationships. *many-to-many* relationships may be supported by using an "artificial record" and making it the member of two one-to-many relationships (See figure 5.6 for an example). Again using the job-related example, the relationship between the record types *Employee* and *Project* is many-to-many. This relationship cannot be captured by adding a field to either record which is an identifying field of the other record.

Figure 5.6 Employee and Project: Many-To-Many

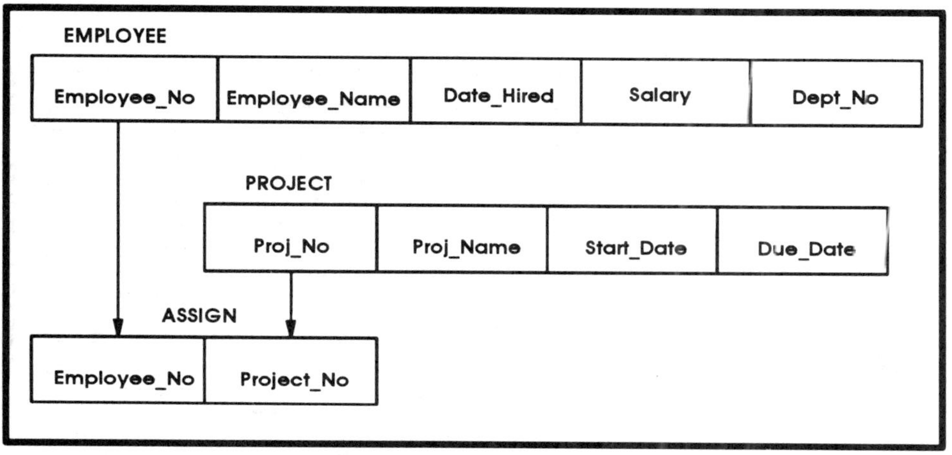

To model this *many-to-many* relationship it is necessary to introduce the record type *Assign*, which has only two fields: an *employee number* and a *project number*. The *Assign* table is used to model a *many-to-many* relationship because there are two *one-to-many* relationships with it.

In most cases the dummy record that is used to model the *many-to-many* relationship can be used for storing useful information about the relationship. Examining the sample data in figure 5.7 should make it clear how *many-to-many* relationships can be modeled using two *one-to-many* relationships.

It is important to create tables that do not cause redundant searches or indexes. For example, consider figure 5.8, which exemplifies the "poor design" of an *employee* database. By creating a table with this structure, you will find it too hard to index. In the previous example, you could index on the *Proj_No* field and do a search like "Find 00124 in the Proj_No field."

This way you'd have to index on *Proj_No1, Proj_No2, Proj_Noxxx*, and then you'd have to search every index. In addition, such a model is a waste of space. What if an individual employee only works one or two projects, but there's space in the record for 25? This type of structure also imposes an artificial limit which is not required if done correctly.

Table 5.7 Example tables for Employee Projects and Assign

EMPLOYEE

Employee No	Employee Name	Date Hired	Salary	Dept No
00001	Smith	05/08/84	98000	00030
00002	Jones	02/04/93	13000	00010
00003	Rukeyser	06/12/91	97000	00030
00004	Kernighan	05/18/92	11000	00020
00005	Ritchie	11/11/85	14000	00020

PROJECTS

Proj No	Proj Name	Start Date	Due Date	Dept No
00123	Solutions Express	08/31/93	12/15/93	00030
00124	Pro/Found	11/11/92	12/15/93	00010
00125	Account Review	03/01/94	04/10/94	00030
00126	I/Fax Plus v2.0	12/01/93	05/01/94	00020

ASSIGN

Employee No	Project No
00001	00125
00003	00125
00004	00124
00004	00126
00002	00124

Figure 5.8 "Poor Design" of *Employee*

Employee_No	Employee_Name	Date_Hired	Salary	Dept_No
Proj_No1	Proj_No2	Proj_No3	...	Proj_NoXXX

Overview Of Pro/Found Database Access Module

In order to focus on the relevance of database design to voice response applications, the remaining portions of this chapter will use examples of how the Pro/Found database access product is used. Due to its award-winning status and popularity, Pro/Found is perhaps the best choice for these examples in addition to its strict adherence to a true client-server model. Pro/Found allows for connecting databases to voice applications.

The inherent client-server architecture allows support for multiple database types (including all major xBASE formats) without application changes. A range of database operations including searches with multiple indexes is supported. Pro/Found is a product that works alongside *ProVIDE* (TRT's Professional Voice Interactive Development Environment). ProVIDE is both a service creation tool, and a run-time engine for computer telephony platforms.

Pro/Found's client-server architecture is pictured in figure 5.9. The power of this architecture is the ability to relocate one or more server modules from local or *Client AP Systems* to separate, LAN-connected PCs, or *Resource Server Systems*. Using a Novell or NetBIOS-compatible network, the client User Function (add-on module to the *Client AP System*)accesses the database as seamlessly as if they were on the local system. The User Function module is an application-invoked process or routine. Pro/Found, then, uses a client communications element called the CLIMGR to speak to *Resource Server Systems*.

The server communication element in these *Resource Server Systems* is called SVRMGR. A separate database engine module (database server) is selected to match the desired database format.

For example, if the database being accessed is DBIII compatible, the database engine module is called PF_DBIII. This *database engine module* manages all low-level database access. By selecting a different *database engine module*, the same application in the *Client AP System* can access databases with different formats.

Figure 5.9 Pro/Found Client-Server Architecture

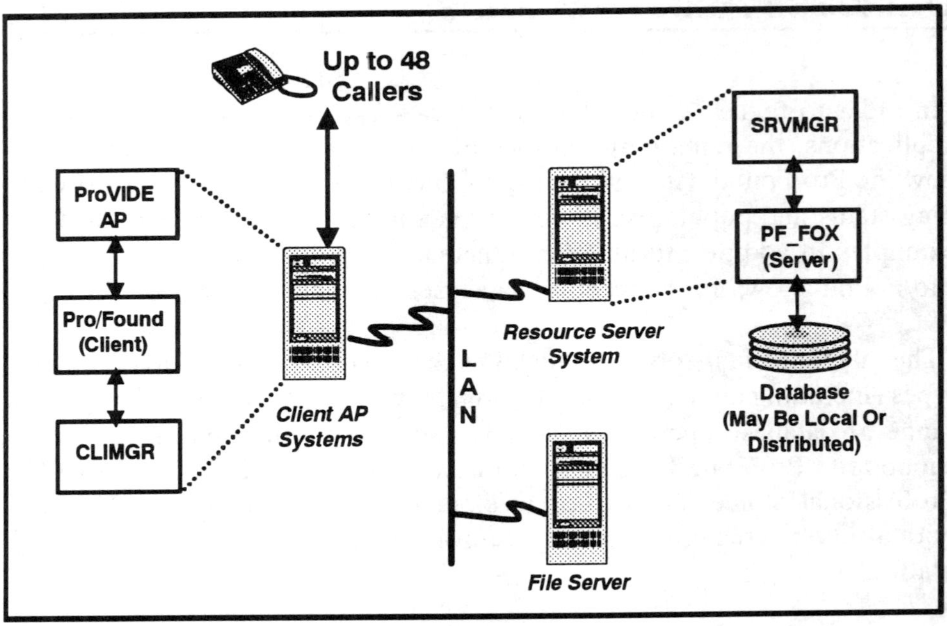

A complete set of database operations is available, including record read, write, append and delete, with full local and network file locking support. Records may be selected directly, by linear access, or by indexed search. Multiple databases, each of which can have multiple indexes, can be used in a single session. Databases may be located on the local system or on a network server. For the best possible performance, all record update operations take place on a buffer copy of the record, minimizing disk and network access.

Topologies

A variety of system topologies can be achieved with the open architecture attributes of a true client-server system. Multiple *database engine modules* can be installed on a single *Resource Server System*, or placed on multiple *Resource Server Systems*.

Single Client / Single Server

The simplest topology is to relocate a single *database engine module* to a *Resource Server System* for use by a single *Client AP System*. The advantage is that the load of database processing is placed on another system, increasing voice system performance.

Single Client / Multiple Server

If multiple *database engine modules* are used, either on single or multiple *Resource Server Systems*, a single *Client AP System* can access an array of database resources too large for a single system.

Multiple Clients / Single Server

If multiple *Client AP Systems* are used with a single *database engine module*, database resources can be easily and flexibly shared among the client systems.

Multiple Clients / Multiple Servers

In a topology with multiple *Client AP Systems* accessing multiple *Resource Server Systems*, almost unlimited voice and database power can be achieved without performance penalties.

Do/Change Function Overview

The application level interface between voice response applications and Pro/Found is the *Do/Change* function. When the Pro/Found User Function module is installed before loading the Application Editor (AE), the database functions are almost seamlessly accessible alongside those of the base ProVIDE package. ProVIDE takes care of the basics of a voice response application by handling multiple telephone lines, voice storage and access, logic flow, and global defaults.

Do/Change functions can be regarded as simple building blocks with which to construct database applications from the elementary to the complex. Although the Pro/Found Do/Change functions are relatively simple to understand when considered individually, it takes a thorough understanding of each and all of them in order to use these “building blocks” to construct a successful application.

Most of the functions either retrieve or write a record, or move a field in a record to or from a Line Register. Line Registers store information specific to telephone line activity and associated processes. A complete understanding of all the available building blocks will greatly enhance development, especially in the application planning stages.

Currency & Record Storage Buffer Changes

Pro/Found operates on the principle of *current* items. Databases, indexes, records, fields and field offsets are first selected. All subsequent Pro/Found operations then use those current selections until another selection is made, either explicitly or as the result of executing another Pro/Found function.

Record Storage Buffers (RSBs) are AP (application processor run-time) line-specific copies of the current database record. When changing field contents using Do/Change: *Store Rxx in Current Field*, changes to the RSB contents are not written to the database until an explicit command to do so is given.

Status Return Codes

All Pro/Found Do/Change functions return a *status* or *error code* in a Status Register. The ProVIDE Status Register is defined by a command line parameter.

Do/Change Function Reference

Pro/Found's Do/Change functions can be separated into six general categories based upon the service each provides. Separated by category, Pro/Found's Do/Changes are listed in the following table:

Figure 5.10 Function Cross-Listing for Pro/Found Do/Change

Do/Change:	Action:
Current Database and Index Selection	
Select Database In Rxx	Select the current database
Select Index In Rxx	Select the current index for the current database
Physical Access	
RecFirst	Retrieve the first physical record
RecNext	Retrieve the next physical record
RecLast	Retrieve the last physical record
RecPrev	Retrieve the previous physical record
Rec In Rxx	Retrieve a specified record number
Keyed Access (Assumes one or more indices have been configured for the current database)	
KeyFirst	Retrieve the first record in index order
KeyNext	Retrieve the next record in index order
KeyLast	Retrieve the last record in index order
KeyPrev	Retrieve the previous record in index order
KeyFind Exact in Rxx	Retrieve a record matching a value
KeyFind Closest in Rxx	Retrieve a record closest to a value
Record Manipulation	
Enable Record Locking	Turn on automatic record locking
Disable Record Locking	Turn off automatic record locking
Write Current Record	Write the Current Record to the database
Append Current Record	Write a new record to the database
Unlock Record	Unlock the Current Record
Unlock Record in Rxx	Unlock the specified record number
Delete Record	Delete the Current Record
Delete Record in Rxx	Delete the specified record number

Do/Change:	Action:
Field Access	
Set Current Field to Rxx	Select the Current Field
Get Current Field into Rxx	Load Register with contents of the Current Field
Store Rxx in Current Field	Load a Record Storage Buffer from a Register
Set Field Offset to Rxx	Set the value for the Current Offset
Clear RSB	Fill Record Storage Buffer with spaces
Fill Regs Rxx with Record	Load a block of Registers with all the RSB fields
Fill Record with Regs Rxx	Load all RSB fields from a block of Registers
Get Rxx Fields	Load block of Registers with selected RSB fields
Store Rxx Fields	Load selected RSB fields from block of Registers
Miscellaneous	
Load Rxx with Record Count	Determine the number of records in the database
Load Rxx with Curr Index	Retrieve the number of the Current Index
Load Rxx with Curr Database	Retrieve the number of the Current Database
Load Rxx with Curr Record	Retrieve the current record number
Move To Rec Num in Rxx	Move to a Specific Record Number
Get Last Error in Rxx	Retrieve last nonzero status return value.

The application level interface between ProVIDE and Pro/Found is the set of Do/Change functions. When the Pro/Found User Function module is installed before loading the *Application Editor* (AE), the database management Do/Change functions are almost seamlessly accessible alongside those of the base ProVIDE package.

Relational Database Model

Most commercial database management systems (DBMS) are based upon what is known as the relational database model, wherein multiple tables in the database may be related to one another through the contents of one or more matching fields. All of the database types supported by Pro/Found are relational.

Relational Database Example

As an example of a database in which two tables are related, consider the following two-table database containing data on the salaries of NBA players and their team win/loss numbers. The first table, *TEAM*, contains information on the various teams in the following fields:

- Team Name
- Wins (games won)
- Losses (games lost)

The second table, *PLAYER*, maintains information on the individual players for each team in the following fields:

- Player Name
- Team Name
- Salary

The current contents of each table are as follows in figures 5.11-12:

Figure 5.11 Relational Model Example: TEAM

Team Name	Wins	Losses
Chicago Bulls	47	19
New York Nicks	50	15
Sacramento Kings	18	47

Figure 5.12 Relational Model Example: PLAYER

Player Name	Team Name	Salary*
Michael Jordan	Chicago Bulls	25,000,000
Scottie Pippen	Chicago Bulls	3,000,000
Patrick Ewing	New York Knicks	12,000,000
* Salaries are approximate and are used for illustration purposes only		

In this example, the two tables can be related using the *Team Name* field, which is the same in both tables. Records will be related by matching the contents of the *Team Name* field for all records in one table to the same field in the other table (The contents of fields used for relation must be unique).

The chief advantage of relating tables in this manner is that it minimizes data duplication. If a single, unrelated table was used, it would not be possible, for example, to match salary information to win/loss ratios without duplicating the information in more than one place.

The problem with such data redundancy is that it wastes hard drive space and causes update inefficiencies. For example, when the New York Knicks win their fifty-first game the database would be updated to reflect this information.

With the relational approach, a single change made to the *TEAM* database is all that is required. With the single-table approach, however, every occurrence would need to be updated to reflect the additional victory, increasing the possibility of incomplete or mismatched data.

Maintaining Indexes

When a database is specified in the configuration file as consisting of a data file and one or more index files, Pro/Found will automatically maintain the specified indexes as records are inserted, deleted, or updated.

Record Storage Buffers

Pro/Found maintains a *Record Storage Buffer* (RSB) for each installed telephone line which is running on the *Client AP System*. Each line's RSB will contain the data most recently read from any database. The use of RSBs allow Pro/Found applications to read an entire record from a database and store it in memory. This in turn minimizes performance-degrading disk access and speeds many subsequent data manipulation operations (As the application needs data from fields from within the current record, the contents of the desired field can be retrieved from the Record Storage Buffer without having to access the disk-based database).

Database Operations & the RSB

This section explains how Pro/Found's basic database operations such as reading, writing and searching for records interact with the RSB.

Reading Records

When an application executes Pro/Found Do/Change functions which read records (e.g., Do/Change: *KeyFind Exact in Rxx* or Do/Change: *RecFirst*) the Record Storage Buffer will be updated to contain the data from the record that was read. If a "read" Do/Change function is not successful, the Record Storage Buffer will be marked as empty and subsequent calls to the Do/Change: *Get Current Field into Rxx* will fail by returning the value 7 (PF_RSB_EMPTY) in the *Status Register*.

Writing Records

Writing or appending a record to the database does not affect the current state of the line's Record Storage Buffer. Regardless of whether the Do/Change function succeeds or fails, the record storage buffer will be left intact. When records are written or appended to a database, the contents of the Record Storage Buffer are converted into the format used by the installed *database engine module* (database server) and the record is then written to disk.

Switching Databases

Whenever an application selects a new database using the Do/Change: Select Database in Rxx function, the Record Storage Buffer is blanked.

Transferring Data

Pro/Found contains a series of Do/Change functions that move data between the RSB and Line Registers. To move data from a single RSB field to a Line Register, execute the Do/Change: Get Current Field into Rxx function. To move data into the RSB from a Line Register use Do/Change: Store Current Field in Rxx. There are four Do/Change functions which move data between the RSB and a block of Line Registers:

- Do/Change: Fill Regs Rxx With Record will copy data into a block of Line Registers from successive fields in the RSB. One register is used for each field.

- Do/Change: Fill Record With Regs Rxx will copy data into the fields of an RSB from a block of Line Registers. One register is used for each field.

- Do/Change: Get Rxx Fields will copy data into a block of Line Registers from successive fields in the RSB. The quantity of fields to copy and the field at which to start copying may be specified.

- Do/Change: Store Rxx Fields will copy data from a block of Line Registers into successive fields in the RSB. The quantity of fields to copy and the field at which to start copying may be specified.

Database Access

Pro/Found offers a variety of methods for accessing database records. Records may be accessed either in the order in which they are stored in the data file (physical access) or based on keyed values as stored in index files (keyed access). Keyed access cannot be used unless there is at least one index defined in the configuration file for use with the associated database. Pro/Found allows applications to manipulate databases using either physical or keyed access, or a combination of both. If multiple databases are used, each can be manipulated using physical or keyed access independently of the others. These database access methods are controlled by currency tables.

Currency

For each line and each database, Pro/Found maintains Current Record and Current Index settings. When an application switches between databases, the *Current Record* number and *Current Index* selection are restored for the newly selected database. This allows an application to temporarily switch from one database to another and then return to the first database with currency intact.

The only information that will be lost by such a change will be the contents of the Record Storage Buffer, which is blanked whenever the current database is changed. The Current Field and *Field Offset* will both be set to 0 (first field, no offset).

Currency Example

An example of currency will clarify how it affects an application's operation. Imagine an application which has selected database 1 and is processing a series of Levels (application logic steps) that perform operations on each successive record in that database. It processes the records sequentially until it reaches record number 5.

Then, based on some field of interest within that record, the application needs to select database 2 and update record number 322 in that database. The Do/Change: *Select Database in Rxx* function is used to switch to database 2, and the update is performed.

The application then executes the Do/Change: *Select Database* function again to return to database 1. At that time, the *Current Record* will be restored to record number 5, which is precisely where it left off while working through database 1's records. The application can then resume execution with the Do/Change: *RecNext* function to move to record 6.

Index Currency

Each active line also maintains a *Current Index* value. The *Current Index* can be selected with the Do/Change: *Select Index In Rxx* function, and the value of the *Current Index* may be loaded into a *Line Register* with Do/Change: *Load Rxx with Current Index.*

Each time an application executes the Do/Change: *Select Database in Rxx* function, the *Current Index* is reset to the default index for the newly selected database. The default index is the first index file specified in the configuration file, or none if no indexes were specified for that database.

Field Currency and Field Position

In order to facilitate the movement of data between *Line Registers* and fields in a line's Record Storage Buffer, Pro/Found uses a *Current Field* indicator. This is used for all field manipulation functions. The *Current Field* is set by the Do/Change: *Set Current Field to Rxx* function. Whenever the Do/Change: *Select Database in Rxx* function is executed, the *Current Field* value is reset to 0, making the first field in the database record the *Current Field*, and the *Current Field Offset* is also reset to 0.

The *Current Field Position* value is used to store an offset into the current field within a record. To set the *Current Field Position*, use the Do/Change: *Set Field Offset to Rxx* function. This offset will be reset to 0 each time a database is selected.

Physical Access

Accessing the records in the order in which they are stored in the data file or table is known as *physical access*. Physical access is useful when an application needs to access all records in the database without regard to a particular field sequence. Since the physical order of the records is usually the order in which the occurrences were added to the database, physical access can be useful when an application needs to retrieve records in chronological order.

Pro/Found uses the following Do/Change functions for performing physical access:

- Select Database In Rxx
- RecFirst
- RecNext
- RecLast
- RecPrev
- Rec In Rxx

Physical Access Example

By using a high-level language, such as TRT's *Pro/Script*, an application fragment to iterate through all records in a database would look like this:

```
#definePF_STATUSR1
start
{
ufunc(PROFOUND, PF_RECFIRST) ;
if(PF_STATUS = PF_SUCCESS)
loop;
else
pf_error;
}

loop
{use// use  record data here
ufunc(PROFOUND, PF_RECNEXT);
if(PF_STATUS = PF_SUCCESS)
loop;
else
pf_error;
}
```

Keyed Access

By using an index or key file to access a database, you can change the application's logical view of the data file. This allows you to access the data file in virtually any order, assuming you have an index that provides that ordering. *Keyed access* to data files also allows an application to quickly search for and retrieve specific records from the database.

Pro/Found uses the following Do/Change functions for performing keyed access:

- Select Index In Rxx
- KeyFirst
- KeyNext
- KeyLast
- KeyPrev
- KeyFind Exact in Rxx
- KeyFind Closest in Rxx

Keyed Access Example

Again using *Pro/Script*, an application fragment to step through all records in the order specified in the first index file (as specified in the configuration file when Pro/Found was loaded from the command line) would look like this:

```
#definePF_STATUSR1
// (Database previously selected)
start
{
r1 = 1;
ufunc(PROFOUND, PF_SELECT_NDX##01);
ufunc(PROFOUND, PF_KEYFIRST);
if(PF_STATUS = PF_SUCCESS)
loop;
else
pf_error;
}
```

```
loop
{// use record data here
ufunc(PROFOUND, PF_KEYNEXT);
if(PF_STATUS = PF_SUCCESS)
loop;
else
pf_error;
}
```

Exact vs. Closest Matches

Pro/Found offers two "find by key value" functions: Do/Change: *KeyFind Exact In Rxx* and Do/Change: *KeyFind Closest in Rxx.* These functions both search for a specific occurrence of a value within an index, but with an important difference. The Do/Change: *KeyFind Exact in Rxx* function will return a status value of 0 and read in a current record only if an exact match is found. If an exact match is not found, an error value will be returned and the RSB contents will remain unchanged.

Figure 5.13 Exact Vs. Closest Matches

Operation	Reason
Select Database in R1	Select TEAM as the current database.
RecFirst	Retrieve the first record in the current database (the record for the Chicago Bulls).
Get Current Field into R2	The Current Field is 0 (by default) which is the team name field. After this operation, R2 will contain "Chicago Bulls."
R1 = "PLAYER"	Set database selection
Select Database in R1	Select PLAYER as the current database.
R1 = "Team Name"	Set index selection.
Select Index in R1	Select Team Name as the current index.
KeyFind Exact in R2,	Find and load the first record whose index field contents match the contents of Line Register R2 ("Chicago Bulls"). The record for "Michael Jordan" will be loaded into the RSB.
R1 = 2	Set Current Field selection.
Select Current Field in R1	Select field 2 (Salary) as the Current Field.
Get Current Field into R3	The text "25,000,000" will be loaded into R3.

If the Do/Change: *KeyFind Closest In Rxx* function does not find an exact match, it will load the next record into the Record Storage Buffer. The result with an ascending alphabetical index of last names might be that a failed search for "Johnson" would return the first "Jones" record instead.

For example, using the *TEAM* and *PLAYER* tables described previously, a likely operation might be to accumulate salaries of all players on a given team. This could be accomplished through the Pro/Found operations listed in figure 5.13.

At this point, the application could enter a loop that performed Do/Change: *KeyNext* operations until the returned status value indicates that the last record has been retrieved (i.e., is a value other than 0 [PF_SUCCESS]).

Record Locking

Pro/Found is fully network-aware and implements record locking to prevent record access by more than one process. When a line locks a record, that record is protected from other processes on the network as well as from actions by other ProVIDE AP (Application Processor) lines. For example, if AP Line 3 locks a record, that record is locked from Line 4 and from access by off-line database programs.

The record locks implemented in Pro/Found are *write-only* locks, meaning that other lines and processes can *read* the locked records but cannot *lock* or *write* to them. This may vary depending on the installed Pro/Found *database engine module* (e.g., PF_DB3.EXE, PF_CLIP.EXE, database servers, etc.)

Automatic Record Locking

Pro/Found's default is to not lock records. This may be changed using the Do/Change: *Enable Record Locking* function. After this function is executed, all Do/Change functions which successfully retrieve records from the database will also lock the retrieved record. At the end of each AP call, automatic record locking is disabled. Applications which need to make use of automatic record locking should enable it before record access functions are used.

If automatic record locking is enabled, attempts to read records locked by another process will fail, since two processes cannot lock the same record. (If the application needs only to read the records in a particular database, automatic record locking should not be enabled.)

Automatic locking can be disabled using the Do/Change: *Disable Record Locking* function. When an application is done using a record, it should unlock the record using either Do/Change: *Unlock Record* to unlock the Current Record, or Do/Change: *Unlock Record in Rxx* to unlock a specific record by number.

End Of Call Unlocking

At the end of each AP *Voice Card* or *Non-Voice Card* line call, all records locked by the line will be unlocked. This allows applications to be written so that records are never manually unlocked, but are unlocked automatically by Pro/Found's end of call *cleanup process*. Despite this feature, applications should unlock records they have locked as soon as they are finished manipulating them. Doing so is a generally accepted good practice which will enhance the maintainability of the application and prevent record access problems for other lines or processes.

In writing applications which use record locking it is important to avoid a situation known as deadly embrace, in which two processes (either AP lines or external programs) are each waiting for the other to unlock a record. The result is that each process will find itself looping indefinitely, waiting for the other process to unlock its record. To avoid this situation, design applications so that they always time out or otherwise fail gracefully after a certain number of attempts to lock a record. Also try to avoid having records locked for lengthy periods of time.

Deleting Records

Pro/Found allows applications to *delete records* but does not allow for deleted records to be *undeleted* (Some external database managers allow a deleted record to be recovered, even if deleted by another process such as Pro/Found). Generally, deleted records are not physically removed from the database but are only marked as deleted. To physically remove a record from a database, a program other than Pro/Found must be used to *pack* the database.

LAN Communication and the Integrated Call Center

In this example, a VRU (Voice Response Unit) equipped with Pro/Found eliminates the need for traditional CTI links. By splitting the application processing between the enterprise database applications and the computer telephony client itself, an interesting twist on the client-server paradigm can be achieved. In this case, service agents have access to a customer database via "front-end" applications that work on their desktop PC. For example, they may be accessing a Clipper database through a program like Telemagic or ACT!. This data base holds information about the callers' previous purchases, the telephone number, account number, and other identifying information which helps the agent to navigate the caller through subsequent transactions.

In many cases it is this same data base of information that is needed by the VRU in order to automate the call. This approach allows the VRU to use the database on the LAN as a communication I/O mechanism in order to "trade" real-time transaction data with the desktop application. In a typical integrated call center scenario, the voice response unit will answer a call and either collect ANI digits or prompt the caller for their customer I.D. # with the aid of a voice processing resource. There are a virtually infinite number of ways to design databases, both separate and relational, for communication between processes. A relatively simple example might use the following record structure:

Figure 5.14 Example of "Exchange" Database

Field	Type	Size
Owner	Numeric	4
Sender	Numeric	4
Flag	Numeric	1
Data1	Character	20
Data2	Character	20

The field "Owner" contains a 4 digit number that identifies the node and line number that owns the record, in the format *nnxx*, where *nn* is the participating node number (01, 24, 65, etc.) and *xx* is the AP line number. (This value can easily be constructed within an application by concatenating a node number stored in a Constant Register and the current AP line number). This field should never be changed by any application. The field "Sender" identifies the provider of the current data, in the same *nnxx* format used for the previous field. This field is written by the sending node. The field "Flag" is a single-digit semaphore value used to control use of the record. A simple system for using this flag value might be:

- 0 Line or Node not available.
- 1 Waiting for data (written by owner).
- 2 New data ready (written by sender).

The fields "Data1" and "Data2" contain whatever data needs to be exchanged by the two participating nodes. This data can be anything: semaphore values, file names or credit validation numbers. Additional data fields can be added if necessary, but should be kept to 20 characters (the size of a *Line* or *Constant Register*) for easy manipulation.

Database Specifics

For inter-node communication, the *EXCHANGE* database must be located on a server whose files are accessible by all participating nodes. There must be one uniquely identified record for each line on each node. The identifier field should be indexed for rapid access. To prevent data corruption, each process that writes to the *EXCHANGE* database should use record locking. A brief summary of record locking steps for such an application might be as follows:

- The application enables record locking by executing Do/Change: Enable Record Locking before attempting to select a record.

- The application selects the appropriate record in the EXCHANGE database. If the record is not currently selected by another process, it will be read and locked. If the record is currently locked by another process, the application should wait a few seconds and try again to read the record (No process should have to have an EXCHANGE record locked for more than a few moments).

- The application reads or writes data from the record's fields, as appropriate, and sets the semaphore field to the proper value.

- The application should then write the record to disk and immediately unlock it using Do/Change: Unlock Record.

Fast ANI Lookups

In a ProVIDE-based system, some users may find it necessary to perform application steps based on the ANI (Automatic Number Identification) data provided by the phone network. One of the fastest ways to make efficient use of ANI data is to do a database lookup.

Simple AreaCode Lookup

A simple application for database lookup of ANI data would be to create a database with records containing just two fields as depicted in figure 5.15 below:

Figure 5.15 Example of ANI Routing for Call Center

Field	Type	Size
AreaCode	Numeric	3
Priority	Numeric	1

The field *AreaCode* would be used to hold, in successive records, all area codes currently in use. For the fastest possible lookups, this field should be indexed. The field *Priority* would hold a ranking value from 0 to 9. How this ranking is used is up to the application. The ANI data captured from incoming calls would be stripped down to an area code, and the result compared to the lookup table database. A priority value of 0 to 9 would be returned.

One possibility is that calls from area codes assigned a 0 priority would be refused, while those with ranks from 1 to 9 would be handled to minimize the call costs (most distant zones handled first, local calls handled at lowest priority).

Complete Number Lookup

A more complex use of ANI lookup would be to match the entire caller telephone number to a database entry to determine call handling. The database record format described in figure 5.16 could be used:

Figure 5.16 Example of ANI Ranking for Call Center

Field	Type	Size
ANI	Numeric	10
CustID	Alphanumeric	20
Priority	Numeric	2

The field *ANI* would contain all known customer phone numbers, each in a separate record. An index would be created for this field to facilitate fast lookup. The field *CustID* would contain an associated customer identification string that would allow the application to locate customer data in another database. This data could be presented to whoever answers the call, allowing them to instantly assist the caller without having to spend time getting a name and manually looking up a record. The *Priority* field would contain a ranking code from 00 to 99. This value could be used to determine the relative importance of the customer and thus the level of service representative to assign the call to, or could be a specific reference to a particular department or extension to which to route the call.

Using this as a basis, applications can be written to use the database access module to create an entry in a temporary communication database, by writing a record number into one of the fields associated with the appropriate service agent.

Because the client PC associated with the service agent is attached to the LAN, it can be set-up to "poll" both the *EXCHANGE* and *ANI Ranking* tables in order to prioritize the disposition of the call. As discussed above, the data fields in the *EXCHANGE* table acts as a dynamic communication I/O link between the VRU application (the *Client AP System*) and the client-based application in the service agent's PC. Once the disposition or priority of the call is decided by the service agent, the *Client AP System* will route the caller over the station interface to the telephone associated with that service agent. The same can be achieved by locating the *Client AP System* behind a PBX or ACD as an adjunct, so that it behalves as an automated attendant or call sequencer. An implementation similar to this is pictured in figure 5.17.

Figure 5.17 Example of Pro/Found in Call Center

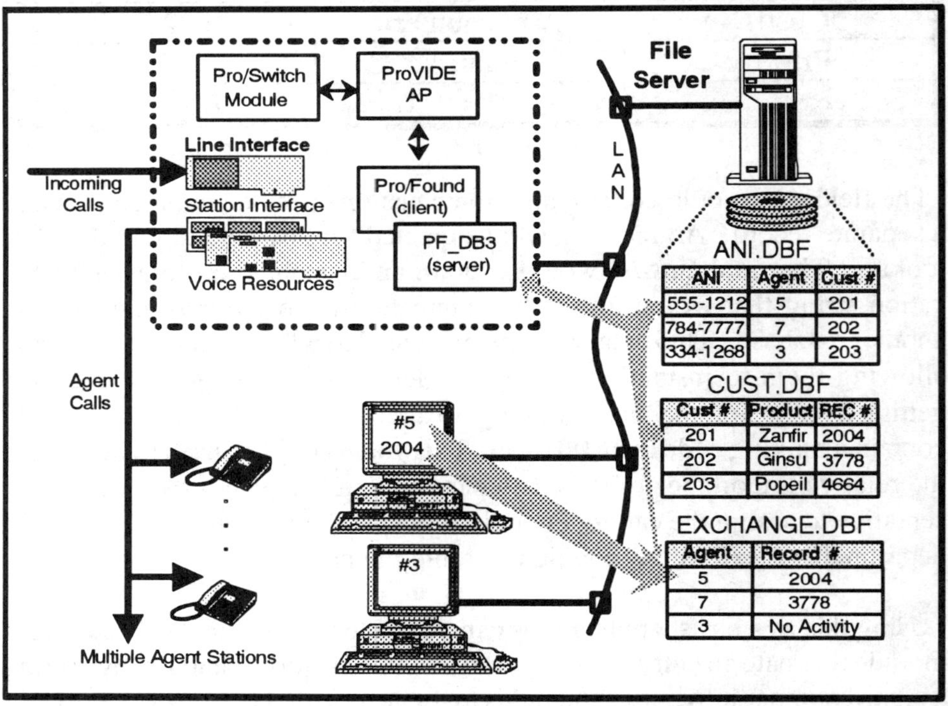

Depending on the complexity of the records, anything from simple status information to complex information requests between systems can be exchanged. Because the constancy and file locking conventions used in such a system are straight-forward, any number of clients with similar or different application can access, change, and append to the records in the aforementioned databases.

The database design and Pro/Found implementation details in this chapter are courtesy of Mike Cohn and Chris Hockett of Telephone Response Technologies.

Mike Cohn is Vice President of Engineering at Telephone Response Technologies, Inc. (TRT). Mike spearheads all strategic product development and project management for the company. A steadfast quality champion, Mike has developed a solid infrastructure at TRT for the most resilient software in the industry. His development team has produced award-winning products, such as the Pro/Found database access servers. Prior to joining TRT, he worked for Arthur Andersen in the Los Angeles and New York offices working with multi-gigabyte databases. Mike's paper on object-oriented programming will be presented at the Pacific Northwest Software Quality Conference in October, 1994. He holds an M.S. in computer science from University of Idaho and an M.A. in economics from Claremont Graduate School.

Chris Hockett is TRT's Chief Scientist. His primary research interests are ISDN, real-time switching, and advanced memory techniques. He is the inventor of TRT's RMEP (Reduced Memory Expansion Pointer) technology and he designed a suite of leading-edge client-server products for the company. Prior to TRT, Chris was recruited by Arthur Andersen's research and development team, where he became expert at large legal database design and LAN-based implementation. As an avid railway enthusiast, he was inspired to invent an enhanced arrivals and departures system for AMTRAK, and an on-line recording system for the Chicago Transit Authority. He holds a B.S. degree in computer science from California State University.

6

Computer Fax
Preamble to Networked Multimedia

The beginning of facsimile technology is traceable to 1843, when the first successful fax device was patented. Commercial fax service began in France, in 1865. Over the 1930s and 1940s, fax evolved into the form we recognize today. Computer-based fax (CBF) is a technology that is readily available and a sure means to upgrade any customer service initiative. This chapter focuses on the relevance of CBF to computer telephony, and how it can be incorporated into client-server architectures.

Understanding Fax Technology

Originally, CBF was viewed as a way for PCs to emulate fax machines. Now, CBF boards enable PC users not only to send and receive faxes, but to print as well as create them, using graphic and text files. A major advantage of CBF is in the reproduction quality at the receiving end. Material run through an ordinary fax machine's scanner is degraded in sharpness. Text and graphics originating from a PC are almost always superior to anything coming from a regular fax device. Another advantage lies in the capability to broadcast high volumes of faxes at times when telephone rates are most advantageous.

Although today fax is rightly thought of as being universal, the fact remains that for any type of fax device to be allowed to be connected to the public telephone network of another country, it must first be approved by the national Post Telephone and Telegraph administration, which is usually controlled by that country's government.

There are many factors going into the making of a successful modern fax call. Among the most important of these is compression technology. The various compression encoding schemes used for fax make it possible to remove redundancy from the material being scanned, and restore the data at the receiving end, shortening transmission times and reducing errors.

The future of fax is evolving toward higher transmission speeds and added features, such as color. Group 4 is a standard written to implement some of these features into future fax devices. However, Group 3 machines today do most of the things envisioned for Group 4 devices, and are compatible with the more than 25 million machines across the world, whereas Group 4 devices are not.

Eventually, industry observers believe there may be a merging of fax and X.400, the store-and-forward messaging protocol defining a framework for the distribution of data between networks. Group 3 information would then be packaged as part of an E-mail message and sent over the worldwide X.400 hierarchy of circuits.

As requirements increase and faxes become more fully digitized, a form of multimedia fax will appear providing high resolution, color, voice and motion, working with E-mail and offering encryption for sensitive data.

Facsimile or fax technology has ceased to be a curiosity or solely a business tool. Particularly over the last three years, it has become a utility, much like the telephone or piped water, and like these conveniences, fax machines and computer-based fax (CBF) are making an appearance everywhere, including the home.

However, unlike that of the automobile and the airplane, the history of fax is not a recent one. Fax technology has traveled a long and difficult road on its way to becoming another of those background miracles we pay little attention to.

From Telegraph to Client-Server

The first successful fax was patented in 1843 by a Scottish inventor, Alexander Bain. His "Recording Telegraph" worked over a telegraph line, using electromagnetically controlled pendulums for both a driving mechanism and timing. At the sending end, a stylus swept across a block of metal type, providing contact scanning wherever the type stood out from the block. This caused a voltage to be applied to a similar stylus at the receiving end, reproducing an arc of the image on a block holding a paper saturated with an electrolytic solution which discolored wherever an electric current was applied through it. The blocks at both ends were lowered a fraction of an inch after each pendulum sweep until the image was completed.

Bain's device transmitted strictly black and white images: it was unable to produce a scale of grays in between, but almost two centuries ago this was not of too vital importance, compared to the capability to send an image over telegraph wires. Soon after Bain's invention, several versions of his idea found relatively wide application. The first commercial fax service was started in 1865 by Giovanni Casselli, using his "Pantelegraph" machine, with a circuit between Paris and Lyon, which was later extended to other cities.

By the 1930s, systems using photoelectric sensors and rotating drums were commonplace in newspaper offices and law enforcement agencies to send and receive photographs and other graphic material over telephone wires. The first versions of what we would recognize as an electronic (rather than purely electromechanical) fax machine used photoelectric tubes to measure the brightness of each spot on a document's surface as it was quickly rotated on a drum. This allowed it to transmit gray-scale information.

These strictly analog devices worked basically by producing a varying voltage based on the output of the photoelectric tube, with the process being reversed at the receiving end. A problem with this system was that since there might be variations in brightness at a frequency below that of the audio range of telephone lines, the public switched telephone network could not be used. DC-coupled leased-line circuits were necessary. After the Second World War there was great interest on the part of newspapers in using fax technology to send newspapers directly to subscribers' homes, but the coming of television as well as technical problems forced an abandonment of the idea.

We are accustomed to the machines which appeared during the course of the last decade, when scanners and thermal printers did away with spinning drums, making fax technology available to those outside of journalism, the military, and law enforcement. Businesses were the first to profit and, in increasing quantities, personal users. But before this happened the Babel of languages these machines used, which kept them from communicating with each other, had to be brought under control.

The Coming of Standards

It was not until October 1966 that the Electronic Industries Association proclaimed the first fax standard: EIA Standard RS-328, Message Facsimile Equipment for Operation on Switched Voice Facilities Using Data Communication Equipment. This "Group 1" standard as it later became known, made possible the more generalized business use of fax. Although Group 1 provided compatibility between fax units outside North America, those within still could not communicate with other manufacturers' units or with Group 1 machines. Transmission was analog, typically it took between four to six minutes to transmit a page, and resolution was very poor.

U.S. manufacturers continued making improvements in resolution and speed, touting the "three-minute fax." However, the major manufacturers, Xerox and Graphic Sciences, still used different modulation schemes - FM and AM - so, again, there were no standards. Then, in 1978, the CCITT came out with its Group 2 recommendation, which was unanimously adopted by all companies. Fax had now achieved worldwide compatibility and this, in turn, led to a more generalized use of fax machines by business and government, leading to a lowering in the price of these units.

When the Group 3 standard made its appearance in 1980, fax started well on its way to becoming the everyday tool it is now. This digital fax standard opened the door to reliable high-speed transmission over ordinary telephone lines. Coupled to the drop in the price of modems - an essential component of fax machines - the Group 3 standard made possible today's reasonably priced, familiar desk top unit.

The advantages of Group 3 are many; however, the one that quickly comes to mind is its flexibility, which has stimulated competition among manufacturers by allowing them to offer different features on their machines and still conform to the standard.

The improvement in resolution has also been a factor. The standard resolution of 203 lines per inch horizontally and 98 lines per inch vertically produces very acceptable copy for most purposes. The optional fine vertical resolution of 196 lines per inch improves the readability of smaller text or complex graphic material.

Group 3 fax machines are faster. After an initial 15-second handshake that is not repeated, they can send an average page of text in 30 seconds or less. Memory storage features can reduce broadcast time even more. The new machines also offer simplicity of operation, truly universal compatibility, and work over regular analog telephone lines, adapting themselves to the performance characteristics of a line by varying transmission speed downward from the standard 9,600 bps if the situation requires it.

International Certification

The Post Telephone and Telegraph (PTT) administrations, usually controlled by their governments, provide telephone and telecommunications services in most foreign countries where these services are not privately owned. In TSS documents, these are the entities referred to as "Operating Administrations." It is not a simple thing to obtain approval from the PTTs to sell and use telecommunication equipment of any kind in their countries. The world is far from being one in the field of telecommunications.

Meeting international requirements typically means providing hardware and software modifications to the product, unique to each country, and then going through an extremely rigorous approval process that can average between six to nine months per country. The approval process requires products to meet both safety regulations and compatibility requirements of each country's telephone systems.

The Fax Call

What takes place before, during and after a fax transmission may seem to fall into the realm of magic, but is in reality a very carefully orchestrated procedure.

With small variations, a modern fax machine's call is made up of five definite stages as defined by the TSS T.30 specification: Phase A, the call establishment; Phase B, the pre-message procedure; Phases C1 to C2, consisting of in-message procedure and message transmission; Phase D, the post- message procedure; and Phase E, call release. Figure 6.1 provides a road map of the five stage of a fax call that are described in more detail below.

Figure 6.1 "Fax Conversation" - The Handshaking Process

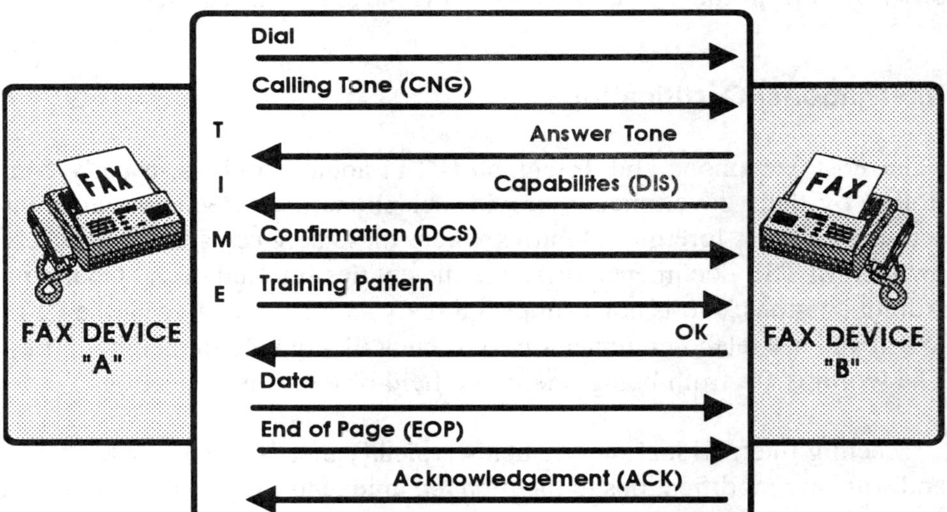

Phase A takes place when the transmitting and receiving units connect over the telephone line, recognizing one another as fax machines. It is here that the "handshaking" procedure begins between the transmitting and receiving units. This is accomplished through a piercing, 1,100-Hz tone (the calling tone or CNG), sent by the caller machine. Virtually everybody is well-acquainted with this mating call, having heard it either by dialing a fax number by mistake, or waiting to hear the answering love warble of the machine at the other end before activating your own to transmit the message. It is here that the caller machine sends its Called Station Identification (CED) and the answerer replies with its own, a shrill 2,100-Hz tone. Once this has been accomplished, both machines move on to the next step.

In Phase B, the pre-message procedure, the answering machine identifies itself, describing its capabilities in a burst of digital information packed in frames conforming to the High-Level Data-Link Control (HDLC) standard. Always present is a Digital Identification Signal (DIS) frame describing the machine's standard TSS features and perhaps two others: a Non-Standard Facilities (NSF) frame which informs the caller machine about its vendor-specific features, and a Called Subscriber Identification (CSI) frame. At this point, optional Group 2 and Group 1 signals are also emitted, just in case the machine at the other end is an older Group 1 or Group 2 device unable to recognize digital signals.

This is very rare, however, and chances are that both devices will be Group 3 machines, in which case they will proceed from the identification section of Phase B to the command section. Here the caller responds to the answerer's initial burst of information, with information about itself. Previous to transmitting, the caller will send a Digital Command Signal (DCS) informing the answerer how to receive the fax by giving information on modem speed, image width, image encoding, and page length. It may also send a Transmitter Subscriber Information (TSI) frame with its phone number and a Non- Standard facilities Setup (NSS) command in response to an NSF frame.

Then the sender activates its modem which, depending on line quality and capabilities of the machines may use either V.27 (Phase Shift Keying - PSK) modulation to send at a rate of 2,400 or 4,800 bps, or V.29 (Quadrature Amplitude Modulation - QAM) modulation to transmit at 7,200 or 9,600 bps.

PSK and QAM are phase modulation techniques used to change a signal's phase to carry information. QAM uses variations in signal amplitude that allow data-encoded symbols to be represented as any of 16 or 32 states. PSK is one of three ways (AM, FM, and PM) to changes a sine wave or L signal to let it carry information. In this case, the phases of the sine wave is changed as the information to be carried is changed.

A series of signals known as a "training sequence" is sent to let the receiver adjust to line conditions, followed by a Training Check Frame (TCF). If the receiver receives the TCF successfully, it uses a V.21 modem signal to send a Confirmation to Receive (CFR) frame; otherwise it sends a Failure-to-Train signal (FTT) and the sender replies with a new DCS frame requesting a lower transmission rate.

Phase C is the fax transmission portion of the operation. This step consists of two parts - C1 and C2 - which take place simultaneously. Phase C1 deals with synchronization, line monitoring, and problem detection. Phase C2 is devoted to data transmission. Since a receiver may range from a slow thermal printing unit needing a minimum amount of time to advance the paper, to a computer capable of receiving the data stream as fast as it can be transmitted, the data is paced according to the receiver's processing capabilities.

An Error Correction Mode (ECM) procedure encapsulates data within HDLC frames, providing the receiver with the capability to check for - and request the retransmission of - garbled data. If there are errors in the transmitted data, ECM adds time; however, although ECM adds an overhead, it uses no fill, so this overhead does not lengthen transmission time.

Once a page has been transmitted, Phase D begins. Both the sender and receiver revert to using V.21 modulation as during Phase B. If the sender has further pages to transmit, it sends a frame called the Multi-Page Signal (MPS) and the receiver answers with a Message Confirmation Frame (MCF) and Phase C begins all over again for the following page.

After the last page is sent, the sender transmits either an End Of Message (EOM) frame to indicate there is nothing further to send, or an End Of Procedure (EOP) frame to show it is ready to end the call, and waits for confirmation from the receiver.

Once the call is done, Phase E, the call release part, begins. The side that transmitted last sends a Disconnect (DCN) frame and hangs up without awaiting a response.

Compression Technologies

When digital techniques were developed for fax technology, it became practical to use encoding techniques to remove redundancy from the page being scanned, and restore the data at the receiving end. This helped reach the sought-after results of error reduction and shorter transmit times.

The TSS specifies that Group 3 machines incorporate modified Huffman run-length encoding of scan lines. In a scan line a white picture element, or pixel, is likely to be followed by a long string of the same, before reaching a black pixel. In typed or printed material, these white strings (or runs) generally continue across the entire page.

A white or black pixel represents 1 bit of information. The early fax machines would transmit 1728 bits of information for every white line across a page. Now, instead of sending all 1728 bits to represent a white line across a page, modified Huffman (MH) produces a 9-bit code word representing that white run, thus compressing this information 192 times. The result is that only 92 binary codes are needed for white runs of 0 to 1728 pixels, and another 92 for the black ones. The shorter binary codes are assigned to the longest, and most commonly occurring runs, in this way saving even more transmit time. The receiving fax units then decode this information, reproducing the original run.

A typical Group 3 fax image can have a total of 1,973,376 pixels - 1728 from side to side and 1,143 from top to bottom. Were this image to be sent uncompressed at 9,600 bps, under ideal circumstances, it would take almost three-and-a-half minutes to transmit. This is not practical and it can get very costly, in terms of telephone time and personnel, to take over ten minutes to fax a three-page document.

Today, Group 3 fax machines use two compression technologies. One of these, the modified Huffman code, is an encoding scheme that takes advantage of the similarities between pixels on the same line but not between pixels in succeeding lines. It uses a combination of run-length and static (not adaptive Huffman encoding). In this process, the sender searches for transitions from black to white (or vice versa) and reports the number of pixels since the previous transition.

To prevent blotching in the event of an error, the line must always start with a "white" run length (which can be zero if the first pixel is black). The code for a run of black pixels is not the same as for an equal number of white ones because they are not as statistically likely since runs of black pixels tend to be shorter than runs of white ones in most printed documents.

If the run is longer than 63 pixels, a special "makeup code" is prefixed to the code word. Each makeup code adds a multiple of 64 pixels to the run length. One makeup code plus one normal run-length code is enough for a run of up to 2623 pixels long (wider than a normal A4-page fax transmission).

Modified Huffman compresses only one scan line at a time; it looks at each scan line as if it were the only one. Each line is viewed by it as a separate, unique event, without referencing it in any way to previous scan lines. Because of this single-line operating characteristic, modified Huffman is referred to as a "one-dimensional compression" encoding technique.

The second encoding scheme, MR, or modified READ (Relative Element Address Differentiation), uses the previous line as a reference, since most information on a page has a high degree of vertical correlation; in other words an image, whether it is a letter or an illustration, has a continuity up and down, as well as from side to side, which can be used as a reference. This allows modified READ to work with only the differences - the variable increments or rates of change - between one line and the next. This results in a rate of about 35 percent higher compression than is possible with modified Huffman. Modified READ's operation may seem a complex concept to grasp, but it really is not. Imagine for example, a white sheet of paper with a black circle in the middle. The sheet, being all white, can be effectively compressed because, after the first compression, there is no change in the following lines so the modified READ algorithm just repeats the line.

When modified READ starts scanning the circle, black run lengths begin and, as it proceeds downward, the circle scan gets increasingly larger. However, since modified READ uses previous lines as a reference, instead of counting all the black pixels to encode them as the modified Huffman technique would, the modified READ algorithm only notes the rate of change between lines.

Therefore, the difference between modified Huffman and modified READ is, essentially, that the latter uses a "knowledge" of previous lines to reference its vertical compression. Because modified READ works vertically as well as horizontally, it is called a "two-dimensional compression encoding technique."

Two-dimensional encoding, even with all the necessary safeguards against errors, can reduce transmission time by as much as 50 per cent. Actual sending time depends on the number of coded bits per line and modem speed. It now becomes possible to compress the image data Modified Huffman down to a more compressed form, Modified Modified READ (MMR), providing as much as twice the compression of one-dimensional encoding.

Getting Hard Copy

When the receiver modem decodes the received analog fax signal it regenerates the digital signal sent by the fax transmitter, the MH/MR/MMR block then expands this fax data to black-white pixel information for printing. Overall, there are two ways to convert a fax into hard copy: through a thermal printer, or a regular printer (the latter covering everything from pin to the preferred laser printer formats).

Each inch of a thermal printer's print head is equipped with 203 wires touching the temperature- sensitive recording paper. Heat is generated in a small high-resistance spot on each wire when high current for black marking is passed through it. To mark a black spot, the wire heats from non-marking temperature (white) to marking temperature (black) and back, in milliseconds.

About the only advantage of thermal paper is that, since it comes in rolls, a thermal printout has the advantage of adapting itself to the length of the copy being transmitted: if the person on the other end is sending a spreadsheet, the printout will be the same size as the original. With sheet-fed printers, such as a laser printer, the copy is truncated over as many separate sheets as necessary to download the information.

In general, thermal printouts offer less definition, thermal paper is inconvenient to handle due to its tendency to curl, and if the copy is to be preserved, it must be photocopied because thermal paper printouts tend to fade over time. Then, most important of all, there is the matter of cost: thermal paper printouts are between five to six times more expensive than those made on plain paper. Plain paper fax machines using laser printer technology are becoming increasingly popular, particularly in the U.S.

Computer-Based Facsimile

GammaLink originated PC fax technology in 1985 when the company released its first PC-to-fax hardware and software products. An increasing number of developers now use PC-based fax boards to create systems adding them to their proprietary hardware and software products. Originally, fax boards from GammaLink and other vendors were viewed just as a way for standalone PCs to emulate fax machines, and applications were limited to the transmission of ASCII files. Although fax transmission has always been used for highly visual data, poor quality reproduction was a fact of life until the advent of CBF.

CBF boards enable users to receive faxes, print them, store them on a hard disk, as well as to create them using text and graphics files, and then transmit them. Depending on system configuration, these boards can act as fax servers for vast computer networks, sending, receiving, and routing faxes for entire multinational companies. Figure 6.2 shows how this technology is put into place from a topological perspective.

Figure 6.2 Adding a Fax Server to Your Network

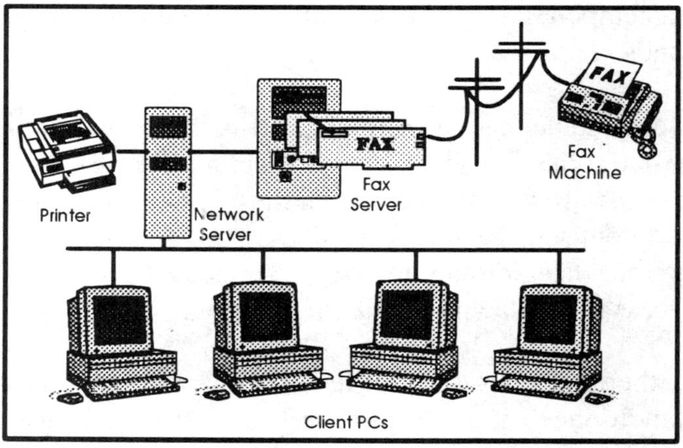

One of the major advantages of CBF is in the quality of reproduction at the receiving end. Text and graphics that are run through a fax scanner are inevitably degraded in sharpness. It does not matter whether the reproduction medium at the other end is thermal paper or a laser printer - it is the scanning process at the transmitting end that degrades the image. Text and graphics produced on a PC, however, are almost invariably superior. Also, it is possible to preview received faxes on the computer display before printing or discarding them, an increasingly useful feature as fax comes to be used more frequently for purposes of every kind.

Another major advantage is in the capability to broadcast large numbers of faxes. Often, it may be necessary to do a mass broadcasting of faxes to clients, suppliers, etc. With CBF systems this becomes a simple matter: a list is created using the phone book utility, and the computer is instructed when to send out the faxes to the people and companies on the list. This last feature is useful if the user prefers to transmit at a time when phone rates are at their lowest. Besides this automation feature, other benefits lie in the ability to track fax expenses as closely as any other business expense and the customization of CBF for different purposes, enabling the user to find novel applications for faxes as selling tools, marketing purposes and, in the case of fax on demand applications, to make information available to staff and customers at remote sites 24 hours a day.

The Future of Fax

In the swift evolution of fax technology, the Group 4 standard is viewed by some as the next significant step. Proposed in 1987 by TSS standard-makers, to allow the transmission of fax over non-analog circuits using X.25 packet switching networks as well as others, the standard has been set. Group 4 is expected to work with ISDN, switched data networks, or dedicated digital circuits. It is a layered standard, laid out in terms of the Open Systems Interconnection Reference Model, and is expected to provide high-speed transmission, outstanding error control, and features such as gray-scale and color imaging.

Group 4, however, is a standard written before a real machine was made and only a group of experts well-versed in its arcane ins-and-outs know how to implement it. Currently, there is no way to use it over ordinary voice grade phone lines, and it will not interoperate with Group 3, 2, or 1 machines. At present, there is no available modulation standard or scheme for Group 4. Absent, also, is a protocol for initial handshake. Applications for Group 4 seem rather limited, particularly in view of Group 3 technology's continued evolution. Group 3 is now expected to provide many of the features once promised only by Group 4, such as tighter compression, gray scale, color, and faster transmission. Work has been concluded by the TSS on a new, faster modem standard, V.17, which gives Group 3 the capability to operate in the 12,000 to 14,400 bps range. Many industry experts are dubious about Group 4's future, arguing that the continued evolution of the T.30 protocol and Group 3's capability to deliver speed, error control, and higher resolution - the very features that made Group 4 attractive - has rendered Group 4 outmoded even before its implementation in the real world.

Primary objections to Group 4 are its inability to communicate with Group 3 machines and work over ordinary telephone lines. Before any consideration can be given to any radical alteration in fax standards, the first thing that must be dealt with is the existence of somewhere between 20 to 25 million Group 3 machines all over the world today. This is a considerable installed base, particularly when one considers these machines are not upgradable nor can they be changed in any significant way. What is more, they run satisfactorily, and users show no intention to discard them for several years to come.

Given that there is such an enormous installed base of unalterable machines, what is going to happen? They cannot be upgraded by adding new keyboard features or new LCD displays, they will not accept new software, there is nowhere one can send in a few dollars and get a new control panel for them. And, like Everest, they are there. Even if the protocol committees were to come out with faster modem definitions, higher resolution pages, etc., a fact of life is that these machines are going to be around well into the 21st century.

The only way users might be led to discard this installed base in any significant way would be if there were some truly fundamental economic reason to do so. This happened to the majority of Group 2 fax machines which were disposed of because transmission time for Group 3 was a third or less than for Group 2. There was a significant telephone cost difference in going from a three-minute to a one- minute fax. The more knowledgeable experts do not believe, however, that this will happen with Group 3.

Once the fact that there exists a large infrastructure of installed machines that is not going to change is accepted, and that any software innovation and fax system planning has to take place taking that reality into consideration, it becomes easier to plan what uses to put the technology to, as well as what sorts of services to offer with it. Thus, services like fax on demand and others have come into being around that reality. Hardly a day goes by that new ways to use fax do not come into existence. These are very innovative and useful applications, but do not require changes in Group 3 technology.

Group 3 Evolves

That being stated, it must be also pointed out that Group 3 technology is not static but is also evolving. There are extensions being added to it. These involve agreements by the standard-making bodies - from various countries and administrations - and, ultimately the world's manufacturers, for additions to the Group 3 protocol set. Group 3 fax machines now boast faster, 14.4 kbps modems. It is estimated that now perhaps two to four percent of the installed base consists of fax machines with the higher speed modems, and this is increasing. Also coming are new resolution capabilities. It is expected that this year 300-dot-per-inch resolution will be approved by the standard-making bodies. Some of these machines may make their appearance as early as next year.

As the technology continues evolving, new capabilities are added to Group 3: there are new routing codes, binary file transfer capabilities, and superfine resolution, just to mention a few.

Although market inertia is considerable, some of these new features may be of particular importance to some users, who will invest in machines offering them, slowly obsoleting existing machines. Higher speed modems and error-correction were features first introduced not too many years ago, which are now well-entrenched in the marketplace.

Where is CBF Going?

It would appear from all this that computer-based fax by being, in effect, part of a computer and therefore more amenable to enhancements and software upgrades would find itself in a privileged position. This is the case, up to a point. The fact remains that an estimate of all LAN-based fax servers, and even all the PC fax boards, sold barely reaches the half-million mark. It is projected that by the end of the current year there will be about a million of various versions of CBF installed. Although this is by no means a small amount, and market acceptance is growing literally by leaps and bounds, the fact remains that anyone wanting to use the capabilities of these computer/fax hybrids must still deal with an overwhelming installed base of external standalone units that cannot change. So, while software for laptops or desktops can add features to CBF, unless these features can find their way to the rest of the industry, into the installed base, they will evolve very slowly.

The Digitalization of Fax

It is very clear that there is a trend towards digital fax by the end of the century. Everything seems to be working toward it - the economics of the technology, as well as the integration of fax with the computer/communications community and other networks and circuits available for the transmission of digital data. To take advantage of all this, fax must become digital. The only question is whether this is going to require yet another new standard, or whether Group 3 will gradually evolve into a form of digital standard. The extensions under proposal suggest that Group 3 itself may migrate and become the all-digital standard.

Probably the biggest growth area for fax today is in the area of its digitalization. There are several proposals out now for consideration by the various standard-making bodies, which provide for the transmission of fax over non-analog circuits. Group 4 was the first one of these. There are Japanese fax machines sending Group 4 fax over ISDN B (Bearer) circuits at 64 kbps. However, in practice, it is only in Japan that any significant population of these fax machines is found, and even there it is very small, in the tens of thousands. The reason is that Group 4 requires digital circuits that are not commonly available. Also, these fax machines have 400-dot print scanners and sell for about $10,000 or $12,000, a price most businesses find difficult to justify, particularly when the ongoing additions and expansions taking place within the Group 3 protocol continue making Group 4 seem less desirable.

While Group 4 machines are intrinsically faster, the speed difference between a 14.4 kbps and 64 kbps message may not be all that critical. While it is true that instead of taking 30 seconds to send a page a Group 4 fax can do it in ten, it is still necessary to wait 20 seconds for call setup procedures; Group 4 is a very complex protocol and machines must exchange some 20 messages before they begin transmitting and receiving. An industry observer compared Group 4 to the Concorde: "A three-hour flight to Europe does not make that much difference when you spend four hours waiting in the airport." And, of course, there is that $12,000 price tag and the fact Group 4 machines do not operate over ordinary telephone lines and have no compatibility with the great infrastructure of installed Group 3 machines.

There are other digital standards, such as Group 3 bis and Group 3/D, which keep the standard Group 3 protocols and resolutions, provide a fast handshaking, and make all digital, full-duplex transmission possible. These standards are also ISDN-compatible. The X.38 and X.39 standards offer another way of digitizing Group 3 fax, working with an X.25 transport layer.

The Merging of Fax and X.400

X.400 is a store-and-forward electronic messaging protocol defining a framework for distributing data from one network to several others. It allows end-users and application processes to send and receive messages which it transfers in a store-and-forward manner. An X.400 message consists of a message envelope and message content.

The message envelope carries addressing, routing, and control certification information. The message content part involves methods of encoding simple ASCII messages, as well as more complex data. It may contain fax4, graphics, text, voice, or binary data structures. X.400 is being increasingly viewed as a delivery platform for a variety of services, including E-mail, electronic data interchange (EDI), and others.

Industry observers agree X.400 fax (Group 3 messages with raster-encoded information payloads) will play a major role in the next generation of facsimile machines. They look at a combination of fax and digital fax with the X.400 E-mail standard. In such a setup, a Group 3 message would be packaged as part of an X.400 E-mail message and sent over the X.400 hierarchy of circuits. There are presently over 100 international carriers that can exchange this type of traffic. X.400-based fax store-and-forward networks are already in operation. The user would transmit a fax locally to a store-and-forward switch that would capture, encapsulate, and send it over high-speed circuits later to be recreated as a fax and delivered.

The concept of sending fax raster images as part of an X.400 E-mail message makes sense, because X.400 already exists as a world standard. It is now in its third division and no further standards have to be implemented to put in fax raster into X.400 traffic. X.400 fax traffic would parallel E-mail traffic generated by corporations. It is not unlikely that in the near future, traveling side-by-side, there would be an E-mail message followed by fax, and a combined fax and text message, then by a voice mail mail message, etc., all of these intermixed in one circuit. Compressed TV, and animation are not too far off, either. In short, X.400 will become the ideal pipeline for multimedia communications.

Figure 6.3 Store and Forward Configuration

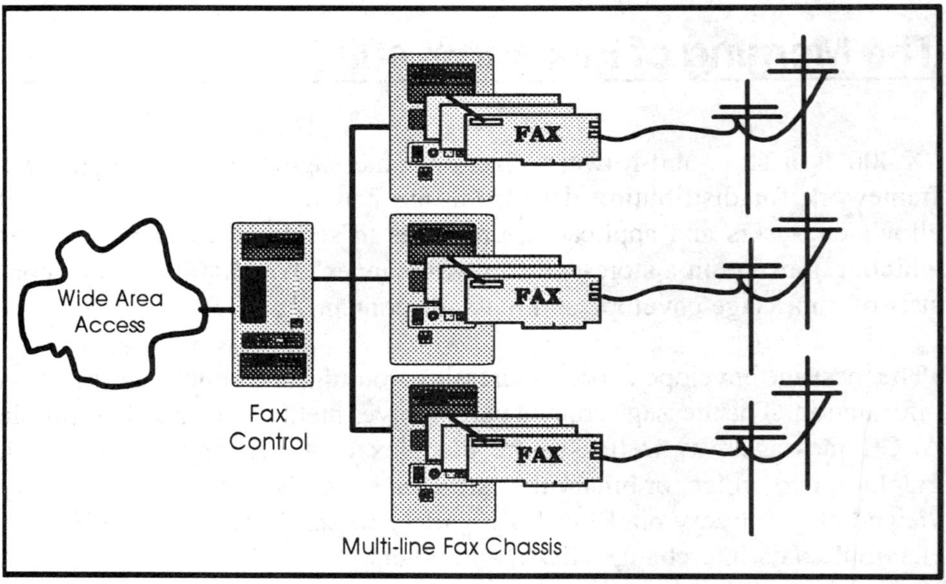

The problem with X.400 today is that it is principally used as a backbone to connect disparate E- mail systems. There are few good user interface packages available, addressing is extremely complicated, as are the options. The tendency has been to install LAN mail systems that use X.400 if needed, and X.400 has not gained the role it deserves. As an industry observer put it, “It is just the Esperanto used to get all these E-mail systems communicating with each other.”

Another problem with X.400 today is that it is primarily a store-and-forward system as pictured in figure 6.3. One of the things people like most about fax is its real-time immediacy. After receiving a transmission confirmation, the user walks away from a fax machine with 99.99 percent certainty that a piece of paper is in the person’s machine at the other end, and that if he picks up the telephone and calls to discuss the fax, it will be there.

This is not always the case with X.400. Although the user may get a local transmission confirmation, it may be another 20 minutes before the message works itself across the various hierarchies of X.400-land and arrives at the recipient’s mailbox. It may find itself at the end of a queue waiting for channels to clear, or pause behind a long file transmission. The existing X.400 standard does not have the immediacy that fax users have grown accustomed to expect. This is not an insurmountable problem in many applications such as the broadcast of faxes overseas, however, and X.400 will survive and evolve as a real commercial, end-user standard. Eventually, there will be a large EDI population of users. It is a superb backbone for E-mail systems, and recognition of its capabilities to handle fax and raster traffic is slowly taking place.

Very little color facsimile equipment is available at present. Among the reasons for this are the complexity and cost associated with color scanning and printing, as well as a long transmission time. Another obstacle to color fax is a lack of standardization for areas such as color components, transmission sequence, bilevel vs. continuous tone, and encoding algorithms.

Widespread use of color fax will probably take place within the X.400 framework, because of this architecture’s evolution into a multimedia E-mail vehicle. X.400 is, for all intents and purposes, evolving into the international standard for multimedia communications.

Remaining Obstacles

Forward-looking corporations have already come to the realization that in order for fax to achieve a flawless integration with telephone and computer technologies, one of the things that is going to have to take place is for both these communities to stop looking down at fax as an orphan of the other. The merger of these technologies has to take place. The computer world with Windows and OS/2 and the Macintosh has gone the way of raster, bit maps, and graphical images. Fax and fax machines can no longer be considered as a separate communication service with a separate network of its own. Image traffic from Windows workstations on computer networks and raster imagery generated by fax machines must merge. It is no longer practical for a company to have a telecom department that deals with fax problems, separate from its MIS department which handles computer and E-mail traffic. These areas must converge: they are holding back people and the technology. There can no longer be disparate networks.

As requirements increase, and faxes become digitized, a form of multimedia fax will make an appearance, providing high resolution, color, working with E-mail, and offering the security of encryption. All the tinker toy pieces are here now, all that is needed is for consumer demand to reach critical mass.

Fax Markets

As fax technology continues developing and finding new applications, new markets appear to fill the demands of business, government, and personal users. While by no means all-encompassing, below are what is generally considered as the major growth and application areas for CBF.

Network Fax Servers

As more companies rely on fax communications to get their work done, network fax servers are providing them with the means with which to control and optimize their fax communication. With a network fax server, any business that regularly sends and receives faxes can increase productivity while saving time and money.

Network fax servers make it possible to send faxes right from the user's workstation. Figure 6.4 shows how a typical computer-based fax server is put together. The primary elements are a dedicated PC, fax server software, and PC-based fax boards. Many fax servers even let the user fax documents right from the applications that created them. The user simply indicates the fax number, and the fax server does the rest, leaving the person free to resume work.

Figure 6.4 Computer-Based Fax Server

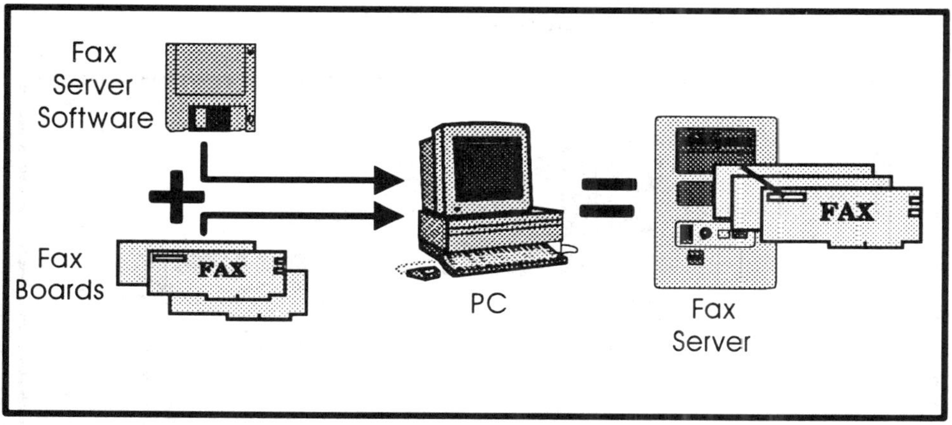

Incoming faxes can be directed back to individual workstations as well. Different fax server products offer different ways of handling incoming faxes: a fax can be received by an operator who then forwards it to the individual workstation, a unique fax extension can be assigned to each workstation.

E-Mail Fax Gateways

As companies look to bring CBF to their computer network, many find it easier to implement and train users on a system when it is simply an extension of their electronic mail. With an E-mail fax gateway a business can expand its mail system by adding fax as an additional messaging capability. This extends the convenience of E-mail communications beyond the network's boundaries. Figure 6.5 shows the interconnection between LAN-based workstations and the associated mail server and *E-mail fax gateway.*

With an E-mail fax gateway, all users can send and receive faxes from within the E-mail package. Because the fax messaging is integrated directly into the system, fax users have virtually no new software to learn. With one place to turn to for all messaging needs, users have all the features that they have come to depend on in E-mail, such as workgroup distribution lists, the capability to attach graphics files to text messages, support for different-user operating systems on the network, and instant notification of received messages. With an E-mail fax gateway, the same message can be sent to both mail users and fax recipients.

Figure 6.5 E-Mail Fax Gateway

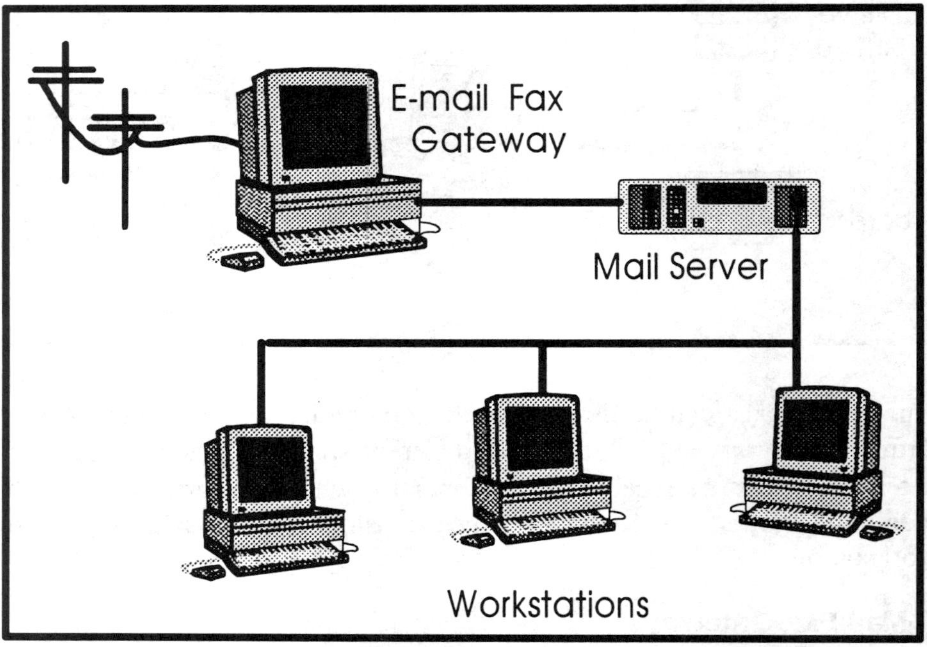

Mini/Mainframe Fax Servers

When it comes to CBF communications, each business has different needs. Although many companies generate and store information on mainframes or minicomputers, most CBF hardware is PC-based. With third-party applications running on PC front ends, computer telephony systems produced with CBF technology meets the communications needs of these customers, bringing the benefits of CBF to the mini/mainframe world. This is consistent with the idea of systems integration as a means to *phase* into client-server implementations as discussed in the first chapter. Figure 6.6 shows how CBF technology acts as an "intelligent front-end" to mainframe and mini-computers.

Many mini/mainframe fax servers work in the same way as LAN-fax servers: users can send and receive faxes from their terminals, saving both time and money while improving the quality of their fax transmissions. In addition to providing fax services to user terminals, mini/mainframe fax servers have carved out a niche for themselves through direct integration into specific applications. By being on the same computer system as an organization's data, mini/mainframe servers are positioned to provide an EDI-like component for large, vertical applications such as accounting or purchase order systems, broadening the electronic reach of these programs to any recipient with a fax machine.

Figure 6.6 Mini/Mainframe Fax Server Configuration

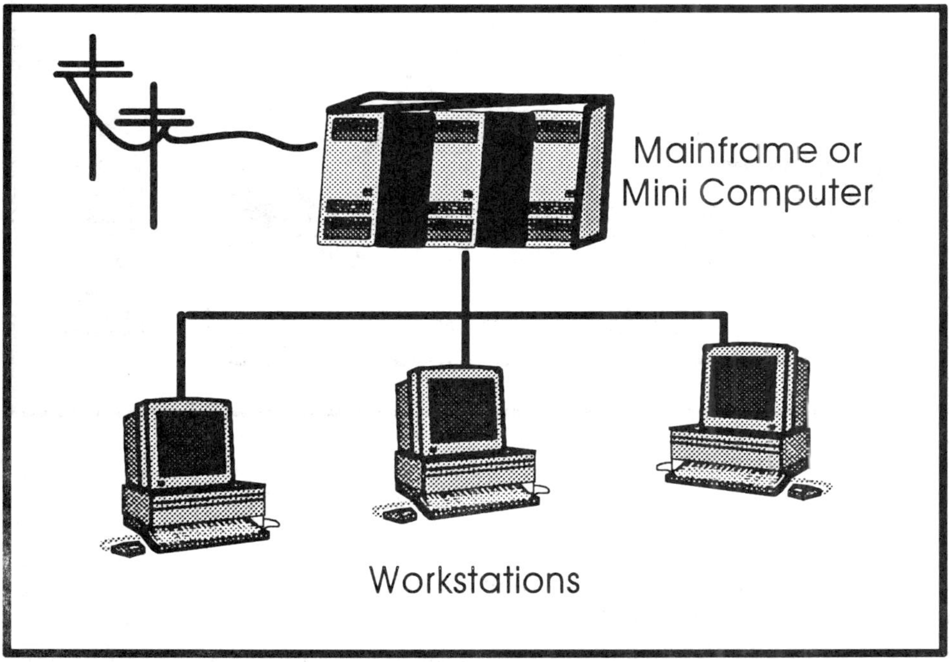

Fax Store-and-Forward Systems

The benefits of a centralized system for unattended faxing - high-volume broadcasting, batch faxing during off-peak hours, integration into database management systems for generating distribution lists, and accounting reports - make fax store-and-forward systems an attractive solution for companies wanting to manage high-volume fax activity.

With such a fax store-and-forward system, companies can centralize the transmission, reception, and management of faxes. Figure 6.7 shows how multiple chassis, equipped with CBF, can be controlled by a fax control server. This server acts as a communications gateway between LAN/WANs and the regular PSTN (Public Switched telephone Network).

Figure 6.7 High-Volume Broadcasting - Unattended Faxing

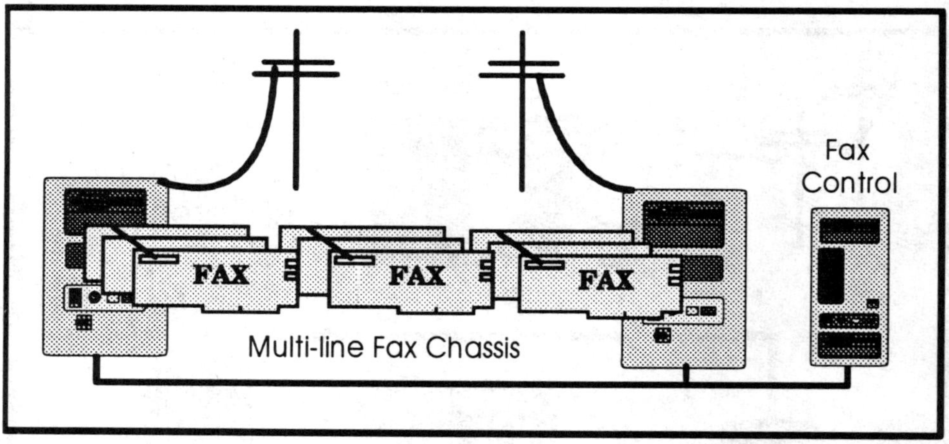

Fax store-and-forward systems range in size and functionality from large, multiple-line turnkey switches capable of sending thousands of fax pages a day, to flexible PC-based fax broadcast applications that can run on an existing computer system and be easily expanded to handle large broadcasts.

Enhancements, Utilities, and Hardware Accessories

Companies like GammaLink and other CBF providers meet most of the needs of a diverse group of customers. However, because businesses are unique and have different fax requirements, developers are creating a wide array of products to help address the needs of a business's particular CBF application.

These products fall into three major categories: software enhancements that extend fax board capabilities, such as printing accelerators; mail merge or memory expansion utilities; and hardware accessories such as large chassis, for multiline fax systems.

Image Systems

For a growing number of firms, imaging technology has become a crucial component of their information systems. Consisting of input, storage, retrieval, processing, and output components, imaging systems provide organizations which rely heavily on paper-based information with a way to make business operations more efficient and competitive. By taking advantage of this technology, firms provide customers with better service by accessing information regardless of how or where it is stored. A typical implementation of an imaging system configuration is pictured in figure 6.8 below.

Figure 6.8 Image System Configuration

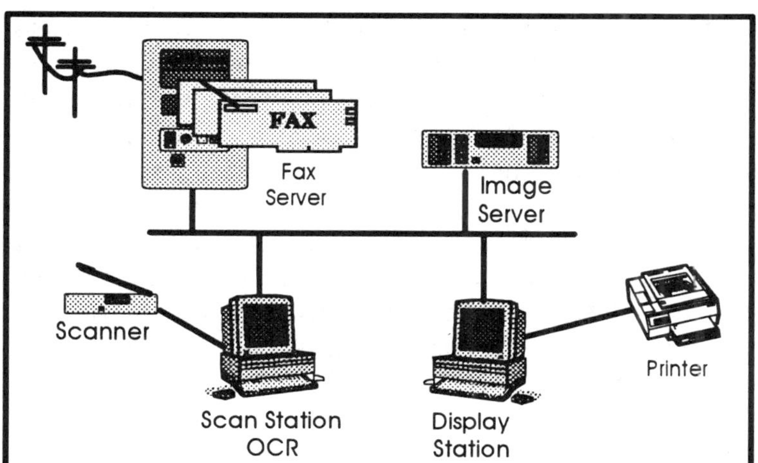

Addressing both the input and output components, CBF technology is increasingly becoming a part of the overall image system. Any company that has an image system in place, or is considering installing one, may find fax integration vital.

By integrating fax into the image system, businesses can receive fax documents directly into their image system for further processing. Similarly, any information stored on the image system can be easily retrieved and transmitted to any fax machine.

Integrated Voice/Fax Systems

At the intersection of two of the fastest growing communications technologies - CBF and voice response. Here lies a new application applications for computer telephony that are likely to revolutionize the way information is delivered to businesses and individuals. With the integration of voice and fax, the delivery of information stored in a computer to any fax machine in response to telephone prompts. Integrated voice/fax systems increase a business's ability to service customers. With a voice/fax system, customers initiate the calls and select the information they wish to receive. This means that they get the information they want at a time of their choosing, when the interest level is at its peak. In turn, by having routine inquiries handled by an automated system, sales representatives are free to concentrate their efforts on those areas and clients needing their expertise the most.

This cooperative merger of technologies manifests the idea of upgrading customer service by providing instant information access via self-navigation. This is central to the theme of client-server computer telephony and what it can provide in terms of enhancing customer service excellence. Figure 6.9 shows how client-server implementations of CBF and voice response can be used to deliver documents as a result of voice response and telephone input. In this scenario, the voice response system (fax-on-demand unit) acts as a client on a LAN. In fact, each telephone caller is a client who uses the fax-on-demand unit as a virtual client to request fax transactions for the fax server. The fax server is a server in the truest sense, because its shared resources are made available as a result of client (communication elements) submissions for service.

Figure 6.9 Client-Server Fax-On-Demand

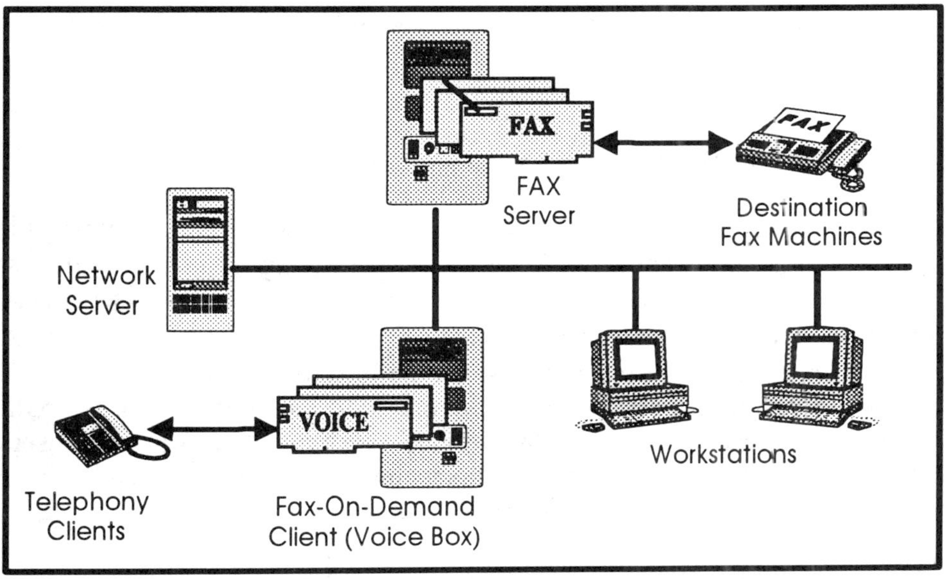

This is enabled as a result of CBF manufacturers, fax server vendors, and fax-on-demand suppliers working together for true client-server interoperability. Currently, only a handful of companies (such as Telephone Response Technologies, and Nuntius) are producing fax-on-demand clients that work with existing fax server environments.

Most other vendors are attempting to compete with fax server manufacturers by incorporating all of the requisite technologies into one monolithic system. Of course, proprietary implementations are quickly fading from popularity, as is the case with any technology over time. A voice/fax system not only helps automate existing communications, but because it is so convenient for customers to use and so cost-effective for the business to implement, it can become a marketing tool that allows a company to offer clients even more service.

Vertical Fax Applications

Vertical fax applications bring the benefits of high-quality faxing to specific corporate functions such as accounting, materials management, or sales contact management. Designed solely for use in one particular area, vertical fax applications can more closely match the needs of that business function.

CBF integrated directly into vertical applications provides a high level of automation capabilities. For instance, fax integrated into a purchase order system allows a business to fax purchase orders to a vendor with one command.

Public Fax Services

Developments in CBF technology have led to a growing market for providers of public fax services. This market, consisting of service bureaus, telephone carriers, and value-added network service providers, offers many advanced fax applications for public use, including broadcast services, fax-on-demand information services, fax mailboxes, fax bulletin boards, fax diagnostic services, and specialized subscription services, such as credit approval applications. Public fax services are typically targeted at users who want to take advantage of newer fax technologies but have not purchased existing technology for a variety of reasons.

These users may not be in a position to integrate fax on their existing networks or to support the technology, or they may not have enough demand for the application to warrant the investment. Finally, for many users, public services can provide the ability to use a large number of fax lines at any one point in time, without having to own and operate them all of the time.

In summary, computer-based fax is a key element to improving overall productivity for business who wish to upgrade their product and service offerings. A variety of developers and systems integrators can help businesses to put together custom systems that meet specific requirements in a particular environment, for a special need or a customized application. Developers can customize systems such as mini/mainframe gateways for EDI, custom voice/fax response systems, custom broadcast systems, or they can provide assistance in customizing existing applications to incorporate fax capabilities to automate faxing and thus improve productivity.

Editorial contributions for this chapter courtesy of Hank Magnuski and John Taylor of GammaLink, Sunnyvale, California. GammaLink is part of Dialogic Corporation, makers of PC-based computer telephony products and stewards of the Signal Computing System Architecture standard.

Hank Magnuski is GammaLink's Chief Technical Officer and a co-founder of the company. As a pioneer of the computer fax industry, Hank was responsible for the development and launch of the industry's first PC-based 9600bps fax modem. Hank is a strong proponent of open architecture and participated in the MVIP Standards Committee. He also co-chaired the TIA, TR.29 committee to establish guidelines for interoperability of computer telephony and fax-based subsystems. At Bell Laboratories, he was a Research Manager and developed a variety of emerging technologies for service-based implementation. Hank holds a Ph.D. in electrical engineering from MIT, with post-doctoral work at Stanford University. His work in computer based fax led to the PC-fax board being accepted into the Smithsonian Institute.

John Taylor is GammaLink's Vice President of Engineering. His leadership at the company was critical in the introduction of high-density PC-based facsimile products, including the now popular 4-port versions of the technology. John's current position was preceded by his work as the company's Senior Software Manager. He was also involved in facsimile systems consultancy with Xerox, Ricoh, and TRW. John holds a B.A. in Biophysics from San Francisco State University, and is a Ph.D. candidate at UCSF.

7

The Computer Telephony Standard: SCSA

Client-server computer telephony would not be complete without a *Framework* for communication between various components. With over 200 endorsers, the *SCSA* (Signal Computing System Architecture) standards initiative has begun to show the fruits of much labor. Notably, the *Telephony Application Object* (TAO) Framework.

This chapter will act as a prelude to several introductions to the most popular computer telephony APIs. In keeping with the spirit of this book, they are all consistent with the client-server model. They include Novell's TSAPI, Sun's XTL, and Microsoft's Windows Telephony APIs. But no other company has done more to champion PC-based computer telephony like Dialogic, so for that reason, the discussion starts with the software part of the *SCSA*. The *TAO Framework* is made up of four components:

First, a set of standard *SCSA Application Programming Interfaces* (SCSA APIs) that defines the way client and server applications access the Message Protocol to communicate with server resources and *System Services*.

Secondly, the *Message Protocol* that defines a standard way for passing messages among applications, system resources, and *System Services*.

A third set of core *System Services* include resource management, switching, event and error handling, configuration management, session management, and security.

The fourth element of *TAO* is a set of *Service Provider Interfaces* (SPIs) that defines the way *System Services* and *Resources* (the *Service Providers*) access the *Message Protocol.*

Other key features of the *SCSA Telephony Application Object Framework* are:

- It is an open software architecture
- It is designed specifically for multiple application client server environments, where multiple distributed applications use the same server resources
- It has sophisticated application management capabilities
- It facilitates both simple and complex application development
- Its core *System Services* and technology-specific resource APIs are interoperable
- It is object-oriented and operating system independent
- It is hardware independent and can be implemented on top of different hardware platforms, like the SCSA Hardware Model, *MVIP*, or proprietary hardware platforms
- It has been defined by leading computer telephony industry technologists to support current and future technology requirements

The *SCSA TAO Framework* simplifies the process of building rich application solutions for computer telephony industry demands. It benefits application developers by allowing them to create robust applications in the shortest development time. *SCSA TAO* applications are scalable and extensible, and they are compatible with the *SCbus, MVIP*, and other hardware architectures.

SCSA Introduction

Client server environments are becoming more and more the standard way of approaching computer telephony system design. Computer telephony hardware allows computers to make and receive calls, record and play voice messages, detect and generate tones, and to support speech recognition, text-to-speech, fax, video, and a range of other media processing and telephony technologies. The distributed nature of client server environments are ideal for computer telephony, where many applications can share the same computer telephony resources.

Signal Computing System Architecture (*SCSA*) is a blueprint of the best way to match resources and services to applications in a distributed environment. It is a comprehensive software and hardware architecture whose mission is to simplify the development of computer telephony systems that can incorporate multiple technologies with standard open interfaces. *Signal computing* describes the computer manipulation of not only discrete numbers and text, but also of streams of real-time signals such as audio or video. *SCSA* as such is an open architecture and provides an infrastructure for signal computing into which suppliers can integrate their own products.

SCSA is designed for both standalone and distributed computing environments, providing support for the complex requirements of client-server architectures. *SCSA* systems may be configured to support media data located in a computer telephony server, or on a network client computer accessible by the server over a computer network.

The *SCSA* client-server architecture provides a flexible topology for system suppliers. By writing applications to the *SCSA* APIs, system developers can configure systems to meet the needs of their customers without being constrained by any "local vs. remote" issues in the structure of the programming interface, or by the host platform of the application.

SCSA standards have been developed through cooperative efforts by multiple companies throughout the computer telephony industry. Each technology covered by *SCSA* is defined by a unique working group consisting of leading vendors and users of that particular technology. The specification development process has been iterative, working through several draft versions of the specifications internally by the *Working Groups* and by a larger group of companies comprising the *SCSA Advisory Council*, prior to release to the general public. As of the time of printing of this paper, the exact specifications had not been released out of the *Working Groups* and *Advisory Council*, but the bulk of the architecture and application model has been defined.

Further *SCSA* benefits include the following:

- ***Location independence.*** Resource location is transparent to the application.
- ***Scalability.*** Systems can be scaled-up by adding additional nodes without rewriting the application.
- ***Extensibility.*** Standard interfaces insure that hardware from different vendors can be combined within the same system and new technologies can be easily added.
- ***Portability.*** SCSA APIs are object-oriented, operating system independent, and can support multiple operating systems and different system topologies.

SCSA *Elements*

SCSA comprises a software model and a hardware model. The hardware model describes a high-speed, high bandwidth bus, a switching fabric, and the capability to connect multiple system nodes into one large, distributed "virtual" system.

For a complete description of the *SCSA Hardware Model*, see the *SCSA* Specification available from Dialogic, or get the book by the same title at Telecom Library. The software model, the *SCSA Telephony Application Object* (*TAO*) *Framework* is described in detail below.

Figure 7.1 The *SCSA* Software Model

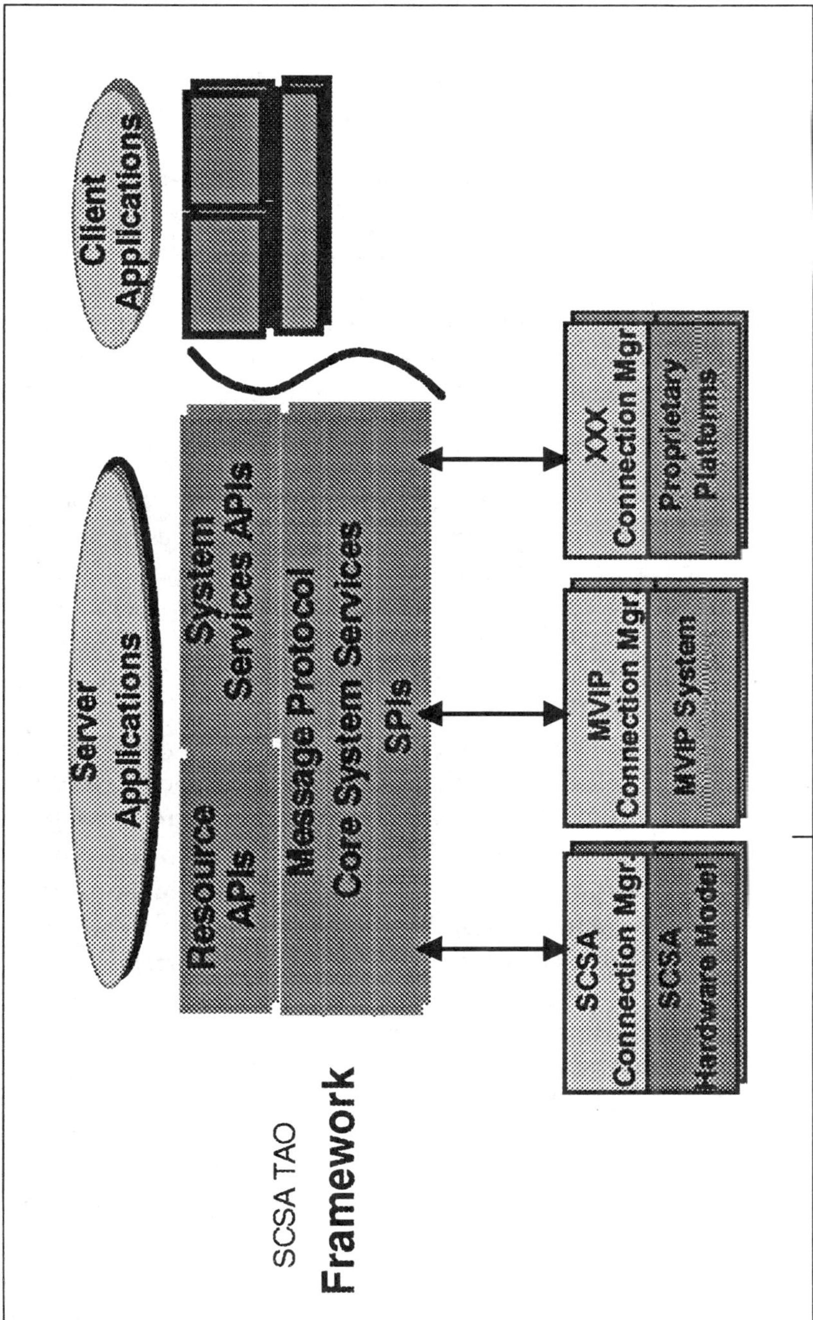

What Is the *TAO Framework*?

The *TAO Framework* includes the following elements, shown in figure 7.1.:

Client Application: The client is the user of the service. The client application sits on top of, and is not considered part of the *TAO Framework.* Clients may be user applications or system applications.

SCSA ***APIs:*** The *SCSA* APIs are the interface that *SCSA* presents to the application. The *TAO Framework* contains *System Services* APIs and *Resource* APIs. Specifically, the APIs are the interface to the *Application Interface Adapter.*

Application Interface Adapter: The *Application Interface Adapter* provides the client application with an interface to the services provided by the system. The *Application Interface Adapter* converts application function calls into standard *SCSA Message Protocol* messages. Optionally, the *Application Interface Adapter* may also perform local preprocessing such as argument validation or the opening of streams.

SCSA Message Protocol (or SMP***):*** The *SCSA Message Protocol* is an abstract component which takes the procedural messages passed through the *Application Interface Adapter* and bundles them into messages to be passed across the network. The *SMP* is responsible for physically moving the messages to and from the *Service Provider.* It also supports asynchronous data streaming. Although *SCSA* allows different implementations of *SMP*, each will present a consistent *Service Provider Interface.*

Service Provider Interface (or ***SPI):*** The *Service Provider Interface* defines a standard, message-based interface between the application, each *Service Provider*, and the *SCSA Message Protocol.*

Addressable Modules *(AMs).* Each *Addressable Module* is an element capable of using or providing services to other *AMs* which can be addressed via the *SCSA Messaging Protocol* (*SMP*). These *Service Providers* may be subdivided between *Technology Resources* (i.e. vendor-specific instances of fax, tone services, speech recognition, text-to-speech, etc.), and *System*

Services, which provide system support services such as allocating and tracking *Resources* and *Groups. The SMP* messaging layer (which may be physical or conceptual) allows these elements to request services or send information to each other. Communication between *AMs* is defined in terms of messages (*not* as functions); this allows asynchronicity and better facilitates location independence.

Figure 7.2 The SCSA *TAO Framework*

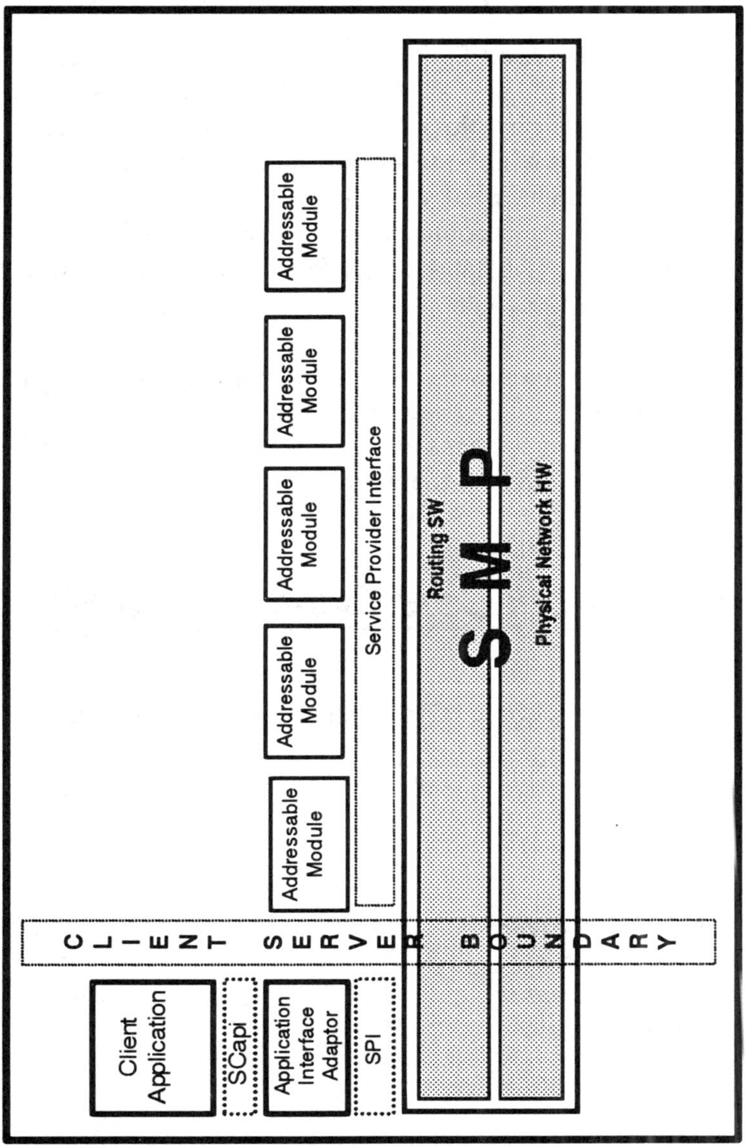

Independent modules communicating via standardized interfaces is a key feature of the *SCSA* architecture. This design allows new services and support for new technology to be added with minimum impact on other components. The technology *Resource*s required by a specific application can be freely selected from the range of *SCSA* compliant products. Similarly, new *System Services* can easily be added or existing *System Services* replaced with different implementations.

The modularity of the *SCSA* architecture also allows it co-exist or integrate with other industry standards as they are developed. Systems using call control services defined by Novell's TSAPI or Microsoft's TAPI, for example, could use AIAs which present the non-*SCSA* interface to the application and translate function calls into *SCSA SMP* messages. Alternatively, an *SCSA*-based application could run on a system which contained a *Call Control Resource* that translates *SCSA SMP* messages into function calls that drive a non-*SCSA* device.

This rest of this chapter will concentrate on the core *System Services* provided by the *SCSA TAO Framework*, the *SCSA* APIs that mediate between the applications, *System Services* and *Technology Resource*s, and the *SCSA Application Model* underlying the architecture.

TAO Framework Core System Services

The *SCSA Telephony Application Object Framework* provides the following *System Services*:

- ***Session Manager***
- ***Group Manager***
- ***Connection Manager***
- ***Simple Call Router***
- ***System Administrator***
- ***Container Manager***

1. Session Manager

The *Session Manager* establishes and maintains the integrity of the connection between the client and server and ensures that clients are authorized to use a particular service. *SCSA* uses a "login" (registration) procedure for client processes to resolve security issues involved in allowing a server process to perform actions on behalf of a client process. The login provides a new session ID (to identify the new service) and is used to resolve any ambiguities between services and name space clashes.

2. *Group Manager*

The *Group Manager*, which contains the *Resource Allocation Service* (RAS), allocates *Resource*s into *Groups* for an application based on the *application profile* the application provides. An application constructs *Resource Groups* containing all the *Resource*s necessary for the management of a particular call. *Groups* are built and configured dynamically according to the changing needs of the application. *Resource*s can be attached or removed from the group at any time.

The *Group Manager* is open to the addition of new technology modules, either from new, competing vendors of existing services, or from vendors of totally new technologies. Vendors for new technologies must also furnish APIs which applications can call. These APIs, and all communications with the technology modules, must conform to the *Service Provider Interface*

3. Connection Manager and *Call Control*

The *Connection Manager* controls the switching fabric of the underlying hardware platform. Its interface is not specific to a particular hardware implementation, and makes no assumptions about the underlying switching architecture, except that it must be capable of providing a reliable circuit-switched connection between the switch ports on two *Resource*s within the server. It can run a switch fabric with any number of stages, which may be distributed or centralized. Examples include SCbus and *MVIP*. The *Connection Manager* also allows for the connection between two *Groups*, monitoring the connection between two *Groups*, and the conferencing of multiple *Groups*.

4. *Simple Call Router*

The *Simple Call Router* (*SCR*) performs the routine routing tasks associated with computer telephony applications, allowing those applications to concentrate on their particular responsibilities. It obtains control of some or all network interface devices at system initiation time and then uses the inter-application hand-off mechanism to pass calls to applications waiting on certain types of calls. This relieves each application of the responsibility for waiting for and sorting incoming calls, and seizing and verifying lines for outgoing calls. The *SCR* also takes care of constructing *Resource Groups* appropriate for calls in various application contexts.

Applications are not required to use the *SCR*. A server supporting only a single application could be controlled completely by that application, without an *SCR* front end. Likewise, a multi-application server where *Resource*s are statically assigned to each application would not require independent allocation of inbound or outbound trunks. Finally, the *SCR* may be replaced entirely with a different trunk controller written using the low-level functions of the *SCSA Telephony Interface Control* (*TIC*) API.

5. *System Administrator*

The *System Administrator* provides a centralized set of services for all system administration functions. In most cases these functions will be performed by other services. The functions performed are

- Installation and removal of system and application packages
- Start up and shut down of *SCSA* core *System Services*
- Monitoring and collection of statistics on the system
- Creating and maintaining the *Server File System*

6. *Container Manager*

The *Container Manager* provides support for special *SCSA File System Services*. A *Container* is treated as a type of *File System*. *File System Services* include the following:

- Location-independent access to files; all references to files by the applications are by names.

- High-level abstraction of media (typed files). *Containers* and data objects have selectable attributes. Data objects also have setable parameters.

- A standard name-space convention.

- Administrative services such as *File System* backups.

Vendor-Specific Technology Resources

Access to vendor-specific Technology *Resource*s is via *Resource*s APIs which are part of the *TAO Framework.* These *Resource*s are the signal processing *Resource*s for the server. They include

- Automatic Speech Recognition
- FAX send and receive
- Player/Recorders (such as audio and text-to-speech)
- Tone generation and detection
- Video

SCSA APIs

The *SCSA* Application Programming Interface (*SCSA* API) portion of the *SCSA TAO Framework* is the application programmer's window into the *SCSA* architecture. *SCSA* APIs provide a toolbox of *Resource* control and system management functions that is rich in core functions for computer-based telephony applications.

This core functionality is non-restrictive, with an architecture that allows existing components to be replaced or new components added. Software developers may also choose to implement higher-level application development environments on top of the *SCSA* APIs to offer value-added capabilities, to provide compatibility with other APIs, or to offer APIs targeted at specific application classes.

The *SCSA* APIs are designed to provide

- Support for multiple technologies
- Open architecture, insuring growth and flexibility
- Hardware independence
- Application and data location independence
- Scalability
- Support for multiple applications, with call sharing between independent applications.
- Application flexibility — high-level abstraction of *Resource* behavior without restricting the development of any class of application.

Figure 7.3 *SCSA* APIs - Current Release

API	Functionality
SYSTEM SERVICE APIs	
Connection/Conference Management	Controls the connection relationship between Groups on a switch fabric.
Data Management	Provides control for reading and writing SCSA data structures.
Group Management	Creates, configures and destroys Groups.
Session Management	Creates and destroys sessions with a logical SCSA Server, and controls server security.
Simple Call Router	Allocates trunk lines to outbound applications, calls to inbound applications, and transfers calls between applications.
TECHNOLOGY RESOURCE APIs	
Automatic Speech Recognition	Enables command and control of applications via speech recognition.
Container	Manages the storage and interchange of data.
Facsimile	Send and receive fax images.
Player/Recorder	Play and record audio data of different encoding types, text-to-speech, ADSI, and TDD
Signal Detector/Generator	Detect and generate tones for purposes of caller input and control.
Telephony Interface Control	Provides control of telephone network interface devices for the purposes of establishing and terminating telephone calls.

The *SCSA* APIs may be broken down into two separate types of APIs — Technology *Resource* APIs, which provide access to the technology offered by multi-vendor *SCSA Resources*, and *System Services* APIs, which provide the core services shared by Technology *Resource* APIs and used by all applications. Figure 7.3 summarizes the current release of the *SCSA* APIs. The following system functions in figure 7.4 are also enabled by APIs.

Figure 7.4 API-Enabled System Functions

Features	Functionality
Event Handling	Detecting changes in system states or application functional errors, and notifying the application.

Figure 7.5 depicts examples of additional APIs that will be defined in future releases of the *SCSA* API:

Figure 7.5 Future *SCSA* API Releases

API	Functionality
Administration	Monitoring system services and controlling application behavior.
Configuration	Defining and configuring system object characteristics.
Diagnostics	Detecting system operation failures.
Macros	Combining API functions to improve performance in Client/Server systems.
Paging	Activating and delivering messages to paging terminals
SNMP	SCSA system performance reporting for Network Management applications.
Video	Send and receive video information.

SCSA *TAO Application Model*

The *SCSA TAO* application model is derived from the *SCSA* architecture and an analysis of some of the common tasks done when developing computer telephony applications. It emphasizes services and facilities that provide these common tasks in a useful and flexible manner. The model is designed to provide a framework that makes the task of writing a computer telephony application easier, and the application more portable.

Applications interact with an *SCSA* server through *Resource* APIs, which actually provide control of the call and its associated hardware, and *System Services* APIs. The application model is a simple one of configuring *Groups* of *Resource*s and defining connections between these *Resource*s.

Overview

Each *SCSA* Application will go through the same basic structure of setup, operation, shutdown, and handling of calls.

First, an application provider supplies an *Application Profile*, which defines the default minimum *Resource*s that it requires to process each call. This profile will most likely be a text file, separate from the application executable. As a text file, the systems administrator can optionally edit the file to meet the custom requirements of a particular installation and configuration before running the application. The file is then read during runtime when the application is loaded.

Once an application is loaded, the first thing the application defines is how to handle events and exceptions by defining event handlers. *SCSA* APIs are designed to support either synchronous programming models, or asynchronous programming models. In a synchronous programming model, functions do not return control to the application until the operation completes. With an asynchronous programming model, functions return control immediately to the application. In addition, asynchronous programming models provide function completion notifications to the application. In this case, applications receive of a specific asynchronous completion event associated with that function.

The application then establishes a session with an *SCSA* server by logging in. The *SCSA Session Management* API provides the basic functions to control or deny access to either an *SCSA* system, or to specific *Resource*s on the system.

When the application has a session established and it is ready to accept calls, it registers its interest with the *Simple Call Router*. Inbound calls are then handled by the *SCR* and passed to the application, pre-configured with the correct *Resource*s as defined in the application's application profile. The application may then choose to use *SCSA Resource* Management functions to change the configuration of the group, attaching and detaching *Resource*s as needed to process the call. When the application is done processing the call, it hands the call back to the *SCR*, and the *SCR* handles call teardown and marks *Resource*s contained in that call's *Groups* as available for handling other calls. *SCSA* also defines the process by which one application can hand off a call to a different application - the group may not necessarily be destroyed by the *SCR*, it may be handed off to a different application for further processing.

Alternatively, applications may bypass the *SCR*, and use the *SCSA Telephony Interface Control* interface to manage trunks on the system directly. In such a case, the application becomes responsible for all the functions otherwise handled by the *SCR* - answering the call, negotiating any network protocols to obtain ANI or DNIS information, allocation of *Resource*s, and eventual call teardown.

Application Profile

Since the underlying multiline computer telephony hardware in a system is potentially shared by multiple applications each with a distinct set of requirements, an application must make its *Resource* requirements known in a concise manner, prior to execution, to allow for the proper configuration of the system. This is analogous to the installation of any application which is installed in a networked environment which requires access to shared *Resource*s. There may be *Resource*s of the same class, but which have different characteristics and capabilities, due to differences among vendors or products.

The matching of *Resources* to application needs is accomplished through an *application profile*. The application profile is a file external to the application's code which contains the following:

- The *Resource Template* consisting of the specifications of the characteristics required for *Resources* to be used by the application.

- The *Group Template* which contain sets of group configurations where each configuration is defined as a specific assembly of *Resources*.

- The application installation instructions to be used by the *System Administrator* in defining how the application should be set up.

The application writer must provide an application profile which accurately represents its requirements to allow the *System Administrator* to install the application. The *System Administrator* will then ensure that the necessary dependencies are installed to meet the needs of an application.

The majority of the detail information found in the application profile is provided by the vendor of the hardware in the server or the *Service Provider*, but an advanced developer has the option of modifying this information to gain more precise control.

At runtime, the application can query a group about a *Resource* contained within its configuration to determine the *Resource*'s characteristics or capabilities. It is this ability that allows an application to determine which of the optional characteristics and capabilities were actually provided to it. Applications will typically assume that the characteristics and capabilities which it required in its profile are actually provided.

Applications and Session Management

The *Session Manager* allows the application to establish a session with the server by logging into the server. This process is required whether the actual server process is local (running in the same machine as the application) or remote (running in another machine over a LAN).

A session gives an application the following:

- Access to a collection of *SCSA System Services* and *Resources*. The aggregation of these services is referred to as the *SCSA server* or simply *server*.
- A common event queue with a set of portable event handling methods.
- Simple security.

A single session may service one or more application instances of one or more application *classes*, but typically, the model of a single session per application instance will be used to simplify event routing.

Applications and *Resource Management*

One of the most complex problems facing computer telephony application developers is the management of scarce *Resource*s such as voice recognition or facsimile devices in a system. The *SCSA* programming model provides *Resource Management* facilities to ease the development of multi-*Resource* applications. The *Resource Management* scheme used by *SCSA* provides the following features:

- ***Dynamic Resource Allocation.*** Applications may reserve *Resources* between calls, or use a *Resource* for the full length of a call, a portion of the call, or for simply the length of a given *Resource* operation. *Dynamic Resource Allocation* is crucial to sharing expensive *Resources* in a system among multiple applications which may not need the services of that *Resource* continuously.
- ***Resource Location Independence.*** As long as a communications path (preferably a time division multiplexed, or TDM, path) is established between the multiple *Resources* handling a call, the separate *Resources* may be distributed in different computer chassis or located remotely from the application.

- ***Scalability.*** Applications associate *Resources* to handle a single call. By increasing the available *Resources* in a system, applications can handle more calls without having to change their interface.

- The ability to ***transfer calls and Resources associated with processing those calls between applications.*** In a multiple application system environment, different applications may be used to handle specific transactions on a given call. For example, one application may be responsible for answering all incoming calls and distributing them to different applications based on ANI or DNIS information. Those other applications in the system may be responsible for automated technical support inquiries, voice messaging service, or document retrieval fax processing. All these applications may be supplied by different suppliers, but when combined together can provide an end user with a more efficient method of offering higher levels of customer service.

Applications and Group Management

After a session has been established the system's signal processing *Resources* must be harnessed. In an *SCSA* system, "*Resources*" represent the underlying hardware or software devices that perform the actual work. An *SCSA Resource* is an abstraction of a standardized vendor-independent interface for a physical device used for computer telephony.

Resources are assumed to have at a minimum one input or output of circuit-switched isochronous data on the internal switch fabric of the server. *Resources* are shared in the sense that multiple applications may contend for access to a *Resource*; however, once granted access, the application has exclusive ownership until it explicitly releases it.

The exact capabilities of *Resources* may vary from vendor to vendor. All *Resources* use standard methods for querying for the existence of a parameter name and the range of values it supports. As an example of this, the player *Resource* implements the method *play( )* which plays audio data. All player *Resources* must implement the play method. However, different vendors might implement different audio coder types and an application could be sensitive to this difference because of the format of its data.

Resource Groups (or just *Groups*) provide a means for an application to reserve *Resource*s it needs for processing a call. A *Group* is defined as a dynamically configurable set of *Resource*s that are used within an application to service a call.

Groups are *Container*s of *Resource*s of different types for purposes of application control. *Groups* expose the capabilities of their *Resource*s to the application and guarantee the existence of the *Resource*s at all times.

Groups may be thought of as an abstraction of a piece of automated telephone terminal equipment, since that is how they are frequently used. *Resource*s in a *Resource Group* are allocated to the exclusive use of that *Resource Group* until freed. The *Group* provides three services to the application:

- Implicit management of TDM relationships between *Group* members, relieving the application from having to switch between multiple *Resources* in a *Group*.
- Representation of a single entity to the application (the *Group* ID), saving the application the chore of maintaining separate handles or IDs for each *Resource* in the group and a common path for events from the *Resources* in a *Group*.
- Reservation of all physical *Resources* (CPU, memory, connections) required to provide the application with guaranteed service for the duration of the call or beyond.

Figure 7.6 Illustration of a Group of Resources.

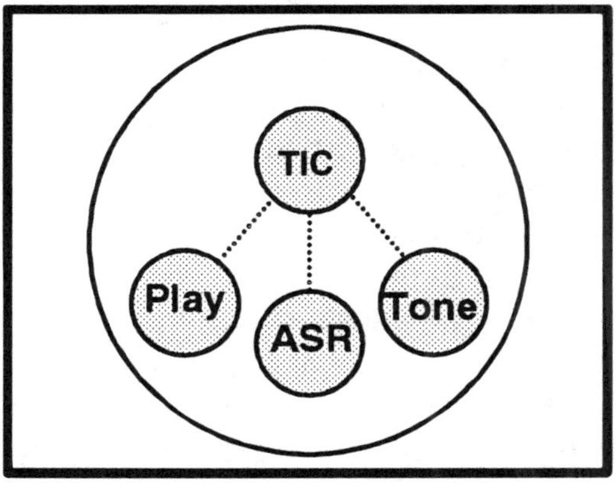

All members of a *Group* are *Resources*. A *Group* has a single primary member which is distinguished only through its connection relationship to the other members of the *Group*. All members listen to the primary member and the primary member listens to whatever member of the *Group* is currently talking (transmitting). This assumes, of course, that there is only one member that talks at any point in time, but that is a reasonable model of how most physical implementations work; having multiple talkers is actually conferencing between *Groups*.

For example, an incoming telephone call might need a trunk interface, voice recognition services, and a audio playback capability. The application simply creates a *Group* by assembling the *Resources* according to a *Group* configuration in the application profile. When the call is complete, the application releases the *Resources*, allowing other applications to have access to them.

The *Group Management* API provides functions for obtaining characteristics and capabilities of *Resources* within the group, as well as changing the current value of a *Resource* characteristic (provided the *Resource* allows for settable characteristics).

Applications and Connection Management

While *Groups* provide a means for implicit (hidden from the application's view and control) connections between *Resources*, the connection management interface provides a means for explicit connection management. This allows an application to reserve connections between two *Resources* through the server switch fabric, and to make or break that connection.

The actual connection to a group takes place through a *Resource* known as a *switch port*. The switch port is an implicit member of every *Group*, unless it is explicitly designated as the primary member of the *Group* at creation time. A switch port is an abstraction of the connection of the *Group* into the switch fabric of the server.

Because the orientation is towards connecting *Resources* rather than manipulating physical switching components, the approach is independent of the underlying hardware implementation. The application does not have to manage multiple switch stages or physical addresses on a bus. Also, because the orientation is towards connecting *Resource*s, a connection cannot be made or reserved until a group has been formed, since the system does not know the location of the *Resource*s that it is connecting until they exist.

Connection Management also allows for the creation of conference bridges by connecting the switch fabric in such a way as to allow each talker to listen all the other talkers. Each talker then has a *Group* associated with their leg of the call. All of these *Groups* are interconnected across the switch fabric by the *Connection Manager*. As the conference grows, *Groups* are created to support the new party and the attached to the existing conference bridge. In this way, the size of a conference is only limited by the number of *Resource*s or TDM connections the system has available.

The *Connection Manager* also allows for setting up a listen-only monitoring connection across any two-party connection for attendant supervision applications.

Applications and the *Simple Call Router*

In many cases only simple control of *Groups*, *Resource* and connections is required. The *Simple Call Router* or *SCR* is a *System Service* which provides:

- Inbound call routing to applications
- Outbound call routing to trunks
- A mechanism for moving *Groups* (and the calls that they represent) between applications

An application can choose to use the *SCR* for any of these functions, or none of them.

Inbound Routing

Inbound applications suffer from a special problem when sharing *Resource*s. It is not efficient to dedicate telephony *Resource*s among a large number of applications, since those applications may only be used a few times in a given day. Lines are therefore generally shared and use information extracted from the network about the call (such as Dialed Number) to determine the application to which each call should be connected. Since the clients can be distributed over a LAN, there are potentially a large number of clients each interested only in calls to specific PBX extensions.

The *SCR* may be instructed to route incoming calls to different applications depending upon criteria such as technology or media type, trunk ID, or ANI information. Routing may also take place via user selection or some other application-specific method.

In general, a *System Administrator* who has knowledge of trunk connections and access to user and application profiles would be responsible for establishing the rules which the *SCR* will follow in connecting a call to an application. These rules are called the *routing rules* and are set up by the *System Administrator* at installation time.

Calls may be routed to a whole class of applications, instead of just one. In this case, the *SCR* attempts to route the call to each available application of the specified class (fax servers, for example), until it finds one capable of accepting the call. If no application can take the call, the *SCR* may be instructed to terminate the call, or to pass it to a default application (such as one that plays music).

Outbound Routing

For shared inbound/outbound call handling environments, with multiple applications sharing a single server, the *SCR* may be used to allocate outbound trunks as well. In such an environment, an application wishing to dial out into the network would notify the *SCR*. The *SCR* would then react by creating a Group, seizing a line, perhaps confirm dial tone to avoid glare (that is, to prevent an incoming call on the line interrupting the preparation for outbound dialing), and pass the trunk group to the waiting application. The outbound application would then be free to dial on the outbound line.

The *SCR* may also be instructed to perform the dialing, setting up any international tone template automatically. The *SCR* would then pass the group to the waiting application upon a certain event, such as connection or positive voice detection.

Call Hand-Off

The *SCR* also acts as means for an application to pass a Group (call) to another application. The only piece of information that an application need know is the set of permissible Group configurations currently established by the application to which it is passing ownership of the Group. The operation has the possibility to fail if there is no application instance of the requested type available, or if the proper *Resource*s cannot be attached to the *Group* for the target application class. In the case of failure, the *Group* (call) is returned to the original application so that the caller is not lost.

When the application currently in control of the *Group* hands off the *Group*, it does so entirely, leaving the original application without any reference to the *Group*.

Data Storage and Management Features of the *SCSA* APIs

Data storage and management can cause major problems for application programmers. Poorly designed data management and storage strategies may severely limit an architecture's potential. *SCSA* APIs use *Key Value Sets*, *Containers*, and *Time Varying Media* to maximize flexibility, extensibility, and portability.

Key Value Sets. *Key Value Sets* (*KVS*) encapsulate any data that may be passed between an application and a *Service Provider* Object or vice-versa. For example, parameter information is presented to a *Service Provider* in the form of a *KVS* as are the event blocks which are sent from a *Resource* to an application. The value of *KVS* lie in the fact that they support extensibility – new and unique features can be provided by technology vendors, and accessed by applications programmers in the most flexible way possible.

Key Value Sets are comprised of *Key Value Pairs*, each of which are in turn comprised of a Key and an associated Value. A Key is the name of an item of information to be transferred between an application and a *Service*

Provider Object. The types of data that can be represented by a Value are limited to simple data types such as integers, complex data types such as null-terminated strings, *SCSA*-defined data types (including *Key Value Sets*), and arrays of such data types.

Containers. A *Container* is a logical vessel holding one or more Data Objects. Data Objects are made up of the actual data and a set of attributes (which describes the properties of the data). In many ways *Container*s and Data Objects are analogous to *File Systems* and files within *File Systems*, respectively.

The primary difference is that the *Container* interface is independent of the actual storage strategies employed. It is independent of the storage medium, and of the data type, formatting and organization.

Examples of data types typically stored in *SCSA Container*s include but are not limited to:

- Encoded audio
- Text
- FAX
- Speech Recognition vocabularies

The data types and associated properties that may be stored and accessed through these APIs are predefined. An application may not create new data types using these interfaces. The types and properties are defined by the technologies which they support.

Time-Varying Media (*TVMs*). A *TVM* is simply a type of *Container* Data Object which is an encapsulation of an atomic piece of a time-varying medium to be recorded and played back in real-time. Common examples of Time-Varying Media are:

- Encoded audio data
- Text-to-speech data
- ADSI data
- TDD data
- Full Motion Video data

All of the data within a *TVM* Data Object is of the same format and type. The *TVM* encapsulates all of the information necessary for playing the data. This information is usually stored in the *TVM* when it is created by means of recording.

Conclusions

The *SCSA Telephony Application Object Framework* (which complements the *SCSA Hardware Model* defined in the *Signal Computing System Architecture*) provides a complete and comprehensive software architecture for implementing a broad range of computer telephony applications. In addition to presenting a set of well-defined interfaces at many levels of its structure, the *SCSA TAO Framework* is well-suited for applications in standalone or distributed computing environments. By writing applications using the *SCSA TAO Framework*'s powerful client-server architecture, computer telephony system suppliers can:

- Support the development of simple or complex applications using the same software model
- Provide for application development that is independent of a specific hardware platform
- Develop solutions that enable multiple applications to share the same system *Resources*
- Develop computer telephony systems with sophisticated application management capabilities that integrate distributed *System Services* and *Resources* together into a seamless, logical whole

The *SCSA Telephony Application Object Framework* facilitates the development of computer telephony services by providing a robust software architecture that meets the varied requirements of today's computer telephony systems. It lets developers keep the simple simple, and make the complex possible. The companies below are part of a growing list of leaders from throughout the information processing and communications industries that have announced their support of SCSA.

A+ Systems Corporation
ACCI
Acsys S.A.
Active Voice Corporation
Aculab Ltd.
Acumen Technologies
Advanced Tech. Solutions
ADX MicroSys Corporation
Aerotel Ltd.
Amper Telematica
AMTELCO
Analog Devices, Inc.
AnTeL, Inc.
APEX Voice Communications
Applied Voice Technology
Arcitel SA
Arel Communications
Ashpool Systems
Atlas Telecom
AudioFAX, Inc.
AUDIOtechs, Inc.
Auralog
Axlund Voice Systems
Berkeley Speech Tech.
Bicom
Biscom, Inc.
Bit Works
BMC Group, Inc.
Boston Technology
Brite Voice Systems, Inc.
Brooktrout Technology
Bull, S. A
C-T Link
C3
CadCom Telesystems, Inc.
CALL
Call Completion Technologies
Call Direct
Cascade Technologies, Inc.
CATS Systems
CBI
Channel Vox
CLM Communications
CNET
Comdial Corporation
Computer Talk Technology
Connaught FactsLine
Cook Comm. Corp.
Creative Solutions Group
CSELT Spa
Cypress Research Corp.
DalTech International
Data et Communication
Database Network Services
DataKinetics Ltd.
DataMedia
Datatal
Daytona Communications
DemoSource
Deutsche Aerospace
Deutsche Bundespost
Dialogic Corporation

Digital Equipment Corp.
DIL-DATA OY
Dinova Systems
Discofone
DS Group SRL
EDIBRO
Efrat Future Technology
Elan Informatique
Elektro-Automatikk
Elettronica Telecomunicazioni
ENA Telecommunicaciones
Enera
Enhanced Systems, Inc.
Equal Access Corporation
Ericsson Data
ETSI Telecomunicacion
Euromag
Executone Info. Systems
Expert Systems, Inc.
Falcon Computers
FBH Associates
GammaLink
Genel
Global Communications
Goodwood Communications
Goteborgs Lokal TV-21
GPT
Groupe Cerveau
Harris Digital Telephone
HCL Limited
Hi Tech Marketing
I & D Telefonica
Ibex Technologies
IBM Corp.
ICA Data Systems
ICR
Infologue, Inc.
Infotel S.r.l. Italy
Intellivoice Communications
Inter-Tel Equipment, Inc.
Interact, Inc.
Interactive Speech & Info Sys.
Interconnect, Ltd.
International Connect
International Telesystems
ISG Network Solutions
JMCC International Corp.
Kingston Communications
Kreutler
Lernout & Hauspie
LOCUS Corporation
Logica Cambridge Ltd.
Logica North America
LSH Communications
Macfarlane Systems
Magellan Communications
Managing Information
MediaSoft Telecom, Inc.
Melita International, Inc.
Microlink Communications
Microlog Corporation
Micrologic Solutions

Micrologica
Missing Link
N-Soft
NEC America, Inc.
NEC Corporation CPE Group
New Technology
Nippon CompuTools
Noble Systems
Northern Telecom
Novavox
Offnet
Olivetti Information Tech.
Panasonic Communications
Parity Software
PCBX Systems
PCvoice
Phonetix Corporation
Powerhouse Communications
PRIMA Telematic
Priority Call Management
Probe Research, Inc.
Promptus Communications
PSi
Ring!
RIS Technology
Rochelle Communications
SCII Telecom
Scott Instruments
SDX Business Systems Ltd.
Seltek, Ltd.
Siemens Components, Inc.
Simpact Associates
SoftTalk Communications
Solutions Vocales
Space Connection
Space Connection
SpectraFAX Corporation
Spectron Microsystems
SpeechSoft, Inc.
SRX
Stentor Speech Products
Sterry Communications
Storacall Voice Systems
Stutz GmbH
Summit Telecomm. Corp.
SuperVoice
Synrevoice Technologies
Syntellect, Inc.
Syrinx Speech Systems
Systar/Calvache
T1 Systems, Inc.
Tandem Computers
Technically Speaking
Tecnovoz, S.A.
TECSEL
Teknekron Infoswitch Corp.
Telecorp Systems, Inc.
TeleDirect International
Telenet GmbH Multimedia
Telephone Management
Telephone Response Tech.

TeleTELL Information Svs.
Telia Promotor Infovox
Tern Systems
Texas Instruments
TGA Systems
The Renaissance Group
Transaction Environments
TriGem Info. & Comm. Corp.
Trio Information Systems
2C Com
Univoice
US Army
US Telecom International
Via Tel Systems
Vicorp Interactive Systems
Vicorp International Svs. B.V.
VLSI
Vocalis Limited
Vocatex
Voice Connect Ltd.
Voice Control Systems
Voice Data Systems B.V.
Voice Information Systems
Voice Interfaces
Voice Link Limited
Voice Processing Corp.
Voice Technologies Group
VoicePlex Corporation
VoiceSmart Corporation
Voicetek Corporation
Von Bulow Associates
Votek
VOX-TEL
Voxtron Asia
Winters Development, Inc.
Zenox Communications
Zilphian Technologies, Inc.
Zybel MicroSystems

This chapter was made possible through editorial contributions from Dialogic Corporation (Parsippany, NJ). The Signal Computing System Architecture is a worldwide initiative spearheaded by Dialogic and over 200 industry endorsers including Texas Instruments, Analog Devices, Tandem Computers, Siemens, and IBM to name a few. Although literally hundreds are involved in the ongoing formulation of the standard, special thanks goes to Bill Spain, SCSA Product Manager at Dialogic.

Bill Spain is responsible for a variety of client-server computer telephony offerings at Dialogic. They include the TAO Framework APIs, and the AppServer offerings. Bill has been an open architecture authority and advocate for both the industry and the company since his start there over six years ago. A prolific writer and popular speaker, Bill's support of open architecture is manifest in a variety of white papers and articles in the trade press. Before Dialogic, Bill was an industry analyst working for Probe Research, where he developed his current affinity for computer telephony and telecommunications.

8

Telephony Services - The View From Novell

For many businesses, integrating the features of voice instruments (telephones) with the personal computer could substantially reduce operating and capital expenditures and simplify communications. This chapter gives a general overview of current Computer-Telephony Integration (CTI) technology, and compares the various types of CTI implementations. It then looks at the components of Novell's Telephony Services and lists some of the applications that are being developed for this client-server technology. The end of the chapter gets more specific, with a look at how Novell and AT&T implemented the Telephony Services technology at Novell's headquarters.

Driving Factors for Telephony Services

The telephone and personal computer are communication tools that have coexisted independently on peoples' desks for many years. Together, they represent between 10 and 25 percent of a company's annual budget expenditure. For most businesses, integrating the features of their voice instrument with the personal computer could substantially reduce operating and capital expenditures and simplify communications. Savings could be realized by reduced desktop and back room communication hardware costs, and elimination of duplicate software development and support. In addition, a more efficient use of existing lines, and increased productivity can be realized.

As a foundation for integrating these two desktop "workstations," Novell and AT&T have jointly developed an open systems, server-based, work-group solution. The Novell/AT&T Telephony Server is an inexpensive, standards-based solution that provides call control features to all users on an existing Novell network.

Technology Overview

For many years, the voice and data communications worlds have paralleled each other. As the number of parallel networks grew, so did the expense and inefficiency of managing independent networks.

AT&T offered Integrated Services Data Network (ISDN) as a solution. The ISDN architecture presented a voice-centric plan to combine voice and data into one integrated network. (In IBM's SNA or data-centric network architecture, a PBX was a PU Type 3). Today there are many opinions about the practicality of implementing ISDN, but there is industry consensus that the two worlds of voice and data communications need to come together.

In the absence of a more widely accepted standard for voice/data integration, several proprietary products have been developed. These Computer-Telephony Integration (CTI) solutions focus on a small portion of voice/data integration needs: call control. A number of proprietary, host-based systems have been developed to integrate many telephony functions with customer databases. Because of the development and support expense, typically only sales and major service organizations with high call volumes can justify the cost of these types of systems.

As the power of the personal workstation increased, tasks that were once handled centrally were distributed across a network. Distributed processing has created distributed information, which in turn has increased the need for a "well connected" information network. The joint announcement by Novell and AT&T to provide a cost effective, standards-based, LAN work-group solution for CTI represents a major step in joining two parallel information networks.

Types of CTI Products

An overview of the three major categories of CTI implementation offerings will help to position Novell's Telephony server.

Host-Based Specialized Enterprise Applications. In this category are mainframe- or minicomputer-based enterprise systems that tie groups of phone equipment to a PBX as shown in figure 8.1. Typically used in call centers or customer services centers (such as catalog order, customer support, or service organizations), these systems require a significant investment to develop, deploy, and maintain. Operating the interfaces is complex and nearly always requires custom development to interface with host hardware, the PBX switch, and software applications.

Figure 8.1: Host-Based CTI Solution

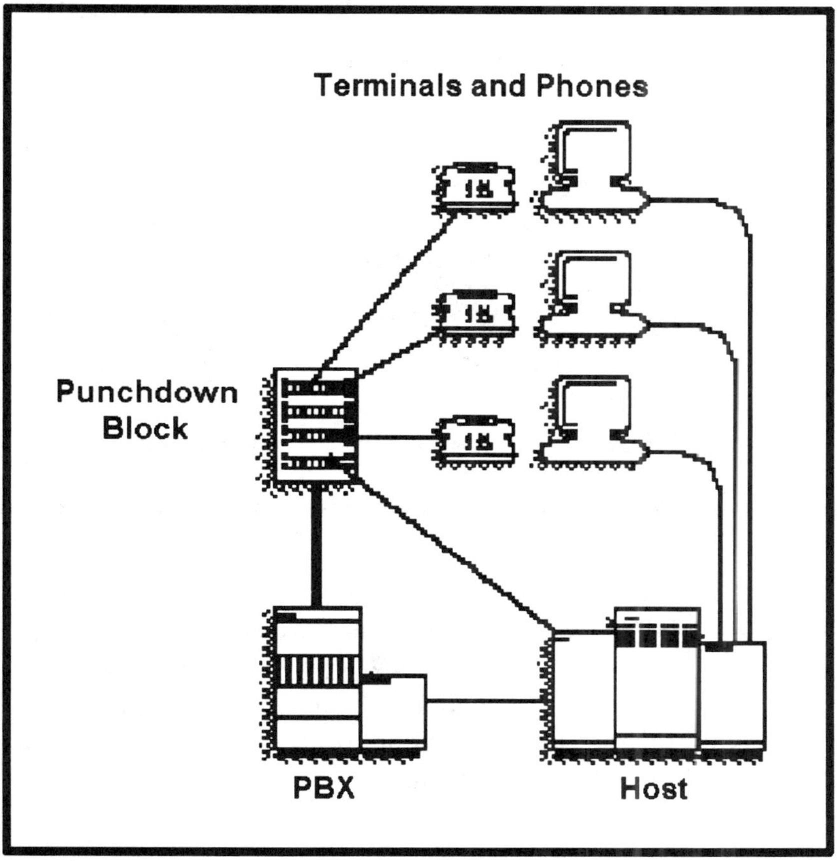

Because of the specialized nature of this type of CTI, end-user access is limited to specific workstations and group members. These services are not generally available to all users. Additionally, ongoing development and support costs are high as discussed in chapter one.

Workstation-Based Standalone Solutions. The workstation solution is a standalone implementation. It generally requires a hardware device and driver for each personal computer as pictured in figure 8.2.

Figure 8.2 Workstation-Based Standalone Solution

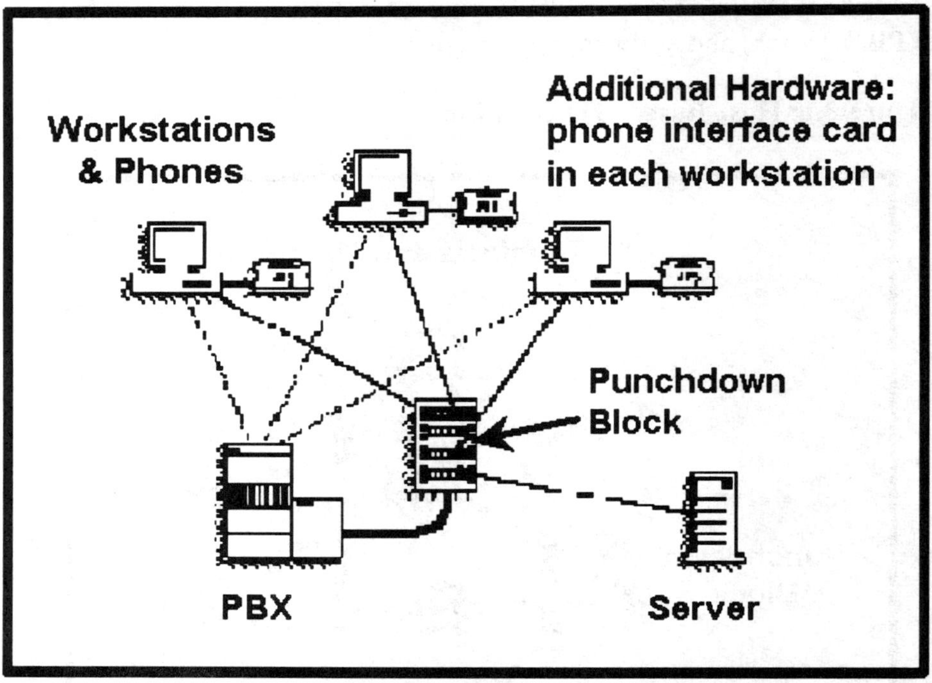

These systems do not typically provide security, call reporting, and other features required for larger installations. The most common implementation is a single-user Windows Telephony API (TAPI)-based application. Because each workstation must be individually installed and administered, and applications are hardware and workstation specific, this solution is generally targeted for small groups or individual users.

Workgroup Solutions. The workgroup solution is a server-based CTI implementation that is centrally administered and managed. This system requires hardware and software upgrades to a file server, and software-only upgrades for the workstations. Novell's "Telephony Server" is a standards-based product that provides service for Computer-Supported Telecommunications Applications (CSTA) and APIs written to the European Computer Manufacturers Association CSTA standards. These standards allow computers to talk directly to a PBX over the data network, rather than going through a dedicated phone as displayed in figure 8.3.

Figure 8.3 Workgroup CTI Solution

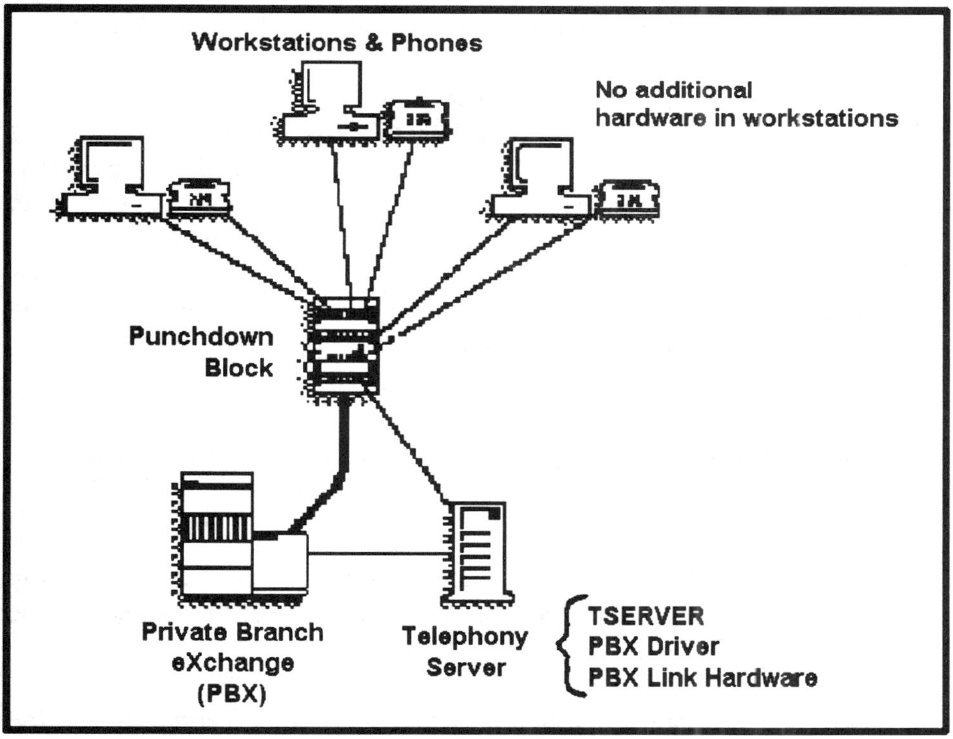

Because the Telephony Server (TSERVER) talks directly to the PBX, information associated with a phone call can be provided to or sent from LAN-attached computer applications. This allows server and workstation applications to talk directly to the PBX. Automatic Number Identification (ANI) information, call reporting, and many other call control features are available to all authorized workstations and/or applications via the data network.

With this capability, users working in MS Windows can have an ANI application running as a background task. When a call comes in, a CSTA request containing ANI information is sent across the network and activates the background application. The application reads the ANI information, goes to a database and retrieve the caller's information, screens the call based on the user's preferences, and displays the caller's name and other information on the screen. The user can either answer the call from the workstation using a speaker phone or handset, or redirect the call.

To illustrate the difference between the workgroup solution and a standalone TAPI-based application, let's compare the dialing capabilities of the two solutions. In the standalone TAPI solution, the workstation emulates a phone. Therefore, it initiates first-party calls from the workstation.

With Novell's workgroup solution, users have the same capability. However, unlike the TAPI-based solution, Novell's workgroup solution allows workstations to talk directly to the PBX through the TSERVER. This means users or applications on the network can place third-party calls without phones or phone line access. This is convenient for conference calling and setting up third-party calls in which the person placing the call is not a participant. It also allows workstation- or server-based applications to run as background tasks without user intervention.

Components of Novell Telephony Services

The Novell Telephony Services software includes an API library and several NetWare Loadable Modules (NLMs). These are loaded on the telephony server.

Client-Server API Suite (Library). The CSTA client-server application interface provides a common library for workstation- and server-based applications. For example, call centers may wish to have a server-based application which dials independent of a client application. Since the APIs for both platforms are common, developing and deploying client-server applications is much faster.

Telephony Server NLM. The Telephony Server (TSERVER) NLM was developed jointly by Novell and AT&T. It provides a CSTA-compliant interface for routing messages between workstations on a Novell network and a PBX, in addition to all network authentication services.

PBX Driver NLM. This vendor (PBX) supplied driver must route and map CSTA requests. Since the design and functionality of the PBX driver NLM are determined by the vendor, it is their responsibility to specify the PBX features supported by their driver.

Part of the PBX Driver is the PBX Driver Interface. This is an open interface that specifies how messages are passed between the TSERVER NLM and any vendor's PBX hardware driver NLM. The PBX Driver Interface routes LAN users' CSTA service requests to the appropriate PBX via the vendor-specific PBX link hardware.

The PBX Driver must also map CSTA requests (whether initiated by the server API or by a client API) to the PBX common control protocol. Since all switch manufacturers handle phone requests in their own way, the driver must know how to complete a request based on the switch manufacturer's hardware and software implementation. For those familiar with a service protocol gateway in NetWare, this is what the PBX driver does. It maps a service from one device to the corresponding service(s) of another device. It must also provide a communication protocol conversion between the devices. This driver is unique because it must be both a server and client: a server to the desktop application and a client to the PBX. This driver must determine whether a CSTA request is supported, and then respond accordingly.

PBX Link Hardware Driver NLM. This driver is a vendor-specific hardware driver for the type of PBX-to-server connection (X.25, synchronous, asynchronous, ISDN, TCP/IP, Ethernet, and so on).

Putting It Together

Examining a real-world scenario may help put this technology into perspective. Suppose that a telephony-authorized administrative assistant has scheduled a conference call between three individuals. Using a PC workstation-based CTI application, the administrative assistant connects the parties as described below. Figure 8.4 provides a diagram of the following steps:

Step 1

The application is started at the workstation (DOS/Windows, OS/2, or Macintosh). The application specifies that the call is a conference type. The request to initiate this call is sent to the telephony server using the Client APIs. It is important to note that if the user is not already authenticated with the Telephony server, he or she is required to verify security clearance to place this type of call. This clearance is checked by NetWare, the NetWare Telephony Server, and the PBX. If the user does not have authorization to place certain types of calls, the request stops at the Telephony server and will not be passed to the PBX. This feature is administered by the Telephony server application. Since applications can access cross-vendor PBXs using standard CSTA authentication calls, developers can query against the vendors' PBX database to verify authorization. Or they may choose to bypass PBX authentication and write their own security function.

Figure 8.4 Step-By-Step Telephony Server Example Scenario

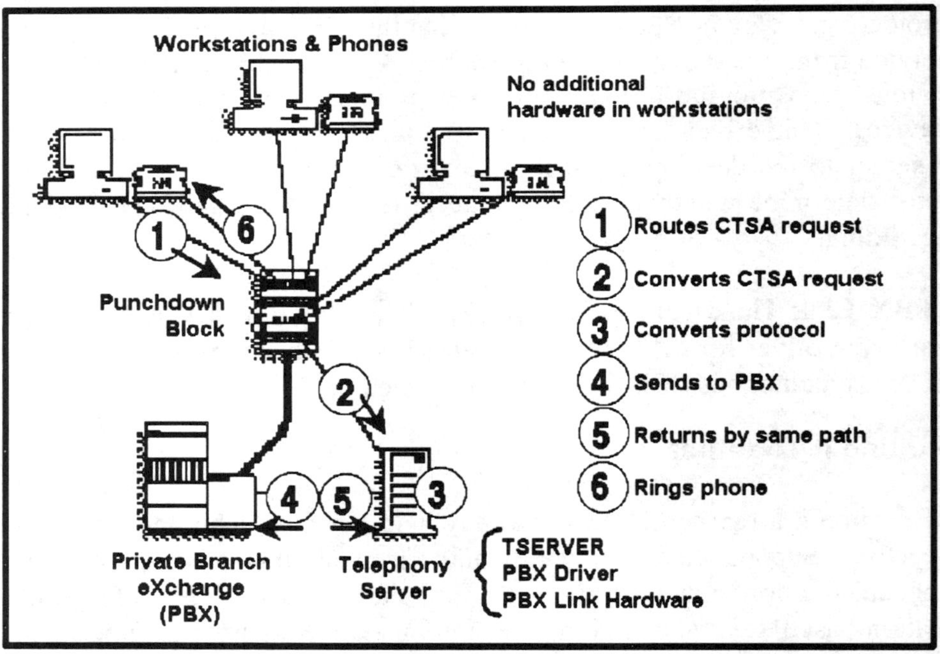

Step 2

NetWare Telephony Services passes the request to the Telephony Server NLM, which identifies the request as a CSTA type request and passes it to the PBX Driver Interface.

Step 3

The PBX Driver Interface routes the request to the specific PBX Driver. (You can have more than one PBX card in the server. This is a similar function to a data router, but it is specific to the PBX driver rather than a network adapter).

Step 4

The PBX Driver converts the request to the corresponding PBX service and resolves the request with a table of available (vendor-specific) services. For example, if the conference call feature is available, the request is readied to forward to the PBX.

If the request is not in the table, a CSTA response is sent to the application noting that the request cannot be completed because either the service is not available or the user does not have authorization to perform the task. Invalid requests are never passed to the PBX. In all cases, the PBX Driver does a protocol conversion in order to talk between the hardware in the server and the PBX.

Step 5

The request is sent to the PBX via the PBX Link Hardware Driver.

Step 6

The PBX sends a response back to the PBX Driver, which formulates a CSTA response and sends it back to the requesting application over the LAN. As mentioned earlier, the PBX Driver acts as both a server to the workstation application and as a client to the PBX.

Applications of Telephony Services Technology

Telephony services can improve your business in several ways. Among other things, this technology can:

- Perform call screening and routing, reduce costs, and help control existing resources

- Incoming calls contain information about the caller. This information can be used to help customer support or account representatives screen incoming calls. Novell's Telephony server can route this information across the data network to LAN users. With this functionality, a bank's customer service representative or a broker could have a server- or workstation-based application that would pull up a customer's information profile based on the ANI information. This information would allow computer-based pre-screening of calls before they are taken. The application could also route calls based on the ANI data.

- Expensive telephone handsets have many features to simplify voice communications, including a variety of displays. Since PC workstations can provide similar display functionality, CTI applications can take advantage of this by displaying information on the PC monitor. For example, users will be able to pull up an electronic phone book, view many names and numbers, and dial with the click of a mouse or a keyboard command. When the call is connected, the user will be able to either speak into a speaker on the workstation or use the handset. Depending on the applications and work requirements of the user, handset cost could be substantially reduced.

- Another cost and time saving benefit for corporations that have their own PBX is the telephony server's ability to talk directly to the PBX. It may no longer be necessary to maintain a corporate employee phone database, as the information can be updated automatically by using the PBX database. Typically the PBX database is the most accurate and up-to-date. As soon as an employee's number is activated in the PBX, all corporate users can look that person up in the directory.

Listed below are summaries of several applications or application features that developers have committed to write for the Novell Telephony services platform. Most of these applications are becoming available in some form.

- Server and client modules that bridge computer networks, telephone systems, voice processing, and desktop computing.

- Workgroup products that seamlessly integrate voice mail, electronic mail, and fax mail.

- Client-server voice management products that enable developers to integrate voice into custom telephone-based applications.

- A PC-based automated conference call bridges. These products will support "dial out/I'll meet you" conferencing, teleconference scheduling, and management.

- Middleware solutions that require no programming. These solutions enable users to receive a call and call-specific records simultaneously, and to perform all telephone functions from their computer keyboard.

- NetWare drivers for use with several vendors' voice and fax boards, along with extending existing APIs to the NetWare environment.

- Server-based NLM applications that will provide contact management capability along with power dialing.

- Server-based products which will enable mutivendor telephony application development.

- Inbound and outbound telemarketing applications that allow complete customization of each telemarketing campaign, including call scripts, screen displays, and call routing.

- Interactive Voice Response (IVR) systems enhancements for integrated with caller ID capability. These are used to dynamically allocate ports and automatically transfer IVR information to agents.

- Inbound/outbound call management applications to provide desktop telephony resources to the call center.

- Development of voice and call processing applications with capabilities which include text-to-speech, advanced fax services, and speaker-independent voice recognition.

- Computer-integrated telephony solutions that enable the exchange, management and processing of fax, voice, data, and video over standard telephone lines.

- Driver development for a Siemens Hicom-300 PBX and the development of a front-end application with basic telephony functions.

- Call restriction software which will provide compliance with state and federal "no sales calls" laws.

- Virtual Translation Device (VTD) technology which will provide Hayes AT modem command set emulation.

- Applications that provide basic and advanced telephone functions from the desktop, such as electronic phone directory with interfaces to central network databases, call logging, and call transfers.

- Customer service and workflow management systems that provide caller ID information, trend analysis, and reporting.

- Packaged applications that include capabilities for interactive voice response (IVR), fax on demand, voice mail, audiotex, controlling call queues, and PBX functions.

- Applications to allow desktop control of the PBX and third-party voice processing servers. Additionally, these solutions provide synchronized call/caller ID presentation to the desktop.

- Groupware applications that provide a full range of telephone capabilities at the desktop, including conference calls, call transferring, and call tracking.

- Network-based voice mail applications that integrate with electronic mail and provide corporate-wide power dialing and voice annotation capabilities.

- Speech recognition engines designed to provide capabilities such as power dialing, conference calls, and transfers, and use of voice commands over the telephone.

In summary, the Novell/AT&T Telephony Services product is an CSTA compliant, LAN-based, workgroup solution. Because it is standards-based, this solution is supported by a wide variety of developers, applications, and PBX manufacturers. In its first implementation, the primary focus is on call control functionality.

In the future, as additional standards are agreed upon, server and workstation applications can bring the worlds of E-mail and voice mail together into one mail or messaging platform. From their workstation monitors, users will be able to browse their mail to see who it is from, when it arrived, whether voice messages have any written attachments or written mail has any voice attachments, the priority of the message, and the FAX number of the sender. The users can then reply either by voice or text message.

Implementing and Configuring Novell/AT&T Telephony Services

This part of the chapter focuses on server and network configuration requirements for the Novell/AT&T Telephony Services product. It provides an overview of the telephony server installation process and shows how these services are currently being used at Novell's corporate headquarters.

Components and Configuration Requirements

The architecture and installation of Telephony Services is similar to that of Novell's NetWare SNA Gateway or NetWare for SAA servers. Like these SNA products, the telephony server uses NetWare's Service Advertising Protocol to advertise its presence across the network (server type 1369). Any authorized user can access these services.

Unlike the SNA environment, the telephony server typically connects to a PBX via a vendor-specific protocol that is not routeable. Because each vendor specifies the hardware and software communication interface to its PBX, the interface may determine where the telephony server may be located relative to the PBX as pictured in figure 8.5.

Figure 8.5 Telephony Server to PBX Interface

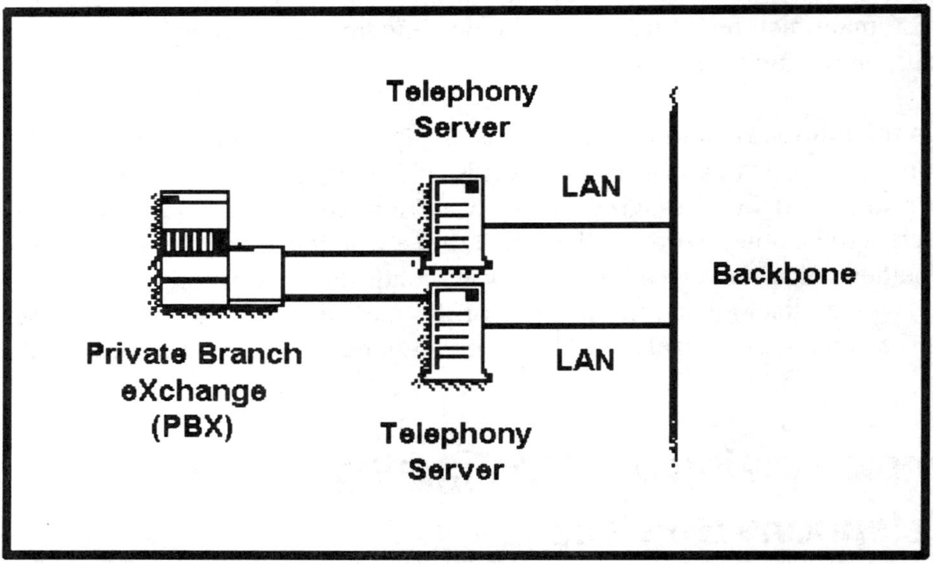

Software Components

The Telephony Services product ships with two diskettes:

- TSRVDSK1, which contains the server components
- TSRVDSK2, which contains the workstation/client components

Figure 8.6 Contents of the TSRVDSK1 Diskette

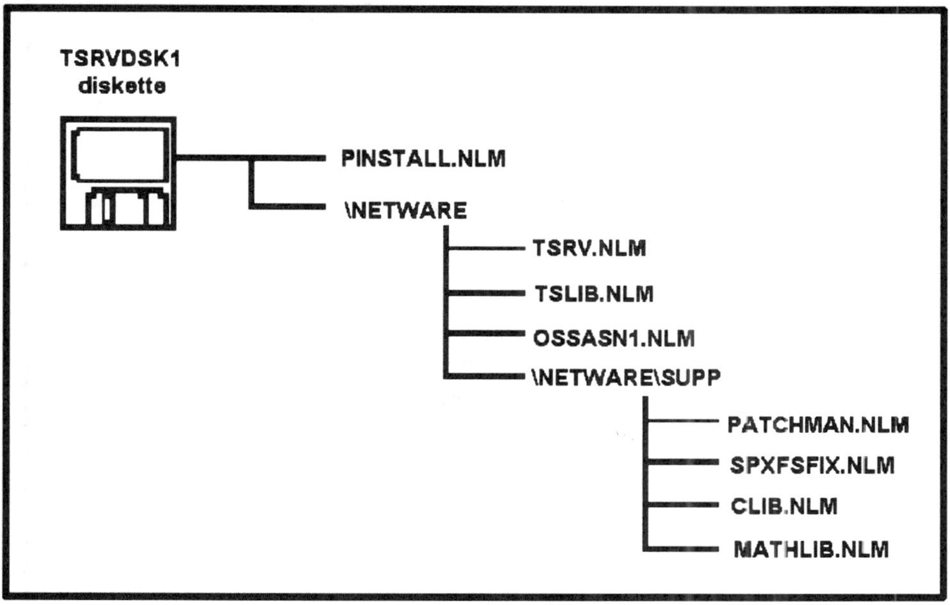

The PINSTALL program on TSRVDSK1 installs the necessary files into the correct directories on the server. Telephony Services consists of three NLMs:

- TSRV.NLM, the NetWare Telephony Server software
- Telephony Services Library for NetWare (TSLIB.NLM), a Windows library for server-based applications
- Telephony Services Encode/Decode Library (OSSASN1.NLM), which provides a CSTA mapping between the vendor's PBX and the client application CSTA requests

The other NLMs on TSRVDSK1 are general libraries and a patch that must be used when loading Telephony Services on a NetWare 3.11 server.

Figure 8.7 TSRVDSK2 Contents

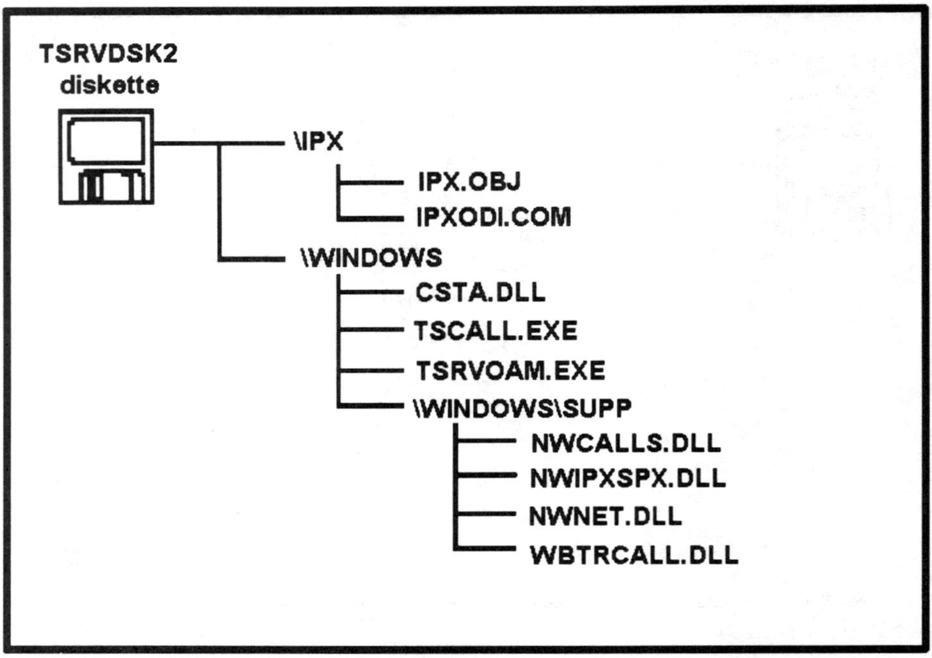

The two client executables on TSRVDSK2 are MS Windows-based applications. TSRVOAM.EXE is an OA&M (Operations, Administration and Maintenance) utility used to configure the telephony server and users. TSCALL.EXE is a simple but useful CSTA Windows application. It is copied into the directory specified by the installer during the installation process. The installation process also copies DLL files, the administrator utility, and some sample OA&M script files.

Server and NOS Requirements

Telephony Services for NetWare requires NetWare 3.1x or NetWare 4.x. In addition, the server must be running CLIB version 3.12 and MATHLIB version 3.12 or later. The SPXFSFIX NLM must be loaded with NetWare 3.11 (apply this patch with the PATCHMAN.NLM utility supplied on TSRVDSK1).

The Telephony Server also uses the Btrieve record manager NLM. Btrieve version 3.12 or greater must be loaded and configured properly. Btrieve parameters for Telephony Services are found in the installation documentation.

To run Btrieve, first load the Btrieve files, then type BSTART at the server console. To verify or modify BTRIEVE parameters, type BSETUP. If any modifications are made, save the changes, type BSTOP, then type BSTART. Btrieve is shipped with the NetWare operating system. For complete documentation on loading, configuring, and running Btrieve, consult the NetWare installation manuals.

Server Memory Requirements

Additional memory requirements for running Telephony Services are minimal. In this first release, Telephony Services supports 500 concurrent connections and uses approximately 700 KB of server memory. (On the Novell corporate telephony server, TSRV.NLM uses approximately 262 KB, TSLIB uses 1 KB, and the driver for the AT&T Definity® G3 PBX uses 444 KB, for a total of 707 KB). Most of this memory is non-moveable. As the number of users increases, very little additional returnable memory is used.

The amount of memory required for the PBX driver will vary depending on the manufacturer and the PBX interface. The suggested minimum amount of server memory for running Telephony Services on a NetWare 3.1x server is 8 MB. This is a minimum memory requirement. As the number of users and applications on the network increases, adding more memory may significantly improve performance.

Workstation Requirements

The two client executables that ship with Telephony Services are Windows-based applications. Therefore, to run these applications, the workstation must have an 80386 microprocessor or better, running MS Windows version 3.1 in Enhanced Mode. The CSTA.DLL (TSLIB for Windows) is not compatible with Windows in Standard Mode nor with earlier versions of Windows. It also requires VIPX.386 version 1.1 and NWIPXSPX.DLL version 1.31.

To connect with NetWare servers, workstations may use dedicated IPX drivers, IPXODI with the NETX shell, or IPXODI with the NetWare DOS Requester (VLMs). When running WSGEN to generate a dedicated IPX driver, use IPX.OBJ version 3.10 or later. For ODI, use IPXODI.COM version 1.02. (These files are included on the TSRVDSK2 diskette). For workstations running the VLMs, use VLMs version 1.0 or later. In the initial release, when running the TSRVOAM application with the VLMs, TSRVOAM.EXE must be copied into the SYS:SYSTEM/TSRV/SDB directory and be run from that directory.

Telephony Server Administration

As with most Novell products, users must be authorized to access telephony services. All telephony services are administered through the TSRVOAM application. In this release, the Telephony Server does not restrict users from running the administration application. This allows any telephony services user the right to perform administrative functions if they have access to TSRVOAM.EXE. Therefore, only authorized users should have rights in the directory where TSRVOAM is located.

Network Traffic

As with other SPX-based applications, the Telephony Server sends SPX "keep alive" packets to each connected client. These are 64-byte packets sent on an average of every 4 seconds. Generally, the Telephony Server adds very little traffic to the network, especially if the caller's database resides on the local drive. For example, dialing from the TSCALL application generates about 10 SPX packets when the database is on a local drive. If the caller database is on the network, calling generates the same number of packets as a local database once the database has been downloaded to the workstation.

Installation Process

The following discussion of the telephony services installation process is not intended to supplant the documentation that comes with the product.

Rather, it serves as an overview to identify the steps and the server processes associated with installing telephony services.

Step 1

Prepare the server hardware components that connect to the PBX and to the network.

Step 2

Run PINSTALL from the server (or from the TSRVDSK1 diskette).

During the installation, the installer will be asked to enter the path where the client software should be copied. The response to this question determines where the Windows components will be copied. If a directory is specified that does not exist, NetWare will create the directory.

Note that NetWare will create only one new directory. For example, suppose the path specified is:

server/SYS:TSCLIENT/CSTA

where TSCLIENT exists as a subdirectory under SYS, but CSTA does not exist. NetWare will create the CSTA subdirectory and install the client components in that directory. Using the same path, if the TSCLIENT directory does not exist, PINSTALL will prompt the installer again for a destination directory.

Step 3

Verify that the proper versions of CLIB, MATHLIB, and Btrieve are loaded (version 3.12 or higher). For NetWare 3.11, the SPXFSFIX patch must also be loaded.

If these NLMs are not currently loaded, they should be copied from the TSRVDSK1 diskette into the SYS:SYSTEM directory. After copying these files, you must reboot the server before continuing.

Step 4

Load the PBX driver provided by the vendor and bind the necessary protocols. Until the protocols are bound to the PBX interface card, the Telephony Server will not advertise its presence.

Step 5

Start the Telephony Server by typing the following commands at the server console:

LOAD TSRV
LOAD OSSASN1

Step 6

Check to see if the Telephony Server is properly installed by typing DISPLAY SERVERS at the server console. The Telephony Server should appear in the list of servers. It will have a name that contains a "#" character. (For example, the name of the telephony server used at Novell for this Application Note was ATT#G3_SWITCH#CSTA#PRV-NMS). If the Telephony Server does not appear, check to make sure the PBX driver interface card is properly bound.

Step 7

Log in to the server as Supervisor, launch Windows, and run the TSRVOAM application found in the telephony directory created during installation. This is the OA&M utility used to configure the server and users. Until this step has been completed, no users will be able to access the telephony services. A sample script file is included with the software that illustrates options for configuring the server. Refer to the Telephony Services documentation for more information.

Step 8

After configuring the server, run the TSCALL application and test for a PBX connection. The application will first ask you to select a Telephony Server and then authenticate you with that server.

Example: Novell's Corporate Installation

The telephony server installed at Novell's corporate headquarters is a COMPAQ DESKPRO 386/33 computer with 16 MB of memory, one NE2000 network adapter, and one AT&T PC/ISDN interface card. Its cache buffers are at 67 percent with 20 active connections. The PC/ISDN card has an on-board MC68000/10Mhz microprocessor and is connected via an RJ41S connection to a single port on a BRI (Basic Rate Interface) card in the G3 PBX switch as shown in figure 8.8.

Figure 8.8 Telephony Server Configuration at Novell Headquarters

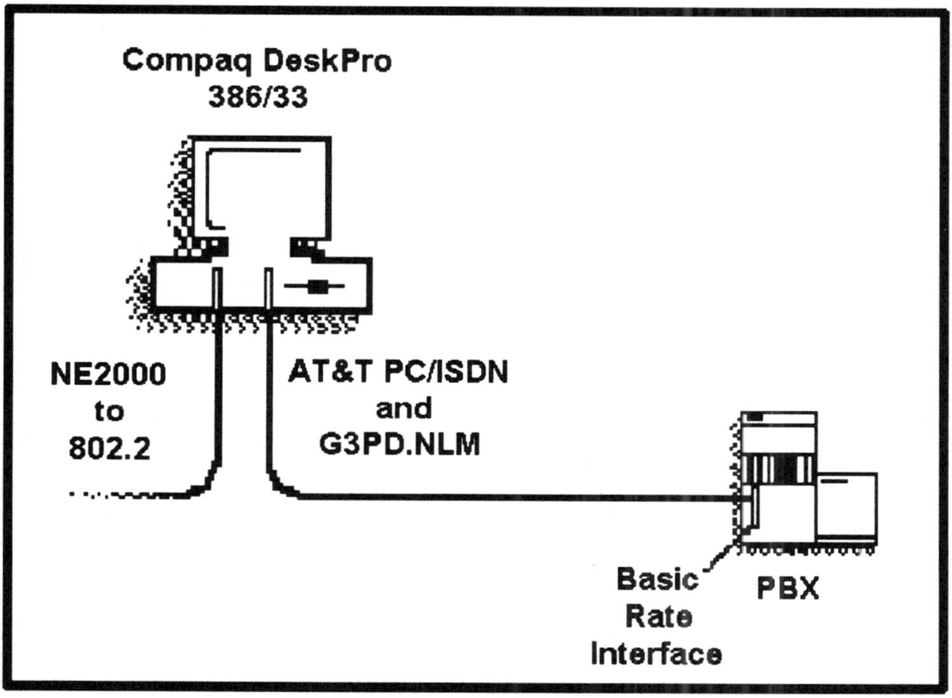

This telephony server is available to all users on Novell's corporate internetwork. However, users located off-site do not have a direct connection to the AT&T Definity G3 PBX located in Provo, UT. So even though users in Salt Lake City or Germany may attach to the server and have the TSCALL application loaded, the PBX cannot ring the handset at the remote site because there is no direct PBX connection.

However, if a remote site did have a data connection and a direct connection to the PBX, the user would be able to use the telephony server. Both a network line and an OPX (Off Premise eXtension) must be in place for this to work. Figure 8.9 shows how OPX and data lines are used to connect secondary sites to a larger site.

Figure 8.9 Telephony Services Solution using OPXs

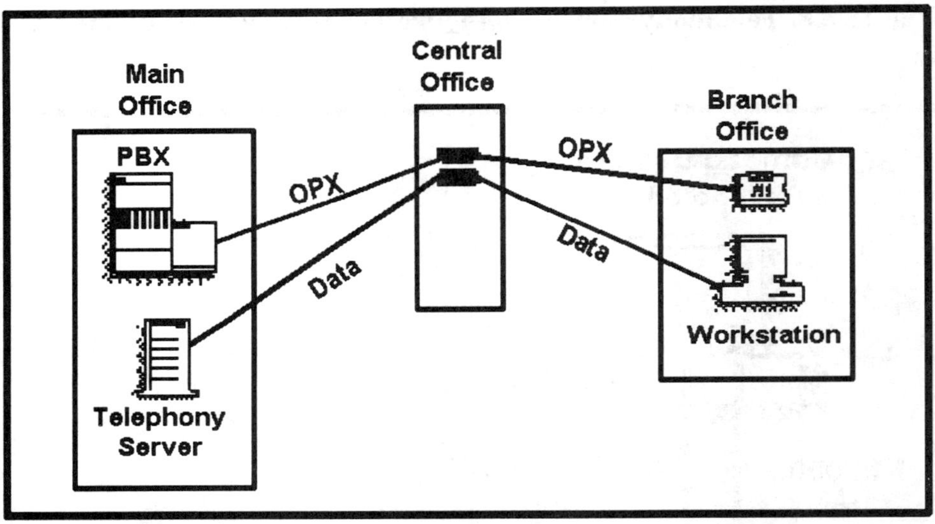

In its first release, Telephony Services for NetWare delivers a full set of client-server, CSTA-compliant APIs that support PBX call control functions. This standards-based platform provides a broad foundation for a variety of applications. At publication time, over 25 developers have signed up to develop to this platform.

As the first cost-sensitive workgroup CTI (Computer Telephony Integration) platform, Telephony Services for NetWare will quickly add new functionality to existing Novell installations and to many call centers currently running customized telephony solutions.

This chapter was made possible from editorial contributions from Novell, Inc. Novell's Myron Mosbarger, Senior Research Engineer, provided much insight into the spirit of this book and provided several application notes which were both relevant and consistent with the overall thrust of client-server computer telephony. The author also thanks Joe Smith, Development Manager, Telephony/NLM; Joe Staples, Marketing Manager, Telephony Services; and Bill Gillman, Senior Software Engineer for their work in putting the material together.

9

Workstation CTI: SunSoft's XTL

Computer workstations capable of connecting to wide area networks are becoming increasingly common. As the hardware and software components for supporting modems, ISDN, Asynchronous Transfer Mode (ATM) and analog telephony increasingly proliferate onto the computer desktop, new applications will come available to exploit them.

The impact of these new applications will likely be felt throughout all areas of computing-from commercial users in the largest corporations, to home users in small, remote communities. The widespread proliferation of the telephone, followed recently by the personal computer, will be joined in the near future by integration between them. The resulting applications for telephony-based applications in the computer-telephony integration (CTI) market is enormous.

Developers of teleservices applications will confront a large range of communication implementation technologies, hardware and software considerations and other complicating factors. To reduce the effort required by developers, while simultaneously freeing them to utilize virtually any communication medium, SunSoft has developed a teleservices product delivery vehicle known as the XTL Teleservices Platform for Solaris.

The XTL platform includes support for teleservices software applications, as well as hardware and driver interfaces for device implementations. The XTL platform provides a stable and robust platform for teleservices applications as they migrate to the client-server, distributed computing desktop.

Workstation *Computer Telephony* Integration

CTI brings together the two most widely used desktop implements (telephones and workstations), enhancing the power and utility of each. Workstations are empowered with access to the wide area, public switched network, telephony applications are enhanced by access to end users environment and data bases.

The key to enabling CTI on workstations is a good architecture and programming platform to allow applications to access telephone technology-independent of the particular topology, telephony interface, or type of phone system being used. Ideally, an application can be written once, and it should work with various wiring configurations and (within reason) with any telephony technology.

XTL Applications and Its Market

XTL is particularly suited for creating personal desktop telephony services: automatic dialing, answering machine, voice mail, automatic call transfers, etc. With appropriate interface cards, XTL can turn a workstation into a personal fax machine. Another common usage would be to use XTL to manage connections from the workstation to other network servers for Internet (IP) connectivity. As network technologies transition to ISDN and ATM, XTL provides an ideal platform for multimedia applications. Because XTL provides access to a variety of network technologies and data types, it is well positioned for developing multimedia applications. Three demonstration or "proving" applications have been developed on XTL:

- Sparcphone (sph): a full featured speed dialing and answer machine application with GUI.
- Talkback: an IVR application that allows users to access email, calendar, etc. when called from remote locations.
- IP/ISDN: a datacomm application that makes ISDN calls and uses them for PPP/IP communications.

In addition, there are example programs that illustrate simple dialing and answering functions.

Overview of XTL

XTL Teleservices for Solaris is the foundation library for applications that use or control telecom data streams. The XTL subsystem and API includes call control functions that establish a call or connection and data stream access methods to control the flow of data over that connection.

On the workstation desktop XTL can be used to control an ISDN line and manage phone calls for various voice applications like a personal answering machine with voice-mail/email integration, a user-friendly GUI for controlling the many features of a typical phone, or speed dialing integrated with local databases. XTL can also be used by non-voice applications like setting up desktop video conference calls, wide area datacomm, or fax.

XTL is designed to allow multiple desktop applications to share access to workstation telephone interfaces and also to allow multiple applications to cooperate in managing an individual call without sacrificing data integrity or security. One application can create or receive a call and pass it to another application for voice processing. XTL allows, but does not require, a single "call manager" application to own all calls and impose a user or site defined policy on the disposition of calls.

XTL does not impose constraints on the content or format of the data stream; the stream is delivered to an application for interpretation. XTL works equally well for audio/voice, fax, video, IP, or other data communications protocols. XTL is the control API for establishing connections on wide-area networks for future multimedia applications.

The XTL teleservices platform realizes a solid foundation for desktop telephone applications. Through object-oriented design, modular interfaces, and easy extensibility, the XTL platform provides standardized interfaces and services for software and hardware developers. This chapter describes the design goals of XTL and how its architecture facilitates the development of desktop teleservices applications.

Goals of XTL Teleservices

The design and architecture of XTL is driven by five goals:

1. Provide an API for developing personal desktop applications. Applications such as a "Feature Phone" GUI, remote access via DTMF, personal voice mail, etc. can share access to a workstation's telephony hardware.

2. Provide transparent porting between analog, ISDN, ATM an other technologies. Applications should not need to be recompiled as network technology is upgraded.

3. Provide easy access to common voice services. The building blocks of voice applications, like DTMF and silence detection must be available easily and efficiently, using "onboard" resources if available.

4. Enable specialized or non-voice services. Many telephony boards also provide fax, modem, or video capabilities.

5. Specify an open, third-party extensible, distributed-object model. The API and system capabilities must be dynamically extensible to utilize new technologies and new protocols as they become available.

The XTL system architecture achieves these goals by defining a clean separation between the application that uses telephony services and the provider of those services. The XTL system services provide object management, message passing and an event notification infrastructure that combine to bind an application to the appropriate teleservices provider.

Components of the XTL Subsystem

The XTL architecture comprises applications that use the XTL API, "providers" of XTL services, and the XTL libraries and system services; see figure 9.1. The details of the system services are hidden from applications and providers by the API and MPI interface libraries. The system services include a message passing "server", a data stream multiplexor streams driver, a provider configuration database, and an tool for administration of that database.

Figure 9.1 **Components of the XTL Subsystem**

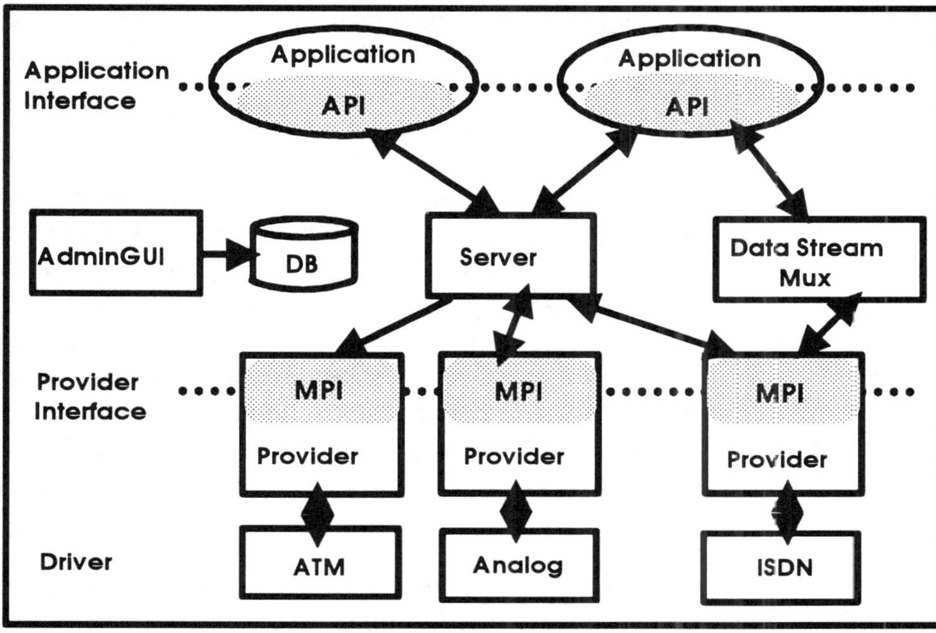

Objects and Processes in the XTL Subsystem

Application developers use the XTL API to create C++ XtlCall objects. Each XtlCall object corresponds to a telephone call. An XtlCall object has command methods that query the current state of the call or request a change in state (for example, to put a call on hold). An XtlCall object also has callback methods for the asynchronous notification of state changes (for example, when a call is disconnected).

An XtlCall object includes accessor methods to determine the local and remote directory numbers associated with the call, the current call-progress state of the call, and the data type or media class associated with the call. Other attributes can be associated with the XtlCall by either the provider or the controlling application. For example, an application may chose to annotate the call object with a customer name and account number.

The XTL API is primarily concerned with call control and the associated capabilities to provide security or shared management of calls when desired by the applications. A secondary aspect of the XtlCall object allows the application to gain access to the data stream associated with the call. The XTL API defines an interface for common usage of voice calls, like detecting DTMF tones or connecting a call to a convenient speaker/microphone. As other media types are utilized (like FAX or Video), the XTL API can be extended to provide access to the required features.

XTL defines the general semantics of a call object and the call establishment protocol, but the actual implementation of a call object depends on the particular telephony technology being used. For this reason, the XTL system delegates the implementation of the call object to the XtlProvider object. The provider implements XtlCall objects that follow the specifications and protocol of the XTL API. The provider is typically a UNIX process or driver supplied by the telephony hardware vendor. Because all XTL providers present the same interface to the application, they can be used interchangeably. The implementation characteristics (latency, bandwidth) may change, but an application can port to a new network Provider without recompilation.

The XTL system services act as the intermediary between the application view of a call object, and the provider's implementation of the call. The XTL server, along with the application and provider libraries, handles the interprocess message passing, object identification and creation, call ownership, security, and asynchronous event notification. The XTL subsystem also manages a database of available providers and helps manage data stream routing and access. A GUI tool is supplied to browse and edit the provider configuration database.

Messaging

The XTL components communicate using asynchronous messages. In the vernacular of RPC, all messages are "one-way". Typically, when an application invokes a command method on a XtlCall object, a message to be sent to the XtlProvider object. When the XtlProvider object detects a change of state in the call, it sends a message up to the application. When an event arrives to an application, the corresponding event method of the XtlCall object is invoked. The event methods are C++ virtual functions that the application writer overrides to specify the appropriate processing. The API and provider libraries include routines to manage I/O signal handling, upcall and downcall dispatching, message marshalling, and the event wait loop.

On a single host, named pipes are used for the IPC message transport. For remote application, standard RPC/TCP/IP technology can be used. The messages are all formatted using XDR data encoding, so messages can be sent transparently between big-endian and little-endian hosts. The messaging system assumes a reliable transport and does not impose any particular time-outs, leaving this to the application if it becomes necessary.

The XTL notification framework is based on the InterViews dispatcher library. In addition, the interprocess (over the wire) packets are generated by an asynchronous messaging protocol compiler based on an abstract definition of the message names and argument types. Once the message set is defined, the C++ code for marshalling and dispatch is generated automatically. The protocol compiler corresponds to the IDL compiler in CORBA; the InterViews dispatcher in conjunction with the messaging support code, comprises the XTL "Object Adapter" layer.

Call Ownership

The XTL system insures that only one application at a time is allowed to control a call. The controlling application is referred to as the "owner' of the call. When an application makes an outgoing call, that application becomes the owner.

An incoming call is initially "owned" by the provider, but the provider immediately "offers" that call to any and all interested applications. An application gains control of an incoming call by issuing a "claim" request. If the claim is successful, the application becomes the owner and the application's Call object is instantiated. The XTL system ensures that only the first claim request is honored for any offer (i.e. "first come, first served").

Applications can share management of calls by passing ownership. The original owner "offers" the call, and another application can "claim" it. The same rules and protocol are used for application-to-application transfer of ownership as is used for claiming an incoming call. Claiming an incoming call is separate from answering the call. Once claimed, the unanswered call can be answered, dropped, or redirected. Or, the call may be annotated, an offered to another application.

Security

XTL was designed to operate on networked personal workstations, and in that environment, security and authentication of users is critical. XTL uses the standard UNIX and UNIX File System security features, making it easy to configure the system to restrict telephone usage to the authorized owner of the workstation and telephone. XTL can also be configured as a network resource, allowing multiple users to share access to telephony resources.

Several layers of security are provided, allowing the user or system administrator to tailor the system to the specific security needs of the site. The first layer of security is access to the XTL server. This is controlled by the UFS permissions on the named pipe used to make contact with the server. By default, only root applications can use the XTL server. A simple script is provided to allow access to particular UNIX group; typically that group would include the workstation owner/user, or a larger group if the workstation is configured as a departmental server. The server limits access to each Provider based on an access control list maintained per provider. Therefore, individual line interfaces can be reserved for specific users. When used as a network server, security is provided by the usual ONC/RPC mechanisms.

Media Channel Access

For each XtlCall object there is a corresponding media channel that contains a call's data stream. The capabilities and utility of the media channel vary depending on the provider and the type of call. Some providers may perform only switching of calls, and not allow application access to the media channel. Other providers may have DSP capability and provide numerous services for voice/analog calls (e.g. DTMF tones, modem, ASR). Typically, the media channel provides a bidirectional UNIX stream that the application can read and write.

Extensibility

The XTL provider interface is open for third-party developers and IHVs. Using the XTL provider library ensures compliance with the basic system protocols. However, the XTL message set can be extended to allow access to provider specific or technology specific or call type specific features.

Every API call and every message includes an optional argument that is a list of arbitrary key-value pairs (an XtlKVlist). The contents and use of the XtlKVlist is determined by the provider, and documented by the provider for the benefit of the application developer. Portable applications may not use the XtlKVlist, but applications that use specific provider features can access them with in the XTL framework using the XtlKVlist extensions.

The XTL API and message set also include a universal extension message, independent of any XTL protocol semantics. By specializing this message and its XtlKVlist argument, any provider-specific features can be accessed.

To avoid a proliferation of provider-specific enhancements and to increase the portability of applications, XTL will be periodically updated to include standards for common features as they become known and used.

Provider Configuration Database

When providers are installed on a system, they are registered in a provider configuration database. The database shows the existence of each provider, how to invoke it (used by the XTL system internally) and describes the specific capabilities and features of that provider. For example, the database would indicate the number of simultaneous lines available, the bandwidth available for datacomm, the types of voice or DSP processing available, etc. If an application has specific requirements, it can query the database to determine the most appropriate provider for its needs. This corresponds roughly to a CORBA interface repository.

The XTL API

The XTL application programming interface (API) is a software library that provides connection management and control over telephony and voice services through an object-oriented interface. The API is suitable for implementing telephony applications that make, receive, control, and terminate phone calls.

The XTL API is a component of the larger XTL platform, which consists of the API, a media platform interface (MPI) library, providers, and configuration databases. The platform is designed to operate with any switch or telephone technology. This platform independence is facilitated by providers, which hide the details of the underlying transmission technology.

Through XTL, you have access to services that allow your applications to:

- Hold, transfer, conference, and drop telephone calls.
- Indicate the progress of a call.
- Enable out-of-band call control for automatic call distribution.
- Enable audio connections to microphones and speakers.
- Detect and generate dual-tone modulated-frequency (DTMF) tones, otherwise known as Touch Tones.

The XTL API is an object-oriented interface accessed using the C++ language. The API includes XtlProvider, XtlCall, XtlCallState, and XtlMonitor objects. These base objects define the command and callback methods of XTL. There are three types of methods on these objects: synchronous requests, asynchronous commands, and asynchronous events. Synchronous requests modify or query information cached in the local C++ object. Command methods send messages to the provider, results or status changes are reported back to the application via the event methods.

An XtlProvider object is the application's representation of an XTL provider. The application registers with the provider object to receive notification of incoming calls, and specifies the provider when creating outgoing calls.

XtlCallState objects represent the identity and a snapshot of state of a call. When a provider has an incoming call, the registered applications receive a XtlCallState object corresponding to that call. The XtlCallState object is not "active"; it does not have command or event methods. If an application wants to monitor or control a call, it creates a XtlMonitor or XtlCall object based on the XtlCallState. In addition to incoming call notifications, an application can get a list XtlCallState objects corresponding to all the calls currently active on a provider.

Monitor objects allow an application to track the status of a call (for logging, statistics, billing, etc.) without actually controlling the call. The XtlMonitor object has notification methods that track the state changes of the call, but there are no command methods to control the call.

An XtlCall object represents a call that is "owned" by the application, with complete command repertoire and event/status notification. In addition to controlling call establishment, a XtlCall object enables an application to configure or get direct access to the data stream. Call objects and call ownership can be passed between cooperating applications.

The XTL API also allows the application to manage the data stream for a call. This can be as simple as providing a UNIX stream for the data being sent and received, or can be a request to connect the call to various hardware or software resources to, for example, detect DTMF tones. The particular data stream capabilities available depend on the provider and the type of data being transmitted by the call. All data stream configuration requests are handled by the Provider, allowing it to do data routing and signal processing as efficiently as it can. For example, the provider may use onboard DSPs, special data busses, or other directly connected hardware resources without the application knowing the specifics.

Distributed Object Activation

When an application creates an XtlCall object, a C++ object is allocated and returned to the application. The actual state and implementation of a XtlCall object is maintained in the provider. Until the provider has created its portion of the object, the command methods of the XtlCall object in the application cannot be meaningfully used.

As part of object creation in the API, a creation request message is sent to the XtlProvider object. When the XtlProvider has completed its object creation and initialization, the application is notified via the activation_ind() method of the XtlCall object. The application's implementation of the activation method typically begins processing of the call.

If the remote aspect of an object should become unreachable (e.g. network or server failure) the application is notified that the object is no longer accessible via the deactivation_ind(). The application's implementation of the deactivation method typically cleans up references and deletes the C++ object.

Comprehensive Description of XTL API Classes

The XTL API features a set of C++ classes to represent various telephony resources. The XTL API uses several important abstractions to represent telephony services and connection. These abstractions are implemented as objects that are created and destroyed with each call.

There is a loose correspondence between the XTL classes and the physical components of a telephone platform: an XtlProvider provides access a telephone technology, an XtlMonitor object allows client applications to monitor the activities of a call, and XtlCall objects with associated XtlCall-State objects represent the information relevant to a phone call.

The XTL platform uses these classes to represent the fundamental elements of a basic telephone platform. These elements are a phone device and the calls made using that device. An XtlProvider object represents a valid initialized phone device ready to make and receive calls. It hides specific device-dependent code running the telephone hardware or device and enables your client application to interact with the telephone device in a device-independent manner.

Your workstation's telephone resources can be shared by many applications. The XTL platform controls access to these resources and maintains call data security while enabling cooperating applications to share telephony devices.

XTL applications use media channels to send and receive data. The XTL platform maintains control of the use of these channels since multiple applications can access and use them. Media channels can transport various kinds of data such as voice, video, and fax.

There are two distinct base XTL classes: *messaging classes* and *utility classes.* These include:

- *Messaging Classes: XtlProvider, XtlCall, and XtlMonitor*
- *Utility Classes: XtlCallState, XtlKVList, XtlByteArray, XtlString, dpIOHandler, and dpDispatcher*

Each XTL class is an abstraction of a telephony resource. Each class is designed to perform a specific telephony function. For instance, an XtlProvider object represents an active telephone device that enables a system to make and receive calls. An XtlCall object represents a call in progress, and an XtlMonitor object continuously updates and monitors the current state of a call. From these base classes, you can create subclasses to customize their behavior. Be aware that the messaging classes contain pure virtual functions, which requires implementation to define specific behavior. The utility classes may be instantiated directly. Here is a brief description of each class:

XtlProvider. An XtlProvider represents an association with a phone device that enables the system to make and receive calls. You must create provider objects in order to create and receive calls.

XtlCall. An XtlCall represents a call in progress and provides an access method to the call's data stream. XtlCall objects can set up, manipulate, and terminate calls.

XtlMonitor. An XtlMonitor enables applications to monitor events on a call. The XtlMonitor object allows an application to monitor all call events on a specific call, which it may or may not own. XtlMonitor objects cannot perform call control functions. When an XtlMonitor object is created, it is automatically registered to receive all events on a specific call.

XtlCallState. The XtlCallState class contains state and identification information of a call associated with a specific provider. This information applies to a specific instance of the call only, so an application can use an XtlCallState object for immediate status only. XtlCallState objects cannot be copied or saved; instead, an XtlMonitor object should be used to save the state of the call. These objects are like handles that enable you to change the ownership of a call and accept incoming calls. All CallState object methods return state values only. CallState objects do not control calls.

XtlKVList. An XtlKVList is a singly-linked list of key-value pairs, which are used to pass parameters to the API. Keys are of type XtlString and values may contain various types. The XtlKVList object is often used to pass provider-specific extension information that may not conform to the standard XTL interface.

XtlByteArray. An XtlByteArray is a reference-counted array of bytes. The reference count allows for efficient use of memory because a single XtlByteArray can be shared among a number of objects without concern about memory allocation. The array is deallocated when its reference count is zero.

XtlString. An XtlString contains a null-terminated string of characters. Like the XtlByteArray object, it is reference-counted to ease memory management when strings are passed by reference between other objects.

dpDispatcher. The dpDispatcher class detects new data on multiple UNIX file descriptors and dispatches the data to the appropriate input and output handlers.

dpIOHandler. The dpIOHandler class is a simple object that gets called by the dispatcher when data is available on a UNIX file descriptor. If you are familiar with the Interviews dispatcher library, this mechanism of handling I/O is similar.

XTL API Characteristics

The XTL API uses an event-driven paradigm where your application is notified of asynchronous events generated by the XTL platform. The XTL API operates across an asynchronous message-passing interface. Sending a message to the platform does not guarantee a response. Messages sent from the platform to the application indicate errors and state changes. The cause of a state change is indeterminable-your application will only know that the state has changed.

You should never assume a request will cause a state change, only that it is likely to change to the requested state. Instead, write programs that react to all possible state change messages that are of interest to your client application. Aside from the possible events generated by a network, user input can also cause a program to react.

For example, your program should not make the assumption that when a user requests to put a call on hold that the call will be put on hold; the network may have disconnected the call for other reasons.

XTL Events

XTL applications are driven by events. Each object receives events through its indication methods. Events are messages sent by the provider to notify an application of changes in call state or call progress. For example, a client can be notified if a call becomes active, on hold, or disconnected.

Event Registration

In order for indication methods to receive events, you must register the events that you are interested in receiving. This is done with the XtlProvider::listen_req() method. Later you can choose to disregard certain events by using the XtlProvider::ignore_req() method.

XTL Object Methods

XTL classes provide two types of virtual functions called request methods and indication methods. These methods generate basic call-control requests that are sent to the provider. Depending on the available telephone resources, the provider may or may not fulfill a request.

Request Methods

Each XTL messaging class uses a set of request methods to make service requests to the provider. These methods have names with the suffix _req, such as connect_req(). An application invokes these methods to manipulate an object. For example, an application program that needs to put a call on hold uses the XtlCall object's hold_req() request method to change the status of the XtlCall object when the call is put on hold.

Indication Methods

Objects receive events from the provider through indication methods. The events notify your application of errors or changes of state on a given call. To handle an event, you must override the indication method of a class. These methods have the suffix _ind, such as event_ind(). In overriding the indication method, you change the behavior of the class so that it can perform distinct tasks. For example, you can derive the XtlCall class to answer a call, play a greeting, and record a message; this behavior imitates an answering machine.

XTL Provider Developer's Kit

XTL Teleservices for Solaris has several providers available, including telephony services for TCP/IP and telephony services on AT&T 5ESS-5E5 ISDN switches.

Other network or telephony technologies may easily be integrated into XTL. Developers of teleservices hardware devices to be integrated into Solaris-based systems typically supply two components: a device driver and provider.

The device driver handles low-level details of the underlying network transfer scheme or telephony device (e.g. ATM, FDDI, analog telephony, etc.), and is written to conform to UNIX System V Release 4 standards. The provider is the code necessary to manage the interface between the XTL subsystem and the associated device-specific driver.

Providing Access to Additional Teleservices Technologies

The task of writing an XTL provider is simplified by using the XTL Media Platform Interface (MPI) library. The provider process uses the MPI to handle all communication and messaging to the XTL system components. The provider developer's sole concern is to translate between the XTL protocol and whatever interface is supplied by the device driver. When devices have additional features not defined by the XTL API/MPI, the provider extension messages can be used to define an access mechanism to allow an application to access the device's features.

Figure 9.2 XTL Provider and Device Driver

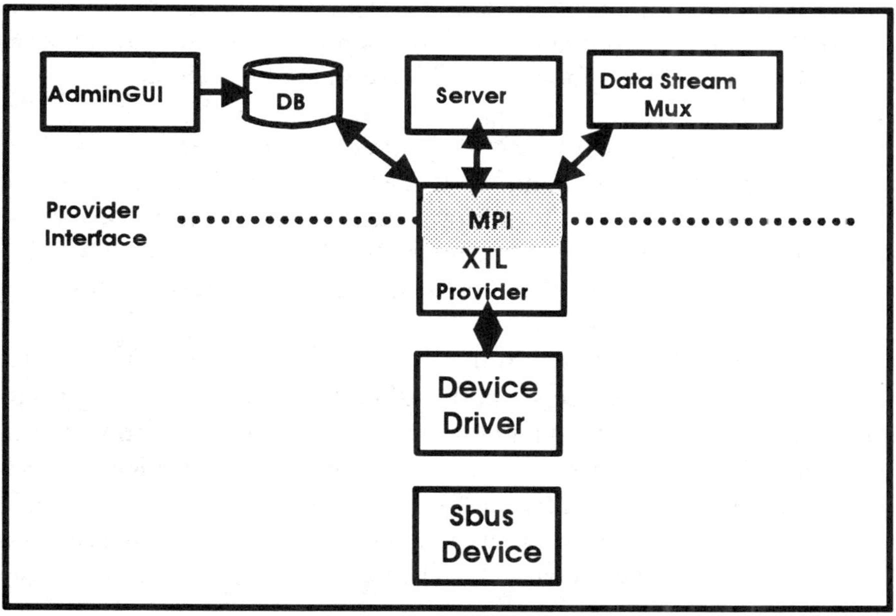

XTL Provider Library

The XTL provider library (MPI) simplifies the task of building an XTL provider. The library isolates the provider code from the intricacies of the XTL system services. Specifically the library supplies interfaces to the provider database, the server messaging system for commands and callbacks, and the mechanisms for making device data streams accessible to applications.

Configuring XTL Resources

XTL Teleservices for Solaris provides hardware-independent telephone call control and voice services for end users. The XTL platform provides a framework to integrate call control, messaging, and specific technologies such as fax, video, and ISDN communications. This document explains how to configure XTL resources, such as providers and the configuration database, after you install your packages.

The XTL teleservices software platform is based on a client-server architecture and includes the following components: XTL-based applications; an application programming interface (API); a server; a media platform interface (MPI) library for providers; and technology-specific providers. See figure 9.3 for a graphical look at the Teleservices Architecture.

The XTL API is implemented as a high-level, object-oriented C++ library. It enables application programmers to design applications that place and receive telephone calls, and to perform basic telephone functions such as to hold, transfer, drop, and conference calls. An XTL application links to the XTL library to use a workstation's Solaris Teleservices resources.

The server, which resides within the XTL cloud in the figure, offers multi-client and multi-device support to XTL applications. It also provides resource management and maintains security. It is the central point of contact for all XTL processes. Each telecommunication device connected to a workstation is managed by an XTL provider. The providers and XTL applications operate by passing and receiving messages. All messages are sent to and received by the server. The server evaluates and administers these messages.

Providers are essential to XTL applications. Applications must use a provider in order to create connections with a telephone device. At installation, the provider and its template file are installed, but not configured. The template file contains key and value information specific to the provider. Using the configuration tools, you can copy the template and create this file. Once you edit and save a template file to the database, it is referred to as this provider's information file. This file should contain all of the information that a server needs to evaluate and use the provider.

Figure 9.3 Teleservices Architecture

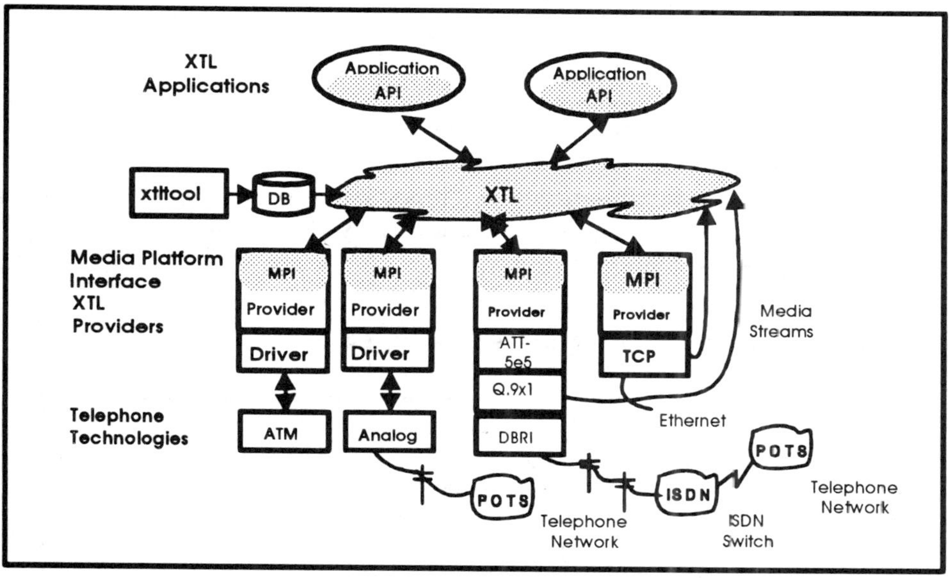

The information file is stored in the database, where the server can access it for information on the provider. This configuration process registers a provider with the Solaris Teleservices server. The database also contains the host configuration file. The host configuration file lists the configured providers on a given host. It is updated every time a provider is configured using the Solaris Teleservices configuration tools. The server can query these database files for lists of the configured providers and for startup and shutdown information on each provider. You can add or load additional provider software and hardware devices at any time. The server cannot find or use these providers until you properly register their information files in the database.

Directory Structure

The Solaris Teleservices runtime hierarchy is installed under the XTLDIR directory; and the host-specific configuration hierarchy is installed under the XTLCONFDIR directory. Because the Teleservices packages are relocatable, the terms XTLDIR and XTLCONFDIR are used throughout this document as placeholders for specifying the path name to the directory trees where Teleservices has been installed. To determine the values for these placeholders on any particular system, use the following commands:

- The absolute path for XTLDIR is: /usr/xtl
- The absolute path for XTLCONFDIR is: /etc/xtl

When you see these directories referenced in the text, substitute their respective path names. Figure 9.4 shows the XTL directory structure that is created for you at installation time.

Figure 9.4 The XTL Directory Hierarchies

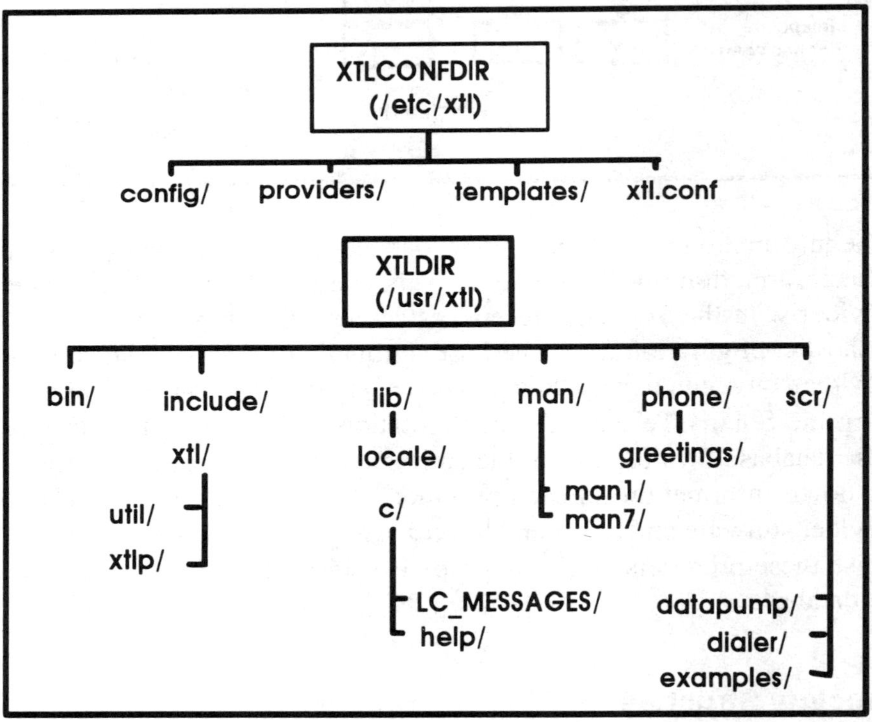

The XTL package contains the following directories:

XTLDIR/lib. This directory contains all of the Solaris Teleservices libraries, including the XTL application programming interface and the XTLP service provider interface. It also contains a locale subdirectory with localization and help files.

XTLDIR/bin. This directory contains the xtltool and config.xtl configuration tools, the change_group and cnx_perm security tools, the XTL server, and the xtlp_sun_ip provider for use over Ethernet networks.

XTLCONFDIR/config. This directory contains the provider information files. This directory is writable by the root user and by a specified group ID. The group ID is set by running the program change_group.

XTLCONFDIR/providers. This directory is available for provider programs to use as desired.

XTLCONFDIR/templates. This directory contains the provider template files listed as *.template. The Solaris Teleservices configuration tools access this directory. When a new template is added to this directory, the tools will add it to their available providers list. The content of each of these template files must include pointers to valid startup scripts or executables so that the server can start up the new provider successfully. The XTLCONFDIR/templates directory is reserved for template files only. The word "template" cannot appear in any provider alias.

All of a host's Solaris Teleservices configuration information is filed under XTLCONFDIR in either the host configuration file or the config subdirectory. The host configuration file is xtl.conf in the XTLCONFDIR directory. This file is created by the Solaris Teleservices configuration tools and may vary from host to host.

Setting Up User and Group Access

At installation, the provider included with your Solaris Teleservices package is automatically installed and the group sys has full read and write permissions. To change the group and user access, you can use tools provided by SunSoft.

Supported Switch and Telephone Configurations

The Solaris Teleservices platform supports the following switch and telephone configurations:

- Voice provider on IP Ethernet
- ISDN protocol stacks

This configuration includes a provider interface that works with a DBRI driver interface.

Using the Provider Configuration Database

This section describes the provider configuration database and how it is configured. The configuration process registers provider information with the XTL server. Without this process, the server cannot identify any installed providers.

Understanding the Provider Configuration Database

The provider configuration database stores information about the names, aliases, capabilities, and configurations of the providers installed on your system. The server uses this information whenever it starts a new provider. The provider configuration database comprises of a host configuration file and a collection of provider configuration files.

How Provider Aliases and Attributes Are Maintained

Each provider must have a primary alias or name. It may also have other secondary aliases, which refer to the same provider. Secondary aliases are useful when referring to a single provider that offers several services. For example, a provider whose primary alias is teldev provides telephone and fax services.

Since the name teldev is not very indicative of what it is capable of doing, you can create more descriptive secondary aliases such as phone and fax. Figure 9.5 shows the relationship between aliases, host configuration files, and provider information files.

Notice that aliases are not tied to the name of the provider executable file xtlp_sun_tel; and the name of the provider information file is the same as the primary alias. The server always invokes a provider and maintains its status using the provider's primary alias. Any client that requests information or wants to invoke a provider may do so by using its primary or any of its secondary aliases. All aliases, which are kept in the host configuration file, must be unique.

Figure 9.5 Provider Aliases and Attributes

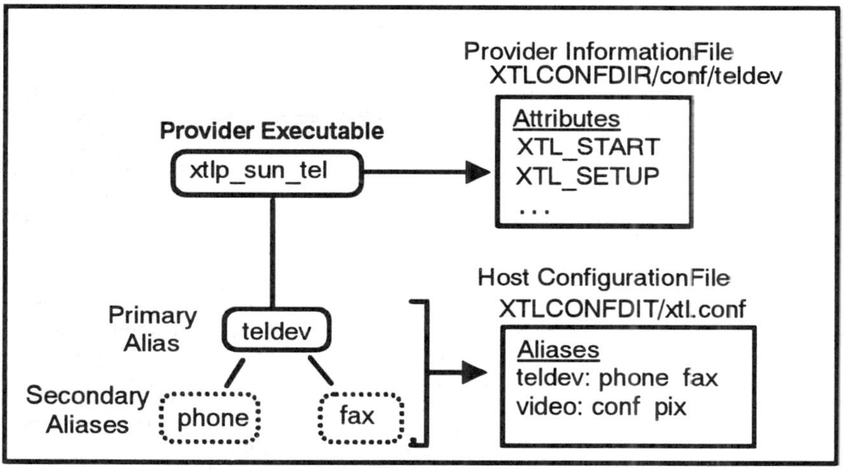

The Host Configuration File

The host configuration file contains a list of primary aliases and any corresponding secondary aliases for the providers available on a host. The primary alias name is also the file name for the provider's information file. The XTL server accesses the host configuration file to determine the available providers and uses that information to start each provider. The host configuration file is modified with the configuration tools described earlier. You should not modify the configuration file directly.

Provider Information Files

The provider information files contain specific attribute values for each provider such as how many different switches a provider can connect to, what types of supplementary services it can support, its primary alias, and any additional information given by the provider's manufacturer. A client can use this information to determine which provider it should use. The XTL configuration tools enable you to view a template file and edit a copy of its contents. When you apply changes to your edits, you create information files for each new provider. Each provider instance requires an individual information file, which is created for you when you configure the provider using xtltool. Even providers that identify similar devices connected to the same switch need their own information files. Each provider information file must include a minimum set of attributes as detailed in figure 9.6.

Figure 9.6 Attribute Values for the Provider Configuration File

Attribute	Example	Description
XTL_FAMILY_NAME	sun_teldev	When a provider executable is run, its process is associated with a provider family name. Multiple providers running in this process are considered part of the same provider family.
XTL_PROVIDER_NAME	sun_teldev	This is the name of the provider; it is the same as its primary alias.
XTL_START	/opt/SUNWx5e5p/scripts/ \ xtlp_sun_5e5.start -p \ xtlp_sun_5e5.0	The value of XTL_START is a fully qualified path name to your provider startup script with any necessary parameters; the XTL_START value cannot be empty.

The server uses the command specified by XTL_START to start the provider. The script may be blocking or non-blocking. At any given time, only one instance of the provider executable will be executing. Consequently, the XTL_START value must be the same for all providers of the same family.

The process started when the XTL_START command is run lasts for the lifetime of the provider. This is important, because the server uses the fact that the process has exited in helping to determine when a provider is done. The server records the process identification (PID) of the XTL_START process and will be informed when this PID finishes execution. Note that the server does not perform block waiting for the XTL_START command to return, but continues running. It will "reap" the process associated with the XTL_START command.

If the XTL platform cannot communicate with your provider process, it invokes the XTL_START script again. When the XTL platform starts your provider, it does so with the following environment:

XTL_FAMILY_NAME=
<family name from configuration file>

This means that any additional environment variables such as PATH, LD_LIBRARY_PATH must be set within the provider script before it executes the provider executable.

<table>
<tr><th>Attribute</th><th>Example</th><th>Description</th></tr>
<tr><td>XTL_CLEANUP</td><td>/opt/SUNWx5e5p/scripts/ \ xtlp_sun_5e5.shutdown \ -p xtlp_sun_5e5.0</td><td>This defines the cleanup script for when the provider is killed. The value for the XTL_CLEANUP attribute can be either null or a full path name, plus any needed command line arguments.</td></tr>
<tr><td colspan="3">If non-null, the value specifies a blocking script that the server will run to perform cleanup tasks. The server will run this command and wait until it finishes before continuing. This is the last operation associated with this provider. The server process retains the process ID of each process it starts up with the XTL_START value. If it receives a SIGCHLD signal for that provider, it knows that the provider process has exited. On the other hand, if the file descriptor through which the server communicates with the provider fails, the server will kill the provider process. Either way, once the provider process has exited, the XTL server executes the script defined by the XTL_CLEANUP attribute.</td></tr>
<tr><td>XTL_DOCUMENTATION</td><td>pageview \ /opt/SUNWx5e5p/\ xtlp_sun_5e5.ps</td><td>This attribute executes a process that displays any on-line documentation that is available for the provider.</td></tr>
<tr><td colspan="3">The value is a fully qualified path to an executable along with parameters for the executable; xttool provides an "Execute Document Command..." button. When the button is pressed, the value of the XTL_DOCUMENTATION key is executed. The documentation command is executed with the same environment as xttool.</td></tr>
<tr><td>XTL_VERSION</td><td>1.0</td><td>This attribute states the release version of XTL with which the provider is compatible.</td></tr>
<tr><td></td><td></td><td></td></tr>
</table>

XTL Provider Overview

The XTL media platform interface (MPI) is a standard programming interface for writing XTL providers. The MPI is implemented as a library called XTLP. This chapter describes the use and role of providers in the XTL architecture and introduces the classes in the XTLP library.

Role of Providers in XTL

An XTL provider is a software entity that enables your telephone device to communicate with the XTL platform and provides XTL applications (herein referred to as clients) access to the services of your telephone device. And for your provider, the MPI is its interface to the XTL platform. In writing your provider, you only need to understand the MPI-in-depth understanding of the API and clients, while useful, is not required.

Providers allow XTL clients to set up, control, and terminate phone calls in a consistent manner. Providers also give clients access to the data associated with a call in a uniform manner. Additionally, value-added capabilities available from your telephone device are accessible to XTL clients through a simple, but powerful extension mechanism.

In terms of the overall XTL architecture, as pictured earlier in figure 9.3, a provider has two entry points (interfaces) to the XTL platform-the MPI and the XTL database interface. Consequently, as a minimum, you do not need to be concerned with the other interfaces in the XTL platform. The only other assumption is that you have a thorough understanding of the telephone device for which you are writing a provider..

In the XTL framework, the MPI acts as an intermediary between your provider and the rest of the XTL platform. Consequently, all communication between XTL clients to your provider is relayed through the MPI. However, you can simplify your view of the provider framework during your programming to the one shown in figure 9.7. Here there are only two entities of concern: an abstract entity called the client and the underlying technology (telephone device).

The MPI (implemented as the XTLP library) is the interface to the client. All communication between the client and the provider occurs through messages call request and indications. The programming model dictates that clients make requests for services to your provider through the MPI, and your provider indicates whether or not it can satisfy such requests by sending indications back to the client through the MPI.

When a client makes a request, the MPI invokes a corresponding callback method on an object; when the request has been serviced, the object invokes another method to indicate the success or failure of fulfilling the request.

The client entity encapsulates all the parts of the XTL platform above the MPI. It is the client that makes requests for the services of your provider and receives the indications your provider sends. The client abstraction is important because it allows you to think of requests as originating from a single source, even though several clients may be making requests.

Figure 9.7 Provider Programming Framework

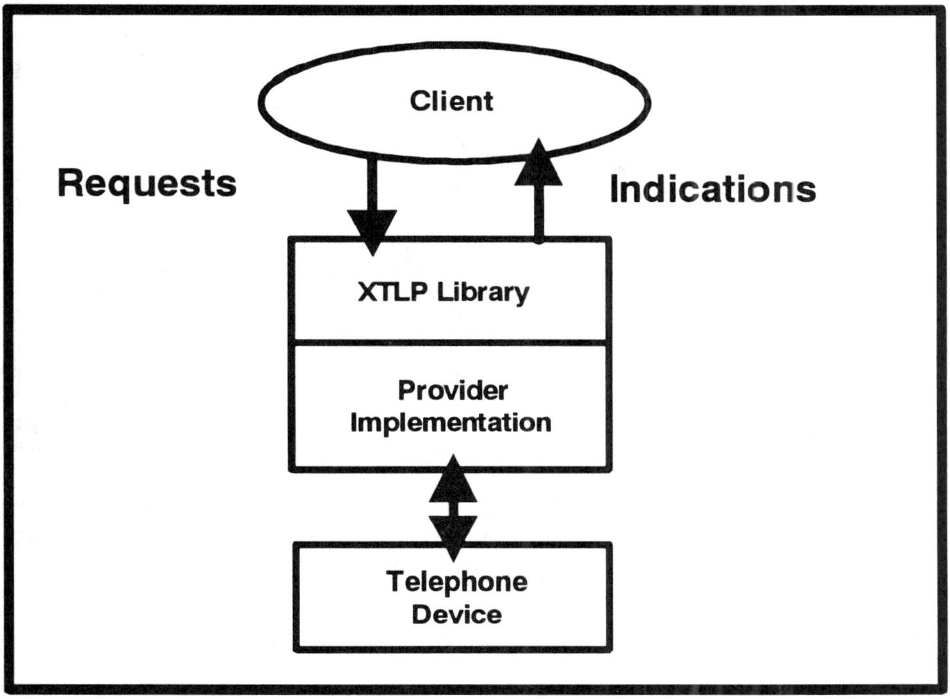

The XtlP Classes

There are four main classes derived from the XtlP base class. Figure 9.8 shows the XtlP class hierarchy.

The XtlPFactory, XtlPProvider, and XtlPCall classes contain virtual methods called request methods that you must implement. A request method is a callback handler whose implementation satisfies some provider service that a client may request. Callback methods that connect, put on hold, or disconnect a phone call are examples of request methods. The derived XtlP classes contain callback methods that you must override with code that implements the functionality of your provider.

Figure 9.8 XtlP Class Hierarchy

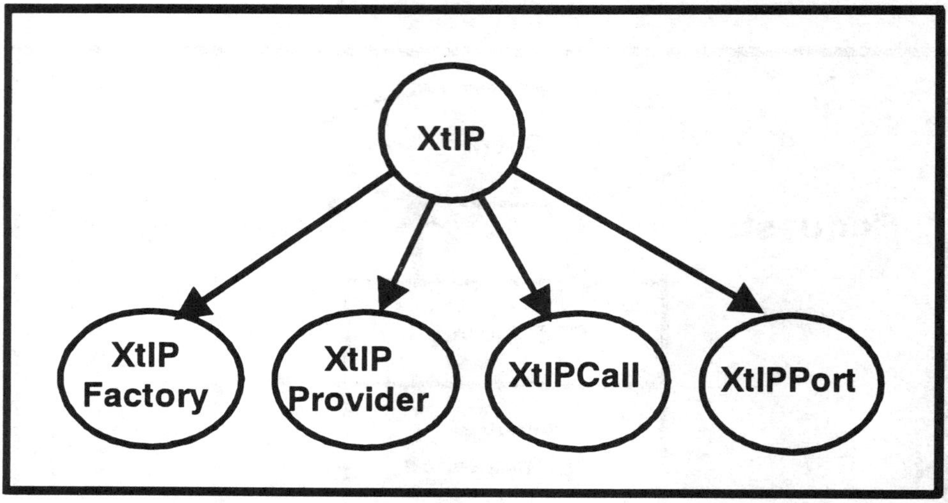

There are also classes and data types that you can use directly without deriving them. Data types that you will see in the process of programming a provider include those detailed in figure 9.9 below:

Figure 9.9 Data Types for Direct Use

Classes	Description
Utility Classes	
XtlKVList	An ordered list structure used to pass parameters between objects.
XtlString	A reference-counted string type.
XtlByteArray	A reference-counted byte array.
Dispatcher Classes	
dpSLDispatcher dpXtDispatcher dpXVDispatcher	Event dispatchers (derived from the InterViews library) for use in various user interface environments.
DpIOHandler	An abstract I/O handler for managing events on a file descriptor (this class is also taken from the InterViews library); however, the dpIOHandler must be derived.
Global Data Types	
XtlFormat	Data type to describe the format of data being transmitted over a call.
XtlCallReference	A unique identifier assigned to a call.

Provider Framework and Concepts

The provider exists between the MPI and the telephone device, as shown previously in figure 9.3. Above the MPI is a client entity that makes requests on you provider for call management services. The MPI is one layer in the larger XTL architecture. Through careful design, each layer in the architecture is modular.

This allows you to program at the provider level without in-depth knowledge of the other layers. Conceptually, the client represents everything above the provider. The provider is only aware of the client above and the device below. The basic function of the provider is to accept requests from the client and to send indications that convey the results of requests back to the client. In other words, the provider is a consumer of requests and a producer of indications.

So far we have used the term provider to name the enabling piece of software that allows a client (encapsulated in the client entity) to manage phone calls using a particular underlying technology. However, providers involve several subtly different and overlapping parts. To better understand the provider framework, it helps to be familiar with the terminology used in this guide:

Provider. A high-level term used to describe the software entity that manages a telephone resource. A resource is the device or underlying technology that you wish XTL clients to use to communicate.

Provider object. A C++ object that is instantiated from a class derived from the XtlPProvider class. A provider object has request methods (to carry out requests) and indication methods (to send events to the client). To define the behavior of a provider object, its request methods must be overridden with provider-specific code.

Provider process. The address space in which one or more provider objects exist.

Provider family. A collection of providers that run in the same provider process and share a common provider family name; you define the provider family name in the template file in the provider package. Provider families are useful when a provider process needs to support multiple physical devices and where it may be convenient to have individual providers manage each device.

Provider package. A collection of files, primarily a provider executable and a provider template file, that is installed by the end user to make use of your specific device or underlying technology.

In general, providers manage calls, which are represented by XtlPCall objects. A provider can control one or more calls, which only exist in the context of the provider; that is, a call is always associated with a provider.

The Provider Programming Model

XTL providers are event driven in a manner similar to X Windows System clients. In that programming model, objects wait for stimuli from external sources and perform an action to carry out a request. The XTL dispatcher library provides the necessary classes to support this event-driven programming model.

Figure 9.10 Sources of Stimuli to a Provider

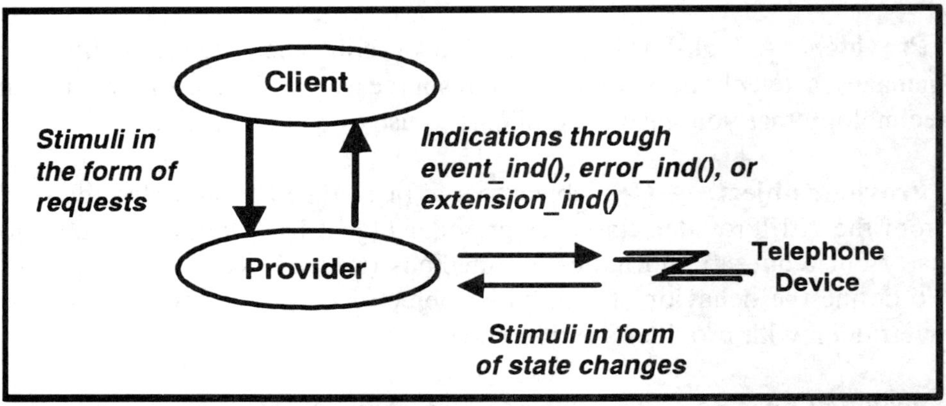

For an XTL provider, an external stimulus may be a client request or a state change in the underlying telephone technology. The provider sends information back to clients (that is, it informs clients of changes in the state of the client, provider, or call objects) by sending the client one of the following indications:

- Event indications through event_ind()
- Error indications through error_ind()

Provider-specific extension indications through extension_ind()

Future Directions in Teleservices

The last several decades have seen the complete ubiquity of the telephone into office and home environments. Given that in less than 50 years, the telephone has been largely taken for granted, it is easy to speculate as to how its merger with the computer will take place.

Telecommunications has had a fundamental and significant impact on modern society, from near-global cellular communications to instantaneous television images from virtually anywhere in the world. The basic medium for communications is no longer always a wire from the local telephone company, and the party on the other end isn't always a person with a telephone.

Teleservices as an integrated part of computing, provides a new paradigm for communications in the corporate world. Taken together with the growing impact of distributed multimedia, teleservices offers improved communication between individuals and groups to foster the exchange of ideas, solving of problems, and management of increasing amounts of information.

Teleservices applications in the near future will provide for integrated desktop applications which include voice capabilities. For example, users will be able to make and accept phone calls directly via their workstation through simple, easy-to-use graphical tools. Features such as voice mail, call forwarding and conferencing will be commonplace.

Users away from their offices will be able to call their workstation and retrieve voice mail, as well as "hear" their electronic mail read to them via integrated text-to-speech applications. Extended features made possible by teleservices include pager services, automated call distribution (via Caller ID), facsimile management and video teleconferencing on the desktop.

As teleservices capabilities are dependent upon the underlying communications media, advanced in network technology will also impact available applications. Technologies such as FDDI, B-ISDN, frame relay, ATM and SONET will provide substantially higher bandwidth to support workstation-based video telephony, large-scale video teleconferencing and true object-based distributed multimedia.

SunSoft sees teleservices as a key component in the future of distributed, client-server computing. The integration of teleservices into the standard Solaris platform provides the basis for next-generation applications destined to improve communications and corporate productivity.

The Solaris Teleservices Platform delivers a stable and robust base for device and media-independent applications and flexible support for new hardware and communications topologies. Developers can begin building their teleservices applications today, confident with the knowledge that they will be supported as new communications technology emerges.

XTL and Emerging Standards for CTI

The XTL subsystem provides a platform for merging with other emerging CTI API standards. The XTL API or an XTL provider can bridge the syntactic and minor protocol differences that distinguish the multitude of otherwise similar call control APIs. By building an API or toolkit on top of XTL, the developer leverages access to all the XTL providers available on a system or network. Furthermore, the XTL subsystem provider the security and shared access that may be missing from other, mission-centric APIs.

SunSoft continues to work with the definers of APIs and the developers of implementations of those systems to ensure compatibility and transportability of applications and services.

The author would like to thank SunSoft and Sun Microsystems marketing and technical publications employees for their assistance in providing editorial contributions to this chapter. Special thanks to David Herrington and Fabian Lubais for their encouragement and guidance in helping to research and compile the subject matter. This portion of the book contains material reproduced with permission from a number of Sun Microsystems publications including:

XTL Architecture Guide (801-7048-01 rev. A 3/4/94)
XTL Administrator's Guide (801-7047-01 rev. A 3/4/94)
XTL Application Programmer's Guide (801-7046-01 rev. A 3/4/94)
XTL Provider Programmer's Guide (801-7049-01 rev. A 3/4/94)

Catalyst are trademarks of Sun Microsystems, Inc., licensed to SunSoft, Inc. SPARC is a registered trademark of SPARC International, Inc. Products bearing the SPARC trademark are based upon an architecture developed by Sun Microsystems, Inc. OPEN LOOK, System V, SVR4, and UNIX are registered trademarks of UNIX Systems Laboratories, Inc. Pentium, i386 and i486 are trademarks of Intel Corporation. GL, Iris GL, and OpenGL are trademarks of Silicon Graphics. PostScript and PostScript Level 2 are trademarks of Adobe Systems. HOOPS is a trademark of Ithaca Software. X Window System, X11, and PEX are products or technologies of the Massachusetts Institute of Technology. All other products referred to in this chapter are identified by the trademarks of the companies who market these products.

10

Windows Telephony

Windows Telephony Rationale

Initially, the desktop computer was a personal productivity tool – first through the use of spreadsheets and word processing programs – and later with additional tools such as databases, project managers, presentation packages and personal information managers. Then local area networks (LANs) connected desktop computers within workgroups and departments, allowing people to share information and resources. In addition, LANs allowed people within a workgroup to communicate electronically, further expanding the role of desktop computers to communicate business information.

The next step in the evolution of the desktop computer is to combine it with one of the most basic business tools – the telephone. Intel Corporation and Microsoft Corporation, in cooperation with many major telecommunications, PC and software companies, have created a standard interface – the Windows Telephony Application Programming Interface (TAPI) – for the integration of telephones and personal computers running the Microsoft Windows operating system.

The API brings the utility and reach of the telephone to the desktop computer. In fact, with the availability of cellular telephone technology, the capabilities are not even limited to the desktop.

Enabling a Broad Range of Applications

The possibilities are exciting for users of both telephones and computers. Products based on the Windows Telephony API will improve existing capabilities, such as:

Visual Interface to Telephone Features. Users can easily access telephone features through the Windows graphical user interface. Telephone providers have been adding features to telephones at a quick pace – call forwarding, call parking, speed dialing, and conference calling. Unfortunately, most people typically use only one or two of the most basic features simply because they can't remember the more sophisticated features – let alone how to use them. Through telephony software applications, users will be able to access even the most complex features with ease. For example, setting up a conference call may be as easy as "clicking" on the names of the conferees.

Personal Communication Management. With a graphical user interface, people can have their PCs handle incoming telephone calls, automatically controlling which calls reach them. For example, people will be able to ensure that they receive important calls by requesting that certain calls be forwarded automatically to locations at which they expect to be working.

Telephone Network Access. Connecting existing applications directly to the telephone network will greatly expand the usefulness of these applications and increase users' productivity. For example, a personal information manager can be used not only to look up telephone number, but also to actually place calls to those numbers.

Additionally, several interesting new applications will be enabled by combining computers and telephones:

Integrated Messaging. With direct connection to the telephone, integrated messaging becomes a reality. Today, when people arrive at the office, they must check three separate "in-boxes": voice mail, electronic mail and the fax machine. With the desktop computer connected to the phone network, users can combine these three forms of messaging into a single in-box. They can review and manage all of their messages – electronic mail, fax and voice mail – from a single place. In addition, voice-mail messages can be accessed randomly, which is far more efficient than the serial access provided on most telephone-based voice-mail systems.

Integrated Meetings. One of the most attractive capabilities of the computer is that it can store, communicate and present information that spans the entire spectrum of media – text, data, graphics, voice and video – in any combination. By itself, the telephone can communicate and present voice information only. By combining the functions of the computer and the telephone, people in geographically separate locations can participate in interactive meetings and share visual as well as audio information. That means they can hold meetings over the telephone network that are nearly as rich in information content as in-person meetings.

These two applications merely scratch the surface of possibilities presented by the integration of the personal computer and the telephone. More will emerge as products are developed on the Windows Telephony API specification.

The Windows Telephony API Approach

One of the major problems in connecting the computer to the telephone is the enormous complexity and diversity found in the underlying telephone network. There is a wide variety of telephone services and equipment, and many incompatible protocols. The analog Public Switched Telephone Network (PSTN), proprietary PBXs, key systems, cellular systems, and Integrated Services Digital Network (ISDN) facilities vary across service networks and switches. The Windows Telephony API provides a standard application programming interface that allows users and application developers to take advantage of the many capabilities and services of the telephone. At the same time, it isolates users and application developers from the complexity and variability of the underlying telephone network.

The Windows Telephony API allows application programs to control telephony functions. This includes such basic functions as establishing, answering and terminating a call. It also includes supplementary functions, such as hold, transfer, conference and call park found in PBXs and other phone systems. The API also provides access to features that are specific to certain service providers, with built-in extensibility to accommodate future telephony features and networks as they become available.

The Windows Telephony API operates independently of the underlying telephone network and equipment. It isolates the application from the network complexity, greatly simplifying the application development task. In addition, the API is independent of the method of connection between the computer and the telephone. This gives maximum flexibility to integrate the PC with the telephone system.

For example, the PC can be connected to the telephone network as shown in figure 10.1. The PC can be connected through a telephone as shown in figure 10.2. Multiple PCs can share telephone resources through a voice server, as shown in figure 10.3. Or a server can be connected through a switch-to-host link, as shown in figure 10.4. Different connection models offer different capabilities to applications. For example, conferencing applications require a connection as shown in either figure 10.1 or figure 10.3, in order for the PC to get access to the information transmitted over the phone line.

Figure 10.1 Connect PC to Network

The Windows Telephony API is part of the Microsoft Windows Open Services Architecture (WOSA), which provides a single set of open-ended interfaces to enterprise computing services. WOSA encompasses a number of APIs, providing applications and corporate developers with an open set of interfaces to which applications can be written and accessed. WOSA also includes services for data access, messaging, software licensing, connectivity and financial services.

Figure 10.2 Connect PC to Telephone

Figure 10.3 Connect PC to Voice Server

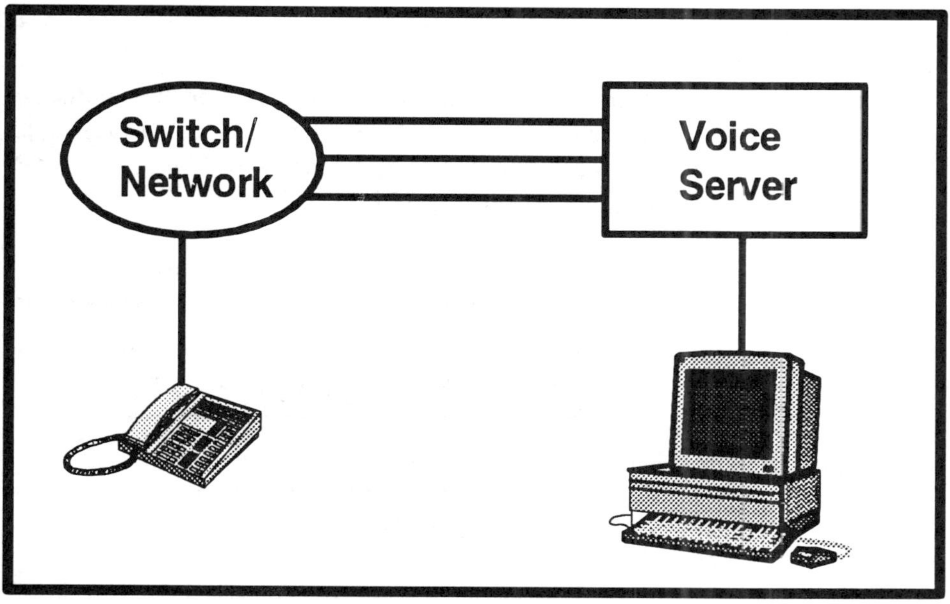

WOSA services such as the Windows Telephony API consist of two interfaces. Developers write to an applications programming interface (API).

Figure 10.4 Connect PC via Switch-to-Host Link

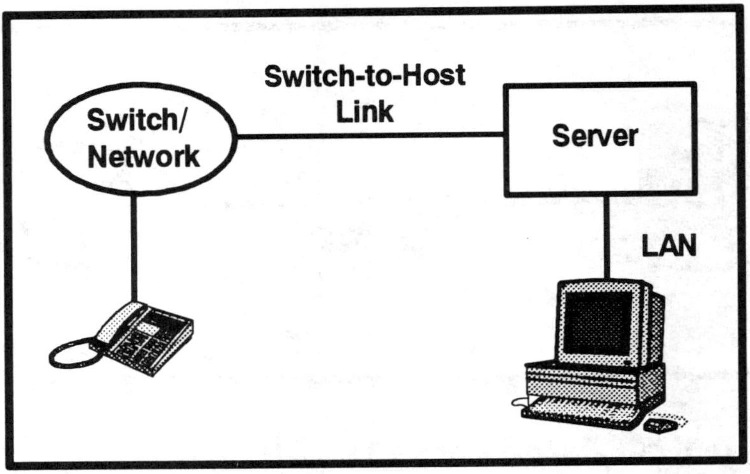

The other interface, referred to as the service provider interface (SPI), is used to establish the connection to the specific telephone network. This model is similar to the computer industry model whereby printer manufacturers provide printer drivers for Windows-based applications. Figure 10.5 shows the relationship between the "front-end" Windows Telephony API and the "back-end" Windows Telephony SPI.

Figure 10.5 Integration of Applications & Telephone Networks

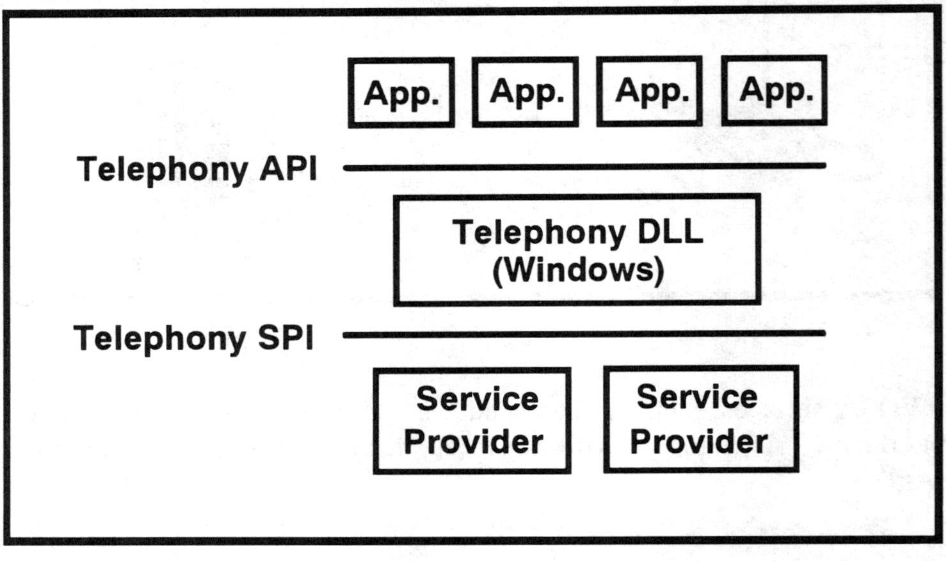

Applications can combine the Windows Telephony API with other capabilities of Windows to provide a combination of services. For example, an application can use the Windows Telephony API to establish a connection and then use the Windows audio functionality to record and play back voice information over the connection.

Picking Up Where Others Have Fallen Short

Windows Telephony is not the first or only telephony application programming interface in the industry. However, most of those that have gone before have faced serious roadblocks to success. These included:

Limited Platforms. Some attempts to integrated telephony into personal computers have used specially-designed PC hardware. In many cases, this hardware was not expandable, insufficiently powerful for general computing needs, and introduced incompatibilities with standard operating systems software and applications. This experience has shown that, to be successful, integration must be based on standard PC hardware and use standard software.

Call Center Focus. Most telephony application programming interfaces concentrate on large, call-center operations in which equipment such as an automatic call distributor is closely coupled with a PBX and mainframe computer to control an entire department. The most basic functions in these APIs are complex due to their "third-party call control" nature.

Limited Media Stream Access; Single Application Focus. At the same time that these legacy APIs are too complex, the overall APIs are insufficient for use in a desktop environment. They lack functions to control media stream input and output on the PC, and are unable to deal with multiple PC applications sharing telephony resources.

Restricted to Single Switching Platform. Virtually all of the telephony APIs in the industry today have been promulgated by an individual switch manufacturer, and require use not only of their PBX but also of interface hardware or server software sold by the same manufacturer. APIs designed by standards committee, while available on a variety of hardware platforms, have nevertheless been generally restricted to a single networking environment, such as PBXs or ISDN, and not portable to other environments such as POTS. This has meant that the market for any particular application written in conformance to these APIs has been small, since different versions (often with quite different user interfaces) were required for each switch or network.

Lack of Extensibility. Those APIs which have been available on multiple platforms (such as those developed by standards bodies) have been narrowly focused. In general, they have not included facilities for manufacturers to expose special, additional features to differentiate their products and make those features available to software developers.

Unfamiliar Programming Model. Many of the existing telephony APIs are based on arcane languages (such as the Hayes® "AT" command set) or involve exchange mechanisms, data structures, and messaging models which are unfamiliar to experienced Windows programmers.

Windows Telephony, on the other hand, addresses all of these issues:

General-Purpose Computing Platforms. Building on the Microsoft Windows foundation, Windows Telephony uses standard PC hardware and software, preserving users investments and allowing the flexibility to which they have become accustomed.

Desktop Focus. Windows Telephony focuses on the "desktop" – generally, a single PC and telephone. The desktop is assumed, in the parameter structure of API functions, to be one endpoint of each call, thereby simplify the API and making it easier for programmers to learn and use. However, the capability of performing "third-party" call control (on behalf of other desktops) is preserved where needed, and future extensions for call center operation are planned. The underlying mechanism of communicating with the network can be either first-party or third-party.

Media Stream Access. Windows Telephony provides linkage between telephony call control operations and existing Windows functions for data communications, fax, digitized audio input and output, and other media streams, thereby facilitating the creation of interactive voice resource, fax-back, and other sophisticated applications. Touch-tone input and output is supported through the API, as well as detection and generation of other tones. The API supports media type detection and reporting and automatic routing of calls to the correct application to handle the detected media mode.

Multiple Application Support. Windows Telephony provides the capability for multiple applications to share telephony devices and to cooperatively control telephone calls. Monitoring and logging applications are supported. Multiple applications can be waiting for incoming calls while outgoing calls are placed on the same device. Control of calls can be handed off between applications.

Network- and Hardware-Independent. Windows Telephony is designed to be a superset of telephone network capabilities, allowing all networks to be modeled: POTS, ISDN, PBX, Centrex, key systems, cellular, wireless, etc.

Applications can use the functions of the API without regard to the underlying hardware configuration, be it PC-based (add-in card), phone-based (smartphone or external module), or server-based (over a LAN).

Differences in capabilities are reflected in data structures available to applications so that user interfaces can properly reflect available operations at any point in time. This permits a single application to be portable across a large number of platforms, so that, for example, a multinational corporation can use the same telephony application at all sites even though different PBXs, phones, and networks are used, cutting support and development costs.

Fully Extensible. Windows Telephony service providers can expose any number of special features to applications. Special device-specific functions and messages are provided, and most data structures and data types include device-specific extensibility. Facilities are provided to detect the extensions supported and negotiate versions of those extensions.

Familiar Programming Model. The Windows Telephony API is based on C-language functions and libraries, data structures, and messages, familiar to Windows programmers. Telephony applications can be developed using standard Windows development and testing tools.

Windows Telephony addresses the major issues which have confronted previous telephony APIs, and provides the basis for the widespread integration of telephony and personal computers.

Benefits of Windows Telephony

Windows Telephony brings benefits to all segments of the telephony and computing industries.

Application Developers. A standard API, providing telephony network- and hardware-independence on the most popular operating system platform, gives the critical market mass to warrant an investment in development of full-featured telephony applications, for both commercial and corporate developers. Developers focus on the value-added, not the plumbing, and need not be concerned with being tied to a particular hardware platform.

Telephony network, switch, and hardware vendors can focus on the area of their expertise – hardware and switching – without needing to come up to speed on Windows user interface programming. Rather than having to sell a limited range of internally-developed applications, a full-range of broad- and vertical-market applications will be available from third parties, greatly expanding the market for telephony hardware for PC platforms and PCs with integrated telephony capabilities.

End Users. Investments in applications software and telephony hardware are protected by the interchangability of components. Competition in telephony application software means that a wide variety will be available at competitive prices, and new features will be continually rolled-out by commercial developers to meet growing user needs.

Broad Industry Support

Over 40 major companies announced support for Windows Telephony when it was made public in 1993. These included:

Acer
Active Voice Corporation
Alcatel Business Systems Group
Ameritech
Analog Devices
Articulate Systems

AT&T Global Business Communications Systems
Bell Atlantic
Centigram Communications Corporation
Compaq Computer Corporation
Contact Software International
Cypress Research Corporation
Delrina
Dialogic
Digital Equipment Corporation
DSP Group, Inc.
Ericsson Corporation
Floreat, Inc.
Fujitsu Business Communications Systems
Harris Corporation
InteCom, Inc.
ISOCOR
Jensen-Jones, Inc.
Lotus Development
Mitel
Motorola Digital Signal Processor Operation
National Semiconductor, Inc.
Natural MicroSystems
NEC Corporation
Northern Telecom
Octel Communications Corporation
OCTuS, Inc.
Polaris Software
Rockwell International Corporation
Siemens Private Communication Systems Group/ROLM
Sequent Computer Systems, Inc.
Smart Technologies
Spectron
Stylus Innovation
TeleInt GmbH
Unifi Communications Corporation
US West Communications, Inc.
VMX, Inc.
Voice Technologies Group, Inc.

These companies, and many others, participated in the open design and review process which resulted in the Windows Telephony API and SPI specifications. Over 10,000 copies of the preliminary specification were downloaded from electronic sources and shipped in hardcopy form, and many more copies of the released specification have already been downloaded. Most major participants in every segment of the telephony industry – switches, desktop equipment, voice processing, network providers, chipsets – as well as personal computers and software, support Windows Telephony, and are actively developing hardware, service providers, and applications.

The Windows Telephony API brings a whole new range of functionality to business users by enabling the integration of the desktop computer with the telephone. Because the API isolates applications from the complexity of the underlying network, application developers can generate network-independent applications. Also, the API is independent of the type of PC-to-telephone connection, giving application developers and users configuration flexibility. Removing these barriers is critical to the development of PC applications that exploit the telephone network.

The availability of Windows Telephony support (via service providers) will soon become a key factor in the selection of PBXs and telephony hardware. Many service providers will become available during the first half of 1994. *Now* is the time for developers to begin working with Windows Telephony, considering new applications to improve services and productivity through computer and telephony integration.

The Windows Telephony Software Development Kit

The Windows Telephony 1.0 Software Development Kit (SDK) includes:

TAPI.DLL, which routes TAPI functions between applications and service providers.

TAPI.LIB, which provides entry points to the functions of TAPI.DLL.

TAPIEXE.EXE, which is an application that is automatically loaded by TAPI.DLL and provides an application context for handling telephony events.

An applet called the **Dialer**, which is a sample call-manager application that provides the most basic telephonic functionality, such as processing requests from applications to make voice calls.

It also has its own user interface that lets users make calls directly. Full source code for the Dialer is provided, and this source code is the starting point from which most programmers will begin programming their own telephony applications.

A **Sample Service Provider** (ATSP.C) that can establish and control a simple call using a Hayes-compatible modem. Its main functions are to help test Windows telephony applications and to provide sample source code for serviceprovider writers.

The **Telephony Control Panel**, a control panel applet (TELEPHON.CPL) which is used through the Windows Control Panel to install, remove, and configure Telephony service providers and to set location and calling-card information used in address translation.

A **number-translation module** (TAPIADDR.DLL) that translates addresses from canonical to dialable format.

Header Files, including TAPI.H for API functions, which must be included by all Windows Telephony applications.

Electronic Documentation, which includes the *Telephony Application Programmer's Guide* and the *Telephony Service Provider Programmer's Guide*. The documentation is provided electronically in Microsoft Word for Windows version 2.0 format, and can be printed on almost any laser printer. No hardcopy documentation is provided with the Windows Telephony SDK.

Help files, for both application programmers and service provider programmers. These Windows Help files contain complete on-line function references of all Windows Telephony API and SPI functions.

The components necessary to run Windows Telephony applications may be redistributed by developers at no cost (no license fees to Microsoft or Intel).

Availability

The Software Development Kit is currently available from several sources:

CompuServe: Either GO MSL (Microsoft Software Library) and search for the keyword "S14400", or GO WINEXT (the Windows Extensions Forum) and download the file TAPI10.ZIP from Library 3.

Internet: Use anonymous FTP to ftp.microsoft.com (198.105.232.1) and look in the directory "/devtools/tapi" for the file TAPI10.ZIP.

Microsoft Download Service BBS. Dial +1 (206) 936-6735, log in, and look for the file "TAPISDK.EXE".

Microsoft Windows Development Platform Level II CD-ROM: This set of four CD-ROMs contains all Microsoft SDKs, DDKs and operating systems. This quarterly offering for developers accompanies the MSDN Level I Development Library, which contains all documentation for the development platform (but no code). For more information, call 1-800-759-5474 in the US or Canada, 05.90.59.04 in France, (0130) 810211 in Germany, (060) 222480 in the Netherlands, (0800) 960279 in the UK. For any other country in Europe call +31 (10) 258 8864. For other countries outside of Europe or the US and Canada, call +1 (402) 691 0173.

TechEd '94 CD-ROM: All attendees of TechEd '94 receive a complete copy of the Windows Telephony 1.0 Software Development Kit for Windows 3.1 on their CD-ROM.

There is no charge for obtaining and using the SDK from network sources except for the cost of connect time for downloading (approximately 3.4 megabytes, compressed). However, do note that the SDK will be available for download for only a limited time, and thereafter will be available only by subscription to the Level II Development Platform CD-ROMs.

Future Versions of Windows

Windows Telephony will be a standard feature of future versions of Microsoft Windows and Microsoft Windows NT. The Windows Telephony Software Development Kit will become a part of the SDK for these future versions as well. A beta release version of the Windows Telephony Software Development Kit for Windows NT is expected to be available in 1994.

Support for Application Developers

Windows Telephony discussions can be found on Section 3 of the Windows Extensions Forum on CompuServe (GO WINEXT). This is the preferred venue for technical support questions, discussion of proposed future features and extensions, contacting other developers, etc. The author of this chapter checks the forum daily and personally answers questions, and other members of the Windows Telephony team also make regular visits. Private questions or feedback about Windows Telephony can be sent via the Internet to "telephon@microsoft.com" (on CompuServe, send to "INTERNET:telephon@microsoft.com"), or via fax to "Windows Telephony Coordinator" at +1 (206) 936-7329. Further information on technical support can be found in the README.TXT file in the Windows Telephony SDK.

Windows Telephony Concepts

Telephony Services

Telephony services are divided into Assisted Telephony services and the services provided by the full Telephony API. In general, the full Telephony API is used to implement powerful telephonic applications and Assisted Telephony is used to add minimal but useful telephonic functionality to non-telephony applications. Telephony's services are divided into the groups shown in figure 10.6.

Assisted Telephony

Assisted Telephony provides telephony-enabled applications with an easy-to-use mechanism for making phone calls without requiring the developer to become fully telephony literate. These functions provide very basic telephony functionality to primarily non-telephonic applications. If your application needs extensive telephonic control or is meant to handle incoming calls, you will need to use the full Telephony API.

Figure 10.6 Overview of Telephony Services

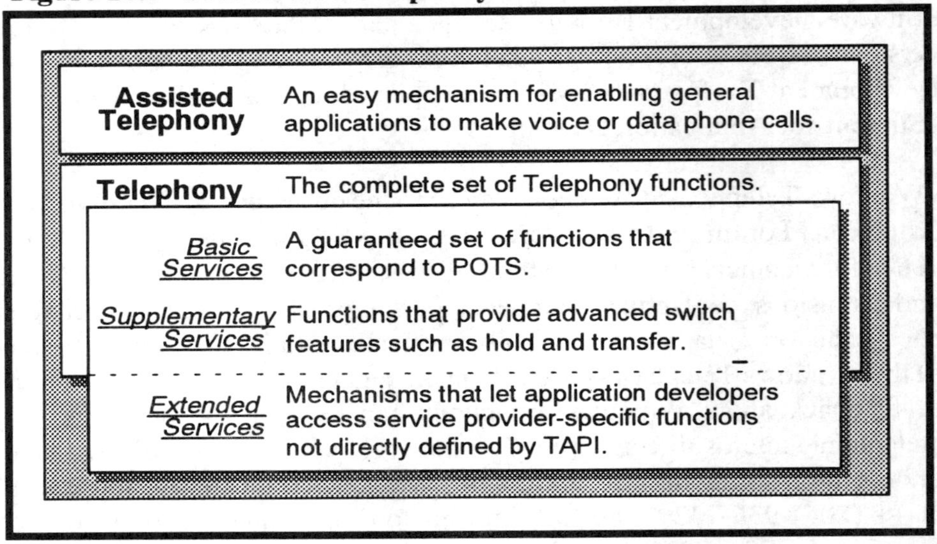

Figure 10.7 shows how requests from telephony-enabled applications are passed through TAPI.DLL to a full-featured call manager application for processing.

Figure 10.7 Path of Assisted Telephony Requests

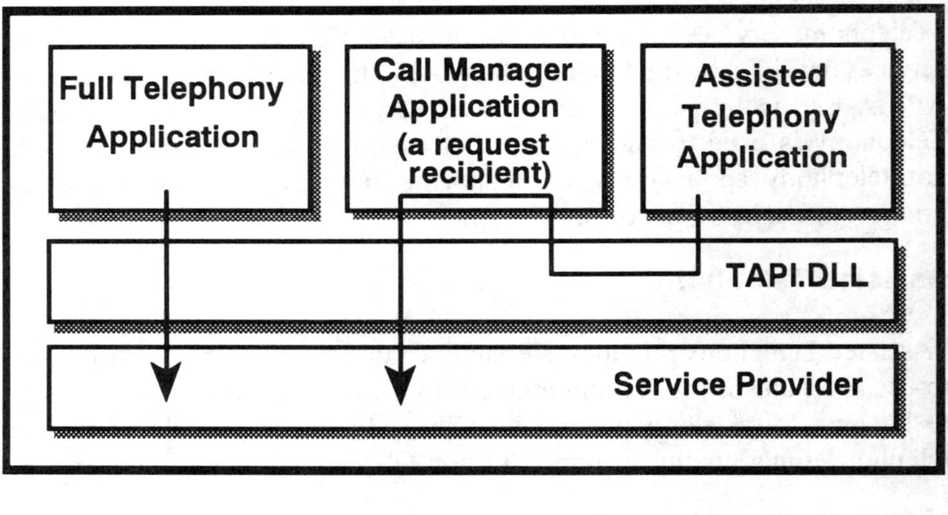

Basic Services

Basic Services are a minimal subset of the Windows Telephony specification. The functionality contained in Basic Telephony roughly corresponds to the features of POTS. Since all service providers must support the functions of Basic Services, applications that use only these functions will work with any TAPI service provider; minor variations in behavior are indicated in device capabilities data structures that can be obtained from the service provider.

The following functions are included in Basic Services:

Fundamental API interactions

- Initialization and shutdown of the telephony API
- Negotiation of API version
- Filtering of status messages to be received
- Opening and closing line devices

Capabilities and Status

- Querying line device and address capabilities, associated media stream devices, icons, etc.
- Querying line device, address, and call status
- Querying and setting media device configurations

Operations

- Translating addresses and setting associated parameters
- Dialing and answering calls
- Dropping calls
- Controlling call privileges and handing off call control

Supplementary Services

Supplementary Services are the collection of all the services defined by the API other than those included in the Basic Telephony subset. It includes features found on modern PBXs, such as hold, transfer, conference, park, and so on.

All supplementary features are considered optional; applications cannot assume that every service provider will support any particular supplementary service. An application can query a line or phone device for the set of supplementary services it provides using functions such as **lineGetDevCaps** or **lineGetAddressCaps**.

Note that a single supplementary service may consist of multiple function calls and messages. It is important to point out that the Telephony API, and not the service provider developer, defines the behavior of each of these supplementary features. A service provider indicates that it provides a Supplementary Telephony service only if it can implement the exact meaning as defined by the API.

Today, many programmers will use only the services provided by Basic Telephony. But others, such as those writing code for PBX phone systems, will need the functions of Supplementary Telephony. Soon, the demand for ISDN and other network services, along with advancements in telephone equipment, will drive even greater usage of Supplementary Telephony.

The following is a summary of the functions included in Supplementary Services:

- Holding and unholding calls
- Transfering calls, both blind and with consultation
- Conferencing
- Forwarding calls
- Parking and unparking calls
- Picking up calls that are ringing elsewhere
- Camp-on and other automatic call completion
- Accepting, rejecting, and redirecting incoming calls
- Securing calls from interruptions
- Generating in-band dial digits and tones
- Monitoring media mode, received DTMF digits, and tones
- Controlling the routing of media stream information
- Sending user-user information (ISDN)
- Changing call parameters on-the-fly
- Controlling the physical phone terminal (speakers, microphones, ringers, display, lamps, buttons, etc.)

Extended Services

The Telephony API contains a mechanism that allows service-provider vendors to extend the API using device-specific extensions. Extended Services (or Device-Specific Services) include all extensions to the API defined by a particular service provider. Since the API defines the extension mechanism only, the definition of the Extended-Service behavior must be completely specified by the service provider.

TAPI's extension mechanism allows service-provider vendors to define new values for some enumeration types and bit flags and to add fields to most data structures. The interpretation of extensions is keyed off the service provider's *Extension ID*, an identifier for the specification of the set of extensions supported, which may cross several manufacturers. Special functions and messages such as **lineDevSpecific** and **phoneDevSpecific** are provided in the API to allow an application to directly communicate with a service provider. The parameters for each function are also defined by the service provider.

Telephony Devices

The Windows Telephony API defines two *device classes*; the *line device class* and the *phone device class.*

The line device class is a device-independent abstraction of a physical line device, such as a modem. It can contain one or more identical communications channels (used for signaling and/or information) between the application and the switch or network. Since channels belonging to a single line have identical capabilities, they are interchangeable. In many cases (as with POTS), a service provider will model a line as having only one channel. Other technologies, like ISDN, offer more channels, and the service provider treats them accordingly.

Just as a line device class is an abstraction of a physical line device, the phone device class represents a device-independent abstraction of a telephone set. TAPI treats line and phone devices as devices that are independent of each other. In other words, you can use a phone (device) without using an associated line, and you can use a line (device) without using a phone.

Service providers that fully implement this independence can offer uses for these devices not defined by traditional telephony protocols. For example, a person can use the handset of the desktop's phone as a waveform audio device for voice recording or playback, perhaps without the switch's knowledge that the phone is in use. In such an implementation, lifting the local phone handset need not automatically send an offhook signal to the switch.

This independence also allows an application to ring the local telephone in a manner that is independent of inbound calls. The capabilities of service providers is limited by the capabilities of the hardware and software used to interconnect the switch, the phone, and the computer.

Media Streams

TAPI by itself provides control only for line and phone devices and does not give access to the information exchanged over a call. To manage this information (known as the "media stream"), developers need to integrate functions from other APIs into telephony applications. In this manner, TAPI works in conjunction with other Windows-based services such as Windows multimedia wave audio, Media Control Interface (MCI), or data APIs. This separation of control provides interoperability with existing audio or data applications.

For example, an application that provides an interface for managing fax or data transmission would use TAPI functions to control and monitor the line over which bits are sent, but the actual transmission of data is accomplished with functions from another API, such as the communications functions (known collectively as the Comm API) of the Windows SDK.

See the Windows SDK documentation for more information about controlling data communication devices. Generally, an API (such as the Comm API) is associated with a particular media stream. For example, the Wave API can handle the voice stream that is transmitted over a TAPI-controlled line.

The media stream in an "interactive voice" call is produced and controlled not by TAPI, but by one human talking to another. However, the line on which that call is established and monitored, and the call itself, remain in control of the TAPI application. The media stream on a "stored voice" call, on the other hand, is routed either to or from the PC (or both), generally using the Wave API.

Figure 10.8 APIs Complement TAPI

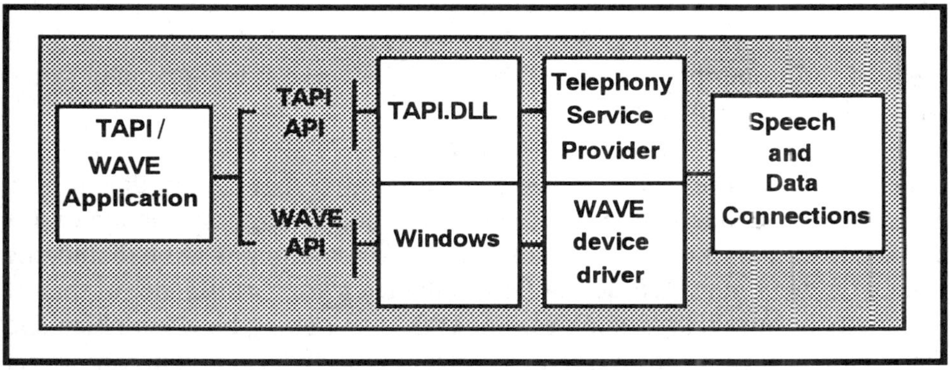

Address Formats and Address Translation

Many users choose to dial people, fax machines, bulletin boards, and other entities by selecting their names from an address book. The actual number that is dialed depends on the geographic location from which a call is to be placed. For example, a user may make calls from a portable or handheld computer and want to use a single, static address book even when calling from different locations or telephony environments. Or, a corporation may keep a master address book which is available to all users, who might be in different area codes or even different countries.

In the past, it was necessary to have separate address book entries, or separate address books, for each location from which a number might be dialed, which is a maintenance nightmare. TAPI's address translation capabilities let the user inform the computer of the current location and the desired line device for the call. TAPI then handles any dialing differences, requiring no changes to the user's address book. An application uses the **lineTranslateAddress** function to convert an address from the canonical address format to the dialable address format.

The canonical address format is intended to be a universally constant directory number. For this reason, numbers in address books are best stored using canonical format. The canonical address format used in TAPI is very similar to the international format for printed telephone numbers defined in ITU-T (CCITT) Recommendation E.123. It includes a "+" character, the country code, the city or area code surrounded by parentheses, and the local number. For example, the main number for Microsoft Corporation would be represented in canonical format as "+1 (206) 882-8080". Various other types of information, such as ISDN subaddresses, can be appended to the end of the canonical address.

The dialable address format describes a number that can be dialed on a given line. A dialable address contains part addressing information and is part navigational in nature. In addition to the actual digits to be dialed, the dialable address may include additional characters for performance of special functions during dialing, such as: hookflash; switching between pulse and tone dialing; pausing for a fixed time; waiting for a second dial tone, quiet answer, or calling card prompt tone; instructing the application to prompt the user to continue dialing; and dividing a phone number into separate dialing instructions. Although an application can use dialable addresses returned by **lineTranslateAddress**, it is not limited to them and can compose its own dialable numbers.

Information related to the current location, such as the country code, area code, and outside line access codes, is entered by the user through the Telephony applet in the Windows Control Panel. The Telephony applet can also store information on telephone calling cards, including card names, numbers, and dialing procedures. Applications can obtain and present to the user a list of available locations and calling cards, and update the Telephony environment based on the user's settings. The selected location and calling card information is then used by the **lineTranslateAddress** function to properly convert numbers in canonical format into the dialable format.

Call Handles and Call Privileges

A call represents a connection between two (or more) addresses. The originating address (the caller) is the address from which the call originates, and the destination address (the called) identifies the remote end point or station with which the originator wishes to communicate.

TAPI identifies a specific call by means of the call's handle, and TAPI.DLL assigns call handles as required. One call handle exists for every call known to an application, and an application can obtain call handles in a number of well-defined ways. Certain TAPI functions create new calls. As they do so, they return any new call's handle to the application. Sometimes, call handles are provided unsolicited in callbacks made to the application from TAPI.DLL, as is the case with inbound calls or calls being handed off by other applications.

Associated with each call handle is the application's *privilege* on the call – either *owner* or *monitor*. At any given time, one or more applications can own a call. While an application has ownership of a call, it is allowed to manipulate the call in ways that affect the state of the call. An application that does not own a call (but has a handle to it) is a monitor of the call and is prevented from manipulating it; it can only perform status- and information-query operations on that call. While one or more applications are owners of a call, still other applications can be monitoring the call.

An application can become an owner of a call in several ways. For example, an application that makes an outgoing call is the initial sole owner of that call. Ownership of an incoming call is assigned by TAPI.DLL to a single application based on the media mode of the call as indicated by the service provider and according to a user-settable priority scheme. Applications which have a monitoring handle to a call can also request to become an owner of the call.

An application that is currently an owner of a call can pass ("hand off") ownership to another application that has the call's line open. Such a hand-off can be to a specific application (by name), or to the highest priority application for a particular media mode. Handing off a call between applications never affects the state of the physical call as perceived by the switch or the service provider. A call can have several owners simultaneously, although the usual situation is for only one application to be the owner of a call.

Programming Examples

In this section, basic techniques for programming applications to use the Windows Telephony API are presented. The topics covered include:

- Using Assisted Telephony from Visual Basic
- Initializing the API
- Receiving and Processing Messages
- Version Negotiation
- Finding a Line Device and Processing Variable-Sized Data Structures
- Opening a Line Device
- Translating Addresses
- Placing a Call
- Tracking Call States
- Finishing a Call
- Closing the Open Line
- Shutting Down the API

Except for the first example, the source code fragments used in all of these examples is taken from the Dialer application which is included with the Windows Telephony Software Development Kit. The reader is assumed to be familiar with programming Microsoft Windows applications in the C programming language.

Using Assisted Telephony from Visual Basic

Assisted Telephony allows any application to be easily "telephony-enabled", or used to initiate telephone calls, even from macro languages and other environments which do not (easily) support functionality such as callbacks and parsing of variable-sized data structures needed to implement an application that uses the full Telephony API. See the description of Assisted Telephony on page for more information on how Assisted Telephony works and when to use it instead of the full Telephony API.

The simplest Assisted Telephony operation is **tapiRequestMakeCall**. This function allows an application to pass a telephone number and related information to the user's preferred call manager application (Dialer, by default) for handling. This programming example shows how this function could be used in a simple Visual Basic application. This sample application accepts a phone number and an optional name string (separated by a slash) from the DOS command line. This allows you to create Program Manager icons to dial frequently-used numbers by placing the appropriate parameters in the Command Line field of the Preferences dialog associated with the icon.

First, it is necessary to declare the function and any constants used. This is done in the general declarations section of the form:

```
Declare Function tapiRequestMakeCall& Lib "TAPI.DLL" (ByVal DestAddress$,
ByVal AppName$, ByVal CalledParty$, ByVal Comment$)
Global Const TAPIERR_NOREQUESTRECIPIENT = -2&
Global Const TAPIERR_REQUESTQUEUEFULL = -3&
Global Const TAPIERR_INVALDESTADDRESS = -4&
```

Here is the complete code for the application. First, it fetches the contents of the command line used to launch the program:

```
Sub Form_Load ()
    a$ = Command$
```

Next, it searches for a "/" (which would indicate a name to go in the Call Log follows), and if one is present, parses the command line into the address to dial (a$) and the name (n$):

```
    n$ = ""
    i = InStr(a$, "/")
    If i  0 Then
        n$ = Trim$(Mid$(a$, i + 1))
        a$ = Trim$(Left$(a$, i - 1))
        End If
```

It then passes these fields to tapiRequestMakeCall. If the result is 0, that means that the request has been accepted; it is up to the call manager application to do any further work.

```
retval& = tapiRequestMakeCall&(a$, "", n$, "")
If retval& = 0& Then End
```

If an error occurs (non-zero result), a dialog box can be displayed to explain what happened. This code builds up an error message string and places it in a dialog box:

```
    Beep
    b$ = "Your request to dial " + Chr$(34) + a$ + Chr$(34)
    b$ = b$ + " could not be fulfilled because "
    Select Case retval&
        Case TAPIERR_NOREQUESTRECIPIENT
            b$ = b$ + "no Windows Telephony dialing application is running and
none could be started."
        Case TAPIERR_REQUESTQUEUEFULL
            b$ = b$ + "the queue of pending Windows Telephony dialing requests
is full."
        Case TAPIERR_INVALDESTADDRESS
            b$ = b$ + "the number you specified is invalid."
        Case Else
            b$ = b$ + "of an unspecified error.   Sorry!"
    End Select
    label1.Caption = b$
 ' Position form on screen
    Left = (Screen.Width - Width) / 2
    Top = (Screen.Height - Height) / 2
 End Sub
```

The form (shown in figure 10.9) consists of simply the label area to contain the error message, an icon (for aesthetics, not function), and an OK button that simply ends the program.

Figure 10.9 Sample Assisted Telephony Application Error Dialog

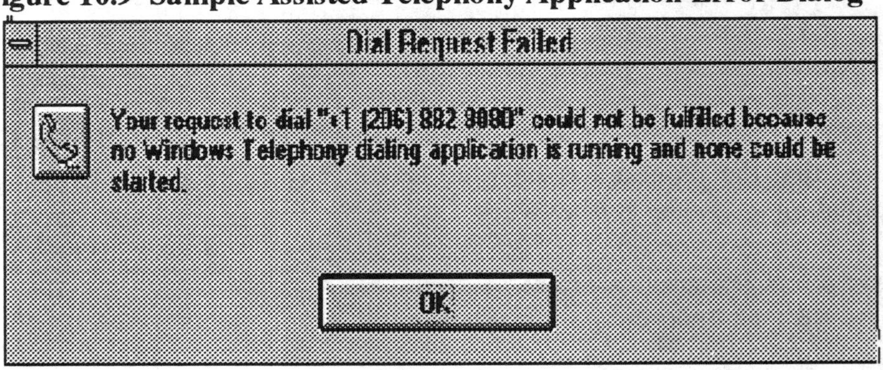

The remaining programming examples in this section apply to applications using the full Telephony API rather than Assisted Telephony.

Initializing the API

Before an application can call the functions of Windows Telephony for using a line device (other than the Assisted Telephony client functions), it must initialize the TAPI environment and enable function callbacks with the **lineInitialize** function. Invoking this function also informs the application of the number of line devices available. In the Dialer application, this initialization takes place in the **ErrStartTapi** routine.

After declaring local variables, **ErrStartTapi** calls **lineInitialize**. This is done as part of a **while** loop, because the function might need to be repeated if TAPI were in the process of reinitializing and waiting for other applications to shut down their use of the API. If the **lineInitialize** function succeeds (the result will be 0) or if some other error is returned, the body of the loop is skipped.

The app passes into TAPI.DLL a pointer to a DWORD where TAPI will return an "application handle" which the app must save and use in other TAPI function calls. It also passes a pointer to its callback procedure, which will be called whenever TAPI has a message for the application (more on that later). A pointer to the application name string is also passed in, as is a pointer to a DWORD where TAPI will return the number of telephony line devices in the system.

```
    while ((lResult = lineInitialize(&(vdts.hApp),hInst, (LINECALLBACK)MakePro-
cInstance((FARPROC)LineCallBackProc, hInst), szAppName,&(vdts.cLines))) ==
LINEERR_REINIT)
        {
        MSG msg;
        if (fFirstTime)
            {
            EnableWindow(HwndDialerMain(),FALSE);
            DisableDialerDesktop(TRUE);
            } /* if */
```

The loop calls **PeekMessage** to give other applications an opportunity to execute while it is waiting to TAPI to reinitialize, if that is necessary.

```
if (PeekMessage(&msg,0,0,0,PM_REMOVE)) {
    {
    TranslateMessage(&msg);
    DispatchMessage(&msg);
    } /* if */
```

Dialer waits for the reinitialization for up to five seconds. If that time expires, the user is given an opportunity to cancel the Dialer startup or continue to wait.

```
if (GetTickCount() - tc = 5000 || fFirstTime)
    {
    char szTitle[cchSzMax], szText[cchSzMax];
    LoadString(HInstDialer(),ikszWarningTitle, szTitle, sizeof(szTitle));
                    LoadString(HInstDialer(),ikszWarningTapiReInit, szText,
sizeof(szText));
    if (MessageBox(HwndDialerMain(),szText,szTitle,
        MB_RETRYCANCEL) == IDCANCEL)
        break;
    tc = GetTickCount();
    fFirstTime = FALSE;
    } /* if */
  } /* while */
if (!fFirstTime)
  {
  DisableDialerDesktop(FALSE);
  EnableWindow(HwndDialerMain(),TRUE);
  } /* if */
```

If an error occurs in **lineInitialize**, the function returns the error code (which is processed in another part of the code and an appropriate error dialog is displayed). Otherwise, it sets a flag show that **lineInitialize** succeeded, but if no lines are set up in the telephony system, an error is synthesized.

```
if (lResult != errNone)
    return lResult;
```

```
vdts.fLineInited = TRUE;
if (vdts.cLines == 0)
    return errNoVoiceLine;
```

Receiving and Processing Messages

An application receives information in two ways: solicited and unsolicited. Solicited information is requested by the application through a function call such as **lineGetDevCaps** or **lineGetAddressCaps**. Unsolicited information arrives in the form of messages – most importantly call-state messages. Often, the two mechanisms are used together, as when an application receives a **LINE_CALLSTATE** message, after which it checks the information contained in the **LINECALLINFO** structure by calling **lineGetCallInfo**.

When a TAPI application initializes its connection to the line service of TAPI.DLL with the function **lineInitialize**, it gives a pointer to the callback function it uses for that line service to TAPI.DLL. This pointer applies to all lines subsequently opened with the same application handle.

The callback function obtains a large amount of information for the application, including asynchronous replies, indications of Assisted Telephony requests, or messages resulting from ongoing monitoring of a line. These messages include indications that the status of a line, address, or call has changed; indication that media, tone, or digit monitoring has detected the requested event; and indication that information about a call has changed.

The callback function used in the Dialer application is called **LineCallBackProc**. It consists of a **switch** statement based on the message type parameter passed into the function by TAPI.DLL. The other parameters of the callback function are the line or call handle (which is passed depends on the message type), an instance value (which the application can optionally provide with the **lineOpen** function), and others which are dependent on the message type. Note that note all parts of the switch statement are shown in this document:

```
void FAR PASCAL _export LineCallBackProc
(DWORD hDevice,DWORD dwMessage,DWORD
dwInstance,DWORD dwParam1,DWORD
dwParam2,DWORD dwParam3)
```

```
{
    switch (dwMessage)
        {
        case LINE_LINEDEVSTATE:
            {
            if (dwParam1 == LINEDEVSTATE_REINIT)
                vdts.fReInitTapi = TRUE;
            break;
            }
```

To keep the size of Dialer's callback function manageable, the processing of call-state messages is performed in a separate function, newCallState, which responds to all call-state messages received by the application. It is in this function that call-state transitions (such as from *connected* to *idle*) are made known to Dialer as notification of the actual call states received from TAPI.DLL and/or the service provider.

```
        /* process state transition */
        case LINE_CALLSTATE:
            {
              NewCallState(dwParam1, dwInstance, dwParam3, (HCALL)hDevice,
dwParam2);
            break;
            }
        case LINE_CLOSE:
            ...
        /* handle simple tapi request.  */
        case LINE_REQUEST:
            ...
```

The **LINE_REPLY** message is sent to an application upon successful or unsuccessful completion of an asynchronous function. Dialer uses only three async functions: **lineMakeCall, lineDial**, and **lineDrop**. Only one of these will be outstanding at any given time, so the processing is as simple as taking note of which was done last and acting on the result. This code appears somewhat convoluted because of the intermixing of processing of calls on behalf of other applications using **tapiRequestMediaCall** (Dialer is an Assisted Telephony server application) and those dialed by numbers entered by the user manually or through **tapiRequestMakeCall** (which are processed as though entered by the user).

```
/* handle the assync completion of TAPI functions
   lineMakeCall/lineDrop */
case LINE_REPLY:
   {
   if (vdcr.requestID != dwParam1)
      break;
```

If the program state is making a call or abandoning the making of a call, the result is processed as being from lineMakeCall or lineDial.

```
   if (vdcr.mcs == mcsMaking || vdcr.mcs == mcsStopMaking)
      {/* reply message for lineMakeCall */
      if (dwParam2 != errNone)
      {
```

If the call was being made as a result of a **tapiRequestMediaCall** request, a failure notification is sent to the client application.

```
         if (vdcr.fIsProxy)
            SendProxyMessage(&vdcr, TAPIERR_REQUESTFAILED);
```

Dialer always closes the line handle it used for making an outgoing call after each call. By keeping it closed when it is not actively using the line, it allows non-TAPI applications and DOS applications to use the resources. It then hides the call status dialog it had displayed while the call was active.

```
         DoLineClose(&vdcr);
         HideCallStatusDlg();
```

If the call failed because no call appearances were available, the user is informed via a dialog that the line is in use. If any other error occurs, a generic error processing function is invoked.

```
         if (!vdcr.fIsProxy)
            if (dwParam2 == LINEERR_CALLUNAVAIL)
               DisplayLineInUseDlg();
            else
```

```
                    DialerErrMessageBox (lkszFromErrCode(dwParam2));
```

The internal program state is then set to show that no call is active.

```
            vdcr.mcs = mcsIdle;
            } /* if */
        else
```

If the call was established, the program state is updated. If the call was being abandoned, it is dropped (the call to lineDrop was deferred until after lineMakeCall asynchronously completed).

```
            {
            MCS mcsOld = vdcr.mcs;
            vdcr.mcs = mcsMade;
            if (mcsOld == mcsStopMaking)
                FDropCall(&vdcr);
            } /* else */
        } /* if */
```

If the message is an asynchronous completion of lineDrop, then the line is closed.

```
        else if (vdcr.mcs == mcsDropping)
            DoLineClose(&vdcr);
        break;
        }
```

Several messages are not supported; these are immediately followed by a break statement. Developers can enhance Dialer's functionality by enabling it to handle these currently unsupported call-state messages.

```
    /* other messages that can be processed */
    case LINE_ADDRESSSTATE:
        break;
    ...
    } /* switch */
} /* LineCallBackProc */
```

Version Negotiation

A Telephony application must negotiate the version of the API to be used during interactions with TAPI.DLL. This negotiation takes place for each line to be used. Dialer does this for all lines in the system, since it monitors activities on all of them for call logging purposes. The function used is **lineNegotiateAPIVersion**.

The application passes as parameters to this function the application handle returned by **lineInitialize**, the line device number for which negotiation is to be performed (which must be between 0 and one less than the number of line devices indicated by **lineInitialize**), the minimum and maximum API versions supported by the application, and a pointer to a DWORD in which TAPI will return the version selected for use with that line. It also passes a pointer to a DWORD where TAPI will return the identification code for device-specific (proprietary) extensions supported by the driver (the application can ignore this value if it doesn't use any proprietary extensions).

```
#define tapiVersionCur0x00010003
      lResult = lineNegotiateAPIVersion(vdts.hApp, iLine, tapiVersionCur, tapiVer-
sionCur, &(vdts.lprgLineInfo[iLine].dwAPIVersion), &lineExtensionID);
        if (lResult != errNone)
            goto Ldone;
```

If the function succeeds, it returns 0; a negative value is returned in case of an error. The most likely cause of an error would be if the range of API versions supported by the application did not overlap the range supported by the service provider for the specific line device – but this itself is actually quite unlikely to occur.

Finding a Line Device and Processing Variable-Sized Data Structures

The Dialer application opens all of the lines in the system for monitoring. It also provides a drop-down list control in the Dialing Options dialog to allow the user to select the line device Dialer is to use to place voice calls. As part of the **ErrStartTapi** function that is used to initialize the TAPI interface, it also scans through all of the line devices, opens them for monitoring, and uses the lineGetDevCaps function to identify those with voice dialing capability. Those that have voice dialing capability are included in the drop-down list.

First, Dialer allocates memory to hold the information it keeps internally about each line, and fails if insufficient memory is available. It sets the allocated memory to all 0.

```
    vdts.lprgLineInfo = (LPLINEINFO) _fmalloc(sizeof(LINE-
INFO)*(int)vdts.cLines);
   if (vdts.lprgLineInfo == NULL)
      return LINEERR_NOMEM;
   _fmemset(vdts.lprgLineInfo, 0, sizeof(LINEINFO)*(int)vdts.cLines);
```

Next, Dialer allows a buffer to store the data returned by **lineGetDevCaps**. An initial size is assumed, which is large enough to hold the information returned by a vast majority of service providers (lcbLineDevCapsInitial is declared as the size of the fixed portion of the LINEDEVCAPS structure plus 1000 additional bytes). If it is successful, the **dwTotalSize** field in the structure is set equal to the amount of memory allocated, to inform TAPI.DLL of the space available for returning information.

```
    if ((lpDevCaps = (LPLINEDEVCAPS) _fmalloc(lcbLineDevCapsInitial)) ==
NULL)
      return LINEERR_NOMEM;
   lpDevCaps-dwTotalSize = lcbLineDevCapsInitial;
```

Dialer then loops through the available lines. It negotiates the API version to use for each line (shown above), and opens each line for monitoring (not shown). It then uses **lineGetDevCaps** to get information on the capabilities of the line device. If errors occur, the startup is abandoned and the function returns the error to the mainline code.

```
 for (iLine = 0; iLine  vdts.cLines; ++iLine)
   {
   LINEEXTENSIONID lineExtensionID;
   char szLineName[cchLineNameMac];
   LPSTR lpszLineName;

   lResult = lineGetDevCaps(vdts.hApp, iLine, vdts.lprgLineInfo[iLine].dwAPIVer-
sion, 0, lpDevCaps);
   if (lResult != errNone)
      goto LDone;
```

If the function completes successfully, Dialer must still check to see if TAPI was able to return all available information about the line device. It does this by checking to see if the value returned in the **dwNeededSize** field in the structure exceeds the amount of memory allocated and indicated in **dwTotalSize**. This is done in a while loop because it may need to be repeated if the variable information changes between calls to the function. (In reality, it is unlikely that the data returned by **lineGetDevCaps** will change between functions, because it returns mostly static information. However, it is quite possible for functions that return structures containing status information to require more memory on consecutive calls. For the sake of consistency, Dialer uses a while loop like this one everywhere it needs to do a "check and reallocate" function.)

```
while (lpDevCaps-dwNeededSize  lpDevCaps-dwTotalSize)
        {
        DWORD lcbNeeded = lpDevCaps-dwNeededSize;
```

The previously-allocated memory is freed, and the new memory is allocated sufficient to hold the number of bytes indicated by dwNeededSize. The function fails if that amount of memory is not available.

```
        _ffree(lpDevCaps);
         if ((lpDevCaps = (LPLINEDEVCAPS) _fmalloc((size_t)lcbNeeded)) ==
NULL)
            {
            lResult = LINEERR_NOMEM;
            goto LDone;
            } /* if */
```

If the memory reallocation succeeds, the new amount of memory available is once again written to **dwTotalSize**, and the function is called again. If it succeeds, the loop cycles to check to see if all of the information was obtained.

```
        lpDevCaps-dwTotalSize = lcbNeeded;
        /* try it one more time */
                lResult = lineGetDevCaps(vdts.hApp, iLine, vdts.lprgLineInfo[iL-
ine].dwAPIVersion, 0, lpDevCaps);
        if (lResult != errNone)
            goto LDone;
```

```
        } /* while */
```

Once all of the information is obtained, Dialer copies into its local storage the parts that it needs to retain – in this case, the number of addresses supported on the line, whether or not the line supports INTERACTIVEVOICE calls, and the name of the line. Note that if no name is indicated, Dialer uses a default name. Note also the mechanism that Dialer uses to obtain the line name from the variable portion of the structure, and that the offset is from the beginning of the entire structure, not from the beginning of the variable portion.

```
        vdts.lprgLineInfo[iLine].cAddr = lpDevCapsdwNumAddresses;
        vdts.lprgLineInfo[iLine].fIsVoiceLine = ((lpDevCapsdwMediaModes & LINE-
MEDIAMODE_INTERACTIVEVOICE) != 0);
        if (lpDevCaps-dwLineNameSize  0)
            lpszLineName = (LPSTR)(lpDevCaps)+lpDevCapsdwLineNameOffset;
        else
            {/* use default name */
        ...
```

The remainder of code in the function is where Dialer selects which line should be initially used for placing voice calls.

Opening a Line Device

As was previously noted, Dialer opens all lines in the system for monitoring so that it can collect information to go into the Call Log. Dialer requests only monitoring privilege on calls on those line handles. When the user asks to dial a call (either through the Dialer user interface, or by a **tapiRequestMakeCall** function from another application), Dialer uses the **lineOpen** function to obtain an additional line handle on the line the user has specific to use for dialing. This occurs in the function **fLocalInitiateCall**.

This function first copies some information stored in Dialer global memory concerning the call to be dialed (not shown here). It then opens the specified line device with **LINECALLPRIVILEGE_NONE**, which means that Dialer is not interested in receiving incoming calls through this line handle, nor in receiving any status information about calls other than those it places itself.

The other parameters passed to **lineOpen** include the application handle originally given to Dialer by **lineInitialize**, the line device number desired, a pointer to a memory location to which TAPI will write the handle to the line, the API version previously negotiated on the line, the version of device-specific extensions desired (Dialer always uses 0, since it does not use any extensions), a callback instance which is passed back to Dialer in all messages pertaining to the line, the media modes for incoming calls the application desires to process (0, since no incoming calls are desired), and a pointer to a **LINECALLPARAMS** structure (which is used only when the **LINE_MAPPER** function is being used to scan for lines by their capabilities, which Dialer does not do, so NULL is passed).

If an error occurs, either an appropriate dialog message is displayed, or a failure message is returned, depending on whether the call was placed by the user or requested using **tapiRequestMediaCall**.

```
        lResult = lineOpen(vdts.hApp, lpdcr-iLine, &(lpdcrhLine), vdts.lprgLine-
Info[lpdcr-iLine].dwAPIVersion, 0, (DWORD)(lpdcr), LINECALLPRIVI-
LEGE_NONE, 0, NULL);
    if (lResult != errNone)
        /* display error or send message */
```

Translating Addresses

Whenever Dialer is going to use place a call, it uses the TAPI **lineTranslateAddress** function to convert the number to dial from the canonical (international) format to a dialable string that can be passed to **lineMakeCall**. It does this in the Dialer function **TranslateAddress**.

The parameters to **lineTranslateAddress** include the application handle that was returned by **lineInitialize**, the line device ID on which the call is intended to be dialed, the negotiated TAPI version, the original number entered by the user, the ID of the calling card selected by the user and a parameter forcing TAPI to use that card number, and a pointer to memory to contain a variably-sized LINETRANSLATEOUTPUT structure.

Dialer uses the same "check and reallocate" process for the **LINETRANSLATEOUTPUT** structure that we discussed with regard to the **LINEDEVCAPS** structure and **lineGetDevCaps**, so the code to reallocate the structure is not repeated here. Dialer also performs some manipulations on the phone number to allow non-canonical phone numbers to be expanded to full canonical format if calling from North America; that code is also not shown here.

```
if ((lResult = lineTranslateAddress(vdts.hApp, lpdcriLine, vdts.lprgLineInfo[0].dwAPIVersion, lpdcrszDialString, vdts.dwCardCur, LINETRANSLATEOPTION_CARDOVERRIDE, lpLineTransOutput)) != errNone)
    goto LTranslateError;
```

lineTranslateAddress returns both a "dialable string" which is passed to **lineMakeCall**, and a "displayable string" which can be safely shown in call status dialog boxes without fear of disclosing the user's calling card numbers to "shoulder surfers". Dialer copies these, and the bits showing the result of the translation to local memory for later use.

```
fstrncpyDialer(lpdcr-szDialString, (LPSTR)(lpLineTransOutput) + lpLineTransOutputdwDialableStringOffset, sizeof(lpdcr-szDialString), lpLineTransOutput-dwDialableStringSize);

_fstrncpyDialer(lpdcr-dialStringDisplayable, (LPSTR)(lpLineTransOutput) + lpLineTransOutputdwDisplayableStringOffset, sizeof(lpdcrdialStringDisplayable), lpLineTransOutputdwDisplayableStringSize);

lpdcr-dwTranslateResults = lpLineTransOutput-dwTranslateResults;
```

Dialer next checks to see if the call is being placed in North America. If it is, it checks to see if the leading three digits are "911", and if so it asks the user if they're sure they want to dial 911. This code is not shown in this example.

Placing a Call

Dialer invokes its internal function **DwDialerLineMakeCall** when it is ready to actually dial a call. It passes in pointers to structures containing the phone number to dial (previously translated from canonical to dialable form using **lineTranslateAddress**).

The most important function performed in **DwDialerLineMakeCall** is the processing of "dial pause" characters that might appear in the dialable string but which are not directly supported by the service provider handling the line device on which the call is being placed. Some telephony hardware cannot detect the call progress tones needed to properly handle these pause requests, but the need for the pauses cannot be ignored. The solution is for the application to prompt the user to indicate when the necessary tone has occurred and to cause the application to continue dialing.

First, the function sets up and initializes some local state variables, and saves off the initial dialable string.

```
/* %%Function:DwDialerLineMakeCall */
static LONG DwDialerLineMakeCall(LPDCR lpdcr,LPLINECALLPARAMS
lpParams)
{
    LONG lResult;
    BOOL fCallMade, fCallAborted;
    LPSTR lpchDialStart;
    char szCtrlCh[2] = {0,0};
    fCallMade = FALSE;
    lpchDialStart = lpdcr-szDialString;
```

Next, the function enters into a loop (which will be eventually exited by a return statement).

```
    while (TRUE)
    {
        LONG dwLineErrCode;
        int ichCtrl;
        char chSave;
```

During the first pass through the loop, the **lineMakeCall** function is used. Once the call is established, if the number has not been completely dialed due to the presence of dial pause characters which are not supported by the line device, **lineDial** will be used to dial the remaining portion of the number, after the user is prompted to tell Dialer when to continue.

```
        /* try to make the call */
        if (!fCallMade)
                lResult = lineMakeCall(lpdcrhLine, &(lpdcrhCall), lpchDialStart, 0,
lpParams);
        else
           lResult = lineDial(lpdcrhCall, lpchDialStart,0);
```

If the **lineMakeCall** or **lineDial** function returned a positive value, it means that the dialable string was accepted, and Dialer must wait for a **LINE_REPLY** message to determine the final outcome of the attempt to establish the call. This function exits, and further processing would occur in the Dialer **LineCallBackProc**.

```
        if (lResult  0) /* async */
           {/* we succeeded */
           lpdcr-requestID = lResult;
           return lResult;
           } /* if */
```

If the dialing attempt failed for any reason other than the presence of a dialing pause character not supported by the line device, the function returns so that the Dialer user interface code can display an appropriate message to the user.

```
        if (lResult != LINEERR_DIALBILLING && lResult != LINEERR_DIALDIAL-
TONE && lResult != LINEERR_DIALPROMPT && lResult !=
LINEERR_DIALQUIET)
           return lResult;
```

If the dialing failed because of an unsupported dial pause character, Dialer must identify the offending character. This switch statement converts the error code into a string containing the offending character.

```
        dwLineErrCode = lResult;
        switch (lResult)
           {
           case LINEERR_DIALBILLING:
              {
              szCtrlCh[0] = '$';
              break;
```

```
        }
    case LINEERR_DIALDIALTONE:
        {
        szCtrlCh[0] = 'W';
        break;
        }
    case LINEERR_DIALQUIET:
        {
        szCtrlCh[0] = '@';
    break;
        }
    case LINEERR_DIALPROMPT:
        {
        szCtrlCh[0] = '?';
        break;
        }
    } /* switch */
```

The saved dialable string is scanned for the offending character. The character is replaced by a semicolon, which will cause the line device to dial up to that point and remain in **LINECALLSTATE_DIALING**. The immediately following character is saved and then replaced with a null to terminate the dialable string.

```
ichCtrl = _fstrcspn(lpchDialStart,szCtrlCh);
lpchDialStart[ichCtrl] = ';';
chSave = lpchDialStart[ichCtrl + 1];
lpchDialStart[ichCtrl + 1] = 0;
```

Now that the offending character has been removed and the dialable string truncated at that point, the call is attempted again. If the original **lineMakeCall** failed, then **lineMakeCall** is used again, otherwise **lineDial** is used.

```
/* try to make the call again */
if (!fCallMade)
        lResult = lineMakeCall(lpdcrhLine, &(lpdcrhCall), lpchDialStart, 0,
lpParams);
else
    lResult = lineDial(lpdcrhCall,lpchDialStart,0);
```

Since the offending character was removed, if the function fails again, the problem is something that can't be handled by this function, so control is returned to the mainline code. Otherwise, Dialer sets up to process the asynchronous completion in **LineCallBackProc**.

```
if (lResult  0)
   {/* we failed again but shouldn't */
   return lResult;
   } /* if */
if (lResult  0) /* async */
   lpdcr-requestID = lResult;
```

Now that dialing up to the point of the desired pause is in progress, Dialer displays a dialog to ask the user whether Dialer should hang up or continue with the rest of the dialing. It passes to the dialog function the original error code indicating the type of pause desired, so that it can display a message indicating what the user should listen for. The dialog function returns 0 if the user indicated to continue dialing, and another value if the call is to be aborted.

```
fCallAborted = (DisplayDialingPromptDlg(dwLineErrCode) != 0);
```

Dialer then sets up the dial the remainder of the dialable string. It restores the character that it had originally replaced with a null, and sets its pointer for the beginning of the string to that position in the string. It also indicates that **lineMakeCall** has already returned, so that **lineDial** will be used to dial subsequent portions of the string.

```
lpchDialStart[ichCtrl] = szCtrlCh[0];
lpchDialStart[ichCtrl + 1] = chSave;
lpchDialStart += ichCtrl + 1;
fCallMade = TRUE;
```

If the user said the abandon the call rather than continue, Dialer drops the call; otherwise, it cycles to dial the next portion of the dialable string.

```
if (fCallAborted)
   {
   FDropCurrentCall();
   return 0;
```

```
        } /* if */
    } /* while */
} /* DwDialerLineMakeCall */
```

Tracking Call States

Once a call is placed using **lineMakeCall**, **LINE_CALLSTATE** messages are sent to the application through the callback function it provided to **lineInitialize** to indicate the state of the call. When Dialer receives such a message, it uses its function NewCallState to parse and process the message.

```
static VOID NewCallState(DWORD newState,DWORD callbackInstance,
DWORD privilege, HCALL hcall,DWORD dwParam2)
```

The first portion of this function involves the processing of messages for calls which Dialer is monitoring for the purpose of call logging. This processing will not be discussed here.

If the **LINE_CALLSTATE** message is for a call that Dialer initiated, it first checks to see if it is a duplicate of the preceding state, and ignores it if so.

```
...
lpdcr = (LPDCR)callbackInstance;
if (lpdcr-lcs == newState)
    return;
```

Otherwise, it saves the state, and then performs specific actions based on the new state.

```
lpdcr-lcs = newState;
switch (newState)
    {
```

If the new call state is **LINECALLSTATE_CONNECTED**, Dialer invokes its **UpdateCallStatusDlg** function to show the connected state to the user, or it invokes its **SendProxyMessage** function to send a message to the application which called **tapiRequestMediaCall** to indicate that the call is connected (note that both of those functions include code to check whether or not the call was made as a result of **tapiRequestMediaCall**, so that code is not included here).

```
        case LINECALLSTATE_CONNECTED:
           {
           UpdateCallStatusDlg(TRUE, lpdcrszCalledParty, lpdcrszDialStringOrigi-
nal);
           SendProxyMessage(lpdcr,TAPIERR_CONNECTED);
           break;
           }
```

If the new call state is **LINECALLSTATE_DISCONNECTED**, Dialer updates the call status dialog (not shown), and then drops the call.

```
        case LINECALLSTATE_DISCONNECTED:
           {
              ...
              FDropCall(lpdcr);
              ...
           }
```

Dialer does not have the capability to automatically redial busy calls, so it treats **LINECALLSTATE _ BUSY** and **LINECALLSTATE_SPECIALINFO** the same as **LINECALLSTATE_DISCONNECTED**. It does this by recursively calling the NewCallState function to set the **LINECALLSTATE_DISCONNECTED** state, indicating the substates for BUSY or UNREACHABLE.

```
        case LINECALLSTATE_BUSY:
           {
            NewCallState(LINECALLSTATE_DISCONNECTED, callbackInstance,
privilege, hcall, LINEDISCONNECTMODE_BUSY);
           break;
           }
        case LINECALLSTATE_SPECIALINFO:
           {
            NewCallState(LINECALLSTATE_DISCONNECTED, callbackInstance,
privilege, hcall, LINEDISCONNECTMODE_UNREACHABLE);
           break;
           }
```

The last state a call enters after it has been dropped in **LINECALL-STATE_IDLE**. When this message is received, Dialer hides the call status dialog or sends a message to the application that called tapiRequestMedia-Call (not shown here). Most importantly, it then deallocates its call handle to free resources in TAPI.DLL used to track the call. It then resets its internal call process state to show that it has no outgoing call in progress, and re-enables the controls on its main window, so that the mainline code will once again be ready to process another call request from the user or an Assisted Telephony application.

```
        case LINECALLSTATE_IDLE:
            {
            ...
            lineDeallocateCall(lpdcr-hCall);
            lpdcr-flsProxy = FALSE;
            lpdcr-mcs = mcsIdle;
            DisableDialerDesktop(FALSE);
            break;
            }
        } /* switch */
} /* NewCallState */
```

Finishing a Call

When the user clicks the Hang Up button in the call status dialog, Dialer calls its **FDropCall** function. If this is done before **lineMakeCall** has asynchronously completed (i.e., Dialer's internal state is not "mcsMade"), the drop is deferred until **lineMakeCall** completes.

```
static BOOL FDropCall(LPDCR lpdcr)
{
    DWORD lResult;
    if (lpdcr-mcs != mcsMade)
        {
        if (lpdcr-mcs == mcsMaking)
            lpdcr-mcs = mcsStopMaking;
        return TRUE;
        } /* if */
```

If an active call is in progress and **lineMakeCall** has completed, Dialer calls the TAPI **lineDrop** function. It does not pass any user-user information (which is indicated by the NULL and 0 parameters). If **lineDrop** returns a positive value indicating that it will complete asynchronous, Dialer sets up to process the matching **LINE_REPLY** message in its **LineCallBackProc**, and disables the controls on its main window while waiting. If the **lineDrop** function fails, Dialer indicates this to the mainline code by returning FALSE as the result of this function, and setting its internal state to IDLE.

```
    lResult = lineDrop(lpdcr-hCall,NULL,0);
    if (lResult  0) /* async */
        {
        lpdcr-mcs = mcsDropping;
        lpdcr-requestID = lResult;
        DisableDialerDesktop(TRUE);
        return TRUE;
        } /* if */
    lpdcr-mcs = mcsIdle;
    return FALSE;
} /* FDropCall */
```

Closing the Open Line

When Dialer is done using a line for an outgoing call, to keep from monopolizing resources that might be needed by non-TAPI-aware and DOS applications (actually, whether or not any such resources, such as serial ports, depends on the underlying implementation of the telephony hardware and service provider, but Dialer nevertheless does its best to be a "good citizen"). This is done in the function **DoLineClose**.

In this function, Dialer simply makes sure that its internal states show that it is idle, and then it invokes the TAPI **lineClose** function. It ignores any result returned by the function, since there's not much it could do about it anyway (whether or not this is ideal programming practice is open to discussion).

```
static VOID DoLineClose(LPDCR lpdcr)
{
    lpdcr-mcs = mcsIdle;
    lpdcr-lcs = LINECALLSTATE_IDLE;
    lineClose(lpdcr-hLine);
} /* DoLineClose */
```

Shutting Down the API

When the user exits Dialer, it calls its function **TapiDone** to disconnect from the Telephony API and release all of its resources. It deregisters as a recipient of Assisted Telephony requests (not shown), closes all of the lines that it opened for monitoring (not shown), and then calls **lineShutdown** to disconnect from TAPI.

If the initial call to **lineInitialize** had failed, then this function returns immediately.

```
void TapiDone()
{
    if (!vdts.fLineInited)
        return;
    ...
    /* disconnect from TAPI */
    lineShutdown(vdts.hApp);
    /* free the rest of the memory allocated */
    if (vdts.lprgdmr)
        _ffree(vdts.lprgdmr);
} /* TapiDone */
```

Special thanks to Toby Nixon, Microsoft's Windows Telephony guru and open architecture advocate. This chapter is based on Toby's white paper entitled: Developing Applications Using the Windows Telephony API. Toby joined Microsoft in January, 1993. He is the principal architect at Microsoft of the Windows Telephony API, and has continuing responsibility for co-ordinating the design and development of extensions, including migrating it to other platforms.

During the preceding nine years, Toby was Principal Engineer at Hayes Microcomputer Products, Inc., and represented Hayes on US and international standards committees on modems, facsimile, and communication protocols. He chaired US and international committees on modem command languages, and had a significant role in the development of several standards including V.42 (error control), V.42 bis (data compression), and the Class 1 and Class 2.0 fax modem command sets. He has worked in the data communication field for 17 years, and was co-inventor of two patents related to computer-modem interfaces. Toby and his wife Irene have five children. A true rebel, he appears to be the single employee in the Microsoft Systems Division to wear a tie to work every day.

11

Industry Players

So far, we have reviewed client-server architecture, telecommunications, and a variety of popular computer telephony APIs. You may be wondering if there are any vendors who can help you put all of this technology to work for your company. In fact, there are literally hundreds of vendors, systems integrators, and consultants you can work with to upgrade you customers service and virtually all aspects of your communication infrastructure.

This chapter provides a snapshot of the top vendors for a variety of technologies and services mentioned in this book. At the end of the chapter, a listing of company contact information is provided for your convenience in getting a hold of these computer telephony experts. Here's an outline of the industry players covered here:

- Telephone Switch Suppliers
- Standalone ACD Suppliers
- Programmable Switch Vendors
- LAN-based Voice Mail System Suppliers
- Interactive Voice Response Suppliers
- Application Generator Vendors
- Voice Processing Board Manufacturers
- Predictive Dialer Vendors
- Voice Processing Algorithm Suppliers
- Fax Processing Suppliers

Telephone Switches

Telephone switches take a variety of forms. If you have a small office, you may be using Centrex lines from the phone company, or a small Key Telephone System. Key Telephone Systems (KTS) provide a visual indication of each telephone line that is accessible for use in the entire system. Typically, you can press a button to put people on hold and "buzz" a colleague on the intercom or press a button to page one another. "Hybrid" KTS systems provide these capabilities and also some more sophisticated ones available on PBXs (Private Branch Exchanges). The PBX concentrates many telephone sets onto a relatively few public telephone lines. An Automatic Call Distributor (ACD) is a specialized type of PBX which is designed to handle a high level of calls of a uniform or specific nature: the caller is not calling to reach a particular person, but rather, is calling about a specific some*thing*.

Standalone ACD Suppliers

Automatic Call Distributors (ACDs) distribute large numbers of incoming calls in a logical fashion. The basic functions of a Automatic Call Distribution system are: Answer calls automatically as they arrive; If telephone Service Representatives (TSRs) are not available, place the call in a queue; switch the calls based on a pre-determined algorithm to a specific TSR group or other functional response unit; gather and make available for presentation, information which characterizes the performing status of the system.

The routing algorithm typically is designed to route the call based on: conditional routing which is tied to real-time traffic and TSR availability; networked directed routing which is based on the number that was called or the number of the calling party; caller directed routing in which a caller identifies the service that they require via an IVR; or data directed call routing in which the caller enters identification information that is looked up in a data base and used to route the caller to the most appropriate place.

An ACD accepts incoming calls and directs them to the TSR that has been idle the longest or to the TSR that has had the fewest number of calls. TSRs are usually grouped into functional units, which are called groups, gates, splits or queues. With the basic ACD function, calls are routed to the agent group that is associated with a particular telephone trunk or group of trunks. If TSRs aren't available to take a call, the ACD system holds the callers in a queue and plays an announcement or series of announcements to the caller. If a caller is in a queue for a pre-determined length of time, the ACD can be programmed to route the call to another TSR group.

Figure 11.1 PBX & Key System Suppliers

Supplier	Product Name	Computer Interface
AT&T	Definity G1/G2/G3	CallVisor ASAI
Comdial	DXP	Switch-to-Host Server Link
Ericsson	MD110	Application Link
Executone	IDS	Computer Port Interface
Fujitsu	F9600	TCSI
Harris	VoiceFrame	Host Interface Link (HIL)
InteCom	IBX/80 Telari	OAI
Inter-Tel	AXXESS	AXXESSLINK
Mitel	SX2000	Host Command Interface (HCI)
NEC	APEX/NEAC	OAI
Northern Telecom (NTI)	DMS-100	CompuCall (SCAI)
NTI	Meridian PBX	Meridian Link
NTI	Northstar	ACCESS
Redcom	MSP	
Rolm	9751 CBX	CallBridge
Siemens	Hicom 300	CallBridge ACL
Solid State Systems (Cortelco)	SR96,224,1000	Telecommunications Applications Bridge (TAC)
SRX	Vision LX	VisionPath
Tadiran	Coral	CoralLINK
Telrad Communi-cations	KeyBx	TelradLINK

Figure 11.2 Standalone ACD Suppliers

Supplier	Product Name	Computer Interface
Aspect	CallCenter	Application Bridge
Rockwell	Galaxy	Galaxy Transaction Link
Telcom Technologies	ECD-6000	Universal Data Link (UDL)
Teknekron Infoswitch	ISD/ACD	InfoExchange

Programmable Switch Suppliers

Programmable Switches provide a general purpose switching capability for a broad range of call processing applications. They are used in large voice mail systems, ACDs, predictive dialers and a variety of other specialized call processing applications.

Programmable switches are switches that are designed to be controlled from a separate computer system. They are available as fully-packaged configurations or as boards.

As discussed in chapter four, computer-telephone interfaces are provided by most of the switch suppliers. There is movement towards standardization with these links, but most were developed independently by each of the suppliers and are proprietary. The physical transport utilized varies from one to another but are standardized interfaces. Although the protocol varies from one CTI link to the next, the information and control functions are similar. The basic functions that are provided by a computer-switch interface include:

- Answer call: allow a call to be completed to a telephone set.
- Create a conference bridge: prepare to build a call having more than the usual two parties.
- Disconnect call: terminate an in-progress telephone call.
- Join existing calls: create a connection between two or more calls already in progress.
- Make call: initiate a connection.
- Place call on hold: temporarily disconnect a call from a telephone set without terminating the call.
- Report call progress: inform the application of call-processing events, such as party disconnect.
- Report station status: inform the application of the state of a telephone set, such as off-hook.
- Retrieve call from hold: reconnect a held call to the original telephone set.
- Transfer call: move a connection from one telephone set to another.

Virtually every one of these functions are available under the umbrella of CTI link protocols. these include CSTA, SCAI, and ASAI as detailed in chapter four. The emergence of the Novell Telephony Services API (CSTA compliant) is becoming a unifying factor since virtually all of the switch vendors are supporting it.

Figure 11.3 provides a snapshot of the primary programmable switch suppliers. Some of these switches are PC-based and use off-the-shelf boards from manufacturers like Amtelco, Dialogic, and Dianatel for the core switching functions. Examples of PC-based systems that are easy to integrate into virtually any topology are the TRT Pro/Switch 96 and the PCBX Systems TelCard. The Pro/Switch system uses analog, digital T-1, or ISDN line interfaces to connect to the telephone network.

Figure 11.3 Programmable Switch Suppliers

Supplier	Switch Product
Amtelco	XDS Switch Matrix Card
Cypress Research	PhonePro
Dianatel	SmartSwitch 96/192
Dialogic Corporation	DMX
Excel	PCX-512, LNX2000
Hays Microcomputer Products	ISDN System Adapter
National Applied Computer Technologies	LCX 120C
Natural Microsystems	VBX 1200
PCBX Systems	TelCard
Redcom	MSP
Rochelle Communications	Caller ID+Plus
Summa Four	SDS-1000
Telephone Response Technologies (TRT)	Pro/Switch 96 Pro/Switch 192

LAN-based Voice Mail System Suppliers

The basic capability that is provided with these systems is the ability for a user to access voice mail messages from the PC. Other capabilities that are provided with some of the systems include call screening and access to LAN E-Mail systems such as cc:Mail or Microsoft Mail.

Figure 11.4 LAN-based Voice Mail Systems

Company	Product	Operating System	
		Server	Client
Active Voice	TeLANphony	OS/2	Windows
Applied Voice	CallXpress Desktop for Windows	OS/2	Windows
AT&T	Intuity	Unix	
Centigram	One View	QNX	Windows
Enhanced Systems	Teloquence	OS/2	Windows
VMX/Octel	VMXmail	VRTX	Windows
VMX/Octel	VMX Desktop for Windows		Windows

Interactive Voice Response (IVR) Suppliers

IVR systems provide the capability for the caller to obtain information over the telephone. They are used to let the caller order something, leave information or obtain information. They are typically either *transaction processing* systems or *inquiry* systems.

Transaction processing systems permit a caller to order/change something or to leave information. *Inquiry* systems are of two types: Host IVR in which the caller is accessing specific account information which is of a private nature; and Information Provider (also referred to as Audiotex), systems which are used to provide 'public' information to a caller.

Figure 11.5 IVR Suppliers

Supplier	*System*	*Processor*	*O.S.*
AT&T	VIS	Intel X86	UNIX
Brite Voice Systems	BVS 2000	Intel X86	QNX
CCS	FirstLine	Intel X86	DOS
DEC	Alpha AXP 150 Voice System	Alpha AXP 150	NT
Edify	Electronic Workforce	Intel X86	OS/2
IBM	DirectTalk/2	Intel X86	OS/2
IBM	DirectTalk/6000	RS/6000	AIX
Intervoice	RobotOperator	Intel X86	OS/2
Microlog	Intela	Intel X86	UNIX
PTC	Vocom 40	Intel X86	UNIX
Periphonics	VPS/sp	SPARC	UNIX
Syntellect	VocalPoint	Intel X86	OS/2
TALX	TALX	Intel X86	OS/2
Telephone Response Technologies (TRT)	ProVIDE/Link	Intel X86	DOS

Application Generator Suppliers

Application generators are a set of tools that are designed to make it easy to develop voice processing applications. They are either Menu-Driven packages or Procedural Language Processors and some of them offer a graphical user interface (GUI). The functions that are performed by most of the application generators are:

- Define the individual Steps of the Script.
- Define the logic flow between the steps.
- Define the action to take at each step.
- Define the parameters associated with each step.
- Provide a display of the status of the call.
- Interface with external data bases.
- Capture statistics and generate reports.

Many application generators have optional packages that provide voice mail, fax processing and data communications capabilities. Figure 11.6 provides a list of the most popular tools. The following is a key to the types of products these vendors offer. Note that most full-featured tools include speech message editors with their respective offerings.

- ***MD - Text menu-driven***
- ***PL - Programming Language***
- ***GUI - Graphical User Interface***
- ***ED - Speech Message Editor Only***

Figure 11.6 Application Generation Tool Kits

Supplier	Product Name	O.S.	Type
Apex Voice Communications	OmniVox	UNIX	MD
Bit Works	Audio Works Station	MS-DOS	ED
Cascade Technologies	CAS Voice	OS/2	MD
CTI Information Services	Apprentice	UNIX	PL
Cypress Research	PhonePro	AppleTalk	GUI
Digital Equipment Corporation	DECvoice Builder	VMS	GUI
Expert Systems	EASE	MD-DOS; UNIX	MD
Infologue	VASE	MS-DOS	GUI
Info Systems	Talkie	MS-DOS	GUI
ITI Logiciel	Multi-Voice	MS-DOS	PL
MediaSoft Telecom	IVS Builder/Server	Unix	GUI
Parity Software Development	VOS	MS-DOS	PL
PCVoice	Assist Pro	Windows	ED
Pronexus	VBVoice	Windows/Visual Basic	PL
SpeechSoft	Speech Master	MS-DOS	PL
Stylus Innovation	Visual Voice	Windows/Visual Basic	PL
Symetrics Industries	ICON-O-Voice	Windows	GUI
Technically Speaking	Show N Tel	OS/2	GUI
Telephone Response Technologies	ProVIDE	MS-DOS	MD/PL
U.S. Telecom International	VAL	MS-DOS	PL
VoiceSmart	VX	MS-DOS	MD
Voice Information Systems	VFEDit	MS-DOS	ED
Voicetek Corporation	Generations	VAX/VMS; SUN	GUI
Winters Development	VoiceKit	MS-DOS	PL

Voice Processing Boards

These are boards that plug into a PC or minicomputer and include a telephony interface for handling all call-processing functions. They receive commands from and provide information to the computer system. The individual products work with specific computer busses (ISA, MCA, VME) and include support for specific operating systems (DOS, OS/2, UNIX, QNX).

Figure 11.7 Voice Processing Board Suppliers

Supplier	*Product Name*
Ava Technology	200L, 200U
Bicom	4LS
Brooktrout Technology	TR112/TR114/TR118
Dialogic	D/41D, D/121D; HD Series
Eletech Electronics	Vlink2
Innovative Technology	nitaAudioboard
Linkon	FC3000
Natural Microsystems	VBXxxx Series; AG Series
NewVoice	NV400, NV800
Pika Technologies, Inc.	AVA-2
Rhetorex	RDS 4108, RDSP/24000
UniVoice	UV-4

Predictive Dialers

Predictive dialing systems are programmed to dial numbers and connect the called party to a telephone service representative(TSR). These systems are connected into a database that contains information about each person that is being called. This information is provided to the TSR when the call connection is made.

Figure 11.8 Predictive Dialers

Supplier	*Product Name*
Davox	Collection Agency System (CAS)
Digital Systems International	MOSAIX, VoiceLink
Electronic Information Systems (EIS)	Call Processor, Call Manager, Gateway, ITC 5000, ITC 7000
Melita International	PhoneFrame
Noble Systems Corporation	Automated Telephone Organization Management System (ATOMS)
Teledirect International	CAT Plus
TeleSystems Marketing	Total Call Management Plus (TCM+)

Voice Processing Algorithm Suppliers

The primary technologies that are available to be licensed are speech recognition and text-to-speech. These vendors have established technology OEM (original equipment manufacturer) type relationships with both board-level vendors and system suppliers. Their chief role is to develop the algorithms and core technology for voice processing that other vendors package for resale.

Figure 11.9 Voice Processing Technology Suppliers

Supplier	*Speech Recognition*	*Text-to-Speech*
Bellcore	•	•
Berkeley Speech Technologies		•
Bolt Beranek & Newman (BBN)	•	
Centigram Communications		•
Digital Equipment Corporation		•
Emerson & Stern	•	•
Lernout & Hauspie	•	•
Voice Control Systems (VCS)	•	
Voice Processing Corporation (VPC)	•	

Fax Processing Suppliers

Chapter six provided a comprehensive overview of fax technology markets and topologies. This section provides a snapshot of the most popular fax processing suppliers including makers of boards, fax response systems and fax servers.

Figure 11.10 Fax Processing Suppliers

Supplier	*Fax Boards*	*Fax Response*	*Fax Server*
Alcom			•
Brooktrout Technology	•		
Faxback		•	
GammaLink	•		
Hayes Microcomputer	•		
Ibex		•	
Intel	•		
Nuntius		•	
Optus			•
PureData	•		
SpectraFax		•	
SofNet		•	•
TRT		•	•
V*Channel		•	•
RightFAX			•

Active Voice, Inc.,
2901 Third Avenue, Suite 500
Seattle, WA 98121
206-441 -4700
Robert Richmond - President

Alcom, Inc.
2464 Embarcadero Way
Palo Alto, CA 94303
415-493-3800
Maurizio Liverani- President

Amtelco
4800 Curtin Drive
McFarland, WI 53558
608-838 -4194
Bernie Torvik - President

Apex
14900 Ventura Blvd.
Suite 200
Sherman Oaks, CA 91403
415-291-0737/800-7APEX70
Ben Levy - President

Applied Voice Technology
11410 NE 112nd Way
POB 97025
Kirkland, WA 98083
206-641 -1760/800-443-0806
Dick LaPorte - President

Aspect Telecom.
1733 Fox Drive
San Jose, CA 95131
408-441-2200/800-541-7799
James Carreker - President

AT&T Global Business Communication Systems
211 Mt. Airy Road
Basking Ridge, NJ 07920
908-953-6422
Mike Lund - Marketing

Bellcore
290 West Mt. Pleasant Ave.,
Livingston, NJ 07039-0486
201-740-6074/800-527-1080
Anthony Lindsay - Marketing

Berkeley Speech Technologies
2246 Sixth Street
Berkeley, CA 94710
510-841 -5083
Dr. Michael O'Malley - President

Bicom
2 Corporate, Suite 202
Trumbull, CT 06611
203-374-0211
Mehmet Binal - President

Brite Voice Systems, Inc.
7309 East 21st North
Wichita, KS 67206-1080
316-652 -6500
Stan Brannan - President

Brooktrout Technology, Inc.,
144 Gould Street,
Needham, MA 02192
617-449-4100
Eric Giler - President

Cascade Technologies, Inc.
1430 Broadway, 7th Floor
New York, NY 10018-3308
212-768-7380
Vigdis Austad - President

Centigram Communications
91 East Tasman Drive
San Jose, CA 95134
408-942-3500
George Sollman - President

Davox
6 Technology Park Drive
Westsford, MA 01886
508-952-0200
Charles E. Carney - President

Dialogic Corporation
300 Littleton Road
Parsippany, NJ 07054
201-334-8450
Howard G. Bubb - CEO

Dianatel Corporation
807 Aldo Ave., Bldg 110
Santa Clara, CA 95054
408-980-8880
Gary Maier - Founder

Digital Equipment Corp.
1 Digital Dr., MK01-2/H10
Merrimac, NH 03054
603-884-2136
Ed Verney - Speech Products Business Manager

Digital Sound Corporation
6307 Carpinteria Ave.
Carpinteria, CA 93013
805-566-2000
Robert Knight - President

Digital Systems International
6464 185th Avenue NE
Redmond, WA 98052-5032
206-881-7544/800-877-VOICE
Michael L. Darland - President

Electronic Information Systems, Inc.
1351 Washington Blvd.
Stamford, CT 06902
203-351-4800
Joseph Porfeli - President

InterVoice, Inc.
17811 Waterview Parkway
Dallas, TX 75252
214-669-3988
David Brandenburg - President

Emerson & Stern Associates
10150 Sorrento Valley Road, Suite 210
San Diego, CA 92121-1604
619-457-2526
Dr. Sandra Hutchins - President

Enhanced Systems Inc.,
6961 Peachtree Industrial Blvd.
Norcross, GA 30092
404-662-1503
Michael Mittel - President

Expert Systems, Inc.
1010 Huntcliff, Suite 2235
Atlanta, GA 30350
404-642-7575
Carlton Carden - President

FaxBack, Inc.
1520 N.W. Greenbriar Parkway
Beaverton, OR 97006
503-690-6390/800-873-8753
Art King - President

First Byte
3333 E. Spring Street
Long Beach, CA 90806
213-595-7006
Ken Mattis - President

Gammalink
133 Caspian Court
Sunnyvale, CA 94089
408-744-1430
Michael Lutz - President

Hays Microcomputer
P.O. Box 105203
Atlanta, GA 30348
404-449-8791

Ibex
P.O. Box 148
Placeville, CA 95667
916-621-4342/800-289-9998
Ney Grant - President

IBM Corporation
IBM UK Laboratories, Ltd.
Hursley Park
Winchester, Hampshire
S021 2JM44
44-962-84-44-33
John Mears - Marketing Mgr.

Lernout & Hauspie Speech Products n.v
800, West Cummings Park,
Woburn, MA 01801
617-932-4118
Yacov Levy - CEO

Linkon Corporation
226 East 54th Street
New york, NY 10022
212-753-2544
Lee W. Hill - President & CEO

Melita International
6611 Bay Circle 220
Norcross, GA 30071
404-446-7800
Aleksander Szlam - President

Microlog Corporation
20270 Goldenrod Lane
Germantown, MD 20874
301-428-3227/800-926-3227
Bill Thompson - President

Mitel
P.O. Box 13089
Kanata, ON K2K 1X3
613-592-2122/800-267-6244
Colin Caton - Marketing Mgr.

Natural Microsystems
8 Erie Drive,
Natick, MA 01760
617-655-0700/800-533-6120
David B. Levi - President

NewVoice
10700 Parkridge Blvd.
Reston, VA 22091-5429
703-648-3181/800-347-6007
Paul Winders

Noble Systems Corporation
3297 Northcrest Road
Atlanta, GA 30340
404-851-1331
James K. Noble Sr. - President

Northern Telecom Inc.
2305 Mission College Blvd.
Santa Clara, CA 95052-8173
408-408-764-2090
Mike Glenn - Vice President

Open + Voice, Inc.
13771 N Central Expressway
Dallas, TX 75243-1017
214-497-9028
Conrad Masterson Jr. -
President

Optus Software, Inc.
100 Davidson Ave.
Somerset, NJ 08873-9931
201-271-9568/800-962-7422
Joseph Avalino - President

Parity Software Development
1721 Chestnut St., Suite 303
San Francisco, CA 94123
415-931-8221
Bob Edgar - President

PCBX Systems, Inc.
3730 South Susan St
Santa Ana, CA 92704
714-668-1180/800-755-7229

Pika Technologies, Inc.
155 Terrence Matthews
Kanata, ON K2M 2A8
613-591-1555
Peter Karneef - President

Pure Data Inc.
1740 South I-35,
Carrollton, TX 75006
214-242-2040

Redcom Laboratories, Inc.
One Redcom Center
Victor, NY 14564-0995
716-924-6500

RightFAX
440 E. Broadway, Suite 312
Tucson, AZ 85711
602-327-1357
Brad Feder - President

Rhetorex, Inc.
1671 Dell Ave. # 208
Campbell, CA 95008
408-370-0881
Alan W. Wokas - President

Rockwell International
1431 Opus Place
Downers Grove, IL 60515
800-722-5959
Jake Chacko - Marketing Mgr.

Rolm Company
4700 Old Ironsides Drive
Santa Clara, CA 95054
408-764-8057
Lorraine Hariton - Brand Mgr.

SRX
3480 Lotus Drive
Plano, TX 75075
214-985-2737

Stylus Innovation
One Kendall Square, Bldg 1500
Cambridge, MA 02139
617-621-9545
Michael Cassidy - President

Summa Four, Inc.
25 Sundial Avenue
Manchester, NH 03103
603-625-4050/800-544-3440
Barry Gorsun - CEO

Talking Technology, Inc.
4383 Piedmont Ave.,
Oakland, CA 94611
510-522-3800
Charles Wall - President

Teknekron Infoswitch
4401 Cambridge Rd.
Ft. Worth, TX 76155
817-354-0661
Michael J. Tamer - CEO

Telcom Technologies
981 Corporate Center Drive
Pomona, CA 91768
714-620-7711/800-366-8352
Al Taibi - President

TeleDirect International, Inc.
5510 Utica Ridge Rd.
Davenport, IA 52807
319-355-6440
Kathleen Kelly - President

Telephone Response Technologies, Inc.,
1624 Santa Clara Drive
Roseville, CA 95661
916-442-1878
Chris Bajorek - President

Texas Instruments
Telecom Systems
12501 Research Blvd.
M/S 2201
Austin, TX 78759
512-250-7111
Peggy Hart - Product Marketing

UniVoice Products, Inc.
1377 Main St.
Waltham, MA 02154-9521
617-736-0030
Scott Stingel - President

U.S. Telecom, Inc.
112 East 32nd Street, Suite D,
Joplin, MO 64803
417-781-7000
J.J. Kelly - President

Voice Control Systems, Inc.,
14140 Midway Road, Suite 100,
Dallas, TX 75244
214-386-0300
Peter J. Foster - President

Voice Information Systems
24 N Merion Ave, #353
Bryn Mawr, PA 19010
215-747-5035/800-234-VISI
Andrew J. Michalik - President

Voice Processing Corporation
One Main Street, 7th Floor
Cambridge, MA 02142
617-494-0100
Merrill Solomon - Chairman

VoiceSmart
The Grant Center
2160 North Central, 2nd Flr.
Fort Lee, NJ 07026
Alex Mashinsky - Vice President

VMX, Inc.
2115 O'Nel Drive
San Jose, CA 95131-2032
408-441-1144
Pat Howard - President

V-Systems, Inc.
39 Brookhollow Dr.
Santa Barbara, CA 92705
714-545-6442
David Droman - President

The author would like to thank Walt Tetschner for his thoughtful research and work which was the basis for this chapter. Walt Tetschner is the founder of Tern Systems, a company that provides market research in the computer telephony arena. Tern Systems is a leading supplier of market reports that address all segments of the voice and call processing industry. Prior to founding Tern Systems, Walt was with Voietek Corporation and Digital Equipment Corporation. He is the author of a book titled <u>Voice Processing</u> (published by Artech House), and his numerous articles on the same subject have appeared in a variety of trade journals and other publications.

12

Evaluating Potential Solutions

This chapter puts into practical perspective the methods you can use to develop computer telephony systems. There are many tools on the market that will make your application development tasks go faster. These tools target Value Added Resellers and OEM's, but any PC-literate person can build systems if the tools are chosen carefully. This chapter will help introduce you to the computer telephony business and give you valuable information about how to build successful, profitable systems.

Computer Telephony Today

Computer telephony (CT) systems today encompass a wide range of functions and capabilities all designed to do one thing: handle phone calls in an automated manner. Hundreds of thousands of times every day, callers place phone calls into automated systems that answer the calls, accept touch-tone commands, and deliver requested information to the caller.

CT systems have become enormously popular among businesses, and for one good reason: the firms who use them save money. A properly-designed computer telephony system can handle an incredible number of calls with little or no live operator intervention. This popularity has come about because these systems pay for themselves, often in less than a year.

Relatively low-cost but reliable PC platforms and high density hard disk storage devices have helped fuel the push of these computer telephony systems into the marketplace. With the advent of sophisticated script and forms-based software tools from companies like TRT, computer telephony application development has never been easier. Computer telephony hardware standards have also emerged that give system developers a relatively broad range of computer peripherals that plug directly into the standard ISA PC bus. These cards provide the interface between the phone lines and the computer - they allow applications to play and record speech messages and handle the generation and detection of touch-tones. Companies like Dialogic Corporation have contributed in major ways to the establishment of these now-mature standards.

Computer Telephony Application Segments

Let's explore the different classes of CT applications. CT systems can be divided into the following segments:

- Voice mail systems
- Automated attendants
- Automated Call Distributors
- Audiotex
- Fax-On-Demand
- Interactive Voice Response

Voice Mail Systems

The "grand-daddy" of all computer telephony applications, voice mail makes it possible for callers to leave messages directly in individual "mail-boxes," electronic repositories for spoken voice messages. Voice mail recipients can save or delete messages at will, while hearing the exact time and date when each message was sent.

Automated Attendant Systems

Automated attendant systems give callers the ability to directly connect to a specific individual at a given business. The caller enters the requested phone extension of the individual they want, and the system automatically dials that extension.

Automatic Call Distributors

Automatic Call Distributor (ACD) systems are designed to handle many incoming calls destined for large groups of live operators (service agents). Typically used by national airline reservation centers and rental car companies, these ACD systems quickly answer incoming calls, play a message to the caller letting them know their call will be handled in the order it was received, and connect the call through to the next agent when available.

Audiotex Systems

Audiotex systems describe a generic class of CT systems that deliver audio information to callers based on touch-tone requests. Corporate information and dial-a-sports-score hotlines are but a few examples. A very popular class of these systems are newspaper information hotlines, where callers select from hundreds of different categories to find out the latest in weather forecasts, regional sports scores, news items, and many other timely topics.

Fax-On-Demand Systems

As discussed in chapter six, fax-on-demand systems are a subset of computer-based fax (CBF), and the technology has significantly changed the way many businesses disseminate information. By combining voice processing along with CBF, it is possible for callers to dial into an automated system by phone and request fax documents to be sent directly to their fax machines. Many businesses face significant challenges delivering information to a large customer or user community, and fax-on-demand systems make it easy to distribute high-quality information to a very large audience.

Companies like Intel Corporation have committed themselves in a big way to using this fax-on-demand technology - virtually every printed ad they run is accompanied by the phone number to call and a document number to request to receive instant details on the advertised product.

Interactive Voice Response

Interactive Voice Response (IVR) is really a catch-all category for CT applications that use voice processing elements. A common thread that runs through many IVR applications is the need to access one or more common databases of information. Here are but a few examples:

Order Entry Hotlines This class of systems makes it possible for callers to place orders for products using their touch-tone phones. Usually, orders are charged to credit cards validated during the phone call.

College Registration HotlinesThese systems make it possible for students to register for classes without leaving their residence. For anyone who has ever registered the "old-fashioned" way (in an auditorium with thousands of other students fighting for classes), this automated method represents a significant reduction in time and frustration.

Choosing The Application Development Method

One of the most important decisions to make is choosing your development method. Here's a summary of the ways you can develop voice applications:

Application Generators (AGs)

For those who are comfortable using spreadsheet and word processing programs but may not be programming-oriented, the so-called Application Generator mode of development offers the best productivity. (Actually, "Application Editor" is a more accurate description - these programs don't "generate" the application for you; rather, you edit application commands into forms or screens.) There are two kinds of AGs: character-based and Graphical User Interface (GUI) based. Unless you absolutely cannot live without sexy-looking graphics, character-based forms let you do things faster. Maintenance costs are important to consider and are usually lowest with this method.

Script Languages

If you have a programming background, you may want to use a script language. Using this method, you create text files using a text editor and high-level statements like:

```
play( GREETING ); get_digs(touch-tone, 1);
```

The advantages of this technique vary depending on user experience. But be wary: language-based products claiming support for every voice card and accessory often only support the hardware manufacturer's low-level programming interface, leaving you to implement really useful features on your own. When inquiring about support for a particular voice card, ask the vendor for a list of ready-to-use functions "out of the box" - these are what truly save you time. Maintenance costs for script-based applications are generally higher than for application generator-based applications.

C Programming

So you're a really experienced programmer and you want to build your dream machine from the "bare-metal" up? Try programming the whole thing in the C language; without question, C is the low-level language of choice for voice system programs. All voice card vendors offer an Application Programming Interface (API) that allows you to execute card functions directly from C. Expect this for free: card vendors make their money on the hardware. Maintenance costs for C-based applications are highest and depend more on the programmer's talents than any other method.

Development Choices

So what is the ideal development choice? Pick a software company that can support several methods. Experience shows that different applications can benefit from different development styles - leave your options open unless you find a compelling reason to go with a vendor that only offers one technique.

Choosing The Operating System

One choice you will be faced with is deciding which operating system to use for your PC-based computer telephony platform. Usually, you will want to go with the operating system that you are most familiar with. Here are a few things to be aware of when making your ultimate choice. Operating systems can be split into two broad categories: some support the ability to run multiple programs simultaneously, some support multiple threads (a piece of a program), and some support both. Computer telephony systems can handle multiple voice lines simultaneously by either using the operating system's ability to run multiple threads (one thread per voice line) or by using a programming technique called state machines.

Microsoft MS-DOS

DOS is an operating system which was developed by Microsoft and has been the main operating system for PCs since they were first introduced. DOS is a single-tasking system which means that it can only perform one task at a time. This, however, does not mean that DOS is unsuitable for use in computer telephony applications. In fact, the vast majority of PC-based computer telephony applications are written to run on DOS-based machines. Programs can be written so that large numbers of callers (up to 48 or more) can be active on a single-tasking DOS-based machine. Although multitasking is not built into DOS, programmers have figured out very efficient methods for adding it themselves. In fact, this is generally done so efficiently that DOS systems can often operate with greater line densities than can other operating systems.

Microsoft Windows

Microsoft Windows is an example of a multitasking operating system which allows for running multiple programs (almost) simultaneously. Switching between running programs happens in a somewhat non-deterministic manner, which is why there are very few Windows computer telephony run-time systems in use today. Currently, Windows is good for single-port speech and game cards, but the operating system runs out of gas above four simultaneous telephone transactions. Windows does provide a suitable environment for CT service creation, however, so it is common for vendors to offer a dual architecture (i.e. DOS for the run-time environment and Windows for development).

Microsoft Windows NT

Microsoft's new version of Windows is called Windows NT (for "New Technology") which adds the concept of preemptive multitasking. This means that various processes running in the Windows NT environment will have a more deterministic control over the frequency and length of the timeslices given to them by the operating system. It may prove to be an excellent choice for CT systems.

UNIX

The UNIX operating system was developed by AT&T and purchased in 1992 by Novell, the world's leading vendor of networking software. UNIX computer telephony systems today enjoy a small but loyal following, especially for service bureau applications. Vendors such as Voicetek, Boston Technologies, and Apex have installed a variety of service-intensive systems for a variety of telephone companies and enhanced service providers with UNIX-based CT systems.

OS/2

OS/2 is an operating system which was developed jointly by IBM and Microsoft but is solely IBM's product at this time. OS/2 is similar to Windows in that it has a Graphical User Interface, or GUI. Like UNIX, OS/2 currently enjoys a relatively small but loyal following of computer telephony system vendors. Companies like Natural Microsystems, IBM, and Intervoice are OS/2 enthusiasts.

Which One Should You Choose?

In determining the operating system on which to build your voice application, the most important factor to consider may be your prior experience. For most applications, there would be little reason to learn a new operating system at the same time you are writing your first computer telephony application. It is generally wisest to stick with the operating system you already know.

Planning The Application

A sad but true fact is that many voice systems are developed with woefully inadequate planning before the application itself is constructed. A number of "tried and true" techniques exist to aid the development of computer telephony applications. The quality of voice systems that follow these guidelines should show a significant improvement over those developed without them. Your customers will notice the difference and you will be rewarded with far fewer support calls. For every hour spent on planning, it will save you more than double that time over the duration of the project.

The Planning Process

Let's get started. In the following sections we will address the steps for ultimately producing a solid plan and a tracking schedule for building successful CT applications. Briefly, here are the steps we will cover:

- Review the customer's list of requirements
- Hold the initial planning meeting
- Develop the Application Specification & Block Diagram
- Determine the phone lines needed
- Create the Development Schedule
- Start building it

Even if you are developing systems for in-house use, the steps discussed in this chapter are quite important to follow. It is not advisable to "jump right in" and start developing without the proper planning. This makes for disappointment and a lot of bugs.

Review the Requirements List

Usually, a written list of desired features or a Request-For-Proposal (RFP) has been generated by the "customer" (or head of the company or department where the voice system will be installed). You should be clear on what the CT system should do and how it should do it. Everyone who will be involved in the application or system development should thoroughly read this list of requirements. If one does not exist, ask for one to be generated. The following is a simplified example of a list of application requirements and objectives that you might get from a typical voice system customer:

XYZ Corporation Order Hotline Requirements

XYZ Corporation would like to have a voice system developed that will be installed at our corporate headquarters behind our phone system. This system is to have the following features in it:

Figure 12.1 Typical Feature/Function List for a CT System

Feature	Requirement Description
1	Answer all incoming calls within one ring and play a brief "Welcome to XYZ Corporation" greeting to callers.
2	A main menu will allow callers to select from one of several operations.
3	From the main menu, allow callers to transfer to any department phone extension using an audio directory of departments. If the party is not in or the extension is busy, allow callers to leave a recorded voice message.
4	Allow callers to press "0" to get connected to a live operator at any voice menu.
5	From the main menu, allow callers to place automated product orders 24-hours a day. Assume that customers who use this service will have a password and a list of product stock numbers in front of them when they call.
6	From the main menu, allow callers to hear product information messages from a list of products they can hear.
7	Maintain a database of orders that will be transferred to the host computer once per day.
8	Allow callers to hang up at any time without losing their entered order information.
9	Handle any caller Touch-tone errors in a friendly manner, encouraging callers to try again.

Since the customer is not the CT "expert" (you will be soon), look for areas in the RFP that need clarification. For example, in the above example requirements list, item #7 indicates that the company wants to maintain a database of orders and upload it to the host once per day. Many additional details would be required before you could estimate how long it would take to implement that feature: the type of host computer, method of transfer, database format, and so on need to be specified in detail. Keep notes on these open areas and prepare a list of questions.

The Initial Planning Meeting

Whether conducted on the phone or in person, this first planning meeting is very important. One of its purposes is to get, with as much detail as possible, answers to all the questions you have about their list of requirements. You also need to get a good idea from the customer as to when they need to have the system installed and running. Often the timing of "going online" is critical. One of the exercises you will be performing after this meeting is determining whether or not all the features they want can be developed within the desired timeframe.

Develop The Application Specification

Now is the time to translate the list of required features into a more complete roadmap of what the application will look like and how it will appear to callers. Without creating this specification, not enough information is available to adequately estimate how long it will take to develop the application. There are three essential parts to this specification: the Application Functional Details, Application Block Diagram, and Application Design Details. Let's explore each in more detail.

Application Functional Details

The purpose of this portion of the application specification is to describe, as accurately as possible, how the application will appear to the caller. This section is not intended to nail down technical details about how it will be implemented, just a clear description of how the caller will be allowed to interact with the application. One approach to preparing this section is to write it as if it were a manual that every caller could read to familiarize themselves with the way things should work when they call in.

Drawing from the Requirements List presented earlier, let's see what an expanded description might look like for one of the items. The following item

2. A main menu will allow callers to select from one of several operations. could thus be expanded in the following way:

2A. After hearing the opening greeting message, the main menu speech prompt will offer the callers five different possible operations:

- Connect to a live operator if they press "0."
- Transfer to any company extension if they press "100-199."
- Place an automated order if they press "2."
- Hear product information messages they choose if they press "3."
- If they press "9," the system will say good-bye and hang up.

2B. After selecting options "2" or "3," when they have completed their transaction they will be returned to the main menu to give them a chance to make another selection.

2C. If a caller does not call in with a touch-tone telephone (or if they do but don't press a touch-tone quickly enough), after 8 seconds the system will automatically transfer their call to the company operator.

2D. If a caller makes an incorrect touch-tone entry at the main menu, they will be allowed to re-enter their selection two more times before the system alerts them that there may be a problem with their phone. Notice that the above explains many details about how the "main menu" section of the application will work. The format of how this information is presented is less important; the content is what counts.

The Block Diagram

Constructing the application block diagram is the next step after completing the functional details. This diagram should show, in reasonable detail, all steps a caller can take in traversing the various menus in the application. The time to develop this diagram is before a single screen or line of application code is written. It will, in effect, be your primary guide as you begin to create the various sections of the application. When completed, it will also give you a good visual feeling of how easy or complicated it might be for callers to navigate the system - that is, how difficult it might be for a caller who wants to do a specific task to actually get there and start doing it.

Drawing the Diagram

There are several ways of actually creating this diagram. One is to get a large piece of heavy paper, a sharp pencil, and an electric eraser. The electric eraser will be needed for the many changes that will be made as you begin to build your application concept.

The preferred way, however, is to use a graphical diagramming program on your PC, such as allCLEAR by Clear Software, Inc. (Newton, MA). This program is moderately priced and very simple in concept but at the same time very powerful.

Choosing Box Names

Choose descriptive names for each block diagram box. This makes it possible for the names to also be used as Labels when creating the application - using either an application generator or a script language.

Labels are the identifiers that help to quickly locate where a particular application statement or screen is. For example, to represent the main menu in an application on the screen, “Main_Menu” would be a good choice.

Application Design Details

After completing both the Functional Details and the Block Diagram, it is a good idea to review them with the customer and get written approval before continuing.

The next major step is to develop the Design Details section. This section's purpose is to describe how all the application's features will be implemented - that is, at a very low level describing the individual specifications and design methods to be used. Keep in mind it is vital for the development schedule to be as accurate as possible - for the customer (so he knows when to expect the delivered system) and for the developer (so you know how much to charge for the project).

So what kinds of details should be developed in this section of the specification? To put it simply, anything that is not fairly obvious (to you) how it will be done. Taking one item again from our requirements list, let's see how it could be expanded: "Maintain a database of orders that will be transferred to the host computer once per day."

This example requirement is leaving out many important details - depending on the answers the task of implementing it could take anywhere from hours to weeks even when high-level development tools are being used. Figure 12.2 lists several questions that you need to answer before moving ahead on the CT application. These are consistent with information provided in chapter five on *making your database talk*:

There are probably several more questions that should be answered before expanding on them in this specification section. After generating the expanded list of questions, consult with the customer and resolve each question. Then take all the information you have gathered and write the application design details section.

Create the Development Schedule

It is now time for the final step: creating the development schedule. No matter whether the application is quite small or very ambitious, this step is an important one. Why do a schedule? Obviously, it will help you determine the duration of the project if it is done properly. This is important for two reasons. First, it gives you the ability to estimate your development costs and hence what you should charge the customer. Secondly, it gives you a benchmark to compare your progress against. If things start slipping, you can quickly alert the customer.

Figure 12.2 Database Questions for CT Application Development

Question	Database Fundamentals
1	What is the format of the database? (including the database record details, number of fields, etc.).
2	How are orders written to the database? (one record per order, one record per item ordered, etc.).
3	Is the database on a LAN or only local to the voice system PC?
4	If it is on a LAN, will other LAN-based processes be reading or writing the database at the same time as the voice system? (if so, this will require record locking to prevent data corruption from occurring.)
5	Is there only one order database file? If yes, what happens if you run out of records or disk space? If not, how many are there and how are they used by the application? (e.g., a different one used each day, etc.)
6	How will the file be transferred to the host? (e.g. RS-232 serial port, copy operation on a LAN, etc.)
7	What times should the file be transferred? (e.g., once per day at midnight, etc.)

Create the List of Tasks

The first step in creating a development schedule is producing an outline of the tasks that each developer will be working on, in the order they will work on them. If there is only one developer (you), then there would be one such outline. Then estimate how long each separate task will take. An example is detailed in figure 12.3 below:

Of course, in this example many more steps could be included. Notice the last two items: "Preliminary tests" and "Rework and retest time." After you have finished developing all the application sections, you will need to set time aside to test everything to be sure it works according to the application specification. During tests, you will undoubtedly discover problems that will need to be fixed, so the "rework" estimate is intended to cover that.

Figure 12.3 Application Task Time Estimate

Program Section	Task Item	Hours
Main menu & Basics	Error handling, transfers, etc	4 hours
Auto-attendant section	Transfer section	2 hours
Auto-attendant section	Audio directory	1 hour
Auto-attendant section	Leave recorded message	6 hours
Order Entry section	Menus, error handling	4 hours
Order Entry section	Database functions	16 hours
Product Info Hotline	Menus, etc	2 hours
Database Host Transfer	Build sample databases	2 hours
Database Host Transfer	Write host simulate program	8 hours
Database Host Transfer	Add functions to application	4 hours
Speech Messages	Create scripts	6 hours
Speech Messages	Record messages	8 hours
Speech Messages	Edit messages	3 hours
Pre-Launch	Preliminary tests	2 days
Pre-Launch	Rework and retest time	2 days
	Total development time	13 days

Scheduling Accuracy - What to Expect

If you have never produced a schedule for developing a voice application before, do not expect perfection with the first one. It is almost guaranteed that you will underestimate one or more tasks. Don't feel bad - even large established development firms miss on their estimates, and sometimes they miss by wide margins. One thing you can do to improve your estimates is to assume you have left something out and compensate for it by adding a "fudge factor." Depending on the relative uncertainty of the project, it is not unreasonable to increase your overall time estimates by 25% or more. As you do more application projects, you should get better and better at estimating what it will take to get the job done. With this knowledge, let's apply a reasonable correction factor to our previous estimates:

- Estimated development time - budget 13 days
- Estimate correction factor (30%) - budget 4 days
- Probable development time - budget 17 days

Produce a Time Line Chart

The final step in producing the development schedule is to take the individual task estimates and plot them on a time line chart, sometimes referred to as a Gantt chart. This chart is a useful visual tool for you and your customer - completion dates (called milestones) are easy to see as well as all the tasks that lead up to each milestone. The final milestone is when the project gets delivered to the customer and is installed. This chart should take into account working versus non-working days and show you the actual date when each task starts and finishes. It can be manually drawn on a large piece of paper and should not take too much time to do. If you prefer, there are several off-the-shelf programs (Microsoft Project is one) that make it possible for you to create this chart in a manner that makes it easy to make changes. You will find that any task changes made will cause all tasks that follow it to shift to the right, which means lots of erasing and redrawing every time a task slips or whenever a new task is added. Figure 12.4 is an example of a possible Gantt chart that you would create for a CT project.

Figure 12.4 CT Application Development Gantt Chart

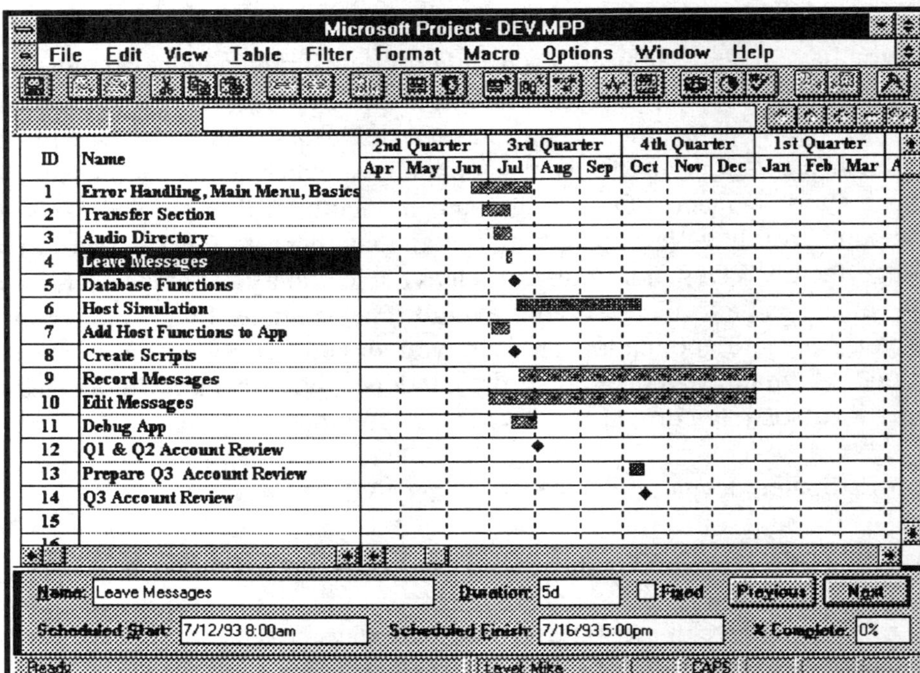

After completing the development schedule, present a copy to the customer and see if the milestones are scheduled to their satisfaction. It is always better to revise things at this stage (before the actual implementation begins) than to wait until development is already underway.

Determine the Number of Phone Lines

This topic is presented here because the determination of how many phone lines will be needed by the system is an integral part of the application planning process. If enough lines are added to a system so a caller never experiences a busy signal, the system is probably over-sized (and thus too expensive). In this case, many of the lines may be idle a good percentage of the time.

To properly determine how many lines are enough, you must decide on a blocking factor and know the average length of each call. This blocking factor is the probability that a caller will experience a busy signal. A typical blocking factor to use is 1% (that is, one out of 100 calls will experience a busy signal), and will usually adequately handle peak hour traffic.

Briefly, here is how to estimate how many lines your system should have for a 1% blocking factor. First, determine the average length of each application call and then estimate the number of calls expected during the peak hour (sometimes you have to take an educated guess).

The following equation will give an approximate idea of how many lines are needed so that very few callers will hear busy signals. Figure 12.5 gives an example of a "thumbnail traffic analysis." More sophisticated traffic modeling for high-density systems can be done with the aid of traffic tables and books on the subject. The *resources* section of this book provides several publications on the subject that provide great detail.

For example, if 250 calls were expected during the peak hour and the average call was 3 minutes long, the number of lines needed would be:

250 * 3 * 0.0238 = 17 (or about 18 phone lines).

Figure 12.5 Thumbnail Traffic Analysis

Lines = Calls/hr * Avg call * 0.023 = 8

where:

- ***Lines = total telephone lines required***

- ***Calls/hr = number of calls per hour during a peak hour***
- ***Avg call = length of an average call in minutes***
- ***0.0238< = constant value***

Once you have calculated how many lines you will need for adequate call handling, you can purchase your speech cards and related hardware.

When to Use Consultants

The mark of any professional computer telephony application developer is knowing when to bring in outside help. How do you know when to do it? One reason might be that the deadline imposed by the customer is impossible with your current level of help. Another is that one or more sections of the application are outside your area of expertise. In either case, finding the right consultant can save your project and make you look very good to your customer.

Where can you find qualified consultants? Start by calling your voice hardware or software firms and asking them for referrals. Usually, they will have a fairly good list of qualified individuals who can work for you on a project-by-project basis.

You should submit your Application Specification to two or three of them, with the tasks you want performed highlighted, and ask for a time and cost bid on the project. After discussing the technical details with each of them and reviewing their bids, the decision should be easy.

Building Applications With a Script Language

Computer telephony script languages were designed to bridge the gap between the flexibility programmers are used to in typical programming languages (e.g., C, C++, Pascal, etc.) and the ease of development afforded by Application Generators. Because of this, script languages offer a viable alternative to programmers who do not relish the thought of such a major undertaking in C, and to non-programmers who consider themselves power users of non-voice software tools (e.g., Lotus 1-2-3).

Skill Level Required

Script languages are not a panacea for all application developers because in addition to combining the best of the other methods, script languages also combine the worst of them. Using a script language you will gain flexibility over an application generator but will face a higher learning curve until you master the syntax of the language.

Similarly, you will trade the integrated development environment of most application generators for the barrenness of a programmer's text editor. You should possess at least the following skills, or acquire them, before undertaking application development with a script language:

Familiarity with common operating system functions. You should not be filled with trepidation and fear whenever you type : COPY C:\TEST*.* D:\TEST

Minimal experience with either a programming language or a macro language such as those included in Lotus 1-2-3 or WordPerfect. Although experience with conventional programming languages like BASIC, C or Pascal is ideal, experience with macro languages is equally suitable experience.

Familiarity with, or access to, an ASCII text editor (not a word processor such as WordPerfect, Microsoft Word or WordStar

Script Language Fundamentals

As with all development methods before you actually begin writing code you should outline the access paths through your application, preferably with a clearly-drawn block diagram. Most script languages are built upon blocks of code generally called functions, procedures or occasionally routines. Regardless of the term used the meaning is the same: these are fragments of code used to perform specific, usually discrete operations. For example a typical application may have functions to hang up, act as a menu, transfer a call, and accumulate statistics. Functions are generally discernible through some syntactic convention and in this example functions are enclosed by curly braces:

```
hangup play(HANGUP); set_hookstatus(ON);

} main_menu {get_response(); get_digits(1); }
```

Figure 12.6 Sample Script Language Code Segment

```
main_menu {
 play (MAIN_MENU_MSG, GET_DIG_TONE);
 get_digs(tt, 1d, 6s, call too_long);
 val_single() {
  case 1:
   goto trans_phone
  case 2:
   goto play_product
  case 3:
   goto leave_voice
  case bad:
   call bad_entry
 }
}
```

The above example shows two functions, "hangup" and "main_menu." Each of these functions makes calls to two other functions; "hangup ", for example, calls the "play" and "set_hookstatus" functions. Each function called by another function in your script must either be written by you (as "hangup" and "mainmenu" are in this example) or provided by the company from which you purchased the script language.

The power of a particular script language is influenced by two crucial factors: the ease with which you can perform low-level operations (e.g., getting a single digit, playing a single message, determining the status of a board, etc.) and the ease with which you can perform high-level operations (e.g., create complex menus, fax a set of requested documents to the caller, etc.). It is important that the set of functions provided by your script language include enough higher-level functions so that it is easy to create common application concepts such as menus.

Rather than build a large number of low-level support functions into their packages, some script language manufacturers choose to provide the low-level support through the ability to access code written in C. Although this approach has its advantages you should weigh it against the fact that you may end up writing some C functions to achieve your goals.

From Design to Code

After you have designed the application, you are ready to begin implementing the application. The first step in doing so is to determine the relationship between the blocks in the block diagram and the functions you will write in the script language. To begin with you should assume that you will have a minimum of one function per box in your block diagram. One of the keys to implementing successful voice applications is the design of these functions and how they will interact with one another.

When moving from a design to actual script statements there are a number of guidelines you can follow which will both speed you through the process and give you a more desirable process when you are finished. The guidelines can be summarized as follows:

- Write modular code
- Structure the flow of control
- Write reusable code
- Keep maintenance in mind
- Test frequently
- Use the tools

Each of these guidelines will now be discussed in greater detail:

Write Modular Code

The functions which make up an application should be written in such a manner that each function provides a single useful, well-defined service to the application. For example, in the typical voice mail application a caller will at some point be asked to enter his ID number and a database will be searched with that number to determine if the caller has any waiting messages. It would be reasonable to expect such an application to contain a function called "ask_for_id," which would play a prompt to the caller and gather tones from the caller. It should not perform the actual database search. The searching of the database should be performed by a second function, presumably called "search_database." The reason for this is that the "search_database" function will be able to provide a useful service to other branches of the program.

Structure the Flow of Control

Early software was often written in what was called "spaghetti code," which was so convoluted with "goto" statements and a general lack of structure that it was almost impossible to follow. The advent of structured programming languages and the lessons learned from them have carried on into most computer telephony script languages.

In large measure spaghetti code can be avoided if the functions created follow the modularity principle outlined earlier. However, you should additionally make use of the loop and control constructs provided by your script language. Looping constructs, such as "while" loops, "do-while" loops and "for" loops allow you to write script functions without using the often confusing "goto" statement. For example the following script statement will play a series of messages (presumably from a voice mail database):

```
not_done = TRUE;  while(not_done) {play(current_msg); if (current_msg == last_msg)
not_done = FALSE; else current_msg = current_msg + 1;  }
```

Using "goto" statements, this same function appears as:

```
not_done = TRUE;  start:  if(not_done) { play(current_msg); if (current_msg = last_msg)
not_done = FALSE; else { current_msg = current_msg + 1; goto start; } }
```

Although the improvement is minor in such a simple function, it should be apparent how the structure imposed on a program through the use of improved control mechanisms like loops will increase the readability of the code.

Write Reusable Code

Never assume that the application you are currently writing will be your last. Even if you are developing an application solely for use within your own company and have no plans for computer telephony beyond the current application you should always try to write reusable code. If you can reuse a function or other code fragment why would you want to waste the time reinventing the wheel?

Keep Maintenance In Mind

You should always write script functions with the idea that you will need to maintain the application, possibly for a number of years. Because of this, you should do what you can while first writing the code to ease that later maintenance burden. All script languages provide some method for adding comments to the actual script statements. You should make liberal use of comments, commenting sufficiently so that anyone reading the script will be able to fully understand it by reading the comments.

Test Frequently

The best way to develop voice applications using a script language is to test frequently. It is not uncommon to test each individual function as it is written. Doing so allows you to detect bugs or problems as soon as they are introduced.

Use the Tools

Hopefully you have selected a script language which provides more than just a language and the compiler to create a program or application from the script files you write; hopefully, the script language vendor has also provided you with tools to record and edit speech messages and to generate reports on the application you have written. It is also desirable to have reports showing if you have any unused (unreferenced) functions in your application. Another report which should be considered a must is one which will verify that required speech messages have actually been recorded and are accessible to the runtime system. Without such a report you must manually verify this or risk running a system which may be missing crucial speech messages.

Strengths and Weaknesses

To many users, application development using a script language offers the best of both worlds. You gain the freedom to use a standard text editor with which you can cut-and-paste text and can comment the script code to your heart's content. However, you lose the protective environment most application generators provide which through their fill-in-the-blanks, form-based approach.

In general, there is no reason to expect a script-based language to perform more or less efficiently at runtime than will an application generator-based application. In fact, some script language vendors like TRT provide compatible application generators allowing you to customize your development approach to a suitable mix of the two approaches.

Compared to development in a general-purpose language such as C, script development will provide a much-faster time-to-market, improved maintainability, and greater reliability at the expense of a potential loss of freedom. However, because most script language vendors provide a means of accessing functions written in C this loss of freedom is generally not a factor.

Using Forms-Based Tools

This section discusses what it is like using forms-based application development tools. These tools are advertised as the ones most likely to save you development time, some claiming to give you the power to create finished, polished applications in days. Do they, and who are they targeted for?

Forms-based tools encompass two fundamental types of voice application development environments:

- Character-based application generators
- Graphical User Interface (GUI) application generators

Each has its own strengths and weaknesses. What they both have in common is that to develop applications you do not write lines of C code or script - rather, you enter commands and parameters by filling in “forms.”

With character-based environments you are usually using pull-down menus to access the various features and functions that allow you to create applications in a step-by-step format: each “step” that is created typically expands to a screen of fields that are filled in by the developer. Each of these fields controls some aspect of the application: what speech prompts to play, how long to record a message from the caller, how many touch-tone digits to gather from the caller, and so on.

It is not uncommon for these screens to have integrated hypertext help and choice lists available to aid the developer in his or her field choices. With GUI tools, you usually use a mouse to click on a portion of the displayed application block diagram, revealing more details and ultimately bringing you to the same “fill-in-the-blanks” forms that are present in character-based environments.

Skill Level Required

Unquestionably, forms-based voice application tools are the easiest to use and require the least programming and technical background to be productive. Much more than script-only packages, forms-based tools can come with a significant amount of integrated tutorial help aimed at the beginner to computer telephony. The level of skill required can be as little as having familiarity with PC spreadsheet and word processing programs.

For the most experienced programmers, significant time can still be saved by developing the first few voice applications using forms-based tools. At some point, however, the forms most of these packages present may feel too "confining" to programmers. After developing a number of applications using "forms," some gravitate toward a script language package while fewer may opt to start building applications directly in C.

While the technical skills required using forms-based tools are the least of all methods, there still is a requirement for the user of the tools to think in a structured way when planning the application. Even when using forms-based tools, it is quite easy to get "lost" in the step-by-step details of constructing a large or complex application. In other words, forms-based tools do not dismiss the need to carefully follow the planning steps outlined earlier in this pamphlet.

Integrated Environments Save Time

A significant advantage of many forms-based software tools is that they are delivered as part of integrated work environments that contain virtually every utility and function needed to build complete voice applications. Tools are provided that allow the creation of applications, generation of documentation listings, editing of speech prompt scripts, and recording and editing of the speech prompts themselves. If the tools are designed right, they will be easily accessible when you need them. This saves the application developer valuable time, which really is the whole purpose of using higher-level tools rather than coding applications in C. If you are interested in going with a forms-based development package, be sure you check to see if the work environment model suits your needs.

Using the Tools

So what are some of the typical features and commands you can expect to use when using forms-based application generators (AGs)? This section presents a list of typical operations you can expect to perform, day in and day out, while developing voice applications:

- Edit the application block (flow) diagram
- Edit the application steps
- Record and edit the speech prompts
- Generate application listings
  - for block diagram of application
  - for step-by-step application details
  - for speech prompt usage
  - for detected application errors

Editing the application block diagram (sometimes referred to as a flow diagram) is most useful when done as part of the application planning effort before the application steps and their associated details are created. While not all AG's have the ability to generate a block diagram, the AG's that do generate this diagram after the application is completed miss the point of this all-important step: namely, to allow you to think about what needs to be developed before the application building starts.

Editing the application steps is the process of actually creating the step-by-step instructions that will guide the caller from the very start of the call to when they finally hang up. When you are in any AG, this is where you will be spending most of your development time. Working with a detailed block diagram as your guide, you will enter the function details that each application section requires.

Some AG products have context-sensitive hypertext help that shows you very specific help text for the field your screen cursor is resting on. If you have a choice, select an AG that has all the required information on-line.

The task of recording and editing speech prompts (and their corresponding scripts) is usually interspersed with the editing of application steps. Whenever you create an application step that "speaks" a speech prompt to the caller, you may want to immediately edit the script for that message, then later record and edit the speech message itself at a later time. AG environments that allow this can save significant development time.

You will typically generate application listings throughout the development process. This is done primarily for the purpose of seeing certain types of application information in front of you rather than having to view it on the screen every time you need it.

Build Modular Applications

Many design and development rules are "universally" valid, and developing forms-based applications in a modular way is no exception. The same rule is quite true for script and C language development. What does this really mean? Simply treat each functional application area as if it were a single stand-alone application. This is a helpful approach, because you can reuse application segments in other applications with little or no editing. In addition, you can fully test each application segment without reliance on other areas of the application.

Let's use the application sample discussed in the "Planning the Application" section as an example. The "XYZ Corporation Order Hotline" has several major features including the product information and automated order areas. Each of these segments was selected from the main caller menu so the application will likely "jump" to two different places in the application based on the caller's choice.

To develop each segment in an independent manner, don't use application variables that are common to multiple segments - if you do, you may need to keep all segments together that use these common variables. Also, don't jump from one segment to locations inside other application segments; rather, if there are common tasks that many segments need to execute, create a common subroutine that all segments can use.

Strengths and Weaknesses

Since forms-based tools are especially strong at constructing "application frameworks" (menus, submenus, and caller error handling processes), if the application you are developing has many such menu "blocks" you can expect these application generators to save you a significant amount of time as compared to script or C development.

If, on the other hand, your application has to interface with one or more time-critical hardware devices requiring interrupt service routines (e.g., analog-to-digital converter cards, pressure transducers, etc.) and these devices are not supported by an off-the-shelf software module from your software vendor, you are probably better off doing one of two things:

1. Write a special add-on software module in C that deals with such devices. Several application generator manufacturers offer add-on libraries that allow new low-level functions to be added to the basic architecture.

2. Write the entire application in C.

Maintainability of applications is another key point of comparison. After the application is "done," months later you may need to add or modify several features quickly. Not all application development methods are the same when it comes to this need. Applications built with forms-based tools are often the easiest to maintain. And because things are more "visual" with this method, maintenance is easier for individuals who were not the original architects of the application.

Recording Speech Prompts

When was the last time you saw a really bad commercial on TV, or perhaps heard a poorly-produced radio spot? If you are like most, it really stuck in your mind and reflected poorly on the company. Unfortunately for computer telephony systems, the very same thing can (and often does) happen.

One of the top deficiencies of CT application developers is failure to recognize the importance of using high-quality speech prompts. Without adequate quality, callers can be less willing to have their calls handled by an automated system. Nothing destroys the perceived quality of a voice system more quickly than hearing prompts that sound too loud, distorted, or unrehearsed. To do the job right, scripting, recording and editing high-quality speech prompts takes real effort and an understanding of what affects their quality.

Creating the Scripts

The first step in this process is to write down each and every word that is to be spoken during the recording session. What you want is for every prompt to be spoken in a clear, unhalting manner. The only way to ensure this is to prepare a script beforehand. Since each "prompt" will be recorded as a discrete message, you will need to clearly identify the prompt name or number, then the prompt text, depending on how your prompt recording and editing program identifies each individual message. For example:

Message 100: Thank you for calling XYZ Corporation.

Message 105: If you know the extension of the person you would like to reach, you may enter it now.

Message 150: That is not a valid selection, please try again.

The absolute best time to create these scripts is during the creation of the voice application itself. This is when you are constructing the application steps and when it is most obvious what each prompt should say.

A few hints for scripting applications:

1. When announcing menu choices to callers, always mention the digit to press at the end of the phrase. For example: "To hear a list of departments, press 5." This makes it easier for the caller to remember what to press.

2. Always refer to special keys on the telephone keypad in the same way. (for example, "star key ", "pound key ", etc.).

3. Try to always use the same error message prompts for similar errors. For example, whenever a caller makes an incorrect selection, always use the same prompt (e.g. "That is not a valid selection, please try again. ")

Choosing the Voices

When it comes time to record the prompts, the best thing to do is locate talent with solid experience in broadcasting to record them for you. These experts have learned to speak quickly, enunciate clearly, and adapt their voices to the style you are after. And because of their training, it is very likely that they will be able to record what you want quickly and without many retakes. Locating this talent can be quite easy. Make a few calls to local radio stations and inquire about the type of talent you are looking for (male, female, straight voice, animated style, etc.). Chances are you will find more than a few who will be quite willing to record your scripts. Now the next question: what kind of voices should you be looking for to match specific applications? Here are a few pointers:

1. Go for clarity. Clarity and intelligibility should be your #1 goals when searching for the appropriate voices to record your speech prompts. Make sure that the voices you choose can enunciate words clearly and distinctly.

2. Males usually sound better. With most computer telephony hardware, male speakers sound better because of the data compression method commonly used. That is not to say that female speakers always sound bad, but most male speakers sound less "scratchy. "

3. Avoid too much bass. Avoid male speakers with too much bass in their voice. Such voices can sound wonderful on the tape but usually sound awful when encoded and played back on computer telephony systems.

4. Avoid "hyped" style. Speakers that sound like "hyped-up" top-40 disc jockeys don't make for popular CT systems. Unless the nature of the application will specifically benefit from this style of speaking, it usually grates on most callers in a very short period of time.

5. Test several voices. Some voices that sound absolutely great on the tape may come across sounding raspy or rough when they are encoded. Test several different voices you think may work.

The Recording Session

Having created your scripts and selected the voices to use, the next step is to record the prompt messages. Here are a few points that should be considered:

1. Record "everything." One of the marks of a good computer telephony system is to have all prompts matching each other - that is, prompts should all have the same volume level, tone, and speech characteristics for a given voice. For this reason, it makes good sense to record prompts that you think are likely to be needed in future revisions of the application.

2. Recording room noise. If you are not conducting the recording session in a real recording studio, find a room that is free from noises like ringing phones, noisy air conditioning vents, etc. In particular, make sure the microphone being used is a good distance away from any PCs: hard disks and cooling fans in these units produce sound that can increase the noise level of any recordings you produce if the mike is too close.

3. Services are available. If you have prepared scripts but do not have the time or resources to do the recordings yourself, recording service bureaus can turn your scripts into professionally-recorded and edited prompts.

Recording Direct to Disk

The easiest way to record speech prompts for your computer telephony application is to run a program or utility that allows the voice talent to record directly to the system hard disk. With this method, the recording and encoding of prompts can be handled in one step. There are three basic classes of programs that allow direct-to-disk prompt recording:

- Integrated development environments
- Record/edit Utilities, software only
- Record/edit Utilities requiring special PC hardware

With the first two choices, the program is designed to run in a PC with at least one speech card installed of the same brand that will be used to run the application.

With the final choice, a special PC card must be installed that interfaces with an external microphone and includes a monitor jack for headphones or speaker amplifier. Each method has its strengths and weaknesses. Figure 12.7 shows a typical screen layout for the many sound editing packages on the market for PC-based components.

Figure 12.7 Screen From PC-based Sound Editor Application

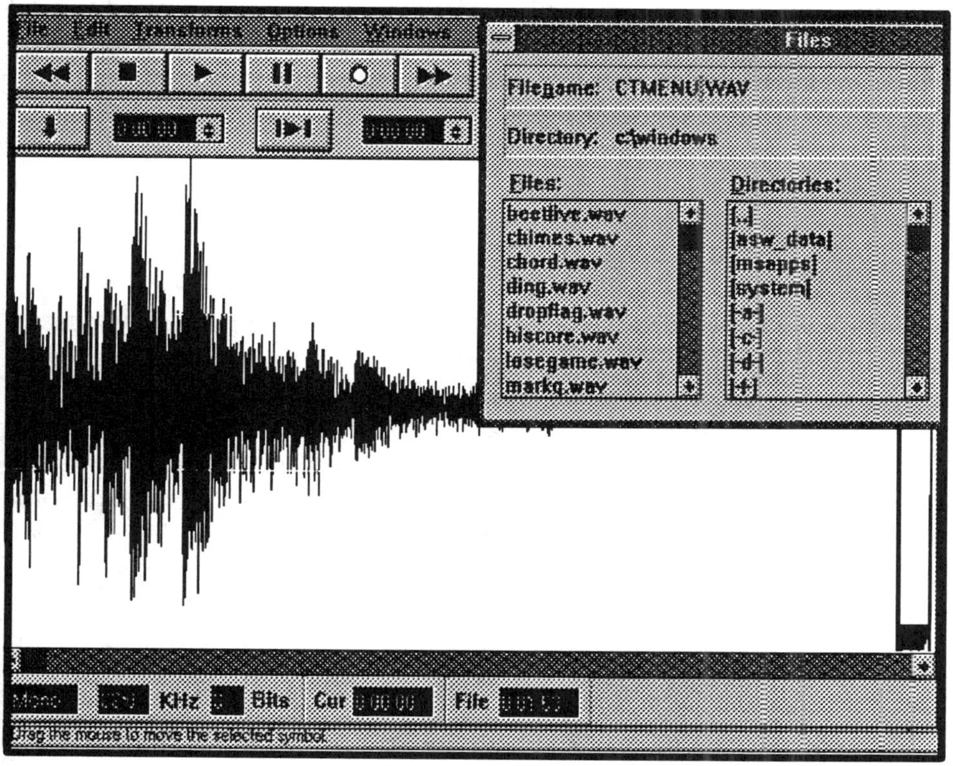

Integrated Development Environments

These "Application Generator" products often include a built-in set of features that enables the application developer to maintain scripts and record them from within a single screen. The advantage of this method is that, because it is fully integrated with the application creation tools, it is relatively easy to jump back and forth between the creation of application steps and the creation of the prompts that each step needs. For an experienced developer this can save significant time.

Record/Edit Utilities

If you have a very large number of prompts to record and edit, need exceptionally high speech quality, need to generate special tones or special effects, or have special editing needs (e.g., cut-and-paste operations), then you will probably want to use one of several products that address these needs.

Bit Works Audio Works Station

This product has earned the reputation in the computer telephony industry as the best set of hardware and software tools to create and edit the absolute highest quality speech prompts. The package includes a PC card with very low-noise high quality circuitry that allows direct recording to disk in a variety of formats. Jacks are provided that allow you to plug in a microphone and headphones directly. The on-card digital signal processing chip works in conjunction with the software to provide real-time filtering, level control, multi-band equalization, and encoding based on settings you choose.

Voice Information Systems VFEdit

This product is a graphical Windows application that gives you the ability to record and edit speech messages using the native speech card that will be running your application. This means you do not have to purchase special hardware to use all the supported operations. VFEdit supports the ability to record and review discrete prompt files as well as Macro File prompts, with thousands of individual prompts in a single file yielding better run-time performance. It is possible to easily edit prompts by "cropping" their beginning and ending regions; or you can use the mouse to grab a segment of a prompt and cut it out and/or paste it into another message.

Recording to Tape

When application scripts are recorded to tape, an additional step must be executed as compared with recording direct to disk. This step is needed to create the actual prompt files that the computer telephony system needs. It is important to record to tape first for several reasons:

Use of different encoding methods. Let's say you recorded the entire application script direct to disk at a particular sampling rate and using a specific speech card or encoding method (e.g., ADPCM, PCM, WAV, VOC, etc.). If you later desire to import the exact same series of prompts to another format, you may not be able to convert the prompt files without causing a significant decrease in speech quality and/or increase in noise. Prompts recorded on tape can easily be used to generate a new set of encoded prompt files using the exact same recorded script source tape.

Original tape - a natural archive If for any reason you need to regenerate a prompt file, the tape of the recorded script is a convenient archive that you can easily access and use.

Tape Recording Hints

Here are a few hints to help you get the most out of your tape recorded scripts:

Choosing the microphone. Any microphone with a relatively flat frequency response between 100 and 10 kHz should be more than acceptable.

Perform silence test first. Each time before you start a recording session, at the start of a fresh tape record:

- 10 seconds of silence with the microphone turned off
- 10 seconds of silence with the microphone turned on

Play the results back and be sure the difference between the two segments is noticeable but not too pronounced.

Keep levels high enough. Be sure you record at sufficiently high levels on the tape. If you do, tape noise will not be a significant percentage of the recorded audio.

Questions and Answers: Buying Computer Telephony Tools

This section presents a series of comprehensive questions you should be asking potential voice software tools vendors before you decide who's software product to use.

Open Architecture Questions

"Does the software vendor let you add ready-to-use "modules" to applications with a minimum of hassle?" Your application should be able to communicate with host computers, access on-line databases, accept credit-card charges, provide fax-on-demand services, handle line switching and resource sharing, and so on. Virtually all voice software vendors charge extra for add-on features like this; you may not need them now, but explore their depth of add-on module coverage. Find out how easy it is to use the functions these modules offer - if it was done right, it will simply extend the command set of the base package.

"Is a C language development toolkit available?" Without it, you can only do things that your vendor has already thought about and supported. Even if you don't write the C code, you should be able to support virtually any new hardware device or software process. Ask how much effort is involved in passing parameters (e.g., touch-tone digits) between user-written modules and your application. Some vendors give you a lean interface that is difficult to use.

Application Generator Questions

"How easy is it to use the program's features, day after day?" Application generators should make these things easy and intuitive. The user interface should use pull-down menus, choice lists, and command "buttons" to make the system easier to navigate.

"Does the vendor offer on-line help for all commands and application functions?" Context-sensitive hypertext help is best. This minimizes the need to look in the technical manuals. When a company says they have on-line help, ask how it works or, better still, get a demo. Some products have a poor concept of what "help" really means. If the vendor says the entire technical guide is on-line, consider it a plus.

"Can you record and edit speech messages and their scripts without leaving the main AG program?" Some do, some don't. If the product forces you to run totally different programs to deal with messages, you're wasting valuable time.

Speech Message Questions

Speech messages, those disk-based "sound bites" that callers hear (and record when they leave messages), are a very fundamental resource to PC-based voice applications.

"Can the vendor handle applications that use thousands of on-line speech messages?" It is most desirable if the vendor can provide this capability. Today's voice/call processing applications must be able to offer callers a multitude of services in a single system, from voice mail to fax-on-demand. The more caller features you offer, the more speech messages you will need. A minimum should be 50,000 to allow for growth and complex applications.

"Is it easy to access messages from separate physical drives, sub-directories, and ram disks?" The answer should be yes if you are concerned at all about performance. Operating systems like MS-DOS cannot efficiently search for more than several hundred speech messages in a single subdirectory, and ram-disks are a great place for your most-often-played messages.

"Is the location (i.e., the drive, directory, and filename) of each speech message "hard-wired" into the application?" Hard-wired speech messages are a thing of the past. You can be faced with a significant editing task every time you want to make significant changes to your application if this is the case..

"Does the vendor support both discrete and "packed" speech message files?" Discrete message files contain speech information for a single message; "packed" message files (sometimes referred to as Macro Files or "VAP" files) contain speech message and script information for hundreds to thousands of speech messages. The latter provide improved access-time and thus better performance - if your application needs thousands of messages on-line, these are the only way to go. If your vendor can handle both types of speech messages, you've got a winner.

"Can you easily create and edit scripts for all speech messages in your application?" Some software tools limit the number of messages that can have scripts, and some don't support script maintenance at all. If you are using an AG product, choose a vendor that lets you maintain scripts directly in the speech message editor.

"Can you reference messages symbolically in applications?" Script languages always allow you to reference messages using symbolic names like "GREETING ", "ENTRY_ERROR ", and the like. Some AG products reference messages by number and others allow the use of names. If this is important to you, be sure to ask.

Script Language Questions

"What do the script language statements look like?" Do they look like the BASIC, C, or PASCAL languages you may be familiar with? Ask to see a sample application listing. The more arcane the language syntax is, the harder it may be for you to learn. The best choice is to have your script language emulate the C language - this should make it relatively easy for your application developers to master it.

"Is it possible to easily move an application between the script and AG environments?" If the vendor supports both script and AG development, you will want the flexibility of taking script-based applications and loading them into the AG (and back to script again). This is especially important if you will have more than one application developer.

"Is an integrated script language development environment available?" This saves even more time - you can edit script files in multiple windows, compile with a single keystroke, and have your cursor directed to each compiler error with a minimum of keystrokes. These environments (like Borland's Turbo C++ product) even allow you to position your edit cursor over a keyword and get instant hypertext help.

Run-Time Engine Questions

After you have developed your application, most voice software products require you to load one or more application files into the companion "run-time" program - that is, the program that executes the step-by-step instructions you created using the development tools.

"How many voice lines can be supported in a single PC?" Most vendors support at least 24 lines (a single T-1 span) in a single PC-based system. If you need support for more than 24 lines, find out how many PC's are required since each additional PC increases your total system costs. If support is claimed for more than 48 lines, ask how they achieve acceptable performance.

"How does your vendor treat system errors?" Most applications must run 24-hours a day, 7 days a week. Callers have little patience for equipment or application failures. Be absolutely sure that run-time failures generate a clear, concise critical error message that alerts the system operator immediately. Not all software vendors consider this important. Some vendors even omit documentation on errors altogether. Ask for a complete listing and description of all possible run-time errors - the longer the list, the more they consider this a key issue.

"Does the run-time system accumulate and save call statistics?" At some point you are going to want call statistics from your run-time system. Without them, you cannot really know how successful your application is. The figure below details a minimum number of CT activity statistics for any system.

"Is it possible to remotely control your run-time system?" Say your customer calls you and needs an urgent change made to his application. How will you respond if you don't have someone at the customer site to help? UNIX application environments have remote console access as a built-in feature of the operating system; MS-DOS platforms do not. Many voice VARs use programs like PC-Anywhere or Carbon Copy to give them dial-in access to customer voice systems. This makes it possible to do everything from uploading new applications to printing statistics reports - all without leaving your cozy office. Be sure your run-time platform peacefully co-exists with remote control programs. Ask what programs have been validated by the vendor.

Figure 12.8 Sample of Call Statistics for Computer Telephony

Item	Call Statistic Type
1	Total daily calls for all lines.
2	Total call-minutes (total calls times the length of each call - this gives you a measure of how much on-the-air time has been consumed by callers)
3	Total time all phone lines were busy (this will let you know if your system is not able to respond to all incoming calls).
4	Total calls for each voice line (this will alert you to hardware or phone line problems if one or a group of lines shows low counts).
5	Number of times specific application areas are executed by callers - this tells you which parts of the application are being used (or not) by callers. It lets you quickly implement changes to help callers through areas that maybe weren't so clear.
6	Call detail statistics: time, date, and duration of each call along with credit card, PIN numbers, etc. Some applications are billing callers based on this kind of information.

Performance Questions

Run-time engines support multiple voice lines at the same time by dividing up the PC's single processor (e.g., an 80386) into a number of "logical" processors: each handles the application for a single line. Whether your vendor uses preemptive multitasking (e.g., UNIX, OS/2, or a special kernel written under DOS) or a multi-line state machine, it should not matter to you. What does matter is how your vendor defines acceptable performance and what tools you have to measure and improve it for each application you develop.

"How does the vendor define "acceptable performance ?" A general *rule of thumb*: if it takes longer than 1 second for a voice system to act on a caller's touch-tone response, it is not acceptable performance. Ask your vendor if he agrees and, if so, what guidelines you should use to achieve this level of performance or better. Expect guidance on what processor your PC should have, minimum access time for your hard disks, and how much PC memory you need - each can have a significant effect on performance. If performance issues are glossed-over by your vendor, not only may touch-tone responses be seriously slowed but speech messages can actually be broken up on a poorly-designed system.

"Are you given tools to measure performance?" If a vendor side-steps the issue, side-step the vendor. At least one vendor provides a special run-time screen that shows a performance index display. If there are no built-in performance tools available, you will have to add your own low-level timers and counters and a method of saving and printing this information periodically.

"Are tools provided to improve performance of applications that need it?" A number of system parameters can usually be changed that will yield a net improvement. While it is true that spending lots of money can help (e.g., buy the fastest PC and hard disk you can afford or buy an expensive memory-intensive caching disk controller), there are more sophisticated ways to approach the problem. One trick: move commonly-accessed speech messages to ram-disks.

"Does the vendor understand the effects of file fragmentation?" If your system is running on an MS-DOS based PC, your vendor should be aware of the effects of file fragmentation on your hard disks - especially if you record speech messages from more than one caller at a time - this is virtually guaranteed to cause fragmentation. Performance is adversely affected since the disk drive head has to move longer distances (and thus consume more time) while recording and playing the message. If recordings are made to LAN-based file server disks, fragmentation is managed by the LAN software itself (e.g. Novell 3.11). Your vendor should give you the ability to automatically run a defragmentation program as an off-line process once a day.

Debugging Questions

No matter how sophisticated your tools are, you still should verify every application step to be absolutely sure your logic and speech messages match perfectly. This process is called *debugging*.

"Are special tools available for debugging your applications?" If not, you will be spending much longer than necessary getting your system up. You will find the depth of application debugging tools varying considerably from vendor to vendor. Some offer virtually nothing in the way of debugging support while a few have fairly sophisticated run-time analyzers to speed the process.

"Is *single-step* debugging of applications supported?" This feature, sometimes called "trace mode," makes it possible to manually execute applications a step at a time, giving you time to compare what is actually happening with what you think should be happening. Typically, a screen displays "source" statements about to be executed. With script-language-only products, you should see several language statements before and after the highlighted one to be executed. If you are using an AG, you should see a representation of the screen step about to be executed and be able to temporarily v ·w application steps before or after this point.

"Does the vendor support *breakpoints*?" You should be able to set a number of breakpoints - symbolic names for application segments where you want to stop if they should be executed. For example, say you wanted to halt execution if particular choices were made at a specific menu. This feature lets you run most of the time at real-time speed but manually single-step after a breakpoint has happened. Be sure you can easily add or delete breakpoints in the middle of a debugging session.

"Are *watch commands* supported? "Watch commands allow you to "watch" the value of selected application variables while the application is executing (e.g., see the last-entered touch-tone digits from a caller). A portion of the single-step screen should display these variables. As well, you want the ability to change any application variable and resume execution - this allows you to override application errors and continue testing without having to edit the application and start your test call over again.

Documentation Questions

Nothing is more frustrating than trying to plow your way through a poorly-written technical guide looking for an answer to a simple question. Here are a few things to look for.

"Can you order the technical guide before you buy the product?" Order the actual technical guide first. Expect to pay $50 or less for each guide. Some vendors give you credit toward the product when you buy. Browse through the guide and get a feel for how it is arranged. Is the table of contents clearly organized? Can you quickly tell what is covered in each chapter by the section titles? Does the guide have a large enough index? Does it make good use of screen captures, illustrations, and tables?

"Is a separate Run-time Reference Available?" If you plan on selling turn-key systems to end-users, you will have to give a basic operation guide to your users. If your vendor has thought about this and provided you with one, it will save you valuable time.

"Is there a separate chapter or section on error handling?" Be sure system error messages are clearly listed and defined in the run-time reference. Some vendors don't document any errors - if an obscure error happens after-hours (they usually do), you're in big trouble!

Technical Support Questions

Until you have to call support, you may not appreciate how valuable a resource they can be in your time of need. Especially if the technical guide can't help, technical support folks should be equipped to give you quick suggestions or resolutions.

"Does the vendor charge for support?" If it's free, great, but many charge for support. Some allow you to purchase support on an hourly basis while others offer two, six, or twelve month plans. You may get a free "introductory" period after your initial purchase. When checking the value of the support plan, ask about discounts for software upgrade releases - some companies offer this. In general, purchasing support in larger blocks should be more cost effective.

"What response time should you expect?" This is closely tied to the above question. If you are paying for support, you should receive faster responses to your calls. If a support person can't take your call immediately, expect a return call in one to two hours at the most.

"What support services are available?" Support services vary from one vendor to another. It may only mean "you can call our bulletin board for help." What you really want is a range of options, including access to support specialists who are trained to do one thing quickly and professionally - answer your product questions.

"What is the size and technical depth of the support staff?" Ask how many full-time support staff are taking calls - if the answer is one or less, be very cautious: your callback may take longer than you want. Ask your vendor how long support staff members are trained - the longer it is, the better the chances they have handled your particular question. Ask how long support staff members have been on the job - the longer, the better (one year or more is desirable).

"How can you get the latest bug and new product release information?" It is essential for you to get this information periodically. Most vendors print quarterly newsletters. Some give you unlimited access to this information via an on-line fax or Bulletin Board System (BBS); BBS's are also useful for downloading new software versions if you "need it yesterday."

Vendor Questions

An important part of your pre-purchase research is qualifying the vendor itself. If you want the relationship with your vendor to be good for the long term, here are a few areas to explore before deciding to go with its products.

"How long has the vendor been in the voice software business?" The voice industry is not actually that "new," the more perspective a potential vendor has, the better they can anticipate your problems and get you on the right path. Three years should be considered an absolute minimum.

"Are price policies clearly-defined?" Ask to see a standard price list. If it takes more than a few minutes to determine how much it will cost to put your application on-line, the vendor may have more hidden costs. Most voice software vendors charge a fee for run-time licenses - that is, every time you install a new system, you purchase a license (usually accompanied with a hardware protection device) specifically for the number of voice lines you want to run. See if you qualify for special OEM pricing.

"How are product returns handled?" Look for a 30-day trial period on all voice software products. If you have to ask for this privilege, be sure you tell the salesman to clearly state the return offer details on your invoice and indicate when the trial period starts (hopefully, it won't start until you receive the package). Keep in mind that hardware purchased from most vendors is not returnable unless special considerations are made beforehand.

"Does the vendor practice full disclosure of all known product problems?" A particularly annoying practice of some software (and hardware) companies is they rarely acknowledge that problems or bugs exist in their products. The hard reality of complex software products is that it is rare when no known bugs exist. Any company that claims otherwise is clearly more worried about public relations issues than they are about your ability to develop reliable applications. Ask to see a copy of the release notes for the last major product release. Were past problems and their solutions openly discussed? If not, you will have no opportunity to intelligently work around them.

"If you discover a software problem, how long will it take the vendor to fix it and get you a new version?" Pose this question to 10 vendors and chances are you will 10 very different answers. What you are looking for here is a general understanding of how a potential vendor treats the subject. A reasonable answer might be anywhere from one to two weeks, but it is common for larger companies to take much longer releasing new software versions.

More Questions To Ask

"If I have absolutely no experience as a programmer, can I still be productive using your tools?" Look for a company that offers a range of tools. Non-programmers may want to start using forms-based tools, then switch to a high-level script environment as the application expands. The best way to make this transition is to use an integrated environment script product - where the text editor, compiler, and hypertext help are all supported from the same environment.

"How long will it take for me to develop an application?" Describe your particular application, then ask this. Since it depends on skill level, the amount of time it will take varies: don't expect an exact number but try to get an idea of what it will take. Ask this question two ways: How long will it take me, and how long will it take an experienced VAR?

"What roadblocks will I run into developing applications?" This is an important question because no software environment is perfect. Look for a truthful answer that acknowledges where users typically run into problems. If the vendor denies that his customers run into any problems, look for another vendor.

"If I am not happy with your software product, what are my options?" Look for an answer that won't leave you high and dry if things don't work out. Expect either a 30-day trial period or request a low-cost demonstration version of the product to help you get familiar with it before you commit the big dollars.

"If I don't have time to do the application myself, can you find someone to help me right away?" Many vendors can refer you to system integrators who will work on your application on a fixed-price or hourly basis. Find out how long they have used the software product you are interested in - one year should be considered a minimum, with two or more even better. Remember, before beginning any such project with a consultant, always state the project requirements in writing and execute a consulting agreement that clearly specifies the project billing rates and terms.

"If I purchase run-time support for a specific number of voice lines, how do I later support more lines?" Since the vendor's development tools presumably make it easy to develop voice applications without regard to how many lines are being handled, find out what must be done to expand to more lines. At a minimum, you need to add more speech cards. Hopefully, only minimal actions need to be taken with the application itself: you may need to edit a few startup parameters to signify the new number of active lines. Expect to pay for the difference between the new number of lines and what you have running currently. Usually, the vendor sends you a new set of disks and a hardware protection device and you return the old device to them.

"Do your software tools allow me to protect my application development efforts from software piracy?" Yes, in this day and age there are still people who would love to take your most feature-rich voice application and use it, royalty free. There are two basic ways protection is offered:

1. Encrypting and password protecting the distributed application files so unauthorized persons cannot edit them.

2. Using hardware protection (dongles) to prevent unauthorized users from running it. Be sure you ask your software vendor if and how he provides this protection.

Adapted from A Guide to Getting Started Profitably by Chris Bajorek.

The author extends special thanks to Chris Bajorek for the use of his time-saving tips and advise represented in this chapter. This material has been used by hundreds of entrepreneurs and companies alike in launching computer telephony systems all over the world.

Chris Bajorek founded Telephone Response Technologies (TRT) in 1986 and is the company's President. His company's mission is to produce high-performance PC-based computer telephony software tools. Under his direction, his team has successfully developed and marketed a robust set of tools for resellers and system integrators that has gained tremendous popularity in the fast-growing computer telephony market. Chris is considered an industry icon, having authored many articles, speeches, and white papers over the past decade. Prior to TRT, he worked for Integrated Office Systems, Inc. where he designed a specialized minicomputer-based voice mail system. He also directed the hardware development effort for Time and Space Processing, Inc., producing low-bit rate voice digitizer products. Chris holds a B.S.E.E. from California Polytechnic State University.

Appendix

Recommended Resources and Bibliography

The publications cited here offer a comprehensive and detailed understanding of some of the subjects covered in this book. Some are listed as a point of interest, and others were used as chief reference material for a number of the chapters. The publisher would like to acknowledge the authors of copyrighted material for the permissions granted to use portions of their work as solicited by the research staff.

An Introduction to Database Systems, Volume 1, Fifth Edition, AddisonWesley Publishing Company, 1990.

Basic Book of Information Networking,
Motorola Codex, Motorola University Press, 1992.

Basic Book of ISDN,
Motorola Codex, Motorola University Press, 1992.

Basic Book of OSI & Network Management,
Motorola Codex, Motorola University Press, 1992.

Basic Book of Frame Relay,
Motorola Codex, Motorola University Press, 1992.

Basic Book of X.25 Packet Switching,
Motorola Codex, Motorola University Press, 1992.

Complete Traffic Engineering Handbook,
Jerry Harder, Telecom Library, 1992.

Computer-Telephone Integration with Novell's Telephony Services,
Novell, Inc., January 1994.

Frames, Packets & Cells for Broadband,
Bill Flanagan, Telecom Library, 1991.

Guide To Getting Started Profitably,
Telephone Response Technologies, Inc., October 1993.

Handbook of Telecommunications,
James Harry Green, Irwin Professional Publishing

Implementing and Configuring Novell/AT&T Telephony Services,
Novell, Inc., February, 1994.

Local & Long Distance Billing Practices,
M. Brosnan & J. Messina, Telecom Library, 1993.

Newton's Telecom Dictionary
Harry Newton, Telecom Library, 1994.

Micro Database Management,
Bonczek, Robert H., Clyde W. Holsapple and Andrew B. Whinston, Academic Press, 1984.

Microsoft At Work Architecture Backgrounder,
Microsoft Corporation, June 1993.

Queuing Systems, Volume II,
Leonard Kleinrock John Wiley & Sons, publisher.

Reference Manual for Telecommunications Engineering,
Roger L. Freeman John Wiley & Sons, publisher.

SCSA - Signal Computing System Architecture,
Edwin Margulies, Telecom Library, 1993.

Signal Computing System Architecture: Specification,
Dialogic Corporation, March 1993.

Speech Recognition,
Pete Foster, Telecom Library, 1993.

Telecommunications Management,
James Harry Green, Irwin Professional Publishing

Telephone Manager Developer's Kit,
Apple Computer

The Guide To Frame Relay,
N. Muller & R. Davidson, Telecom Library, 1991.

The Guide to SONET,
R. Davidson & Nathan Muller, Telecom Library, 1992.

The Guide to T-1 Networking,
Bill Flanagan, Telecom Library, 1990.

Understanding Data Communications,
G. Friend & J. Fike, Telecom Library, 1993.

Understanding Fiber Optics,
Jeff Hecht, Telecom Library, 1993.

Understanding Telephone Electronics,
J. Fike, Telecom Library, 1993.

Voice Processing,
Walt Tetschner, Artech House, publisher.

Windows Telephony API,
Microsoft Corporation, May 1993.

XTL Architecture Guide (801-7048-01 rev. A),
Sun Microsystems, March, 1994.

XTL Administrator's Guide (801-7047-01 rev. A),
Sun Microsystems, March, 1994.

XTL Application Programmer's Guide (801-7046-01 rev. A),
Sun Microsystems, March 1994.

XTL Provider Programmer's Guide (801-7049-01 rev. A),
Sun Microsystems, March, 1994.

All of these Books can be obtained from Flatiron Publishing.

1-800-LIBRARY

1-800-999-0345

212-691-8215

Glossary

10Base2
IEEE standard for baseband Ethernet at 10 Mbps over coaxial cable to a maximum distance of 185 meters. Also known as Thin Ethernet.

10Base-T
IEEE standard for operating Ethernet LANs on twisted pair wiring that appears like telephone cabling. Sometimes old cabling will not work.

A

A & B Bits
Bits used in digital environments to convey signaling information. A bit value of one generally corresponds to loop current flowing in an analog environment. A bit zero corresponds to no loop current, i.e. to no connection. Other signals are made by changing bit values. For example, a flash-hook is set by briefly setting the A bit to zero.

A & B Leads
Additional leads used typically with a channel bank two-wire E&M interface to connect certain types of PBXs (also used to return talk battery to the PBX).

A & B Signaling
Procedure used in most T-1 transmission links where one bit, robbed from each of the 24 subchannels in every sixth frame, is used for carrying dialing and control information. A type of in-band signaling used in T-1 transmis-

sion, A and B signaling reduces the available user bandwidth from 1.544 to 1.536 Mbps. See also PRI.

A4
Basic Group 3 standard defined for the scanning and printing of a page 215 mm (8.5 in) wide. An A5 page is 151 mm (5.9 in) wide, and the A6 is 107 mm (4.2 in) wide.

A LAW
The PCM coding and companding standard used in Europe. See A LAW ENCODING and E-1.

A LAW Encoding
The method of encoding sampled audio waveforms used in the 2048K bit 30 channel PCM primary system, widely used outside North America. See E-1.

Access Tandem
A special type of local phone company central office. It's designed to provide equal access for all the long distance carriers in that area.

Activity Report
Provides a record of transmission time, date, size of the file, recipient's telephone number, transmission success or failure, the sender's name, and other pertinent information. This is a valuable management tool to get an overview of a company's fax traffic and costs.

A/D
Analog to digital conversion.

Adaptive Pulse Code Modulation
A way of encoding analog voice signals into digital signals by adaptively predicting future encodings by looking at the immediate past. The adaptive part of this method reduces the number of bits per second that another rival and more common method called PCM (Pulse Code Modulation) requires to encode voice.

Adaptive PCM is not especially common because, even though it reduces the number of bits required to encode voice, the electronics to do it are expensive. See also PULSE CODE MODULATION.

ADC
Analog-to-Digital Converter.

ADPCM
Adaptive Differential Pulse Code Modulation. A speech coding method which calculates the difference between two consecutive speech samples in standard PCM coded voice signals. This calculation is encoded using as adaptive filter and therefore, is transmitted at a lower rate than the standard 64 Kbps technique.

Typically, ADPCM allows an analog voice conversation to be carried within a 32k-kbit/s digital channel; 3 or 4 bits are used to describe each sample, which represents the difference between two adjacent samples. Sampling is done 8,000 times a second.

ADSI
Analog Display Services Interface. ADSI is a Bellcore standard defining a protocol on the flow of information between something (a switch, a server, a voice mail system, a service bureau) and a subscriber's telephone, PC, data terminal or other communicating device with a screen. The simple idea of ADSI is to add words to, and therefore a modicum of simplicity of use to a system that usually uses only touch tones.

Imagine a normal voice mail system. You call it. It answers with a voice menu. Push 1 to listen to your messages, 2 to erase them, 3 to store them, 4 to forward them, etc. It's confusing. You have to remember which is which. ADSI is designed to solve that. It's designed to send to your phone's screen the choices in words that you're hearing.

You then have the choice of responding to what you hear or what you see. Your response is the same -- a touch-tone button. ADSI's signaling is DTMF and standard Bell 202 modem signals from the service to your 202-modem equipped phone. From the phone to the service it's only touch-tone.

With ADSI, you don't hear the modem signaling because every time the service gets ready to send you information, it first sends a "mute" tone. ADSI works on every phone line in the world.

Advisory Tones
Signals such as dial tone, busy, ringing, fast-busy, call-waiting, camp-on--and all the other tones which your telephone system uses to tell you that something is happening or about to happen.

AEB
Analog Expansion Bus. Dialogic's name for the analog electrical connection between its network interface modules and its analog resource modules. This bus is now "open." Technical specifications are available, thus enabling outsiders to make their own resource modules and/or network interface modules. The AEB interfaces DTI/124 and D/4x voice response component boards which fit in an AT-expansion slot of a PC. See also PEB, which is the more modern digital PCM expansion bus. See also SCSA, which is Dialogic's latest standard.

AGC
Automatic Gain Control. There are two electronic ways you can control the recording of something -- Manual or Automatic Gain Control (AGC). AGC is an electronic circuit in tape recorders, speakerphones, and other voice devices which is used to maintain volume. AGC is not always a brilliant idea, since AGC will attempt to produce a constant volume level.

This means it will try to equalize all sounds -- the volume of your voice, and, when you stop talking, the circuit static and/or general room noise which you undoubtedly do not want amplified. Sometimes it's better to have quiet, when you want quiet. Manual Gain Control is preferred in professional applications.

Alerting Signal
A ringing signal put on subscriber access lines to indicate there's an incoming call.

Algorithm
A prescribed finite set of well defined rules or processes for the solution of a problem in a finite number of steps. In normal English, it is the mathematical formula for a computing operation.

All Trunks Busy
When a user tries to make an outside call through a telephone system and receives a "fast" busy signal (twice as many signals as a normal busy in the

same amount of time), he is usually experiencing the joy of All Trunks Busy. No trunks are available to handle that call. The trunks are all being used at that time for other calls or are out of service. These days, many long distance companies are replacing a "fast" busy signal with a recording that might say something like, "I'm sorry. All circuits are busy. Please try your call later."

AMIS
See AUDIO MESSAGING INTERCHANGE SPECIFICATION. AMIS is a standard for networking voice mail systems.

Amplitude
The distance between high or low points of a waveform or signal. Also referred to as the wave "height."

Amplitude Distortion
The difference between the output wave shape and the input wave shape.

Amplitude Equalizer
A corrective network that is designed to modify the amplitude characteristics of a circuit or system over a desired frequency range. Such devices may be fixed, manually adjustable, or automatic.

Amplitude Modulation
Also called AM, it's a method of adding information to an electronic signal in which the signal is varied by its height to impose information on it. "Modulation" is the term given to imposing information on an electrical signal. The information being carried causes the amplitude (height of the sine wave) to vary.

In the case of LANs, the change in the signal is registered by the receiving device as a 1 or a 0. A combination of these conveys different information, such as words, numbers or punctuation marks.

AMX
Analog Matrix Switch. A Dialogic product. An 8 x 8 analog crosspoint switch on a board used for sharing resources among AEB-based products and for connecting to phones and external audio devices.

Analog
Comes from the word "analogous," which means "similar to." In telephone transmission, the signal being transmitted -- voice, video, or image -- is "analogous" to the original signal. In other words, if you speak into a microphone and see your voice on an oscilloscope and you take the same voice as it is transmitted on the phone line and ran that signal into the oscilloscope, the two signals would look essentially the same.

The only difference is that the electrically transmitted signal (the one over the phone line) is at a higher frequency. In correct English usage, "analog" is meaningless as a word by itself. But in telecommunications, analog means telephone transmission and/or switching which is not digital. See ANALOG TRANSMISSION.

Analog Bridge
A circuit which allows a normal two-person voice conversation to be extended to include a third person -- without degrading the quality of the call. Digital bridges work better.

Analog/Digital Converter
An A/D Converter. Pronounced: "A to D Converter." A device which converts an analog signal to a digital signal.

Analog Facsimile
Facsimile which can transmit and receive grey shadings -- not just black and white. "Analog" facsimile is usually transmitted digitally. But it's called analog because of its ability to transmit what appear to be continuous shades of grey.

Analog Transmission
A way of sending signals -- voice, video, data -- in which the transmitted signal is analogous to the original signal. In other words, if you spoke into a microphone and saw your voice on an oscilloscope and you took the same voice as it was transmitted on the phone line and threw that signal onto the oscilloscope, the two signals would look essentially the same. The only difference between them is that the electrically transmitted signal would be at a higher frequency.

ANI
Automatic Number Identification. A phone call arrives at your home or office. At the front of the phone call is a series of digits which tell you the phone number calling you. These digits may arrive in analog or digital form. They may arrive as touch-tone digits inside the phone call. They may arrive in a digital form on a separate circuit.

Whichever way they arrive, you will need some equipment to decipher the digits AND do "something" with them. That "something" might be throwing them in a database and bringing up your customer's record on a screen in front of your telephone agent as he answers the phone. "Good morning, Mr. Smith." Some large users say they could save as much as 20 seconds on the average IN-WATS call if they knew early on the phone number of the person calling them. They wouldn't need to ask their regular customers for their address, phone number, credit card number, etc.

Announcement Service
Allows a phone user to hear a recording when he dials a certain number. Could be an answering machine. Could be a voice response system. Could also be a solid-state digital announcer. Increasingly, it's a voice response system.

ANSI
American National Standards Institute. A standards- setting, non-government organization which develops and publishes standards for voluntary use in the U.S.

Answer Detect
The use of a digital signal processing technique to determine the presence of voice energy on a telephone line. It is used with call (answer) supervision, to identify an answered line. It is beginning to be used with computerized dialing equipment in business to consumer calling. This technique eliminates the need for a telephone representative to constantly monitor call set-up progress on each telephone line in the event a call is answered. See ANSWER SUPERVISION.

Answer Supervision
Follow this scenario: I call you long distance. My central office must know when you answer your phone, so my central office or long distance phone company can start billing me for the call. It works like this: when

you, the called party, answer your phone, your central office sends a signal back to my central office (the originating CO). This tells my central office to start billing me for the call. This signal is called Answer Supervision.

Before the Divestiture of the Bell System in early 1984, most of the nation's long distance companies -- with the exception of AT&T -- did not receive Answer Supervision. They did not know precisely when the called party answered. So they started their billing cycle after some time -- 20 or 30 seconds after the caller completed dialing. These long distance companies presumed that after this time, some one will have answered and the call will be in progress (and they therefore start timing *and billing* for the call). Without Answer Supervision, their billing of calls is inaccurate. With the Divestiture of the Bell System, and the introduction of Equal Access, most long distance companies now receive true Answer Supervision. See also SOFTWARE SUPERVISION.

Anti Aliasing
A computer imaging term. A blending effect that smoothes sharp contrasts between two regions of different colors. Properly done, this eliminates the jagged edges of text or colored objects. Used in voice processing, anti-aliasing usually refers to the process of removing spurious frequencies from waveforms produced by converting digital signals back to analog.

API
Application Programming Interface. "Hooks" into software. A set of standard software interrupts, calls, and data formats that application programs use to initiate contact with network services, mainframe communications programs, or other program-to-program communications. For example, applications use APIs to call services that transport data across a network.

Standardization of APIs at various layers of a communications protocol stack provides a uniform way to write applications. NetBIOS is an early example of a network API. Also, applications use APIs to call services that transport data across a network. See also WINDOWS TELEPHONY.

Application
A software program that carries out some useful task. Database managers, spreadsheets, communications packages, graphics programs, and word processors are all applications.

Application Programming Interface (API)
A set of formalized software calls and routines that can be referenced by an application program to access underlying network services.

Applications Generator
Basically, software that writes software. Applications generators are software tools that, in response to your input, write software code which a computer can understand. Applications generators have two major benefits: First, they save time. An applications generator is perfect for demonstrating a quick, though not complete, programming application.

Second, they can often be used by non-programmers. Applications generators are often used in programming voice processors. Applications generators come in many flavors. They may be general purpose tools. Or they may provide support for specific application segments such as: connecting voice response units to mainframe databases; voice messaging system development; audiotex system development, etc.

One of applications generators' biggest advantages is that their ability to translate user specified screens and menus into programming code. In essence you produce the screen or menu using an interface as simple as a word processor. Then the applications generator translates that screen into programming code in a language, such as the widely-used ""C." Once translated into C, a programmer proficient in C could go through the code and ""improve" on it.

Applications Processor
A special purpose computer which attaches to a telephone system and allows the telephone system (and the people using it) to do different "applications" things, like voice mail, interactive voice response, etc. We think AT&T invented the term Applications Processor.

Appli/COM
See T.611.

AppServer
A telephony server software program from Dialogic that enables an open SCSA telecomputing LAN server. Multiple applications from multiple vendors may control this server locally or remotely.

Apps Gens
See APPLICATIONS GENERATORS.

ASCII
American Standard Code for Information Interchange.

ASCII Character Set
A character set consisting only of the characters included in the original 128-character ASCII standard.

Asynchronous Communication
A method of data communication in which the transmission of bits of data is not synchronized by a clock signal but is accomplished by sending the bits one after another, with a start bit and a stop bit to mark the beginning and end of the data unit.

The two communicating devices must be set to the same speed-called the baud rate. Asynchronous communication normally is used for transmission speeds under 19,200 baud. Because of the lower communication speeds, normal telephone lines can be used for asynchronous communication.

AT WORK Protocol
Microsoft's integration protocol for linking peripheral office equipment, including telephony services, to Windows applications.

Audio
Sound you hear which may be converted to electrical signals for transmission. A human being who hasn't had his ears blown by listening to a Sony Walkman or a ghetto blaster can hear sounds from about 15 to 20,000 hertz.

Audio Frequencies
Those frequencies which the human ear can detect (usually in the range of 15 to 20,000 hertz). Only those from 300 to 3,000 hertz are transmitted through the phone. Which is why the phone doesn't sound "Hi-Fi."

Audio Menu
Options spoken by a voice processing system. The user can choose what he wants done by simply choosing a menu option -- hitting a touch-tone on his phone, or speaking a word or two. There are basically two ways of organizing computer or voice processing software -- menu-driven and non-

menu driven. Menu-driven programs are easier for users to use. But they can only present as many options as can be reasonably spoken in a few seconds. Audio menus are typically played to callers in automated attendant/voice messaging, voice response and transaction processing applications. See also MENU.

Audio Messaging Interface Specification (AMIS)
Issued in February 1990, AMIS is a series of standards aimed at addressing the problem of how voice messaging systems produced by different vendors can network or inter-network. Before AMIS, systems from different vendors could not exchange voice messages. AMIS deals only with the interaction between two systems for the purpose of exchange voice messages. It does not describe the user interface to a voice messaging system, specify how to implement AMIS in a particular systems or limit the features a vendor may implement.

AMIS is really two specifications. One, called AMIS-Digital, is based on completely digital interaction between two voice messaging systems. All the control information and the voice message itself, is conveyed between systems in digital form. By contrast, the AMIS-Analog specification calls for the use of DTMF tones to convey control information and transmission of the message itself is in analog form. AMIS was discussed in detail in the October 1990 issue of Business Communications Review. AMIS specifications are available from Hartfield Associates, Boulder CO. 303-442-5395.

Audio Response Unit (ARU)
A device which translates computer output into spoken voice. Let's say you dialed up a computer and it said "If you want the weather in Chicago, push button "123," then it would give you the weather. But that weather would be "spoken" by an audio response unit.

Audiotex
A generic term for voice response equipment and services. Audiotex may be passive or interactive. In "passive," the classic applications fall into "Jokes, Scopes and Soaps." Dial a number, hear the joke of the day. Dial a number, hear your horoscope. Dial a number, hear what's happening on your latest TV soap.

In its interactive form, Audiotex is basically another term for Interactive Voice Response. You call a phone number. A machine answers. It presents you several options, "Push 1 for information on Plays, Push 2 for information on movies, Push 3 for information on Museums." If you push 2, the machine may come back, "Push 1 for movies on the south side of town, Push 2 for movies on the north side of town, etc." Or it says, "To hear your present bank balance, touch-tone your bank account number in now." See also INTERACTIVE VOICE RESPONSE.

Audiotext
An alternate, though wrong, saying of AUDIOTEX.

Auto Fax Tone
Also called CNG, or Calling Tone. This tone is the sound produced by virtually all Group 3 fax machines when they dial another fax machine. CNG is a medium pitch tone (1100 Hz) that lasts 1/2 second and repeats every 3 1/2 seconds. A FAX machine will produce CNG for about 45 seconds after its dials. See also CNG.

Automatic Cover Letter
Allows the user to automatically attach a cover letter to the document being sent. This is especially convenient when sending material such as spreadsheets, for example.

Automatic Redial
Provides for the automatic redialing of a voice, data, or fax number in the event the receiving line is busy or an error occurred in sending the data. Some products allow the user to specify the redial attempts and correct specific errors to be used when redialing.

Automatic Routing
Allows incoming fax documents to be automatically routed to the addressed individual on a LAN or centralized system. Current technology provides several methods of accomplishing this using various techniques.

Automated Attendant
A specialized form of an Interactive Voice Response system. An IVR connected to a PBX. When a call comes in, this device answers it, and says something like: "Thanks for calling the ABC Company. If you know the extension number you'd like, push-button that extension now and you'll be

transferred. If you don't know it, push button "0" (zero) and the live operator will come on. Or wait a few seconds and the operator will come on, anyway." Sometimes the automated attendant might give you other options -- like "dial 3" for a directory. Automated attendants are sometimes connected also to voice mail systems ("I'm not here. Leave a message for me."). Some people react well to automated attendants. Others don't.

A good rule: Before you spring an automated attendant on your people/customers/subscribers, etc., let them know. Train them a little. They'll then perceive the automated attendant device a lot more positively. Tip: When you reach an automated attendant and don't know the extension number, dial the person's last name on your touch-tone pad. Better automated attendants will recognize the name and translate it into the extension number.

Automatic Call Distributor (ACD)
A specialized phone system used for handling many incoming calls. Typically used by airlines, rent-a-car companies, hotels, etc. An ACD has four functions. First, it will recognize and answer an incoming call. Second, it will look in its database for instructions on what to do with that call. Third, based on that database's instructions, it will send the call to a recording that "somebody will be with you soon, please don't hang up!" Fourth, it will send the call to one operator of a group of operators -- as soon as that operator has completed their previous call, and/or the caller has heard the canned message.

The term Automatic Call Distributor comes from distributing the incoming calls in some logical pattern to a group of operators. That pattern might be Uniform (to distribute the work uniformly). It also might be Top-down. Distributing calls logically is the function most people associate with an ACD. But it's not the most important. Much more important is the management information which the ACD produces. This information typically is of two sorts -- 1: The arrival of incoming calls (when, how many, which lines, from where, etc.) and 2: How many callers were put on hold, told to wait and didn't.

This is called information on ABANDONED CALLS. This information is very important for staffing, for buying lines from the phone company and also for figuring what level of service to provide to the customer. And what different levels of service (how long for people to answer the phone) might cost. Automatic Call Distributors are now combined with Interactive Voice

Response Systems and ANI (automatic number identification) to give much effective and faster handling of incoming customer calls.

Automatic Call Sequencer
ACS. A device for handling incoming calls. Typically it performs three functions. 1. It answers an incoming call, gives the caller a message, and puts them on "Hold." 2. It signals the agent (the person who will answer the call) which call on which line to answer. Typically, the call which it signals to be answered is the call which has been on "hold" the longest. 3. It provides management information, such as how many abandoned calls there were, how long the longest person was kept on hold, how long the average "on hold" was, etc.

Automatic Callback
When a caller dials another internal extension and finds it busy, the caller dials some digits on his phone or presses a special "automatic callback" button. When the person he's calling hangs up, the phone system rings his number and the number of the original caller and the phone system automatically connects the two together. This feature saves a lot of time by automatically retrying the call until the extension is free.

Automatic Calling Unit
ACU. A device that places a telephone call on behalf of a computer.

Automatic Circuit Assurance
ACA is a PBX feature that helps you find bad trunks. The PBX keeps records of calls of very short and very long duration. If these calls exceed a certain parameter, the attendant is notified. The logic is that a lot of very short calls or one very long call may suggest that a trunk is hung, broken or out of order. The attendant can then physically dial into that trunk and check it.

Automatic Number Identification
ANI. Equipment at your central office which recognizes the telephone number of the person making the call so that information about the call can be sent to the call accounting (i.e. billing) system. There has been some discussion about using ANI capability and sending calling information all over the country along with the call itself. This way the recipient will know who's calling before he/she picks up the phone and answers the calls. So far, this service apparently awaits more universal introduction of ISDN,

more corporate demand, more standardization, more seminars or whatever. See ANI.

B

Backbone
The part of a communications network which carries network traffic between access devices.

Backplane
The high-speed communications line which individual components of a modern electronic system are connected to. For example, all the extensions of a PBX are connected to line cards (circuit boards), which slide into the PBX's cage. At the rear of the PBX cage, there is a connector. Each of these connectors is plugged into the PBX's Backplane. Also called a Backplane Bus.

This backplane bus is typically very high speed, since it carries many conversations, much address information and considerable signaling. These days, the backplane bus is typically a time division multiplexed line -- somewhat like a train with many cars, each of which represent a time slice of another conversation. The backplane's capacity determines the overall capacity of the switch.

Baseboard
A Dialogic voice processing board without any daughterboards attached.

Battery
1. Term used to reference the DC power source of a telephone system. Often called "Talk Battery." 2. Storage battery used with central office switching systems and PBXs serving locations which cannot tolerate outages.

Batteries serve the following purposes: Act as a filter across the generator or power rectifier output to smooth out the current and reduce noise; provide a cushion against periodic overloads exceeding the generator/rectifier capacity; supply emergency power for a limited time in event of commercial power failure.

Baud

The number of changes in signal state (switching) per second in a signal sent by a modem. A baud may contain four or more bits. Sometimes confused with BPS, the bits per second transmitted on the channel.

Baud Rate

The transmission rate of a communications channel. Technically, baud rate refers to the maximum number of changes (switching) that can occur per second in the electrical state of a communications circuit. Under the RS-232C communications protocol, 300 baud is likely to equal 300 bps, but at higher baud rates the number of bits per second transmitted is actually higher than the baud rate because one change can represent more than one bit of data. For example, 1,200 bps is usually sent at 600 baud by sending two bits of information with each change in the electrical state of the circuit.

BISDN

Broadband ISDN (Integrated Services Digital Network) Also see ISDN.

Bit

Binary digit, the smallest amount of information in a binary system, a 0 or 1 condition.

Board

An SCSA definition. Any hardware module that controls its own physical interface to the SCbus or SCxbus. From a programming point of view, a board is an addressable system component that contains resources.

Bong

A tone that long distance carriers and value added carriers make in order to signal you that they now require additional action on your part -- usually dialing more digits.

BPS

Bits per second.

Broadcasting

This procedure allows the user to send a voice message, data file, or fax document to a group of people or companies. Groups can be temporarily or permanently stored in the telephone directories for repeated broadcasting.

Busy
In use. "Off-hook". There are slow busies and fast busies. Slow busies are when the phone at the other end is busy or off-hook. They happen 60 times a minute. Fast busies (120 times a minute) occur when the network is congested with too many calls. Your distant party may or may not be busy, but you'll never know because you never got that far.

Byte
A group of 8 bits, making up a single memory location. Most computers cannot address a bit, they can only address bytes.

C

C
The most common programming language in the voice processing industry. C operates under MS-DOS or UNIX, and other operating systems. It is very powerful and is becoming a standard also for programming telecom switches, PBX and central office.

Cadence
In voice processing, cadence is used to refer to the pattern of tones and silence intervals generated by a given audio signal. Examples are busy and ringing tones. A typical cadence pattern is the US ringing tone, which is one second of tone followed by three seconds of silence. Some other countries, such as the UK, use a double ring, which as two short tones within about a second, followed by a little over two seconds of silence.

Call Center
A place where calls are answered and calls are made. A call center will typically have lots of people (also called agents), an automatic call distributor, a computer for order-entry and lookup on customers' orders. A Call Center could also have a predictive dialer for making lots of calls quickly. The term "call center" is broadening. It now includes help desks and service lines.

Call Control
The establishment and control of telephone links. This involves answering, originating, transferring, conferencing, and terminating telephone calls, and

monitoring their status. The electronic signaling functions that control the setting up, monitoring and tearing down of telephone calls.

Call Processing
Call processing is setting up, connecting, transferring, disconnecting, etc. a phone call. Call processing does not affect the content -- voice or otherwise -- of the conversation. That process is called "voice processing." And that is a broader concept, encompassing everything from compression, storage, editing to recognition.

Call Progress Tone
A tone sent from the telephone switch to tell the caller of the progress of the call. Examples of the common ones are dial tone, busy tone, ringback tone, error tone, re-order, etc. Some phone systems provide additional tones, such as confirmation, splash tone, or a reminder tone to indicate that a feature is in use, such as confirmation, hold reminder, hold, intercept tones.

Caller ID
Signals that identify the telephone number of the calling party; these signals are sent along the telephone line at the start of the call. Not all telephone network connections support caller ID signaling. In a more general sense, caller ID can be obtained by prompting the caller for an identity code.

Calling Party Identification
A new service being tested in some local areas which tells the person being called which number is calling them. They can then decide to answer or not answer the call. See ANI, which stands for Automatic Number Identification.

CALLPATH
IBM's announced telephone system link to IBM's computers. See CALLPATH SERVICES ARCHITECTURE.

CALLPATH CICS
Enabling software that connects your telephone systems with your IBM 370 or 390 (i.e. the mainframe version of CallPath/400, which works on the AS/400 platform).

CALLPATH Host
IBM and ROLM's CICS-based integrated voice and data applications platform which links to ROLM's 9751 PBX. See CALLPATH SERVICES ARCHITECTURE.

CALLPATH Services Architecture
CSA. IBM's program for integrating voice and data technologies. It is both a strategy and set of open architecture commands and interfaces for integrating voice and database technologies. The idea is that with CallPath a call will arrive at a computer terminal simultaneously with the database record of the caller. And such call and database record can be transferred simultaneously to an expert, a supervisor, etc. The first implementation is CallPath/400 which works with the IBM AS/400 minicomputer. CallPath CICS works with IBM mainframes. See OPEN APPLICATION INTERFACE and DIRECTTALK.

Carrier Frequency
The frequency of a carrier wave.

Carrier Wave
A wave having at least one characteristic that may be varied from a known reference value by modulation.

CAS
Communicating Applications Specification. A high-level API (application programming interface) developed by Intel and DCA that was introduced in 1988. CAS enables software developers to integrate fax capability and other communication functions into their applications.

CBF
Computer-Based Fax.

CCITT
Formerly the Comite Consultatif Internationale de Telegraphique et Telephonique (Consultative Committee for International Telephone and Telegraph). See Telecommunication Standardization Sector.

CED
Called Station Identification. A 2,100-Hz tone with which a fax machine answers a call.

Central Office (CO)
Telephone company facility where subscribers' lines are joined to switching equipment for connecting other subscribers to each other, locally and long distance.

Centrex
Centrex is a business telephone service offered by a local telephone company from a local central office. Centrex is basically single line telephone service delivered to individual desks (the same as you get at your house) with features, i.e. "bells and whistles," added. Those "bells and whistles" include intercom, call forwarding, call transfer, toll restrict, least cost routing and call hold (on single line phones).

Centrex is known by many names among operating phone companies, including Centron and Cenpac. Centrex comes in two variations -- CO and CU. CO means the Centrex service is provided by the Central Office. CU means the central office is on the customer's premises.

CFR
Confirmation to Receive frame.

Channel
1. An SCSA definition. A transmission path on the SCbus or SCxbus Data Bus that transmits data between two end points. 2. Typically what you rent from the telephone company. A voice-grade transmission facility with defined frequency response, gain and bandwidth. Also, a path of communication, either electrical or electromagnetic, between two or more points. Also called a circuit, facility, line, link or path.

Channel Bank
A multiplexer. A device which puts many slow speed voice or data conversations onto one high-speed link and controls the flow of those "conversations." Typically the device that sits between a digital circuit -- say a T-1 -- and a couple of dozen voice grade lines coming out of a PBX.

One side of the channel bank will be connections for terminating two pairs of wires or a coaxial cable -- those bringing the T-1 carrier in. On the other side are connections for terminating multiple tip and ring single line analog phone lines or several digital data streams. Sometimes you need channel banks. Sometimes, you don't. For example, if you're shipping a bundle of voice conversations from one digital PBX to another across town in a T-1 format -- and both PBXs recognize the signal -- then you will probably not need a channel bank. You'll need a Channel Service Unit (CSU). If one, or both, of the PBXs is analog, then you will need a channel bank at the end of the transmission path whose PBX won't take a digital signal. See CHANNEL SERVICE UNIT and T-1.

Channel Service Unit
CSU. A device used to connect a digital phone line (T-1 or less) coming in from the phone company to either a multiplexer, channel bank or directly to another device producing a digital signal, e.g. a digital PBX, or data communications device. A CSU performs certain line-conditioning, and equalization functions, and responds to loopback commands sent from the central office. A channel service unit is also called a Data Service Unit. See CSU.

CIG
Calling Subscriber Identification. A frame that gives the caller's telephone number.

CLASS
1. Custom Local Area Signaling Services. It is based on the availability of channel interoffice signaling. Class consists of number-translation services, such as call-forwarding and caller identification, available within a local exchange of Local Access and Transport Area (LATA). CLASS is a service mark of Bellcore.

Some of the phone services which Bellcore promotes for CLASS are Automatic Callback, Automatic Recall, Calling Number Delivery, Customer Originated Trace, Distinctive Ringing/Call Waiting, Selective Call Forwarding and Selective Call Rejection. See also CALLING LINE IDENTIFICATION. 2. In an object-oriented programming environment, a class defines the data content of a specific type of object, the code that manipulates it, and the public and private programming interfaces to that code.

Class 1
The Class 1 interface is an extension of the EIA/TIA's (Electronics Industry Association and the Telecommunications Industry Association) specification for fax communication, known as Group III. Class I is a series of Hayes AT commands that can be used by software to control fax boards.

In Class 1, both the T.30 (the data packet creation and decision making necessary for call setup) and ECM/BFT (error-correction mode/binary file transfer) are done by the computer.

A specification being developed (fall of 1991) Class 2, will allow the modem to handle these functions in hardware. Industry analysts believe Class 2 will be the standard for the long haul, but approval is slow. Even so, some modem makers will shortly deliver data/fax modems. See also CLASS 1 OFFICE.

Clear Channel
A channel which is used exclusively for data transmission, with no bandwidth required for administrative messages such as signaling or synchronization. All SCbus data channels are clear.

Client
The requesting communication element in a distributed computing system. Clients send requests to servers across a network and wait for indication from the server that the request is complete.

Client AP (Application Processor) System
An independent PC linked to at least one Server System via a NetBIOS or SPXcompatible network. Under TRT's ProVIDE environment, for example, each client system must be running a compatible version of the Application Processor and at least one clientserver User Function.

Client-server
A software architecture which splits operation between two component programs and their respective communication elements: the client and the server. Client elements make requests of servers. Servers process the requests and often return processed data to the client. For example, TRT's PROFOUND.EXE is a client while programs such as PF_DB3.EXE and PF_CLIP.EXE are servers.

CNG
Also called Auto Fax Tone, or Calling Tone. This tone is the sound produced by virtually all fax machines when they dial another fax machine. CNG is a medium pitch tone (1100 Hz) that lasts 1/2 second and repeats every 3 1/2 seconds. A fax machine will produce CNG for about 45 seconds after it dials. The CNG tone is useful for owners of fax/phone/modem

switches. Such switches answer an incoming call. If they hear a CNG tone, they will transfer the call to a fax machine. If they don't, they'll transfer the call to a phone, answering machine or perhaps a modem. Depends on how they're set up.

CO

Central Office. In North America, a CO is that location which houses a switch to serve local telephone subscribers. Sometimes the words "central office" are confused with the switch itself. In Europe and abroad, the words "central office" are not known. The more common words are "public exchange." But those words tend to refer more to the switch itself, rather than the site, as in North America. See also CENTRAL OFFICE or PUBLIC EXCHANGE.

CO Lines

These are the lines connecting your office to your local telephone company's Central Office which in turn connects you to the nationwide telephone system.

Compression

Reducing the representation of the information, without losing the information itself. Reducing the bandwidth or bits necessary to encode information. Compression saves transmission time and storage requirements on storage devices such as hard disks, tape devices, and floppy disks.

Compression Algorithm

The arithmetic formulae which convert a signal into a smaller bandwidth or fewer bits.

CO Simulator

A desktop device which pretends to act like a mini-central office. The smallest version will consist of two lines and two RJ-11 jacks. Plug a phone into both jacks. Pick up one phone. You hear dial tone. Dial or touch-tone two or three digits. Bingo, the second phone rings. You pick up the second phone. You can have a conversation with yourself or with a machine -- like a voice processing system.

Most central office simulators can simulate normal on-hook, off-hook, dialing, answering, speaking, etc. Some now can simulate caller ID features -- including number of person calling.

Compiler
A computer program used to convert symbols meaningful to a human into codes meaningful to a computer. For example, taking instructions written in a "higher" level language such as C, BASIC, COBOL or ALGOL and converting them into machine code which can be read and acted upon by a computer.

Compression Algorithm
The arithmetic formulae which convert a signal into smaller bandwidth or few bits.

Computer-Aided Dialing
Another term for Predictive Dialing. See PREDICTIVE DIALING.

Computer Telephony
Computer telephony represents the cooperative merger between telephony and data communications. It is a form of telecommunication that concentrates on the movement of both encoded and voice-related information from one point to another for the purpose of automating transactions between machines and humans, or between machines.

Interactive voice response, voice mail, and every type of host computer-to-switch integration scheme are examples of computer telephony. Because computer telephony requires both computers and telephones to work cooperatively, *data processing* is employed.

Conference Bridge
A telecommunications facility or service which permits callers from several diverse locations to be connected together for a conference call. The conference bridge contains electronics for amplifying and balancing the conference call so everyone can hear each other and speak to each other. The conference call's progress is monitored through the bridge in order to produce a high quality voice conference and to maintain decent quality as people enter or leave the conference.

Cover Page
The cover page is the first page of a fax message. It generally includes a header, typically the sender company's logo; the recipient's name and fax telephone number; the sender's fax and voice telephone numbers; the system's date and time; a message; and a footer.

CPE
Customer Provided Equipment, or Customer Premise Equipment. Originally it referred to equipment on the customer's premises which had been bought from a vendor who was not the local phone company. Now it simply refers to telephone equipment -- key systems, PBXs, answering machines, etc. -- which reside on the customer's premises. "Premises" might be anything from an office to a factory to home.

CPU
The Central Processing Unit. The computing part of a computer. The "brain" of the computer. It manipulates data and processes instructions coming from software or a human operator. See CENTRAL PROCESSING UNIT.

CRP
Command repeat.

CSI (CSID)
Called Subscriber Identification. An identifier whose coding format contains a number, usually the telephone number from the remote terminal used in fax.

CSTA
Computer Supported Telecommunications Applications. This is a set of API calls agreed upon by the ECMA.

CSU
Channel Service Unit. Also called a Data Service Unit. A device to terminate a digital channel on a customer's premises. It performs certain line-conditioning, and equalization functions, and responds to loopback commands sent from the central office. A CSU sits between the digital line coming in from the central office and devices such as channel banks or data communications devices. See CHANNEL SERVICE UNIT.

CTI
Computer Telephone Integration. Basically a polite term for connecting a computer to a telephone switch and having the computer issue the switch commands to move calls around. The most classic application for CTI is in call centers. Picture this: A call comes in. That call carries some form of caller ID -- either ANI or Class Caller ID. The switch "hears" the calling

number, strips it off, sends it to the computer. The computer does a lookup, sends back the switch instructions on what to do with the call. The switch follows orders. It might send the call to a specialized agent or maybe just to the agent the caller dealt with last time.

Customer Premises Equipment
CPE. Terminal equipment, supplied by either the telephone common carrier or by a competitive supplier, which is connected to the nationwide telephone network and resides on the customer's premises.

CVSD
Continuously Variable Slope Delta modulation. A method for coding analog voice signals into digital signals.

D

D/A
Digital to analog conversion.

DAA
Data Access Arrangement. A device required to hook up CPE (Customer Provided Equipment), usually modems and other data equipment, to the telephone network.

Database
A data file and its associated index files. (Occasionally the term is used to refer to multiple data files, each with its own index files.)

Data File
The file used to store the data portion of a database. Data files are usually given the .DBF extension when using any of the xBASE family of database managers.

Database Handle
See *Handle.*

Data Communications
This is a form of telecommunications that concentrates on the movement of encoded information from one point to another. This information is readable by machines, such as modems, computers, and fax machines as opposed to telephony, which is "readable" by the human ear.

dB
Decibel. A unit of measure of signal strength, usually the relation between a transmitted signal and a standard signal source. Therefore, 6 dB of loss would mean that there is 6 dB difference between what arrives down a communications circuit, and what was transmitted by a standard signal generator.

DBMS
Database Management System. An inclusive term for a database format and its management and development software tools.

DCN
Disconnect frame. Indicates the fax call is done. The sender transmits it before hanging up; it does not wait for a response.

DCS
Digital Command Signal. Signal sent when the caller is transmitting, which tells the answerer how to receive the fax. Modem, speed, image width, image encoding, and page length are all included in this frame.

DDS
1. Digital Dataphone Service. 2. Dialogic's Device Driver Server.

Device Driver
A piece of software that expands MS-DOS's ability to work with peripherals. The routines that make peripherals (a mouse, a RAM disk, a print spooler) work. They may be part of another program (many applications include device drivers for printers) or separate programs.

DOS comes with two device drivers: ANSI.SYS and VDISK.SYS. These are things DOS is not used to. The first is to expand the capabilities of the keyboard. The second is used to carve a RAM disk out of the 640K of RAM that MS-DOS can address. In short, device drivers can be used to expand the abilities of DOS. They are loaded from your CONFIG.SYS file when you boot up the computer. Some network operating systems run as device drivers. They do this to get loaded before anything else so they can get the memory space they want. By being loaded as a device driver they are able to tell DOS how to operate certain "network" things, like virtual drives, shared printers, spoolers, print queues and so on. See DRIVER and VOICE DRIVER.

Dial-It 900 Service
A special one-way mass calling service that allows prospects, customers and others to reach you from anywhere across the country. In contrast to 800-service, the caller pays the 900 charge. The caller generally pays one charge for the first minute, with a lesser charge for each additional minute. DIAL-IT 900 Service is a great way to involve your customers and prospects in a promotion!

Premium Billing lets you select a rate above standard DIAL-IT 900 rates. The long distance carriers (through their deals with local phone companies) handle the billing. You, the information provider, may split the revenues with the long distance provider. International DIAL-IT 900 service is currently available from a growing number of countries.

Dial Pulsing
A means of signaling consisting of regular momentary interruptions of a direct or alternating current at the sending end in which the number of interruptions corresponds to the value of the digit or character. In short, the old style of rotary dialing. Dial the number "five" and you'll hear five "clicks." See DIAL SPEED and DTMF.

Dial Speed
The number of pulses that a rotary dial can send in a given period of time, typically 10 pulses per second. A Hayes modem with a communications package, like Crosstalk, can send 20 pulses a second.

Dial Tone
The sound you hear when you pick up a telephone. Dial tone is a signal (350 + 440 Hz) from your local telephone company to you that it is alive and ready to receive the number you dial. If you have a PBX, dial tone will typically be provided by the PBX. Dial tone does not come from God or the telephone instrument on your desk. It comes from the switch to which your phone is connected to.

Dictation Access and Control

A telephone system feature which allows a user to dial a dictation machine and use that machine (giving it instructions by push button) as if that machine were in his office. Typically the material on that dictation machine is taken off by one or several typists out of a centralized word processing pool and word processed into letters, reports, legal briefs, etc. Telephone suppliers usually don't supply the dictation equipment. Newer telephone dictation machinery is, in reality, a specialized application of voice processing equipment. See VOICE PROCESSING.

DID

Direct Inward Dialing. You can dial inside a company directly without going through the attendant. This feature used to be an exclusive feature of Centrex but it can now be provided by virtually all modern PBXs and some modern hybrids.

DID Trunks

DID trunks are employed to reduce the number of channels between the PBX and the telephone company central office. DID trunks are one-way trunks. A PBX perceives the DID trunk as one of its single-line telephones and can interpret four-digit dialing.

Digital Facsimile

A form of fax in which densities of the original are sampled and quantized as a digital signal for processing, transmission, or storage.

Digital Recording

A system of recording in which musical information is converted into a series of pulses that are translated into a binary code intelligible to computer circuits, and stored on magnetic tape of magnetic discs. Also called PCM - Pulse Code Modulation.

Digital Signal Processor (DSP)

A specialized digital microprocessor that performs calculations on digitized signals that were originally analog (e.g., voice) and then sends the results on. The big advantage of DSP lies in the programmability of digital microprocessors. DSPs can be used for compression of voice signals to as few as 4,800 bps. DSPs are an integral part of all voice processing systems and facsimile machines.

Digital Transmission
The use of a binary code to represent information. Analog signals, like voice or data, are encoded digitally by sampling the signal many times a second and assigning a number to each sampling. Unlike an analog signal which picks up noise along the way, a digital signal can be reproduced precisely.

Digital Trunk
Generic name for a telephone connection for which uses digital rather than analog transmission. Common examples are T-1 in North America and E-1 in Europe.

Digital-To-Analog Conversion
A circuit that accepts digital signals and converts them into analog signals. A modem typically has such a circuit. It also has other circuits, such as those doing with signaling. See MODEM.

Digitize
Converting an analog or continuous signal into a series of ones and zeros, i.e. into a digital format.

Digitized Voice
Analog voice signals represented in digital form. There are many ways of digitizing voice. See Pulse Code Modulation for the most common.

Direct Inward Dialing
DID. The ability for a caller outside a company to call an internal extension without having to pass through an operator or attendant. In large PBX systems, the dialed digits are passed down the line from the CO (central office). The PBX then completes the call. Direct Inward Dialing is often proposed as Centrex's major feature. But automated attendants (a specialized form of interactive voice response systems) also provide a similar service.

DIRECT TALK
A family of IBM voice processing products introduced in the summer of 1991. According to IBM, its "new IBM CallPath DirectTalk product line lets businesses automate routine operations and also provide callers with easy access to many kinds of information over the telephone -- at any hour of the day and with greater accuracy. Businesses can raise the level of

service they provide and do it with fewer people and with greater efficiency." According to IBM's press release, the North Carolina Employment Security Commission is using the DirectTalk product to automate the filing of unemployment benefit claims. For several years, the state has allowed claimants to verify their unemployment status by answering a series of questions on a postcard. Based on initial results, Claimants who use the telephone to answer the questions can receive checks up to four days sooner than if they answer by mail.

DIS

Digital identification signal.

Disconnect Supervision

The change in electrical state from off-hook to on-hook. This indicates that the transmission connection is no longer needed.

Distributed Mode

An operational mode possible with clientserver applications, where each client module and each server module runs on a separate PC. One or more server systems can support one or more client systems over a network. The load on each PC is reduced and the performance of the system as a whole is enhanced. See also *Local Mode*.

DMX

Digital Matrix Switch. Dialogic board that provides digital switching among four PEB spans -- for a maximum of 96 channels.

DNIS

Dialed Number Identification Service. DNIS is a feature of 800 lines. Let's say you subscribe to several 800 numbers. You use one line for testing your advertisements on TV stations in Phoenix; another line for testing your advertisements on TV stations in Chicago; and yet another for Milwaukee. Now you get an automatic call distributor and you terminate all the lines in one group on your ACD. You do that because it's cheaper to man and run one group of incoming lines.

One queue is more efficient than several small ones, etc. You have all your people answering all the calls. You now need to know which calls are coming from where. So your long distance carrier sends you the call's DNIS -- the numbers the person dialed to reach you. Those DNIS digits might come to you in many ways, depending on the technical arrangement you have with your long distance company. In-band or out-of-band. ISDN or data channel, etc. Make sure you understand the difference between DNIS and ANI. DNIS tells you the number your caller called. ANI is the number your caller called from.

DOS
Disk Operating System. As in MS-DOS, which stands for MicroSoft Disk Operating System. DOS is the software that organizes how a computer reads, writes and reacts with its disks -- floppy or hard -- and talks to its various input/output devices, including keyboards, screens, serial and parallel ports, printers, modems, etc.

DPI
Dots per inch. A measure of output device resolution. The number of dots a printer can place in a horizontal inch.

Driver
Also called a Device Driver. A piece of software which lets applications software tell a computer's various parts what to do. Those parts might be everything from Dialogic boards to laser printers.

Drop And Insert
That process wherein a part of the information carried in a transmission system is demodulated (dropped) at an intermediate point and different information is entered (inserted) for subsequent transmission.

Dry T-1
T-1 with an unpowered interface.

DS-0
Digital Service, level 0. It is 64,000 bps, the worldwide standard speed for digitizing one voice conversation. There are 24 DS- channels in a DS-1.

DS-1
Digital Service, level 1. It is 1.544 megabits per second in North America, 2.048 Mbps elsewhere. Why there's no consistency is one of those wonderful questions. The 1.544 standard is an old Bell System standard. The 2.048 standard is a CCITT standard. Standard for 1.544 per second is 24 voice conversations. Standard for 2.048 is 30 conversations.

DSP

Display System Protocol or Digital Signal Processor. A Digital Signal Processor is a specialized computer chip designed to perform speedy and complex operations on digitized waveforms. Useful in processing sound and video.

DTC

1. Digital Trunk Controller. 2. Digital transmit command.

DTMF

Dual Tone Multi Frequency. A fancy term for describing push button or touch-tone dialing (touch-tone is a former trademark of AT&T). In DTMF, when you touch a button on a push button dial, it makes a tone, which is actually the combination of two tones, one high frequency and one low frequency. Thus the name Dual Tone Multi Frequency.

In U.S. telephony, there are actually two types of DTMF signaling -- one that is used on normal business or home push button/touchtone phones, and one that is used for signaling within the telephone network itself. When you go into a central office, look for the testboard. There you'll see what looks like a standard touch-tone pad.

Next to the pad there'll be a small toggle switch that allows you to choose the sounds the touch-tone pad will make -- either normal touch-tone dialing or the network version. The eight possible tones that comprise the DTMF signaling system were specially selected to easily pass through the telephone network without attenuation and with minimum interaction with each other. Since these tones fall within the frequency range of the human voice, additional considerations were added to prevent the human voice from inadvertently imitating or "falsing" DTMF signaling digits.

One way this was done to break the tones into two groups, a high frequency group and a low frequency group. A valid DTMF tone has only one tone in each group. Here is a table of the DTMF digits with their respective frequencies. One Hertz (abbreviated Hz.) is one cycle per second of frequency.

	Low frequency	High frequency
1	697 Hz.	1209 Hz.
2	697	1336
3	697	1477
4	770	1209
5	770	1336
6	770	1477
7	852	1209
8	852	1336
9	852	1477
0	941	1336
*	941	1209
#	941	1477

There are four other digits defined in the DTMF system and usable for specialized applications that cannot be generated by standard telephones. They are:

	Low frequency	High frequency
A	697 Hz	1633 Hz.
B	770	1633
C	852	1633
D	941	1633

DTMF Cut-Through

The capability of a voice response system to receive DTMF tones while the voice synthesizer is delivering information, i.e. during speech playback. This capability of DTMF cut-through saves the user waiting until the machine has played the whole message (which typically is a menu with options).

The user can simply touch-tone his response anytime during the message -- when he first hears his selection number, when the message first starts, etc. When the voice processor hears the touch-toned selection (i.e. the DTMF cut-through), it stops speaking and jumps to the chosen selection. For example, the machine starts to say, "If you know the person you're calling, touch-tone his extension in now.." But before you hear the "If you know" you push button in 230, which you know is Joe's extension. Bingo, the message stops and Joe's extension starts ringing.

Dumb Switch
A slang word for a telecommunications switch that contains only basic switching software and relies on instructions sent it by an outside computer. Those instructions are typically fed the "dumb" switch through a cable from the computer to one or more RS-232 serial ports which the dumb switch sports.

The switch makes no demands on what type of computer it talks to, but simply insists that it be able to feed the computer questions and promptly receive responses in a form that it (the switch) can understand. Plain ASCII is OK. For example, the dumb switch might signal the computer, "A call is coming in on port 23, what do I do now?" The computer might reply "Answer it and transfer it to extension 23." Or it might say "answer it and put it on hold," or "answer it, put it on hold and play it recording number three."

In essence, a dumb switch is anything but. It is in reality an empty cage containing whatever network interface cards the user has chosen. Each of these network interface cards is designed to "talk" to one type of telephone line. That line might be a T-1 line. It might be a normal tip and ring loop start line. It might be a tie trunk with E&M signaling. The card may handle one or many lines, but always of the same type. The card knows how to answer a call or pulse out a call on that particular type of line. It has all the telephony smarts.

What it lacks is the intelligence of what to do with the calls. That is provided by the outside computer. Well, almost. Most "dumb" switches do contain rudimentary intelligence -- a small computer and some memory. That computer is usually programmed to handle "default" calls -- and to handle calls should the link to the outside computer fail, or the outside computer itself fail. Dumb switches come in flavors all the way from residing in their own cabinet to being printed circuit cards which reside in one or more of the personal computer's slots.

Dumb switches are programmed to do "specialized" telecom applications, for example emergency 911, added value 800 services, cellular switching, automatic call distributors, predictive dialers, etc. They can, of course, be programmed to be "normal" PBXs. The question increasingly being asked is "If I want to program a specialized telecom application should I use a dumb switch or should I use an open PBX?" And the answer is "It depends." Depends on what you want to do. Depends on what software is available, etc. See also OAI.

E

800 Service
See 800 SERVICE, spelled as EIGHT HUNDRED SERVICE.

E & M Leads
The pair of wires carrying signals between trunk equipment and a separate signaling equipment unit. The "M" lead transmits a ground or battery conditions to the signaling equipment. The "E" lead receives open or ground signals from the signaling equipment. These leads are also known as Ear and Mouth Leads. The Ear lead typically means to receive and the Mouth lead typically means to transmit.

Changes of voltage on these leads convey such information as seizure of circuit, recognition of seizure, release of circuit, dialed digits, etc. In the old days it was the PBX operators who originated trunk calls by asking the long distance carrier for free trunks using their mouth or M lead. If the carrier had a free trunk, the PBX heard about it through its ear or E lead. See also E & M SIGNALING.

E & M Signaling
In telephony, an arrangement that uses separate leads, called respectively the "E" lead and "M" lead, for signaling and supervisory purposes. The near end signals the far end by applying -48 volts dc (vdc) to the "M" lead, which results in a ground being applied to the far end's "E" lead. When -48 vdc is applied to the far end "M" lead, the near-end "E" lead is grounded. The "E" originally stood for "ear," i.e., when the near-end "E" lead was grounded, the far end was calling and "wanted your ear."

The "M" originally stood for "mouth," because when the near-end wanted to call (i.e., speak to) the far end, -48 vdc was applied to that lead. When a PBX wishes to connect to another PBX directly or to a remote PBX or extension telephone over a leased voice grade line, a channel on T-1, the PBX uses a special line interface which is quite different from that which it uses to interface to the phones it's attached directly to (i.e. with in-building wires).

The basic reason for the difference between a normal extension interface and the long distance interface is that the signaling requirements differ -- even if the voice signal parameters such as level and two-wire, 4-wire remain the same. When dealing with tie lines or trunks it is costly, inefficient and too slow for a PBX to do what an extension telephone would do, i.e. go off hook, wait for dial tone, dial, wait for ringing to stop, etc. The E&M tie trunk interface device is the closest thing there is to a standard that exists in the PBX, T-1 multiplexer, voice digitizer telco world. But even then it comes in at least five different flavors. See E & M LEADS.

Eight Hundred Service
800-Service. A generic and common (and not trademarked) term for AT&T's, MCI's, US Sprint's and the Bell operating companies' IN-WATS service. All these IN-WATS services have "800" as their "area code." Dialing an 800-number is free to the person making the call. The call is billed to the person or company being called.

The telephone company suppliers of 800 services use various ways to configure and bill their 800-services. One way: you can buy an 800 line which will ring on your normal phone line. You'll only pay per call, but you won't receive any incoming call if you're making an outgoing one. (You can even terminate an 800 number on your cellular phone.) For other 800 services you might pay a flat monthly rate plus "so-much" (i.e. timed usage) per call. That timed usage may include some calculation for the distance the incoming call traveled. 800-Service is now available for calls from Canada and some countries in Europe.

More and more long distance companies are introducing 800-service. 800 Service works like this: You're somewhere in North America. You dial 1-800 and seven digits. Your local central office sees the "1" and recognizes the call as long distance. It ships that call to a bigger central office (or perhaps processes the call itself). At that central office it's processed, a machine will recognize the 800 "area code" and examine the next three digits. Those three digits will tell which long distance carrier to ship the call to. Each long distance company has been assigned specific 800 three digit "exchanges." For example, MCI has the exchange 999. AT&T has the exchange 542. If you want a phone number beginning with 800-999, then you must subscribe to MCI 800 service. If you want a phone number beginning with 800-542, you must subscribe to AT&T 800 service. Once the 800-call is "passed off" to whichever carrier it belongs to, that carrier sends the call to a switch attached to a huge "translation" database. The call arrives at the switch. The database says the call 800-NNN-XXXX is really 212-555-1234, and sends the 800 line to that number.

As a real-life example, Telecom Library, publishers of this book, has an 800 number, namely 800-LIBRARY (or 800-542-7279). When you call that number, the following number -- 212-206-6870 -- in New York City rings. Dialing 800-542-7279 is effectively the same as dialing 212-206-6870, except that if you dial 212-206-6870 you'll pay. If you dial 800-542-7279, I'll pay. Because 800 long distance service is essentially a database lookup and translation telephone service, there are endless "800 services" you can create.

E-1

Another name given to the CEPT digital telephony format devised by the CCITT that carries data at the rate of 2.048 Mbps (DS-1 level). CEPT format consists of 30 voice channels, one signaling channel, and one framing (synchronization) channel. Since robbed-bit signaling is not used (as it is for T-1 in North America) all 8 bits per channel are used to code the waveshape sample. E-1 is the European version of North American T-1, though T-1 is 1.544 Mbps. See T-1.

Echo

A wave reflected or otherwise returned with sufficient magnitude and delay to be perceived. This is an effect sometimes experienced with long distance calls. It is usually associated with relatively long round-trip delay in the four-wire portion of the circuit so that the unwanted sound is perceived as being separate in time from the wanted one. The phenomenon of echo primarily affects the talker and not the listener. Ghosts on a television picture are a type of echo.

Echo Canceller

The echo suppressor used on circuits with long transmission time. It attenuates the direction of transmission which is not active so that any echoes that are fed into a circuit do not return to the starting point and cause confusion. Echo cancellation stops a received signal from being transmitted back to its origin by constructing a signal closely approximating the echo component and subtracting this from the locally transmitted signal. This avoids double-talking problems. ECM Error Correction Mode. Encapsulated data within HDLC frames providing the receiver with an opportunity to check for, and request retransmission of garbled data.

ECMA
European Computer Manufacturers Association. An independent standards group of computer and PBX manufacturers. Their standards are recognized internationally.

EDI
Electronic Data Interchange. A series of standards providing automated computer-to-computer exchange of business documents (structured business data, editable documents, or electronic transactions such as invoices, purchase order, etc.) between different companies and computers over telephone lines.

E-Mail
Electronic mail. A popular application on both LANs and WANs which provides communication among users. There is a variety of systems which vary considerably in their level of sophistication. E-mail services can include simple message handling as well as complex file sharing.

E-Mail Fax Gateways
With an E-mail fax gateway, all E-mail users can send and receive faxes from within the company's E-mail package. Because the fax messaging is integrated directly into the mail system, fax users have virtually no new software to learn and can take advantage of E-mail features such as workgroup distribution lists, attaching graphics files to text messages, support for different user operating systems on the network, and instant notification of received messages. With an E-mail fax gateway, it is possible to send the same message to both mail users and fax recipients.

Electronic Mail Integration
Integrating computer fax and E-mail technology allows the user to send and receive fax documents using a company's E-mail program. The most popular method uses MHS for Novell networks.;

Electronic Voice Mail
A system which stores messages spoken by a user usually over a telephone, which can be retrieved by the intended recipient when that person next calls into the system. Also called Voice Mail, it operates just like a touch-tone controlled answering machine.

Email-to-fax
Conversion of electronic mail (ASCII text) into fax image format, suitable for sending to a fax machine.

Emulate
To imitate a computer or computer system by a combination of hardware and software that allows programs written for one computer or terminal to run on another. The most common data terminal is a DEC VT-100. Our communications program, Crosstalk, allows us to "emulate" a DEC-VT100 on our IBM PCs and PC clones.

EOM
End of Message frame. A frame from the sender indicating that the message is done, and that Phase B can be repeated. See also EOP.

EOP
End of Procedure frame. A frame indicating that the sender wants to end the call.

ESP
Enhanced Service Provider. A vendor who adds value to telephone lines using his own provided software and hardware. Also called an IP, or Information Provider. An example of an ESP is a public voice mail box provider or a database provider, say one giving the latest airline fares. An ESP is an American term, unknown in Europe, where they're most called VANs, or Value Added Networks. See also INFORMATION PROVIDER.

Ethernet
A LAN used for connecting computers, printers, workstations, terminals, etc., within the same building. Ethernet operates over twisted pair wire and over coaxial cable at speeds up to 10 Mbps.

Event
An unsolicited, asynchronous signal from a device or device driver that reports on a change in the status of the device. Events are generally attention-getting messages, allowing a process to know when a task is complete or when an external event occurs.

Expansion Slots
In a computer there are card slots for adding accessories such as voice processing interface cards, internal modems, extra drivers, hard disks, monitor adapters, hard disk drivers, etc. Most modern PBXs are actually cabinets with nothing but expansion slots. And into these slots we fit trunk cards, line cards, console cards, etc. Some phone systems have "universal" slots, meaning you can put any card in any slot. Some phone systems have dedicated expansion slots, meaning that they expect only a certain card in that slot.

F

Facsimile
Facsimile, or fax, equipment allows information (written, typed, or graphic) to be transmitted through the switched telephone system and printed at the other end. The sending fax scans the material to be sent, digitizing it into binary bits and sending those through a modem to the receiving fax, which essentially reverses the process and outputs it through a printer.

Fast Busy
A busy signal which sounds at twice the normal rate (120 interruptions/minute vs. 60/minute). A "fast busy" signal indicates all trunks are busy.

Fax
Abbreviation for facsimile.

Fax Activity Records
Much of the power and flexibility in GammaFax comes from the Queue Manager. This is a set of programs and files that operate in the background while the user works with GammaFax or other application programs in the foreground. As the Queue Manager handles fax activity, it updates three detailed activity logs that provide the status of each task: the pending log

for tasks still being processed; the received log for incoming faxes; and the sent log for outgoing faxes.

Fax-Back
You go to your fax machine. You dial a voice response unit. It says "Punch in 23 if you want to receive the latest specs on our new XYZ machine. Now when you are ready, hit the 'start' button on your fax machine and hang up." A few seconds later, your fax machine disgorges paper containing the latest specs on the XYZ machine. Welcome to "fax-back."

FaxBIOS
API used for in-application faxing. Developed by WordPerfect Corp.; and Everex Systems, Inc.;

Fax Board
A specialized synchronous modem designed to transmit and receive facsimile documents. Many also allow for binary synchronous file transfer, and V.22 bis communication.

Fax Mailbox
Companies can send facsimiles of documents to be stored for later retrieval to a fax mailbox -- a cousin to a voice mailbox. Travelers can check their fax mailboxes and have the faxes sent to convenient locations, like a hotel front desk.

Fax Server
In a LAN, a PC or a self-contained unit that has fax circuitry accessible to all the network's workstations. The server receives requests for fax services and manages them so that they are answered in an orderly, sequential manner. It is used to send and receive faxes by any network user, sharing the common resource of one or more fax boards.

Depending on application, a fax server may have a specialized interactive voice response system that routes faxes to a fax machine the user designates by touch-tone numbers. The receiving unit may be the user's or one designated by him.

FCC Registration Number
A number assigned to specific telephone equipment registered with the FCC, as set forth in FCC docket 19528, part 68. The presence of this

number affixed to a device indicates that the FCC has approved it as being a compatible device for direct connection to telephone line facilities.

Field

A component of a record. Fields may contain either numeric, string, or date values. Fields are numbered starting with 0 as the first field.

Firmware

Programs kept in semi-permanent storage, such as various types of read-only memory. These programs can be altered, but with difficulty. Firmware is used in conjunction with hardware and software. It also shares the characteristics of both. Firmware is usually stored on PROMS (Programmable Read Only Memory) or EPROMs (Electrical PROMS).

Firmware contains software which is so constantly called upon by a computer or phone system that it is "burned" into a chip, thereby becoming Firmware. The computer program is written into the PROM electrically at higher than usual voltage, causing the bits to "retain" the pattern as it is "burned in". Firmware is non-volatile. It will not be "forgotten" when the power is shut off. Hand-held calculators contain firmware with instructions for doing their various mathematical operations.

Flash

Quickly depressing and releasing the plunger in or the actual handset-cradle to create a signal to a PBX or Centrex that special instructions will follow such as transferring the call to another extension.

Flash Hook

A brief on-hook period. A common use of the flash-hook is in the residential call waiting feature. A new call comes in while a conversation is in progress.

The central office, however, doesn't give the caller a busy signal. The caller hears ringing and the called party, who's having a conversation, hears a special "beep" tone. If he or she chooses, the called party can quickly push the hook-switch on their telephone, sending what the industry calls a "flash hook." The central office puts the original caller on hold and the new dial tone, allowing a three-way conference or call transfer.

Flowchart
A graphic or diagram which shows how a complex operation, e.g. programming, takes place. The flowchart breaks that operation down into its smallest, and easiest-to-understand events.

FOD
Fax On Demand. Dial up a number. hear an voice response unit say, "Would you like a timetable?" You say "Yes." It says put in your fax number. You punch in your fax number and bingo, your fax machine starts receiving a fax of the timetable.

Frame
A group of data bits in a specific format, with a flag at each end to indicate the beginning and end of the frame. The defined format enables network equipment to recognize the meaning and purpose of specific bits.

Frame (Data)
A set of time slots which are grouped together for synchronization purposes. For example, as with SCSA, the number of time slots in each frame depends on the SCbus or SCxbus Data Bus data rate. Each frame has a fixed period of 125us. Frames are delineated by the timing signal FSYNC.

Frame (Message)
A data link layer frame the encapsulates control and signaling data transmitted on the SCbus or SCxbus Message Bus. The form of a Message Bus frame is fully compliant with ISO HDLC UI (Unnumbered Information) Frame specifications.

Frame Relay
Frame relay switching is a form of fast packet switching, but uses smaller packets and requires less error checking than traditional forms of packet switching. Like traditional X.25 packet networks, frame relay networks use bandwidth only when there is traffic to send. Frame relay does not support voice.

Frequency
The number of complete oscillations per second of an electromagnetic wave.

Frequency Response
The variation (dB) in relative strength between frequencies in a given frequency band, usually the voice frequency band of an analog telephone line.

FTT
Failure-to-train signal.

Full Duplex
A communications protocol in which the communications channel can send and receive signals at the same time.

FSK
Frequency Shift Keying. A modulation technique for translating 1s and 0s into something that can be carried over telephone lines, like sounds. A 1 will be assigned a certain frequency of tone, and a 0 another tone. The transmission of the bits keys the sounds to shift from one frequency to the other.

G

GammaFax Cpi
Programmatic version of GammaLink's network-ready board and communication software. This single-port PC fax board supports 16 lines in one chassis and has a 16-bit microprocessor with 512K of RAM enabling 16 boards to be installed in a single chassis, all sending or receiving at 14,400 bps simultaneously.

GammaFax CPD
GammaLink's network-ready answer-only version of the GammaFax CPi that supports (but is not limited to) inbound routing of faxes across a network through the use of polling applications. With a trunk line and a bank of unique fax numbers, the GammaFax CPD can be used in a fax server with software that supports routing applications.

GammaFax Xpi
Network-ready fax board offering four-line capability, broad software support, and compatibility with any PC-based LAN. Its 16-bit microproc-

essor carries out all communication operations and text and PCX file conversion while transmitting at 9,600 bps. Up to four XPi and 16 CPi boards can be installed in a single PC for maximum throughput on even the largest networks. All GammaFax menus and utilities are supported by the XPi.

Glare

Glare occurs when both ends of a telephone line or trunk are seized at the same time for different purposes or by different users. Most embarrassing.

Ground Start

A way of signaling on subscriber trunks in which one side of the two wire trunk (typically the "Ring" conductor of the Tip and Ring) is momentarily grounded to get dial tone. There are two types of switched trunks one can typically lease from a local phone company -- ground start and loop start. PBXs work best on ground start trunks, though many will work -- albeit intermittently -- on both types.

Normal single line phones and key systems typically work on loop start lines. You must be careful to order the correct type of trunk from your local phone company and correctly install your telephone system at your end -- so that they both match. In technical language, a ground start trunk initiates an out-going trunk seizure by applying a maximum local resistance of 550 ohms to the tip conductor. See LOOP START.

Group1

Analog fax equipment, according to Recommendation T.2 of the CCITT. It sends an ISO A4 or (U.S. letter size) 8.5 x 11- inch page in six minutes over a voice-grade telephone line using frequency modulation with 1,300 Hz corresponding to white and 2,100 Hz to black of the original. Because North American six-minute equipment uses a different modulation scheme, it is not compatible with Group 1 equipment.

Group2

Analog facsimile equipment, according to Recommendation T.3 of the CCITT. It sends an A4 or 8.5 x 11-inch page in three minutes over a voice-grade telephone line using 2,100-Hz AM-PM- VSB.

Group3
A digital fax standard that allows high-speed, reliable transmission over ordinary telephone lines. All modern fax devices use Group 3, based on CCITT Recommendation T.4.

Group4
CCITT fax standard primarily designed to work with ISDN. Written before a real machine was made, it is generally considered difficult to implement. Although it offers a transmission rate of about five seconds per page, it requires an ISDN or leased line. Currently, there is no way to use it over ordinary voice grade telephone lines, and equipment from different manufacturers cannot interface.

H

Half Duplex
A communications protocol in which the communications channel can handle only one signal at a time. The two stations alternate their transmissions.

Handle
A string of characters (alphabetic, numeric, or any combination including the underscore), userdefined in the database configuration file, used by Pro/Found to reference database and index files.

Handshaking
An exchange of signals between the fax transmitter and the fax receiver to verify that transmission can proceed, determine which specifications will be used, and to verify reception of the documents sent.

HDLC
High-Level Data-Link Control Standard. It always contains a frame called the Digital Identification Signal (DIS), which describes the standard CCITT features of the machine. It can also contain two other frames: a Non-Standard Facilities (NSF) frame, which tells the caller about vendor-specific features, and, usually, a Called Subscriber Identification (CSI) frame, which contains the answerer's telephone number.

High Level Languages
Essentially any of the computer languages whose code is not unique to the hardware or architecture of a particular computer. High level languages are more like human language than the machine language which computers talk. High level languages translate human instructions into the machine language computers can understand, but which humans don't have to (in order to tell the computer what to do).

Computer languages such as C, BASIC, FORTRAN, COBOL and Pascal are high level languages. They are a number of levels (at a High Level) away from the actual bit manipulation (machine language, also called "bit twiddling" by the Hackers).

HIVR
Host Interactive Voice Response. Tying a voice response unit into a mainframe computer which has lots of data. Applications which can be produced include bank-by-phone, reservations-by-phone, etc.

Hook Flash
See FLASH

Hookswitch
Also called SWITCHHOOK. It's typically the place on your telephone instrument where you lay your handset. When you lift the handset, you are said to be going "off hook." When you place your handset back, you are said to be "on hook." When you lift the handset (i.e. go off hook) you are, in effect, signaling your central office that you'd like to make a call, or that you have answered the incoming ringing call.

Host Computer
A computer attached to a network providing primarily services such as computation, data base access or special programs of special programming languages. The central computer in a time-sharing operation.

Host Interactive Voice Response
Interactive Voice Response system communicating with a host computer (typically a mainframe computer). See HIVR.

Host Processor
Same as HOST COMPUTER.

Hot Key
Refers to TSR utilities in DOS or filters in a Windows environment that allow users to fax without leaving their present application. The ability to send a fax from within an application is one of the most important features of computer fax technology.

Huffman Encoding
A popular lossless data compression algorithm that replaces frequently occurring data strings with shorter codes. Some implementations include tables that predetermine what codes will be generated from a particular string. Other versions of the algorithm build the code table from the data stream during processing. Huffman encoding is often used in image compression. (Q.v., Modified Huffman Code.)

Hunt
Refers to the progress of a call reaching a group of lines. The call will try the first line of the group. If that line is busy, it will try the second line, then it will hunt to the third, etc. See also HUNT GROUP.

Hunt Group
A series of telephone lines organized in such a way that if the first line is busy the next line is hunted and so on until a free line is found. Often this arrangement is used on a group of incoming lines. Hunt groups may start with one trunk and hunt downwards. They may start randomly and hunt in clockwise circles. They may start randomly and hunt in counter-clockwise circles.

Inter-Tel uses the terms "Linear, Distributed and Terminal" to refer to different types of hunt groups. In data communications, a hunt group is a set of links which provides a common resource and which is assigned a single hunt group designation. A user requesting that designation may then be connected to any member of the hunt group. Hunt group members may also receive calls by station address.

Hyperchannel
A data path on the SCbus or SCxbus Data Bus made up of more than one time slot. By bundling time slots into a hyperchannel, data paths with a bandwidth greater than 64 Kbps can be created.

I

ICFA

International Computer Facsimile Association. Formed in 1991, its members include the leading companies in the computer and communications industries.

Idle

A state of the SCbus or SCxbus Message Bus where no information is being transmitted and the bus line is pulled high.

In-Band Signaling

Signaling made up of tones which pass within the voice frequency band and are carried along the same circuit as the talk path that is being established by the signals. Virtually all signaling -- request for service, dialing, disconnect, etc. -- in the U.S. today is in-band signaling. Most of that signaling is MF -- multi-frequency dialing. The more modern form of signaling is out-of-band.

Indexed Database

A database indexed on a key field. Indexing allows for rapid retrieval of records through an index field.

Index Field

The field to be used when indexing a database.

Index File

An (optional) file used for indexing the data in a database. Index files are usually given extensions which identify them as index files. For example, when using dBASE III+, the index files are given the NDX extension.

Index Handle

See *Handle*.

IndexOrder Retrieval

Implies a sequence in which records are read from the database in an order based on the contents of each record's index field.

Information Center Mailboxes
A voice bulletin board on a voice mail system. Here's their explanation: Multiple callers can access, directly or indirectly, recorded announcements containing information that would otherwise have been given live by employees. Callers are frequently "outside" users of the system. One type of "listen only" mailbox simply plays the messages to the callers. This technology, sometimes known as audiotex, makes it possible to create a verbal database so callers can select which information they want to hear.

Another type of Information Center Mailbox prompts callers to reply to announcements. Callers wanting further information can be given the opportunity to leave their names and phone numbers after listening to a product description. They can also be transferred to a designated employee who can immediately take an order. If desired, a password can be required before confidential or controlled access information can be heard.

Information Provider (IP)
A business or person providing information to the public for money. The information is typically selected by the caller through touch tones, delivered using voice processing equipment, and transmitted over tariffed phone lines, e.g., 900, 976, 970. Typically, billing for information providers' services is done by a local or long distance phone company.

Sometimes the revenues for the service are split by the information provider and the phone company. Sometimes the phone company simply bills a per minute or flat charge. A typical "information provider" is American Express, which provides a service -- 1-900-WEATHER. By dialing that number you can touch-tone in city names and find out temperatures, weather forecasts, etc. Calling 1-900-WEATHER costs several dollars a minute.

Interactive Voice Response
IVR. Picture a standard personal computer. You enter information through the keyboard. You see the results of your work on your screen. With interactive voice response, the keyboard, (or data entry device) becomes the touch-tone pad of a telephone (either local, but most likely remote) and the screen (the output device) becomes a voice synthesizer which electronically converts the computer's output (what you'd normally see on the screen) into spoken words.

You call a phone number. A machine answers. It presents you with several options, "Push 1 for information on Plays, Push 2 for information on movies. Push 3 for information on Museums." If you push 2, the machine may come back, "Push 1 for movies on the south side of town, Push 2 for movies on the north side of town, etc." That's a very simple interactive voice response (also called Voice Processing) application.

There are literally thousands of others. A bank might say "Thanks for calling the XYZ Bank, if you'd like your balance, punch in your account number now." A cable TV company might say "Thanks for calling ABC TV, if you'd like to see tonight's feature movie, push 1. $5.00 will be billed to your account." There are applications for Interactive Voice Response in every industry, in every company. Hint: Think customer! What can we do to make our customers' lives easier? Can we help them find our nearest store? Can we tell them where to get the stuff we sell them repaired? Would they like to know where the order is they placed a week ago?

Intercept Service
A service of the local phone in which a phone call is redirected by an operator or a recording to another phone number or a message. Intercept could also be sold to companies who have moved and would like to retain a recording and/or a phone advertisement for many months after they've moved.

Interconnect Companies
Companies which sell, install and maintain telephone systems for end users, typically businesses.

Inter-LATA
Telecommunications services that originate in one and terminate in another Local Access and Transport Area (LATA). Under provisions of Divestiture, the Bell operating companies cannot provide Inter-LATA service, but can provide Intra-LATA service.

Some LATAs are very large. So some "local" phone companies provide the equivalent of long distance service. And some of these phone companies have different pricing packages. Some of these packages are cheap, but not highly-publicized. See also LATA.

IPX

Internet Packet eXchange. A lowlevel network communications protocol used by Novell networks. In most networks, IPX is supplemented and extended by SPX.

ISDN

Integrated Services Digital Network. A collection of standards which define interfaces for, and operation of, digital switching equipment, developed by carriers, equipment manufacturers, and international standards organizations. It is intended to form the basis for the next generation telephone network and is currently being implemented by carriers throughout the world. Instead of one analog telephone line, there would be two 64 kbps bearer lines and one 16 Kbps data line.

Each bearer line could carry voice, video, data, images or combinations of these. As the name implies, it would be a point-to-point digital system. BISDN stands for Broadband Integrated Services Digital Network. It is a packet switching technique which uses packets of fixed length, resulting in lower processing overhead and higher speeds. Also known as cell switching and ATM.

ISO

The International Standards Organization in Paris, devoted to developing standards for international and national data communications. The U.S. representative to the ISO is ANSI.

IVR

Interactive Voice Response.

IXC

InterExchange Channel, or InterExchange Carrier -- as contrasted to the LEC -- the Local Exchange Carrier, a new word for a local phone company. InterExchange Carriers used to be called "Other Common Carriers," except that didn't include AT&T. Now, AT&T, MCI, Sprint and all the Other Common Carriers are called InterExchange Carriers.

L

LAN
Local Area Network. A short distance network (typically within a building or campus) used to link together computers and peripheral devices under some form of standard control. See RING and ETHERNET.

LATA
Local Access and Transport Area; one of 161 local telephone service areas in the United States. As a result of the Bell divestiture that now distinguishes local from long-distance service, switched calls with both endpoints within the LATA (intraLATA) are generally the sole responsibility of the local telephone company, while calls that cross outside the LATA (interLATA) are passed on to an interexchange carrier.

LEC
Local Exchange Company. The local phone companies, which can be either a Bell Operating Company (BOC) or an independent (e.g. GTE) which provides local transmission services. Prior to divestiture, the LECs were called telephone companies or telcos.

Line
See Channel.

Line Powered
Telephone equipment that is powered solely by the CO talk battery supplied in a standard phone line.

Local Loop
The physical wires that run from the subscriber's telephone set, or PBX or key telephone system, to the telephone company central office. Increasingly, the local loop now goes from the main distribution frame in the basement to the phone company. And the subscriber is responsible for getting his/her wires from the box in the basement to his phone system.

Local Mode
A clientserver application with both the client User Function and server modules running on a single PC. (See also *Distributed Mode*.)

Loop
1. Typically a complete electrical circuit. 2. The loop is also the pair of wires that winds its way from the central office to the telephone set or system at the customer's office, home or factory, i.e. "premises" in telephones. 3. In computer software. A loop repeats a series of instructions many times until some prestated event has happened or until some test has been passed.

Loop Current Detection
When a voice, modem, or fax resource seizes the line (i.e., completes the connection between tip-and-ring terminals of the telephone cable), current flows from the positive battery supply in the telephone central office, through the twisted pair in the loop, through the board, and back to the central office negative terminal where it is detected, showing that this telephone line is off hook. The fax board also detects the loop current and can detect problems such as disconnects, shutting down the connection or a busy signal, making it wait and redial.

Loop Start
You "start" (seize) a phone line or trunk by giving it a supervisory signal. That signal is typically taking your phone off hook. There are two ways you can do that -- ground start or loop start. With loop start, you seize a line by bridging through a resistance the tip and ring (both wires) of your telephone line.

Loop Timing
A way of synchronizing a circuit that works by taking a synchronizing clock signal from incoming digital pulses.

Lossless Compression Coding
Coding designed not to lose any data when compressing or restoring an image.

Low Level Language
A programming language that uses symbols -- one step away from the machine language of a computer. Low level computer languages such as Assembler and C which actually manipulate the bits in computer registers. Higher level languages such as Basic and Fortran will take care of the piddling details of doing specific functions when you give it a broad command like "PRINT". In a lower level language, you must provide all

the details of instruction necessary in the code (program) to perform the operation. It is possible to do this by calling standard routines, but still takes up the programmers' time in deciding which routines, and keeping the registers straight as he designs the program.

M

Mailbox
Messages belonging to a single owner in a voice mail system. Today, these will be recorded voice messages, but increasingly mailboxes will include E-mail and fax documents.

MAPI
Messaging Application Programming Interface. Developed by Microsoft.

MCA
Micro Channel Architecture.

MCF
Message Confirmation Frame. Confirmation by the receiver that it is ready to receive the next fax page, starting Phase C again.

Media Processing
The processing of transactions during a telephone call; these transactions may include fax operations, speech recognition and synthesis, Touch Tone recognition, voice and fax store-and-forward messaging, and the conversion of messages from one format to another (such as from text to voice, or from fax to text).

Menu
Options displayed on a computer terminal screen or spoken by a voice processing system. The user can choose what he wants done by simply choosing a menu option -- either typing it on the computer keyboard, hitting a touch tone on his phone, or speaking a word or two. There are basically two ways of organizing computer or voice processing software -- menu-driven and non-menu driven. Menu-driven programs are easier for users to use. But they can only present as many options as can be reasonably

crammed on a screen or spoken in a few seconds. Non-menu driven screens can allow more any alternatives. But they're much more complex and frightening. It's the difference between receiving a bland "A" or "C" prompt on the screen -- as in MS-DOS and receiving a menu of "Press A if you want Word Processing," "Press B if you want Spread Sheet," etc. It's very easy to write menus in MS-DOS using BATch files. See also AUDIO MENUS.

Micro Channel
A proprietary 32-bit bus developed by IBM for its PS/2 family of computers' internal expansion cards. Also offered by Tandy and other vendors.

Microcode
Programmed instructions that typically are unalterable. Usually synonymous with firmware and programmable read-only-memory (PROM).

Mini/Mainframe Fax Servers
Although many businesses generate and store information on mainframes or minicomputers, most computer-based fax hardware is PC-based. With third-party applications running on PC front-ends, GammaFax meets the communications needs of these users, bringing the benefits of computer-based fax to the mini/mainframe world.

Many mini/mainframe fax servers function in the same way as LAN fax servers: users can send and receive faxes from their terminals, saving both time and money while they increase the quality of their fax transmissions. By being on the same computer system as an organization's data, mini/mainframe servers can provide an EDI-like component for large, vertical applications such as accounting or purchase order systems, broadening the electronic reach of these programs to any recipient with a fax machine.

Modem
Acronym for MOdulator/DEmodulator. Equipment that converts digital signals to analog signals and vice-versa. Modems are used to send data signals (digital) over the telephone network, which is usually analog. A modem modulates binary signals into tones that can be carried over the telephone network. At the other end, the demodulator part of the modem converts the tones back to binary code.

Modified Huffman Code (MH)

A one-dimensional data compression technique that compresses data in an horizontal direction only and does not allow transmission of redundant data. Huffman encoding is a lossless data compression algorithm that replaces frequently occurring data strings with shorter codes. Often used in image compression.

Modified READ (MR)

Relative Element Address Differentiation code. A two-dimensional compression technique for fax machines that handles the data compression of the vertical line and that concentrates on space between the lines and within given characters.

Modified Modified READ (MMR)

A two-dimensional coding scheme for Group 4 fax, but now finding use with Group 3 machines.

Modulation

The process of varying some characteristic of the electrical carrier wave as the information to be transmitted on that carrier wave varies. Three types of modulation are commonly used for communications, Amplitude Modulation, Frequency Modulation, and Phase Modulation. And there are variations on these themes called Phase Shift Keying (PSK) and Quadrature Amplitude Modulation (QAM).

MPS

Multi-Page Signal. A frame sent if the sender has more pages to transmit.

MSI

Modular Station Interface. A Dialogic board that interfaces analog phones to PEB-based products.

MTBF

Mean Time Between Failure. The length of time a user may reasonably expect a device or system to work before an incapacitating fault occurs.

MTTR

Mean Time to Repair. The average time required to return a failed device or system to service.

Multiplexer
Electronic equipment which allows two or more signals to pass over one communications circuit. That "circuit' may be a phone line, a microwave circuit, a through-the air TV signal. That circuit may be analog or digital. There are many multiplexing techniques to accommodate both.

MVIP
Multi-Vendor Integration Protocol. A proposed standard for digital switching technology that permits the design of sophisticated applications such as voice, fax, speech recognition, and others. The technology was developed by Mitel, and the standard was proposed by Natural Microsystems.

N

NAP
Network Applications Platform (Unisys, Blue Bell, PA, term). A public telephone network service with the ability to send and receive facsimile documents to standard Group 3 fax machines.

NetBIOS
The Network Basic Input Output System. An IBMdeveloped standard for network communication. Most nonIBM networks require a NetBIOS compatibility module or utility to use NetBIOS communication and protocols. (See also *SPX*.)

Network
1. Networks are common in our lives. Think about trains and phones. A networks ties things together. Computer networks connect all types of computers and computer-related things together -- terminals, printers, modems, door entry sensors, temperature monitors, etc. The networks we're most familiar with are long distance ones, like phones and trains.

But there are also Local Area Networks (LANs), which exist within a limited geographic area -- like the few hundred feet of a small office, or they can span an entire building, or even touch a "campus," such as a university, or industrial park. There are also Metropolitan Area Networks (MANs). See LAN.

Network Board

A board device designed to act as an interface between a computer-based signal processing system and a telephone network.

Network Fax Servers

A network fax server allows users to send faxes from their network workstations. Many fax servers allow the faxing of documents from the applications that created them, leaving users free to continue with their work. Incoming faxes can be directed back to your workstation as well.

Different fax server products offer different ways of handling incoming faxes, but most use one of the following: the fax can be received by an operator who forwards it to the proper workstation, a fax extension can be assigned to particular workstations for touch-tone routing, or there can be a direct fax telephone line accessed through a Direct Inward Dial (DID) line.

Network Interface

The point of inter-connection between Telephone Company communications facilities and terminal equipment, protective apparatus or wiring at a subscriber's premises. The network interface or demarcation point shall be located on the subscriber's side of the Telephone Company's protector, or the equivalent thereof in cases where a protector is not employed, as provided under the local telephone company's reasonable and nondiscriminatory standard operating practices.

Network Interface Module

Electronic circuitry connecting a workstation (typically a personal computer) to the telephone network. Network interface modules come in as many flavors as there are ways of connecting to the telephone network -- from simple loop start phone lines to complex primary rate interfaces (PRI) on ISDN. Usually, the network interface module slides into one of the expansion slots inside a personal computer. The card transmits and receives messages from the resource modules connected to the telephone network.

NNX/NXX

A three-digit code to identify the central office in which N is any digit 2 to 9 and X is any digit. The first three digits of a North American telephone number. Originally only NNX codes were used. Now subscriber dials 1+

in making a direct distance dialed toll call and the code may be NXX. Area codes are also being changed to NXX codes.

Node

1. A point of connection into a network. In LANs, it is a device on the network. In packet switched networks, it is one of the many packet switches that form the network's backbone. 2. An independent SCSA unit in a distributed processing SCSA network, consisting of one or more resource and/or network boards, and one or more SCxbus adapter boards. Communication between nodes take place via the SCxbus. From a device programming point of view, a node is simply an addressable system unit which contains boards connected by an SCbus.

Noise

Unwanted electrical signals introduced into telephone lines by circuit components or natural disturbances that tend to degrade the line's performance.

NonIndexed

A database which is not indexed on a key field.

Novell Telephony Services

Novell's telephony server product, providing a single standard client-server call control interface (including an API for programmers) to many of the diverse PBX systems on the market today.

NSC

Non-Standard Facilities Command. A response to the called fax DIS response.

NSF

Non-Standard Facilities.

NSS

Non-Standard Facilities Setup command, a response to an NSF frame.

O

OAI

Open Application Interface. Basically an opening in a telephone system that lets you link a computer to that phone system and lets the computer command the phone system to answer, delay, switch, hold etc. calls. The term is also called PHI -- as in PBX-Host-Interface. The term OAI was first used by PBX makers, NEC and InteCom. And now the term has become somewhat generic, like all good things. Essentially every manufacturer of phone systems is evolving towards open application interfaces of their own.

OA&M

Operations, Administration and Maintenance. This term refers to PBX management.

Octet

The CCITT standard term for byte.

Off-Hook

When the handset is lifted from its cradle it's Off-Hook. Lifting the hookswitch alerts the central office that the user wants the phone to do something like dial a call. A dial tone is a sign saying "Give me an order." The term "off-hook" originated when the early handsets were actually suspended from a metal hook on the phone.

When the handset is removed from its hook or its cradle (in modern phones), it completes the electrical loop, thus signaling the central office that it wishes dial tone. Some leased line channels work by lifting the handset, signaling the central office at the other end which rings the phone at the other end. Some phones have autodialers in them. Lifting the phone signals the phone to dial that one number. An example is a phone without a dial at an airport, which automatically dials the local taxi company. All this by simply lifting the handset at one end -- going "off-hook."

Off-Hook Signal

In telephone switching, a signal indicating seizure, request for service, or a busy condition.

One-Dimensional Coding
A data compression scheme that considers each scan line as being unique, without referencing it to a previous scan line. One-dimensional coding operates horizontally only.

On-Hook
When the phone handset is resting in its cradle. The phone is not connected to any particular line. Only the bell is active, i.e. it will ring if a call comes in. See ON-HOOK DIALING and OFF-HOOK.

On-Hook Dialing
Allows a caller to dial a call without lifting his handset. After dialing, the caller can listen to the progress of the call over the phone's built-in speaker. When you hear the called person answer, you can pick up the handset and speak or you can talk hands-free in the direction of your phone, if it's a speakerphone. Critical: Many phones have speakers for hands-free listening. Not all phones with speakers are speakerphones -- i.e. have microphones, which allow you to speak, also.

OPEN
An acronym for **O**pen **P**latform **EN**vironment. A term coined by Dialogic to denote its commitment to open standards, formalizing its customers' access to information and improving the overall utility of its various voice processing platforms.

OPEN Development Program
Companies belonging to Dialogic's Open Development Program can purchase technical specifications for Dialogic's PEB, AEB, SC, and SCx expansion busses and installable Device Driver Server (DDS). Get a list from Dialogic.

OPEN Solutions Developers
These are companies which build complete turnkey call processing solutions for end users. Get a list from Dialogic.

OPEN ToolKit Developers
These companies provide applications generators in several operating systems, including MS-DOS, UNIX, OS/2 and Windows. See Chapter 12.

Operator Services
Any of a variety of telephone services which need the assistance of an operator. For example, such services typically include collect calls, third-party billed calls, person-to-person calls.

Out-Of-Band Signaling
Signaling that is separated from the channel carrying the information -- the voice, data, video, etc. Typically the separation is accomplished by a filter. The signaling includes dialing and other supervisory signals. Out-band-band hardware signaling takes place on its own data path, without the necessity of "bit robbing" or other methods of mixing signals into a data stream.

P

Packet
A bundle of data, usually in binary form, organized in a specific way for transmission.

Packet Switching
Sending data in packets through a network to a remote location. The data are subdivided into individual packets of data, each with a unique identification and individual destination address. This way each packet can take a different route and may arrive in a different order than it was shipped. The packet ID allows the reassembling of data in the proper sequence. This is an efficient way to move digital data. Although it has been used with fax messages, is not yet useful for voice.

PABX (PBX)
Private Automatic Branch Exchange. Originally, PBX was the word for a switch inside a private business (as against one serving the public). PBX means a Private Branch Exchange. Such a "PBX" was typically a manual device, requiring operator assistance to complete a call. Then the PBX went "modern" (i.e. automatic) and no operator was needed any longer to complete outgoing calls. You could dial "9." Thus it became a "PABX." Now all PABXs are modern. And a PABX is now commonly referred to as a "PBX." Some manufacturers have tried to make their PBX appear different by calling it something else.

Siemens/Rolm calls theirs the "CBX" (Computerized Branch Exchange). Some others call theirs the "EPABX" (the electronic Private Automatic Branch Exchange. Then there are the special ones, like SRX's SRX, NEC's IMS (Information Management System), etc.

PAM

Pulse Amplitude Modulation. The process of representing a continuous analog signal (a voice conversation) with a series of discrete analog samples. This concept is based on the information theory which suggests that the signal can be accurately recreated from a sufficient sample. Why bother? Sampling allows several signals to then be combined on a channel that otherwise would only carry one telephone conversation.) PAM was used as part of a method of switching phones calls in several PBXs. It is not a truly "digital" switching system. PAM is the basis of PCM, pulse code modulation. See PCM.

Part 68 Requirements (Registration)

Specifications established by the FCC as the minimum acceptable protection which communications equipment must provide the telephone network. Meeting these requirements does not certify that equipment performs any task. Equipment which is sold for connection to the public network in the US must conform to Part 68.

PBX (PABX)

Private Branch eXchange. A private (i.e. you, as against the phone company owns it), branch (meaning it is a small phone company central office), exchange (a central office was originally called a public exchange, or simply an exchange). In other words, a PBX is a small version of the phone company's larger central switching office.

A PBX is also called a Private Automatic Branch Exchange, though that has now become an obsolete term. In the very old days, you called the operator to make an external call. Then later someone made a phone system that you simply dialed nine (or another digit -- in Europe it's often zero), got a second dial tone and dialed some more digits to dial out, locally or long distance. So, the early name of Private Branch Exchange (which needed an operator) became Private AUTOMATIC Branch Exchange (which didn't need an operator). Now, all PBXs are automatic. And now they're all called PBXs, except overseas where they still have PBXs that are not automatic.

PCM

Pulse Code Modulation. PCM is a method of taking an analog voice signal and encoding it into a digital bit stream. First, the amplitude of the voice conversation is sampled. This is called PAM, Pulse Amplitude Modulation. This PAM sample is then coded into a binary (digital) number. This digital number consists of zeros and ones. It can then be switched and transmitted digitally. There are three basic advantages to PCM voice. They are the three basic advantages of digital switching and transmission.

First, it is less expensive to switch and transmit a digital signal. Second, by making an analog voice signal into a digital signal, you can interleave it with other digital signals -- such as those from computers or facsimile machines. Third, a voice signal which is switched and transmitted end-to-end in a digital format will usually come through "cleaner," i.e. have less noise, than one transmitted and switched in analog. The reason is simple: An electrical signal loses strength over a distance. It must then be amplified. In analog transmission, everything is amplified, including the noise and static the signal has collected along the way.

In digital transmission, the signal is "regenerated," i.e. put back together again, by comparing the incoming signal to a logical question: Is it a one or a zero? Then, the signal is regenerated, then it is "amplified and sent along its way. PCM refers to a technique of digitization. It does not refer to a universally accepted standard of digitizing voice. The most common PCM method is to sample a voice conversation at 8000 times a seconds. The theory is that if the sampling is at least twice the highest frequency on the channel, then the result sounds OK. Thus, the highest frequency on a voice phone line is 4,000 Hertz. So one must sample it at 8,000 times a second. Many PCM digital voice conversations are typically put on one communications channel. In North America, the most typical channel is called the T-1 (also spelled T1). It places 24 voice conversations on two pairs of copper wires (one for receiving and one for transmitting). It contains 8000 frames each of 8 bits of 24 voice channels plus one framing (synchronizing bit) bit which equals 1,544,000 bits per second. i.e. 8000 x (8 x 24 + 1) equals 1.544 megabits.

Europe uses a different scheme for multiplexing voice conversations. It is based not on 24 voice channels, but on 32 channels. This scheme keeps two of the 32 channels for control and actually transmits 30 voice conversations at a data rate of 2,048,000 bits per second. The European system is calculated as 8 bits x 32 channels x 8000 frames per second. European PCM multiplexing is not compatible with North American multiplexing. The two systems cannot be directly connected. Some PBXs in the U.S. conform to the U.S. standard only. Some (very few) conform to both. Both the European and North American T-1 "standards" have now been accepted as ISDN "standards." In addition to PCM, there are many other ways of digitally encoding voice. PCM remains the most common. See E-I, T-1 and VOICE COMPRESSION.

PCM-30
Short name of international 2.048 Mbps T-1 (also known as E1) service derived from the fact that 30 channels are available for 64 Kbps digitized voice each using pulse code modulation (PCM).

PEB
PCM Expansion Bus. Dialogic's name for the digital electrical connection between its network interface modules and its resource modules. This bus is now "open." Technical specifications are available, thus enabling outsiders to create their own resource modules and/or network interface modules. See also AEB, which is Dialogic's Analog Expansion Bus.

Pel
Picture Element. A pel contains only black and white information, no grey shading.

Personal Identification Number
PIN number. 1. An AT&T term meaning the last four digits of your AT&T, MCI Bell operating company Credit Card -- the card you use for making long distance numbers. 2. Some banks and financial institutions issue credit cards for machine, teller-less banking. These machines, called Automated Teller Machines, ask you for a password consisting of several numbers or characters. These are not on your credit card. These numbers or characters, called PIN numbers, are designed to make sure the right person is using your card. It's not a good idea to use your birthday as you PIN number.

Phase A
In a fax machine's call process, the call establishment, when the transmitting and receiving units connect over the telephone line, recognizing one another as fax machines. This is the start of the handshaking procedure.

Phase B
In a fax machine's call process, the pre-message procedure, where the answering machine identifies itself, describing its capabilities in a burst of digital information packed in frames conforming to the HDLC standard.

Phase C
In a fax machine's call process, the fax transmission portion of the operation. This step consists of two parts-C1 and C2-which take place simultaneously. Phase C1 deals with synchronization, line monitoring, and problem detection. Phase C2 includes data transmission.

Phase D
In a fax machine's call process, this phase begins once a page has been transmitted. Both the sender and receiver revert to using HDLC packets as during Phase B. If the sender has further pages to transmit, it sends an MPS frame, and the receiver replies with an MCF and Phase C recommences for the following page.

Phase E
In a fax machine's call process, the call release portion. The side that transmitted last sends a DCN frame and hangs up without awaiting a response.

Phonemail
A ROLM term for Voice Mail. Rolm's PhoneMail is a voice messaging system that provides (1.) telephone answering (with the user's own greeting), (2.) the capability to store and forward voice messages, and (3.) the capability to turn on a message waiting light or message on the recipient's phone. PhoneMail can be used positively -- to speed the flow of information. It can also be used negatively -- to allow the user to "hide behind" the system and avoid the outside world and anyone in the outside world who might actually want to buy something. See also VOICE MAIL.

PIN
Procedure interrupt negative.

PIN Number
Personal Identification Number. A group of characters entered as a secret code to gain access to a computer system, such as the one that completes long distance calls. See PERSONAL IDENTIFICATION NUMBER.

Pixel
Picture Element. The smallest area of an original sampled and represented by an electrical signal. A pixel has more than two levels of greyscale information.

Phone Book
This is a special file for fax telephone numbers and other transmission information for people with whom the user regularly communicates. It has Category and Class fields to organize contacts into groups and subgroups. With the Phone Book it is not necessary to type numbers and names each time a fax is sent. It can be used to send to a single number or to more than one fax number broadcasting purposes.

PIP
Procedure interrupt positive.

Polling
Refers to some form of data or fax network arrangement whereby a central computer or fax machine/board very quickly asks each remote location in turn whether they want to send some information. The purpose is to give each user or remote data terminal an opportunity to transmit and receive information on a circuit or using facilities which are being shared. Polling is typically used in a multipoint or multidrop line. It is done mostly to save money on telephone lines.

Pop-Up
See Hot Key.

Port
An entrance to or exit from a network, the physical or electrical interface through which one gains access. The interface between a process or a program and a communications or transmission facility. A point in the computer or telephone system where data may be accessed. Peripherals are connected to ports.

PostScript
A page description language for PCs, which is standard for many graphics and desktop publishing applications. It allows the creation of elaborate documents. Other applications such as spreadsheets, word processors, and databases rarely require this sophistication.

POTS
Plain Old Telephone Service. The basic service supplying standard single line telephones, telephone lines and access to the public switched network. Nothing fancy. No added features. Just receive and place calls. Nothing like Call Waiting or Call Forwarding. They are not POTS services. Pronounced POTS, like in pots and pans.

Predictive Dialer
See PREDICTIVE DIALING.

Predictive Dialing
An automated method of making many outbound calls without people and then passing answered calls to a person as the calls are answered. Here's the story: Imagine a bunch of operators having to call a bunch of people. Those calls may be for collections. They may be for employee call-ups. They may be for alumnae fund raising. When it's done manual, here's how it works: Before each call operators spend time reviewing paper records or computer terminal screens, selecting the person to be called, finding the phone number, dialing the numbers, listening to rings, listening to phone company intercepts, busy signals and answering machines.

Operators also spend time updating the records after each call. Predictive dialing automates this process, with the computer choosing the person to be called and dialing the number and only passing it to an operator when a real live human being answers. There are enormous productivity gains made by screening out answering machines, busy signals, network busy signals, non-completed calls, operator intercepts etc. The result is productivity increases of 300% to 600%. According to generally accepted industry lore, a well-run manual dialing center can get its people talking on the phone for 25 minutes an hour. With a predictive dialer you can get them on the phone making sales, collecting money, etc. for 55 minutes an hour. It's a major productivity gain.

True predictive dialing should not be confused with automated dialing. True predictive dialing has complex mathematical algorithms that consider, in real time, the number of available telephone lines, the number of available operators, the probability of getting no answer, a busy signal, a disconnected number, operator intercept or an answering machine, the time between calls required for maximum operator efficiency, the length of an average conversation and the average length of time the operators need to enter the relevant data. Some predictive dialing systems constantly adjust the dialing rate by monitoring changes in all these factors. Some people don't like the term "predictive dialing," since they think it's getting "a bad rap" in Washington, DC by being associated with junk phone calls. As a result some people would prefer to call it Computer Aided Dialing.

Preview Dialing
Preview dialing is a term used to describe an automatic dialer. Preview dialing is also called "screen dialing" or "cursor dialing." Typically the prospect's account information and/or phone number appears on the screen BEFORE the call is made. Thus the agent can "preview" the number, the screen, the customer. If the agent wants to make the call, the agent hits a key, such as "Enter" and the computer dials the number.

In some preview dialing equipment, the agent must hit a key if he/she DOESN'T want the number dialed. Contrast preview dialing with Predictive Dialing where the computer makes all the dialing decisions and presents the calls to the agent only after they are connected. Predictive dialing is a lot faster than preview dialing. See PREDICTIVE DIALING.

PRI
See PRIMARY RATE INTERFACE.

PRI-EOM
Procedure interrupt-end of message.

PRI-EOP
Procedure interrupt-end of procedures.

PRI-MPS
Procedure interrupt-multipage signal.

Primary Rate Interface
PRI. The ISDN equivalent of a T-1 circuit. The Primary Rate Interface (that which is delivered to the customer's premises) provides 23B+D (in North America) or 30B+D (in Europe) running at 1.544 megabits per second and 2.048 megabits per second, respectively. There is another ISDN interface. It's called the Basic Rate Interface. It delivers 2B+D over either one or two pairs. In ISDN, the "B" stands for Bearer, which is 64,000 bits per second, which can carry PCM-digitized voice or data.

Printed Circuit Board
PCB. Flat material (fiberglass/epoxy) on which electronic components mount. A PCB also provides electrical pathways, called traces, that connect components. Printed circuit boards are what PBXs and computers are made of these days. Be careful when you're replacing PCBs. They're usually very sensitive to static electricity. Handle them only when you're attached to a static electricity strap that is properly grounded. Lay them down only on a surface you're sure is static electricity free. And don't touch the components on PCBs whatever you do.

Printer Emulation
Enables the mimicking of a printer-generated document. This way, the outgoing fax will look as if it has come from the printer attached to a computer. This can include full formatting, as well as letterhead, signature, and different graphic images.

Private Branch Exchange
PBX. Term used now interchangeably with PABX. See PABX.

Program Logic
The particular sequence of instructions in a program.

Programming Language
A language used by a programmer to develop instructions for the computer. It is translated into machine language by language software called assemblers, compilers and interpreters. Each programming language has its own grammar and syntax.

Prompts
1. Recorded instructions delivered by voice processing units. Prompts may include MENUS or other information that is played each time you get into the system. 2. Messages from the computer instructing the user on how to use the system. See MENU and AUDIO MENU.

Prosody
Intonation. In text to speech, prosody refers to how natural it sounds -- the ups and downs of the sentence.

Protocol
A specified set of rules, procedures, or conventions, relating to format and timing of data transmission between two devices. A standard procedure that two data devices must accept and use to be able to understand each other.

PSK
Phase Shift Keying. A method of modulating the phase of a signal to carry information.

PSTN
Public Switched Telephone Network. An abbreviation used by the CCITT.

PTT
Post Telephone & Telegraph Administration. The PTTs, usually controlled by their governments, provide telephone and telecommunications services in most countries.

Pulse Amplitude Modulation
PAM. A technique for placing binary information on a carrier to transmit that information. PAM is a technique for analog multiplexing. The amplitude of the information being modulated controls the amplitude of the modulated pulses. Samples of each input voltage are placed between voltage samples from other channels. The cycle is repeated fast enough so the sampling rate of any one channel is more than twice the highest frequency transmitted. See also PAM and PCM.

Pulse Code Modulation
PCM. The most common and most important method in North America in which a telephone system samples a voice signal and converts that sample into an equivalent digital code. PCM is a digital modulation method that encodes a Pulse Amplitude Modulated (PAM) signal into a PCM signal. See PCM and T-1.

Pulse Density
In T-1, since "O"s are represented by no pulse and "1"s by alternating pulses, pulse density refers to the number of no pulse ("O") periods allowed before a pulse ("1") must occur. Typically, no more than 15 no pulse periods ("O"s) are allowed before a pulse ("1") must occur.

Pulse Dialing
One or two types of dialing that uses rotary pulses to generate the telephone number.

Pulse Dispersion
The spreading out of pulses as they travel along an optical fiber.

Pulse Duration Modulation
PDM. That form of modulation in which the duration of the pulse is varied in accordance with some characteristic of the modulating signal.

Pulse Link Repeater
A signaling set that interconnects the E and M leads of two circuits. In E & M signaling, a device that interfaces the signal paths of concatenated trunk circuits. Such a device responds to a ground on the "E" lead of one trunk by applying -48Vdc to the "M" lead of the connecting trunk, and vice versa. This function is a built-in, switch-selectable option in some commercially available carrier channel units.

Pulse Overshoot
In T-1, the amount of signal voltage that can remain at the trailing end of a pulse. It can be no more than 10-30% of the pulse amplitude. Also called afterkick.

Pulse-Position Modulation
PPM. That form of modulation in which the positions in time of the pulses are varied in accordance with some characteristic of the modulating signals, without modifying the pulse width.

Pulse Repetition Frequency
PRF. In radar, the number of pulses that occur each second. Not to be confused with transmission frequency which is determined by the rate at which cycles are repeated within the transmitted pulse.

Pulse Stuffing
When timing signals on digital circuits get out of whack, some method of allowing mismatches must be provided. In time division multiplexing, this is called pulse stuffing. One stream of data has bits added to it so its final rate is the same as the master clock.

Pulse Train
The resulting electronic impulses that transmit encoded information.

Pulse Width
In T-1, refers to the width (at half amplitude) of the bipolar pulse (typically 324 + or -45 nsec).

Q

QAM
Quadrature Amplitude Modulation. A modulation technique that uses variations in signal amplitude, allowing data-encoded symbols to be represented as any of 16 or 32 different states. Some QAM modems allow dial-up data rates of up to 9,600 bps.

Quantize
The process of encoding a PAM signal (Pulse Amplitude Signal) into a PCM signal (Pulse Code Modulation). See QUANTIZING and QUANTIZATION.

Quantizing
The second stage of pulse code modulation (PCM). The waveform samples obtained from each communication channel are measured to obtain a discrete value of amplitude. These quantized values are converted to a binary code and transmitted to a distant location to reconstruct the original waveform. See QUANTIZATION.

Quantization
Take an analog voice signal, sample it and put numbers on those samples. That's called quantization. Here's an explanation from Understanding Telephone Electronics: "A circuit called a quantizer takes in the analog signal and produces an equivalent number.

Threshold levels are established and numbers are assigned to the analog samples as their amplitudes fall within the bands formed by the threshold numbers. (For example, everything within the range 1000.05 and 1000.06 Hz is given the number 14568.) The assigned number in most costs is an approximation rather than a true value because the true value would require many more bits (i.e. more threshold limits) in the binary code...

This approximation causes an error which is the difference between the approximate number and the true sample. This quantization error adds noise to the signal, called quantization noise, which is heard in the telephone as hissing. Quantization noise can be reduced by making the threshold bands narrower...However, providing more intervals requires more bits in the binary code. Therefore, more bandwidth is needed. There is a tradeoff between small quantizing intervals (higher bandwidth, lower noise), and fewer intervals (lower bandwidth, higher noise).

Quantization Noise
Signal errors which result from the process of digitizing (and therefore ascribing finite quantities to) a continuously variable signal. See QUANTIZATION.

Queuing
The act of stacking or holding calls to be handled by a specific person, trunk, or trunk group.

R

RAM
Random Access Memory. The primary memory in a computer. Memory that can be overwritten with new information. The random access part of the name comes from the fact that the next bit of information in RAM can be located-no matter where it is-in an equal amount of time, making access to it considerably faster than to information in other storage media, such as a hard disk.

Raster Scanning
The method of scanning in which the scanning spot moves along a network of parallel lines, either from side to side or top to bottom.

Real Time
A voice telephone conversation is conducted in Real Time. That is, there is no perceived delay in the transmission of the voice message or in the

response to it. This concept often applies to interaction between a computer and a terminal. See also REAL TIME CAPACITY. In data processing or data communications, real time means the data is processed the moment it enters a computer, as opposed to BATCH processing where the information enters the system, is stored and is operated on a later time.

Record
An entry in a database. Records contain fields. Records may be retrieved in either recordorder or keyorder.

RecordOrder Retrieval
Implies a sequence in which records are read from the database in the order in which they were added to the database.

Record Storage Buffer (RSB)
A storage area allocated within the Pro/Found User Function which is used to store the last record read from a database. The contents of the record storage buffer can be moved into registers on a fieldbyfield basis. Each AP line has its own RSB.

Reference Line
The first scanning line in memory. The location of each black pixel of this line is kept in memory for the next scanned line. Depending on the compression technique used, more or fewer scan lines are necessary.

Registration Number (FCC Part 68)
Approval number given to telephone equipment to certify that a particular device passes the tests defined in Part 68 of the FCC Rules. These tests certify the phone won't cause any harm to the public network. They do not attest to the commercial value of the product, nor whether it will (or won't) sell.

Relational Database
A database composed of multiple table files, linked or related by the contents of a single "key" field duplicated in each.

Remote Diagnostics
You own a phone system. You have a service company. There's some problem with it. Instead of sending a technician out, your service company dials your PBX from a data terminal or PC and "asks" your PBX in

computerese what's wrong with it. If it isn't too broken, it will come back and give you some indication. This is called remote diagnostics.

Remote Programming
Dial your phone system with your friendly personal computer, modem and a communications software package and you can change the telephone system's programming remotely. This feature is great for companies with telephone systems in many locations. They can all be run from one central point. This feature is also great. You may want some changes made on your system. It's obviously a lot cheaper for your vendor to make those changes from his office than having to visit yours. It's also a lot faster. See REMOTE DIAGNOSTICS.

Resolution
A measure of capability to delineate picture detail.

Resolution Levels
Provides for high- and low-resolution levels (CCITT Group 3 standard is most popular) up to 400 dots per inch. Most computer fax products allow users to select which resolution meets their needs.

Resource Module
A Dialogic term referring to devices which perform specific voice processing functions, such as voice compression, voice recognition, facsimile transmission and reception and conversion of computer text to spoken words over the phone. Resource modules are typically connected to the telephone network through devices known as "network interface modules."

Resource Server System
An independent PC linked to at least one Client AP System via a NetBIOS or SPXcompatible network. Each resource server system must be running a compatible version of SRVMGR and at least one server module.

Ring
1. As in Tip and Ring. One of the two wires (the two are Tip and Ring) needed to set up a telephone connection. 2. Also a reference to the ringing of the telephone set. 3. The design of a Local Area Network (LAN) in which the wiring loops from one workstation to another, forming a circle (thus, the term "ring"). In a ring LAN, data is sent from workstation to workstation around the loop in the same direction. Each workstation (which

is usually a PC) acts as a repeater by re-sending messages to the next PC in the ring. The more PC's, the slower the LAN.

Network control is distributed in a ring network. Since the message passes through each PC, loss of one PC may disable the entire network. However, most ring LANs have a way of recovering very fast should one PC die or be turned off. If it dies, you can remove it physically from the network. If it's off, the network senses that and the token ignores that machine. In some token LANs, the LAN will close around a dead workstation and join the two workstations on either side together. If you lose the PC doing the control functions, another PC will jump in and take over. This is how the IBM Token- Passing Ring works.

Ringing Voltage
In addition to talk battery, a Central Office provides ringing signaling. Ring Voltage is generally 70 to 90 volts at 17 Hz to 20 Hz.

RJ-11
RJ-11 is a six conductor modular jack that is typically wired for four conductors (i.e. four wires). Occasionally it is wired for only two conductors -- especially if you're only wiring up for tip and ring. The RJ-11 jack (also called plug) is the most common telephone jack in the world.

The RJ-11 is typically used for connecting telephone instruments, modems and fax machines to a female RJ-22 jack on the wall or in the floor. That jack in turn is connected to twisted wire coming in from "the network" -- which might be a PBX or the local telephone company central office. RJ-22 wiring is typically flat. None of its conductors (i.e. wires) are twisted. You cannot use flat cable for high-speed data communications, like local area networks. See also RJ-22 and RJ-45.

RJ-14
A jack that looks and is exactly like the standard RJ-11 that you see on every single line telephone. Whereas the RJ-11 defines one line -- with the two center, red and green, conductors being tip and ring, the RJ-14 defines two phone lines. One of the lines is the "normal" RJ-11 line -- the red and green center conductors. The second line

RJ-45

The RJ-45 is the 8-pin connector used for data transmission over standard telephone wire. That wire could be flat or twisted. And it's very important that you know what you're working with. You can easily use flat wire for serial data communications up to 19.2 Kbps. Up to that speed you're connecting with your wire to a data PBX, a modem, a printer or a printer buffer. If you wish to connect to a 10BaseT local area network, which you also do with a RJ-45, you must use twisted wire.

You can typically tell the difference by looking at the cable. If it's flat grey satin (like a typical phone wire, only bigger) than it's probably untwisted. If it's circular, then it's probably twisted and therefore good for LANs. RJ-45 connectors come into two varieties -- keyed and non-keyed. Keyed means that the male RJ-45 plug has a small, square bump on its end and the female RJ-45 plug is shaped to accommodate the plug. A keyed RJ-45 plug will not fit into a female, non-keyed (i.e. normal) RJ-45. See RJ-11 and RJ-22.

Robbed-Bit Signaling

This explanation from Gary Maier of Dianatel: ISDN is the key to future sophisticated telephone network services with its dynamic, highly configurable T-1 connection (also called PRI connection). Since T-1 is a common method of carrying 24 telephone circuits, many wonder about the uses for ISDN, especially when they learn ISDN signaling requires an entire voice channel, reducing today's T-1 from 24 voice channels to 23.

But the popular signaling mechanism of "robbed bit" signaling in T-1 has serious limitations. Robbed bit signaling typically uses bits known as the A and B bits. These bits are sent by each side of a T-1 termination and are buried in the voice data of each voice channel in the T-1 circuit. Hence the term "robbed bit" as the bits are stolen from the voice data. Since the bits are stolen so infrequently, the voice quality is not compromised by much. But the available signaling combinations are limited to ringing, hang up, wink, and pulse digit dialing. In fact, the limitations are obvious when one recognizes DNIS and ANI information are sent as DTMF tones. This introduces a problem: time.

Each DTMF tone requires at least 100 milliseconds to send, which in a DNIS and ANI situation with 20 DTMFs will take at least two full seconds. There is also a margin for error in transmission or detection, resulting in

DNIS or ANI failures. With the explosion of telephone related services, the telephone companies are turning to ISDN PRI to provide the more complicated and exact signaling required for new services. ISDN employs a more robust method of signaling. ISDN uses a T-1 circuit as 23 voice channels and one signaling channel.

The term 23B plus D refers to 23 bearer (voice) channels and 1 Data (signaling) channel. The data channel carries the signaling information at a rate of 64 kilobits per second. This speed is many times greater than some of the most powerful modems available. Because of this high speed, telephone calls can be placed more quickly, and because of the protocol used, DNIS or ANI transmission failures are impossible.

Additionally, since no bits are "robbed" from the voice channels, the voice quality is better than that of Robbed Bit signaling on today's T-1 circuits. Also, computer modems and high speed faxes can use the voice channel for sending digital data instead of the traditional analog bit "noise." Therefore, ISDN PRI offers the end user countless new service capabilities. One channel could be used for faxing, another for modem data, several for video, another for a LAN and the remainder for voice. Suddenly, the average T-1 circuit becomes a pipeline for all communications! Increasingly long distance carriers are using ISDN PRI to provide inbound 800 calls with ANI and DNIS and re-routing skills. Dianatel makes some of the most sophisticated ISDN interface equipment around.

Rotary Dial
The circular telephone dial. As it returns to its normal position (after being turned) it opens and closes the electrical loop sent by the central office. Thus it generates pulses for each digit dialed. You can hear the "clicks". The number "seven," for example consists of seven "opens and closes," or seven clicks.

You can dial on a rotary phone without using the rotary dial. Simply depress the switch hook quickly, allowing pauses in between to signify that you're about to send a new digit. It's a good party trick.

Routing
The process of selecting the correct path for a message.

RS-232
A set of standards specifying various electrical and mechanical charac teristics for interfaces between computers, terminals, and modems. It applies to synchronous and asynchronous binary data transmission.

RSB
See Record Storage Buffer.

RTN
Retrain negative.

RTP
Retrain positive.

S

Sampling Rate
The number of times per second that an analog signal is measured and converted to a binary number -- the purpose being to convert the analog signal to a digital analog. The most common digital signal -- PCM -- samples 8,000 times a minute.

Scanner
A device used to input graphic images in digital form. A fax machine's scanner determines the brightness of a document's pixels for transmission

Scheduled Transmission
A feature allowing the user to schedule a fax transmission at a specific date or time in the future. Key benefits are convenience and cost savings. Scheduling jobs at a period of low telephone rates can have immediate considerable savings.

SCSA
Signal Computing System Architecture. A new standard for the tele-com/voice processing/computing industry announced by Dialogic in early Spring 1993. The SCSA standard is remarkable for several things: 1. On the day of its announcement over 70 telecom and voice processing companies publicly endorsed SCSA, committed to work with it and are clearly planning

to work it. Today, over 200 companies are endorsing SCSA. 2. With SCSA -- a standard for PC/LANs and VME-backplaned computers -- you can build much larger telecom switches and much larger call and voice processing boxes.

Previous standards, like AEB, PEB and MVIP, were basically limited to what you could do with one PC. Now PCs can be joined together. With SCSA, you can put 16 T-1 lines, or 512 voice lines in one PC and join together 16 PCs, for a total of 16 x 16 x 24 = 6,144 lines! That's a central office built out of networked PCs. A mainframe built out of a LAN. The SCSA joining is not via LAN or LAN-emulation. That would be too slow and the transmission too bursty (great for data, lousy for voice). It's via an SCbus -- something that looks and works like a PBX backplane.

3. SCSA incorporates virtually every other standard in PC-based switching -- including the most popular ones, Mitel's ST-Bus, MVIP, Siemens PCM Highway, AEB and PEB. 4. It's a lot faster and more reliable. All signaling is out of band. There's clock fall-back and time slot bundling. It's more modular, meaning you can start with one PC and grow one at a time. That makes it more "modular" (scalable is the new word). It's also hot pluggable. You don't have to turn off to upgrade. 5. It has applications portability. Tandem, the highly-successful fault-tolerant mini-computer maker, has an SCSA application in a call center. They call it the Tandem Non-Step Call Center. It uses the Tandem 2400 VRU and the 4800 VRU. SCSA is open, truly open. All its specs and all levels of its specs are available. To that extent, SCSA represents a remarkable gamble by its creator, Dialogic, a telecom/voice processing hardware company. It is encouraging competing manufacturers to build hardware to its specs and gambling that it won't be left in the dust, as IBM was with its PC. (Compaq, not IBM, built the first '386 PC.) SCSA, as an idea, is revolutionary (for telecom).

No one in telecom has ever promulgated an open standard everyone can adopt -- hardware and software vendors. Dialogic has done it to create opportunities by providing great economies of scale for the developers. Write one application, create one applications generator, design one piece of hardware. Erector set telecom/voice processing! Build small. Build large. Just join the bits and pieces together.

SDLC
Synchronous Data-Link Control.

Server
A communications element providing a service such as shared access to a file system, a printer or an E-mail system to LAN users. Usually a combination of hardware and software. A process in a distributed computing system that provides a service in response to requests from clients.

Server Module
A module within a clientserver architecture system that provides resources or resource management for one or more client modules. Server modules may be located on the same system as the client AP (Local Mode), or on a separate resource server PC linked via a network (Distributed Mode).

Service Control Points
SCPs. The local versions of the national SMS/800 number database. SCPs contain the intelligence to screen the full ten digits of an 800 number and route calls to the appropriate, customer-designated long distance carrier.

Sidetone
A part of the design of a telephone handset which allows you hear your own voice while talking on the telephone. The idea of doing this is to give you a little feedback that the telephone you're speaking on is working. Too much sidetone becomes an echo and is bad. Too little sidetone makes the channel unerring.

Signal Errors
Signal errors indicate the return status of a Do/Change function. Despite the name, signal errors do not always indicate an error condition. If a signal error is encountered and the k command line option specifies a Level to go to, the application will continue from the specified Level.

Signaling
Pertains to the transmission of electrical signals to and from the user's premises and the telephone company central office. Examples of central office signals to the user's premises are ringing (audible alerting) signals, dial tone, speech signals, etc. Signals from the user's telephone include off-hook (request for service), dialing (network control signaling), speech to the distant party, on-hook (disconnect signal), etc.

Signal-To-Noise Ratio
The ratio of the usable signal being transmitted to the noise or undesired signal. Usually expressed in decibels. This ratio is a measure of the quality of a transmission.

SIR (ASR)
Speaker Independent Recognition. See SPEAKER INDEPENDENT RECOGNITION.

SIT Tones
1. Standard Information Tones. These are tones sent out by a central office to a pay phone to indicate that the dialed call has been answered by the distant phone, etc. 2. Special Information Tones. These are tones for identifying network provided announcements. Here's Bellcore's explanation: Automated detection devices cannot distinguish recorded voice from live voice answer unless a machine-detectable signal is included with the recorded announcement.

The CCITT, which specifies signals that may be applied to international circuits, has defined Special Information Tones for identifying network provided announcement. The SIT used to precede machine-generated announcements also alerts the calling customer that a machine-generated announcement follows. Since SIT consists of a sequence of three precisely defined tones, SIT can be machine-detected, and therefore machine-generated announcements preceded by a SIT can be classified.

At least four SIT encodings have been defined: Vacant Code (VC), Intercept (IC), Reorder (RO) and No Circuit (NC). With the exception of some small Stored Program Control Systems (SPCSs) and some customer negotiated announcements, Bell operating companies in North America now precede appropriate announcements with encoded SITs to detect and classify announcements.

SMS/800
The national database Service Management System that will retain all 800 records. This database provides long distance carriers a single interface for 800 number reservations and record maintenance. Developed by Bellcore, the database has been in use by various Regional Bell Operating Companies (RBOCs) since 1988. The FCC has mandated that a neutral third party administer the database.

Software Supervision
"Answer Supervision" is knowing when the person at the other end answers the phone. The main reason for wanting to know this is so that a phone company can start billing the call. There are two ways of doing answer supervision. You can get it from the nation's phone system, i.e. the distant office signals back across the country when the called person picks up the phone. Or you can fake it with "software supervision."

Essentially this means there's electronics which "listens" to the call. If it "hears" voice or something like voice, it assumes the conversation has started and it's time to start billing the call. Software supervision is not accurate. But when you haven't got access to real answer supervision (for whatever reason) it's better than the previous alternative, which was "timeout." In timeout answer supervision, the carrier simply assumed the call had begun after a certain number of seconds -- like 30 -- had elapsed with the calling person hanging up. This meant, for example, if you called Grandma and she wasn't there, but you left it ringing, 'cause you knew she took time to answer the phone, then you'd be charged for the call -- even though she didn't answer phone! See also ANSWER SUPERVISION.

Source Code
A computer program which can be translated by another program into a program that will run on a particular computer. The program which finally runs on that computer is known as the object code.

Span
1. Refers to that portion of a high speed digital system than connects a C.O. (Central Office) to C.O. or terminal office to terminal office. 2. Also called a T-Span Line. A repeatered outside plant four-wire, two twisted-pair transmission line.

Span Line
A T-1 link.

Speaker Independent (Voice) Recognition (ASR)
SIR. Technologies for the automated conversion of speech to accurate and meaningful textual information (typically ASCII). SIR is typically used to accept input from callers to voice processors where the callers are using rotary dial phones instead of touch-tone -- Dual Tone Multi-Frequency (DTMF) -- phones. SIR can substitute for the numbers on the DTMF keypad

and can add the benefit of a few basic voice commands, e.g., Yes, No, Help, etc. Because computer processing demands are formidable with speaker independent recognition, accurate speaker independent products are created with limited vocabularies. In contrast, trainable or speaker dependent recognizers can feature larger vocabularies at lower prices.

SIR has been slowly gaining acceptance in telephone applications. SIR is increasingly used in automated operator assistance applications. SIR will see increased use as system builders respond to pressures to provide voice processing functions to the enormous rotary phone installed base domestically and abroad.

Speech Concatenation
A term used in voice processing for economical digitized speech playback that uses independently recorded files of phrases or file segments linked together under application program control to produce a customized response in natural sounding language. For example, order status, bank balances, bus schedules or lottery results, etc.

Concatenation is done for speed and economy. It lends itself to limited and structured vocabularies that are best stored in RAM (Random Access Memory) or speedily accessible from disk. Concatenation does not replace Text-To-Speech (TTS) as a method of getting the voice processor to deliver its responses. Concatenation, however, can be an excellent complement to TTS when a voice application demands broad, real time vocabulary production. See TEXT-TO-SPEECH.

Speech Synthesis
See TEXT-TO-SPEECH.

Spooler
A program that controls spooling. Spooling, a term mostly associated with printers, stands for Simultaneous Peripheral Operations On Line. Spooling, temporarily stores programs or program outputs on magnetic tape, RAM, or disks for output or processing.

On a LAN, a printer is controlled by a spooler. The spooler places each print request on the LAN in the print queue and prints it when it reaches the top of the queue.

Springboard
Dialogic's term for a general purpose computing engine designed for a wide range of powerful voice processing applications. It contains two Motorola 56001 DSPs (Digital Signal Processors) and one Intel 80286 12.5 MHz microprocessor. It allows Dialogic's Technology Partners to extend D/12x functions.

SPX
Sequenced Packet eXchange. A connectionoriented session protocol for network data exchange that uses the IPX (Internetwork Packet Exchange) communication protocol. (See also *NetBIOS*.)

Standards
Agreed principles of protocol. Standards are set by committees working under various trade and international organizations. RS standards, such as RS-232-C are set by the EIA, the Electronics Industries Association. ANSI standards for data communications are from the X committee.

Standards from ANSI would look like X3.4-1967, which is the standard for the ASCII code. The CCITT does not put out standards, but rather publishes recommendations, owing to the international personalities involved. V series recommendations refer to data transmission over the telephone network, while X series recommendations, such as X.25, refer to data transmission over public data networks.

State Machine Programming
To control multiple telephone lines in a single voice processing program, a new program structure is required. Dialogic calls this technique state machine programming. Computer Science called state machines "Deterministic Finite State Automata."

Station
A dumb word for a telephone. Also called an instrument, or a telephone instrument. An extension station is one connected "behind" a PBX or key system. In other words, the PBX or key system is between the station and the telephone central office. We tried to remove the word "station" from this dictionary, but failed. We suspect the word comes from the very old days when the telephone industry was regulated by the Interstate Commerce Commission, (the ICC) which also regulated the railroad industry.

Station Adapters
Cables and interface assemblies for connecting Dialogic network interface and switching products to telephones or analog telephone lines.

Station Set
Another word for a common desk telephone.

Store And Forward
In communications systems when a message is transmitted to some intermediate relay point and stored temporarily. Later the message is sent the rest of the way. Not very convenient for voice conversations, but useful for telex type, and other one way transmissions of messages. Telephone answering machines, as well as voice mailboxes are considered forms of Store and Forward message switching.

Supervised Transfer
A call transfer made by an automatic device such as voice response unit which attempts to determine the result of the transfer -- answered, busy, ring no answer -- by analyzing call progress tones on the time.

Supervision
Supervision of a phone call is detecting when a called party has picked up his phone and when that party has hung up. Supervision is used primarily for billing purposes. Not all long distance carriers have supervision capability. It depends on how "equal accessed" they have chosen to be. See ANSWER SUPERVISION and SOFTWARE SUPERVISION.

Switch
A mechanical, electrical or electronic device which opens or closes circuits, completes or breaks an electrical path, or selects paths or circuits.

Switched Network
A network providing switched communications service; that is, the network is shared among many users, any of whom may establish communication between desired points when required.

Switchhook
A switchhook was originally an electrical "switch" connected to the "hook" on which the handset (or receiver) was placed when the telephone was not in use.

Switch Hook Flash
A signaling technique whereby the signal is originated by momentarily depressing the switch hook.

Synthesized Voice
Human speech approximated by a computer device that concatenates basic speech parts (or phonemes) together.

T

T-1
Also spelled T1. A digital transmission link with a capacity of 1.544 Mbps (1,544,000 bits per second). T1 uses two pairs of normal twisted wires, the same as you'd find in your house. T1 normally can handle 24 voice conversations, each one digitized at 64 Kbps. But, with more advanced digital voice encoding techniques, it can handle more voice channels.

T1 is a standard for digital transmission in North America. It is usually provided by the phone company and used for connecting networks across remote distances. Bridges and routers are used to connect LANs over T1 networks. There are faster services available, such as T2 and T4, but these are not used much. T1 links can often be connected directly to new PBXs and many new forms of short-haul transmission, such as short-haul microwave systems. It is not compatible with T1 outside the United States and Canada. In Europe T-1 is called E-1 or E1.

Outside of the United States and Canada, the "T-1" line bit rate is usually 2,048,000 bits per second. Japan, France and West Germany impose slight variations that make their formats unique. Only one element remains constant -- the DS-0. The 64 kilobit per channel is universal. Most often it represents a PCM voice signal sampled at 8,000 times per second. However, the form of PCM encoding differs between T-1 (mu-law) and E-1 (A-law companding).

According to Bill Flanagan's book, the differences are not so great that a multiplexer cannot convert between them. Conversion of E-1 to T-1 involves both the compression law and the signaling format. At the higher rate of 2,048,000, 32 time slots are defined at the CEPT interface, but two are used for signaling and other housekeeping chores. Typically 30 channels are left for user information -- voice, video, data, etc. CEPT is the Conference of European Postal and Telecommunications administrations. Standards-setting body whose membership includes European Post, Telephone, and Telegraphy Authorities (PTTs). For a full explanation of T1 see Bill Flanagan's book The Guide to T-1 Networking.

T2

A digital transmission link with a capacity of 6.312 Mbps. T2 can handle at least 96 voice messages.

T3

A digital transmission link with a capacity of 44.736 Mbps. T3 can handle 672 voice messages simultaneously. T3 runs on fiber optic cable.

T.4

CCITT recommendation for Group 3 machines, using T.30 and various V series standards. It also describes compression methods (Modified Huffman and Modified READ).

T.6

CCITT recommendation for Group 4 machines. It defines the facsimile coding schemes and their associated coding control functions for black and white images.

T.30

CCITT recommendation. This handshake protocol describes the overall procedure for establishing and managing communication between two fax machines. It covers five phases of operation: call setup, pre-message procedure (selecting the communication mode), message transmission (including phasing and synchronization), post-message procedure (EOM and confirmation), and call release.

T.35

CCITT recommendation proposing a procedure for the allocation of CCITT members' country or area codes for non-standard facilities in telematic services.

T.611
Also known as Appli/COM. A messaging standard proposed by France and Germany, defining a programmable communication interface (PCI) for Group 3 fax, Group 4 fax, teletext, and telex service.

Table
See *data file.*

Table-Driven
Describing a logical computer process, widespread in the operation of communications devices and networks, where a user-entered variable (e.g. a password) is matched against an array of predefined values (a table of acceptable passwords) and checked for access, authorization, etc. A frequently used process in least cost routing, in network routing, in access security, and in modem operation.

Tag
Some database formats use individual DOS files for each index. Others, such as dBASE IV and FoxPro, combine multiple indexes into a single file. Each such index within the index file is known as a tag. Two parameters are required to access a tag within an index file: the name and extension of the index file, and the name of the desired tag within it.

Talk Battery
The DC voltage supplied by the central office to the subscriber's loop to operate the carbon transmitter in the handset.

Talk Path
The tip and ring conductors of a telephone circuit.

Talk-Off
Talk-off is one hazard of in-band signaling. Talk-off occurs when your voice has enough 2600 Hz energy to activate the 2600 Hz tone- detecting circuits in the central office. The 2600 Hz tone is used for in-band signaling.

TAO
See TELEPHONY APPLICATION OBJECT FRAMEWORK

TAPI
See Windows Telephony API

TCF
Training Check Frame. Last step in a series of signals called a training sequence, designed to let the receiver adjust to line conditions.

Technology Developers
Dialogic term for companies which make specialized voice processing devices which can be used with Dialogic products to build end user products. Technology partners include those with skills in facsimile, voice recognition and text-to-speech. Their products will work with Dialogic products.

Telco
The local telephone company. Often a term of endearment.

Telecommunications
Telecommunications, or telecom for short, is the transmission or reception of signals, images, sounds, or intelligence of any nature by wire, radio, light pulse, or electromagnetic system. That just about covers virtually any means of transmission, regardless of source, channel, or media type. *Telephony* and *data communications* are subsets of telecommunications that are specific to computer-type transmissions and telephone-type transmissions, respectively.

Telecomputing
Telephony services administered by a computer. These services include call control and media processing operations.

Telecomputing Server
A server software program that allows client applications to take advantage off call control and media processing hardware remotely. See AppServer for an example.

Telefax
European term for fax.

Telecommunication Standardization Sector (TSS)
One of four permanent parts of the International Telecommunications Union (ITU), based in Geneva, Switzerland. It issues recommendations for standards applying to modems, packet switched interfaces, V.24 connectors, etc. Although it has no power of enforcement, the standards it recommends

are generally accepted and adopted by industry. Until March 1, 1993, the TSS was known as the CCITT (see above).

Telecopier
European term for fax.

Telemarketing
Marketing and sales conducted via the telephone. There are two sides to telemarketing -- incoming and outgoing. Incoming telemarketing is largely run through 800 toll-free IN-WATS numbers and local FX (foreign exchange) lines. Outgoing telemarketing is organized over OUT-WATS lines. Everything from computers to clothes is now sold over the phone.

An expanding range of telecom gadgetry is being developed to automate telemarketing -- including automated outbound dialers, voice processing technology, and automatic call distributors. The tone recognition, voice detection and transaction Audiotex and transaction processing capabilities of voice processing gear can be used to enhance all telemarketing applications.

Telephone Manager
Apple's telephony API for the Macintosh environment.

Telephony
Taken from Greek root words meaning "far sound," telephony is the discipline of converting or transmitting voice or other signals over a distance, and then re-converting them to an audible sound at the far end.

Telephony Application Object (TAO) Framework
TAO is the software part of the Signal Computing System Architecture (SCSA). The TAO Framework is made up of four components: 1) A set of standard SCSA Application Programming Interfaces (SCSA APIs) that defines the way client and server applications access the Message Protocol to communicate with server resources and system services. 2) The Message Protocol that defines a standard way for passing messages among applications, system resources, and system services.

3) A set of core System Services that includes resource management, runtime control, switching, event and error handling, configuration management, session management, and security. 4) A set of Service Provider

Interfaces (SPIs) that defines the way System Services and Resources (the Service Providers) access the Message Protocol. Other key features of the SCSA Telephony Application Object Framework are: It is an open software architecture; It is designed specifically for multiple application client server environments, where multiple distributed applications use the same server resources; It has sophisticated application management capabilities; It facilitates both simple and complex application development; Its core system services and technology-specific resource APIs are interoperable; It is object-oriented and operating system independent; It is hardware independent and can be implemented on top of different hardware platforms, like the SCSA Hardware Model, MVIP, or proprietary hardware platforms; It has been defined by leading computer telephony industry technologists to support current and future technology requirements.

Telephony Database Transactions
The use of telephony terminal equipment (phone and/or fax) as input/output devices to operate on a computer database.

Telephony Server
A server software program that allows client applications to take advantage of call control hardware remotely. See Novell Telephony Server for an example.

Telephony Workgroup
A group of people with a common telecomputing requirement: for example, a technical support group might need an application that automatically links incoming calls to client records on a database.

Terminal Emulation
A microcomputer or personal computer mimics, pretends to be (i.e. emulates) a data terminal. It does this with special printed circuit boards inserted into its motherboard and/or special software.

Text-To-Speech (Speech Synthesis)
TTS. Technologies for converting textual (ASCII) information into synthetic speech output. This technology is used in voice processing applications that require the production of broad, unrelated and unpredictable vocabularies, e.g., products in a catalog, names and addresses, etc. This technology is appropriately used when system design constraints prevent

the more efficient use of speech concatenation alone. See SPEECH CONCATENATION.

TIFF

FileFormatTagged Image File Format. TIFF provides a way of storing and exchanging digital image data. Current TIFF specifications support three main types of image data: black-and-white data, halftones or dithered data, greyscale data and, more recently, color.

Tip & Ring

An old fashioned way of saying "plus" and "minus," or ground and positive in electrical circuits. Tip and Ring are telephony terms. They derive their names from the operator's cordboard plug. The tip wire was connected to the tip of the plug, and the ring wire was connected to the slip ring around the jack. A third conductor on some jacks was called the sleeve. That's it. Nothing more sinister. Nothing more interesting.

Tone Dial

A push button telephone dial that makes a different sound (in fact, a combination of two tones) for each number pushed. The correct name for tone dial is "Dual Tone MultiFrequency" (DTMF). This is because each button generates two tones, one from a "high" group of frequencies -- 1209, 1136, 1477 and 1633 Hz -- and one from a "low" group of frequencies -- 697, 770, 852 and 841 Hz. The frequencies and the keyboard, or tone dial, layout have been internationally standardized, but the tolerances on individual frequencies vary between countries.

This makes it more difficult to take a touch-tone phone overseas than a rotary phone. You can "dial" a number faster on a tone dial than on a rotary dial, but you make more mistakes on a tone dial and have to redial more often. Some people actually find rotary dials to be, on average, faster for them. The design of all tone dials is stupid. Deliberately so. They were deliberately designed to be the exact opposite (i.e. upside down) of the standard calculator pad, now incorporated into virtually all computer keyboards.

The reason for the dumb phone design was to slow the user's dialing down to the speed Bell central offices of early touch tone vintage could take. Today, central offices can accept tone dialing at high speed. But sadly, no one in North America makes a phone with a sensible, calculator pad or computer keyboard dial. On some telephone/computer workstations you can dial using the calculator pad on the keyboard. This is a breakthrough. It a lot faster to use this pad. The keys are larger, more sensibly laid out and can actually be touch-typed (like touch-typing on a keyboard.) Nobody, but nobody can "touch-type" a conventional telephone tone pad. A tone dial on a telephone can provide access to various special interactive voice response services and features -- from ordering your groceries over the phone to inquiring into the prices of your (hopefully) rising stocks.

ToolKit
A Dialogic word for an Applications Generator.

ToolKit Members
An company which has written one or more applications generators for use with Dialogic products. Get a list from Dialogic.

Touch Tone
A term coined by AT&T for Tone Dialing.

TTS
Text To Speech. A term used in voice processing. See TEXT-TO-SPEECH.

Trellis Coding
A method of forward error correction used in certain high-speed modems where each signal element is assigned a coded binary value representing that element's phase and amplitude. It allows the receiving modem to determine, based on the value of the preceding signal, whether or not a given signal element is received in error.

Trellis Code Modulation (TCM)
A version of quadrature amplitude modulation (QAM) that enables relatively high bit rate signals to be used on ordinary voice-grade circuits. When used as a modem modulation technique in which algorithms are used to predict the best fit between the incoming signal and a large set of possible combinations of amplitude and phase changes. TCM provides for transmission speeds of 14.4 Mbps and above on single voice-grade telephone lines.

Trunk

A communication line between two switching systems. The term switching systems typically includes equipment in a telephone company's central office and PBXs. A tie trunk connects PBXs. Central office trunks connect a PBX to the switching system at the central office.

TSI

Transmitting Subscriber Information. A frame that may be sent by the caller, with the caller's telephone number (may be used to screen calls).

T-Span

A telephone circuit or cable through which a T-carrier runs. See T-1.

TSR

Terminate and Stay Resident. A term for loading a software program in a DOS computer in which the program loads into RAM and is always ready for running at the touch of a combination of keys.

TTI

Transmit Terminal Identification. The telephone number and words on top of a received fax document, identifying its point of origin. This information does not originate with the telephone company, but with the sender, who programs it into the fax.

Twisted Pair

Two insulated copper wires twisted around each other to reduce induction (thus interference) from one wire to the other. The twists, or lays, are varied in length to reduce the potential for signal interference between pairs. Several sets of twisted pair wires may be enclosed in a single cable.

In cables greater than 25 pairs, the twisted pairs are grouped and bound together in a common cable sheath. Twisted pair cable is the most common type of transmission media. It is the normal cabling from a central office to your home or office, or from your PBX to your office phone. Twisted pair wiring comes in various thicknesses. As a general rule, the thicker the cable is, the better the quality of the conversation and the longer cable can be and still get acceptable conversation quality. However, the thicker it is, the more it costs.

Two-Dimensional Coding

A data compression scheme that uses the previous scan line as a reference when scanning a subsequent line. Because an image has a high degree of correlation vertically as well as horizontally, two-dimensional coding schemes work only with variable increments between one line and the next, permitting higher data compression.

Two-Wire Circuit

A transmission circuit composed of two wires -- signal and ground -- used to both send and receive information. In contrast, a four wire circuit consists of two pairs. One pair is used to send. One pair is used to receive. All trunk circuits -- long distance circuits -- are four wire. A four wire circuit costs more but delivers better reception. All local loop circuits -- those coming from a Class 5 central office to the subscriber's phone system -- are two wire, unless you ask for a four-wire circuit and pay a little more.

U

Unified Messaging

A telecomputing application that treats incoming and outgoing electronic mail, voice messages, and fax messages together. A mixed-media messaging control mechanism.

UNIX

An immensely powerful and complex operating system for computers. UNIX is developed, marketed, championed and trademarked by AT&T. UNIX is very powerful and very complex to use. Because of its power it needs a computer with a large amount of RAM memory. It has been extensively used in universities, and is only now emerging onto the business scene.

UNIX allows a computer to handle multiple users and multiple programs simultaneously. It works on many different computers. This means you can often take applications software which runs on UNIX and often move it -- with little changing -- to a bigger, different computer, or to a smaller, different computer. This process of moving programs to other computers is known as "porting." UNIX was developed in 1969 by Ken Thompson of AT&T Bell Laboratories.

V

V.17
CCITT recommendation for simplex modulation technique for use in extended Group 3 facsimile applications only. Provides 7,200, 9,600, 12,000, and 14,400 bps trellis-coded modulation.

V.21
CCITT recommendation for 300 bps duplex modems for use on the switched telephone network. V.21 modulation is used in a half-duplex mode for Group 3 fax negotiation and control procedures.

V.22
CCITT recommendation for 1,200 bps duplex modems for use on the switched telephone network and on leased lines.

V.22bis
CCITT recommendation for 2,400 bps duplex modems for use on the switched telephone network. V.22bis also provides for 1,200 bps operation for V.22 compatibility.

V.27ter
CCITT recommendation for 2.4/4.8-kbps/s modem for use on the switched telephone network. Half-duplex only. It defines the modulation scheme for Group 3 facsimile for image transfer at 2,400 and 4,800 bps.

V.29
CCITT recommendation for 9,600 bps modem for use on point- to-point leased circuits. This is the modulation technique used in Group 3 fax for image transfer at 7,200 and 9,600 bps. V.29 uses a carrier frequency of 1,700 Hz which is varied in both phase and amplitude. V.29 can be full duplex on four-wire leased circuits, or half duplex on two-wire and dial-up circuits.

V.32
CCITT recommendation for 9,600 bps two-wire full duplex modem operating on regular dial-up lines or two-wire leased lines. V.32 also provides fallback operation at 4,800 bps.

V.32bis
CCITT recommendation for full-duplex transmission on two-wire leased and dial-up lines at 4,800, 7,200, 9,600, 12,000, and 14,400 bps. Provides backward compatibility with V.32. It includes a rapid change renegotiation feature for quick and smooth rate changes when line conditions change.

V.33
CCITT recommendation for 14.4 kbps and 1.2 kbps modem for use on four-wire leased lines.

V.42
CCITT recommendation, primarily concerned with error correction and compression for modems. The protocol is designed to detect errors in transmission and recover with a retransmission.

Vari-A-Bill
A new 900 service of AT&T whereby the call's price varies depending on certain events -- the caller punching out some tones on his phone, or a service technician coming on line, etc. Telephone Response Technologies (TRT) supports this feature with their call processing module called Pro/ISDN.

V.fast
A modem standard under development. Once approved by the CCITT, it will raise modem speeds to 19.2 kbps.

Visual Voice Mail
An application displaying and controlling voice messages on a desktop computer. Usually associated with unified messaging.

Voice Board
Also called a voice card or speech card. A Voice Board is an IBM PC- or AT-compatible expansion card which can perform voice processing functions. A voice board has several important characteristics: It has a computer bus connection. It has a telephone line interface. It typically has a voice bus connection. And it supports one of several operating systems, e.g. MS-DOS, UNIX. At a minimum, a voice board will usually include support for going on and off-hook (answering, initiating and terminating a call); notification of call termination (hang-up detection); sending flash hook; and dialing digits (touch-tone and rotary). See VRU.

Voice Circuit

The typical analog telephone channel coming into your house or office. It has a bandwidth between 300 Hz and 3000 Hz. This is not sufficient for high fidelity voice transmission. You'd probably need at least 10,000 Hz. But it's sufficient to recognize and understand the person on the other end.

Voice Digitization

The conversion of an analog voice signal into binary (digital) bits for storage or transmission.

Voice Driver

A Dialogic product that comes for MS-DOS, OS/2 and UNIX. In MS-DOS, it is a terminate and stay resident (TSR) program which acts as a central server for MS-DOS based applications. It provides all of the services required to support installable device drivers for each hardware component and for the application. See also DEVICE DRIVER.

Voice Frequency

VF. An audio frequency in the range essential for transmission of speech. Typically from about 300 Hz to 3000 Hz.

Voice Integration

Allows computer fax solutions to be store and forward hubs for both image as well as voice communication. Many of these products work on PC-based systems and offer all the capabilities of a message center.

Voice Mail

A specialized form of Interactive Voice Response. Includes Voice Messaging and Automated Attendant systems. Denotes customer premise or central office systems that are aimed at automating and enhancing message taking and ATTENDANT console styled services. See VOICE MAIL SYSTEM.

Voice Mail System

A device to record, store and retrieve voice messages. There are two types of voice mail devices -- those which are "stand alone" and those which profess some integration with the user's phone system. A stand alone voice mail is not dissimilar to a collection of single person answering machines, with several added features; you can instruct the machines (voice mail boxes) to forward messages amongst themselves; you can organize to allocate your friends and business acquaintances their own mail boxes so they can dial, leave messages, pick up messages from you, pass messages to you, etc; you can also edit messages, add comments and deliver messages to a mailbox at a pre-arranged time. In addition, messages can be tagged "urgent" or "non-urgent" or stored for future listening. The range of voice mail options varies among manufacturers.

An integrated voice mail system includes these features. First, it will tell you if you have any messages. It does this by lighting a light on your phone, and/or putting a message on your phone's alpha-numeric display. Second, if your phone rings for a certain number of rings (which number you set), the phone will transfer your caller automatically to your voice mail box, which will answer the phone, deliver a little "I am away" message and then receive and record the caller's message.

Voice Message Service
A service typically over dial up phone lines which provides the ability for a phone user to access a voice mail system and leave a message for a particular phone user. See VOICE MAIL SYSTEM.

Voice Messaging
Recording, storing, playing back and distributing phone messages. New York Telephone has an interesting way of looking at voice messaging. NYTel sees it as four distinct areas: 1. Voice Mail, where messages can be retrieved and played back at any time from a user's "voice mailbox"; 2. Call Answering, which routes calls made to a busy/no answer extension into a voice mailbox; 3. Call Processing, which lets callers route themselves among destinations via their touch-tone phones; and 4. Information Mailbox, which stores general recorded information for callers to hear.

Voice Processing
1) Term which applies to all forms of technology used for the digitization, decoding, storage, or manipulation of the human voice. 2) Form of Computer Telephony which uses interactive voice response elements and/or call processing elements in order to interconnect computer-based information to telephone callers. See also INTERACTIVE VOICE RESPONSE.

Voice Recognition
The ability of a machine (obviously a computer) to understand human speech.

Voice Response Unit
VRU. Another term for INTERACTIVE VOICE RESPONSE. Think of a Voice Response Unit as a voice computer. Where a computer has a keyboard for entering information, an IVR uses remote touch-tone telephones.

Where a computer has a screen for showing the results, an IVR uses a digitized synthesized voice to "read" the screen to the distant caller. An IVR can do whatever a computer can, from looking up train timetables to moving calls around an automatic call distributor (ACD).

The only limitation on an IVR is that you can't present as many alternatives on a phone as you can on a screen. The caller's brain simply won't remember more than a few. With IVR, you have to present the menus in smaller chunks. See TELECOMPUTING; VOICE BOARD.

Voice Store And Forward
Voice mail. A PBX service that allows voice messages to be stored digitally in secondary storage and retrieved remotely by dialing access and identification codes. See VOICE MAIL SYSTEM.

Voice Switched
A device which responds to voice. When the device hears a voice, it turns on and transmits it, while muting the receive side. The most common voice-switched device is the common desk speakerphone.

With voice switching, it's easy to hog a circuit. Just keep making a noise. Watch out for voice hogging. If you're calling someone and waiting for them by listening in on your speakerphone, mute your speakerphone. This way you'll hear them when they answer.

VS&F
Voice Store and Forward. Voice is digitally encoded, sent to large storage devices and later forwarded to the recipient. See VOICE MAIL.

W

WAN
Wide Area Network. A network using common carrier-provided lines that cover an extended geographical area. WANs are data networks typically extending a LAN outside the building, over telephone common carrier lines to link to other LANs in remote buildings or other geographic areas.

WATS
Wide Area Telecommunications Service. WATS is basically discounted toll service. It is provided by all long distance and local phone companies. AT&T started WATS but forgot to trademark the name, so now every supplier uses it as a generic name.

There are two types of WATS services -- in and out WATS, i.e. those WATS lines that allow you to dial out and those which allow you to receive incoming calls (the typical 800 line service). You subscribe to in and out-WATS services separately. In the old days you needed separate in and out lines to handle the in and out WATS services. But these days you can choose to have in and out WATS on the same line. This is not particularly brilliant traffic engineering, since you can't receive an incoming 800 call if you're making an outgoing call.

Windows Telephony API
Microsoft's standard call control programming interface for the Windows environment. Microsoft and Intel introduced Windows Telephony as a concept in the Spring of 1993.

The announcement included a joint specification that has three elements: 1. An API, Application Programming Interface for applications developers. 2. A SPI, Service Provider Interface for service providers and network interface cards. 3. Windows DLL, software code to be incorporated into Microsoft Windows.

Wink
A momentary interruption in SF (single frequency) tone indicating the distant central office is ready to receive the digits you just dialed.

Wink Operation
A timed, off-hook signal, normally of 140 ms, which indicates the availability of an incoming register for receiving digital information from the calling office.

Wink Release
On most modern central offices when the person or device at the other end hangs up, your local central office will send you a single frequency tone. That tone is called wink release. Such a tone can be used to alert a data device that the device at the other end has hung up. (Remember it can't tell by just listening -- like you and me.) When a data device hears a wink release, it usually takes it as a signal to hang up also.

Wink Start
Short duration off-hook signal. See Wink Operation.

WOSA
Windows Open Architecture. Developed by Microsoft.

X

X.5
CCITT recommendation on digital data communication networks and services, dealing with interfaces.

X.25
Possibly one of the most important international standards ever recommended by the CCITT. From the beginning, it has provided a common reference point by which mainframe computers, word processors, minicomputers, VDUs, microcomputers, and varied equipment from different manufacturers can operate together over a packet switched network.

X.25 defines the interface between a public data network and a packet-mode user device. Typically used to connect WANs, packet switching breaks network data into smaller packets and sends them from point to point through interconnected switches. X stands for packet switched network.

X.38
CCITT recommendation for the access of Group 3 facsimile equipment to the Facsimile Packet Assembly/Disassembly (FPAD) facility in public data networks situated in the same country.

X.39
CCITT recommendation for the exchange of control information and user data between a Facsimile Packet Assembly/Disassembly (FAPD) facility and a packet mode data terminal equipment (DTE) or another pad, for international internetworking.

X.400
CCITT recommendations for the transmission of electronic text and graphic mail between unlike computers, terminals, and computer networks. Briefly, X.400 describes how mail messages are encoded, and X.25 sets up how they are transmitted.

X.500
The CCITT standard defining directory services, most commonly for E-mail systems. It provides for common naming and addressing in the networks of large-scale enterprises.

xBASE
The collective term for all database management systems using dBASE-compatible (.DBF format) data files, with a variety of enhancements and differing index formats (e.g., dBASE III+, dBASE IV, FoxBASE, FoxPro, Clipper).

XENIX
Microsoft trade name for a 16-bit microcomputer operating system derived from AT&T Bell Labs' UNIX.

Y

Yellow Alarm
A T-1 alarm signal sent back toward the source of a failed transmit circuit in a DS-1 2-way transmission path. A yellow sends 0's (zeros) in bit two of all time slots. See also T-1.

Yellow Pages
A directory of telephone numbers classified by type of business. It was printed on yellow paper throughout most of the twentieth century until it was obsoleted in the late 1990s by dial-up yellow page directories operated by voice processing systems and in the early 21st century by electronic directories delivered on disposable laser disks.

As a concession to history, the laser disks are now painted bright yellow. Actually, yellow pages remain one of the phone companies' most lucrative sources of revenues. Advertising rates are not cheap. There is now competition. There are many "Yellow Pages" directories, since AT&T never trademarked the term "Yellow Pages." Some "yellow page" directories are better value than others. And some are more legitimate than others. Some actually never get printed or, if they are printed, are not printed in great quantity and are not distributed as widely as their sales literature implies.

Many businesses have been suckered into paying money for listings and advertisements in directories that never appeared. This fictitious directory scam also has happened with "telex" and "fax" directories. This "scam" is fraud by mail and is heavily stomped upon by the US Postal Service. As a result, many fake directories (especially the telex ones) are "published" abroad.

Z

Zero Code Suppression
The insertion of a "one" bit to prevent the transmission of eight or more consecutive "zero" bits. Used primarily with digital T1 and related telephone-company facilities which require a minimum "ones density" keep the individual subchannels of a multiplexed, high-speed facility active. Several different schemes are currently employed to accomplish this. Proposals for a standard are being evaluated by the CCITT. See also ZERO SUPPRESSION.

ZeroFill
A traditional fax device is mechanical. It must reset its printer and advance the page as it prints each scan line it receives. If the receiving machine's printing capability is slower than the transmitting machine's data sending

capability, the transmitting machine adds fill bits (also called zero fill) to pad out the span of send time, giving the slower remote machine the additional time it needs to reset prior to receiving the next scan line.

Zip Tone
Short burst of dial tone to an ACD agent headset indicating a call is being connected to the agent console.

Index

#

A

B

C

D

E

G

H

I

K

L

M

N

O

P

S

T

U

V

W

U

V

W

X

Other Books We Publish

Flatiron Publishing publishes books and magazines and organizes trade conferences on computer telephony, telecommunications, networking and voice processing. It also distributes the books of other publishers, making it the "central source" for all the ablove materials. Call or write for your FREE catalog.

ATM Users' Guide
Complete Traffic Engineering Handbook
Customer Service Over the Phone
Frames, Packets and Cells in Broadband Networking
The Guide to Frame Relay
The Guide to SONET
The Guide to T-1 Networking
Local & Long Distance Telephone Billing Practices
Moore's Imaging Dictionary
Newton's Telecom Dictionary
PC-Based Voice Processing
SCSA
Speech Recognition
Telephony for Computer Professionals
VideoConferencing : The Whole Picture

Quantity Purchases

If you wish to purchase this book , or any others, in quantity, please contact:

Christine Kern, Manager
Flatiron Publishing, Inc.
12 West 21 Street
New York, NY 10010
212-691-8215

1-800-LIBRARY facsimile orders: 212-691-1191

Flatiron Publishing, Inc.
12 West 21 Street
New York, NY 10010
212-691-8215 1-800-LIBRARY